BLANK COMIC BOOK FOR CHILDREN

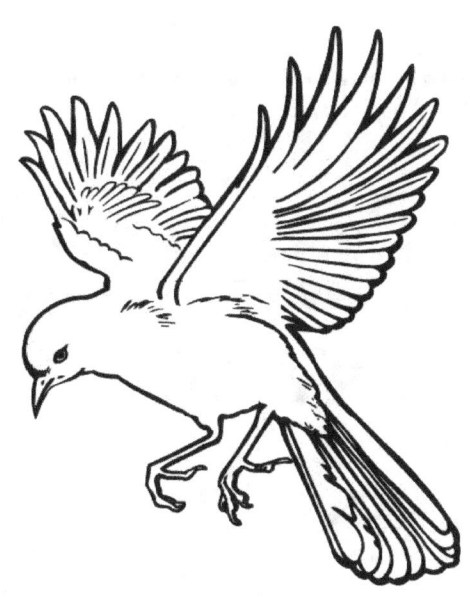

The Blank Shaped Comic Book Journal is Awesome for creating kinds of comics and manga. There exist several options to select from with different layouts. Get inspired by the different panel layouts. Get perfect Blank Shaped Comic Book Journal for your story.

THIS Blank Comic Book Belongs

To

....

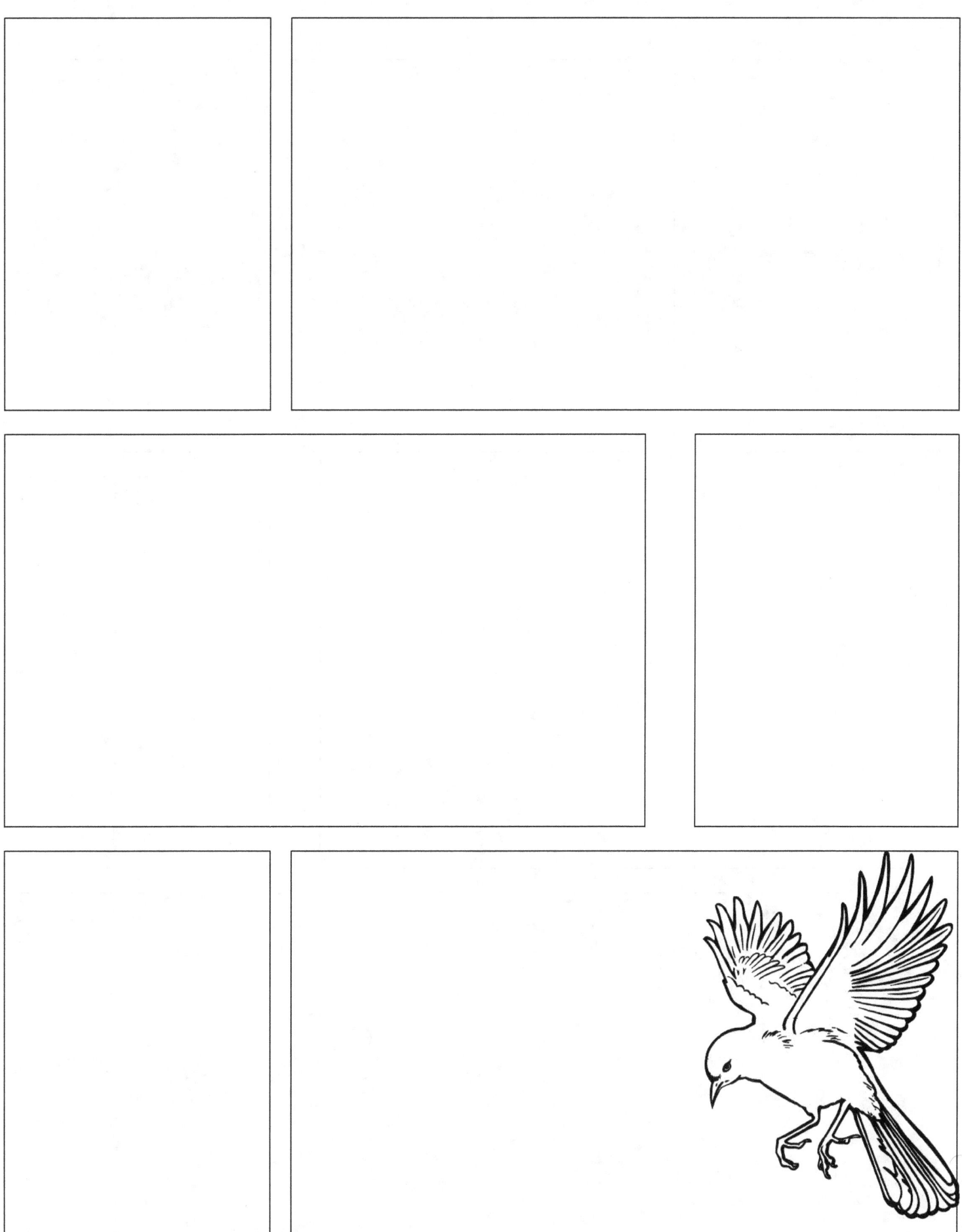

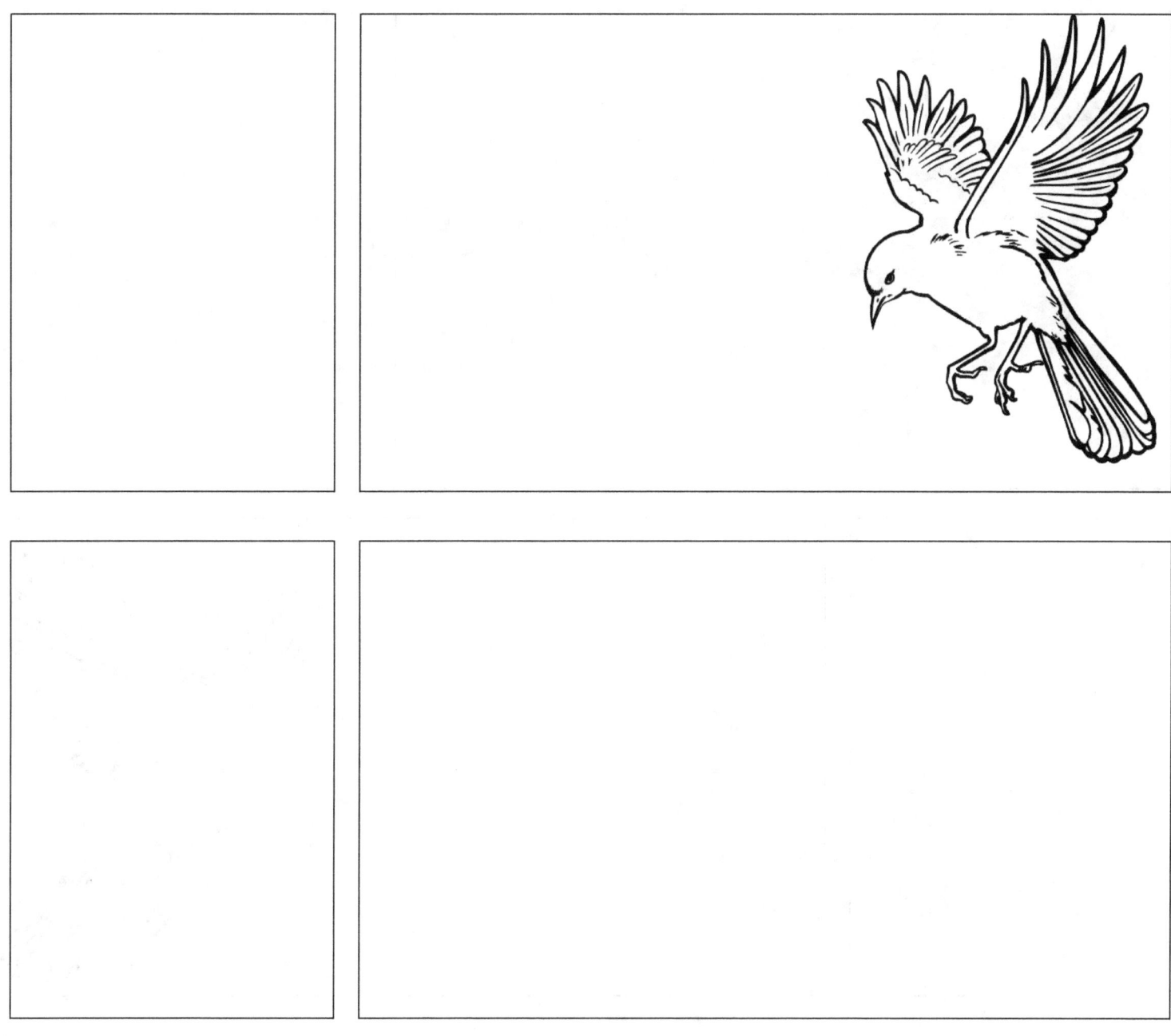

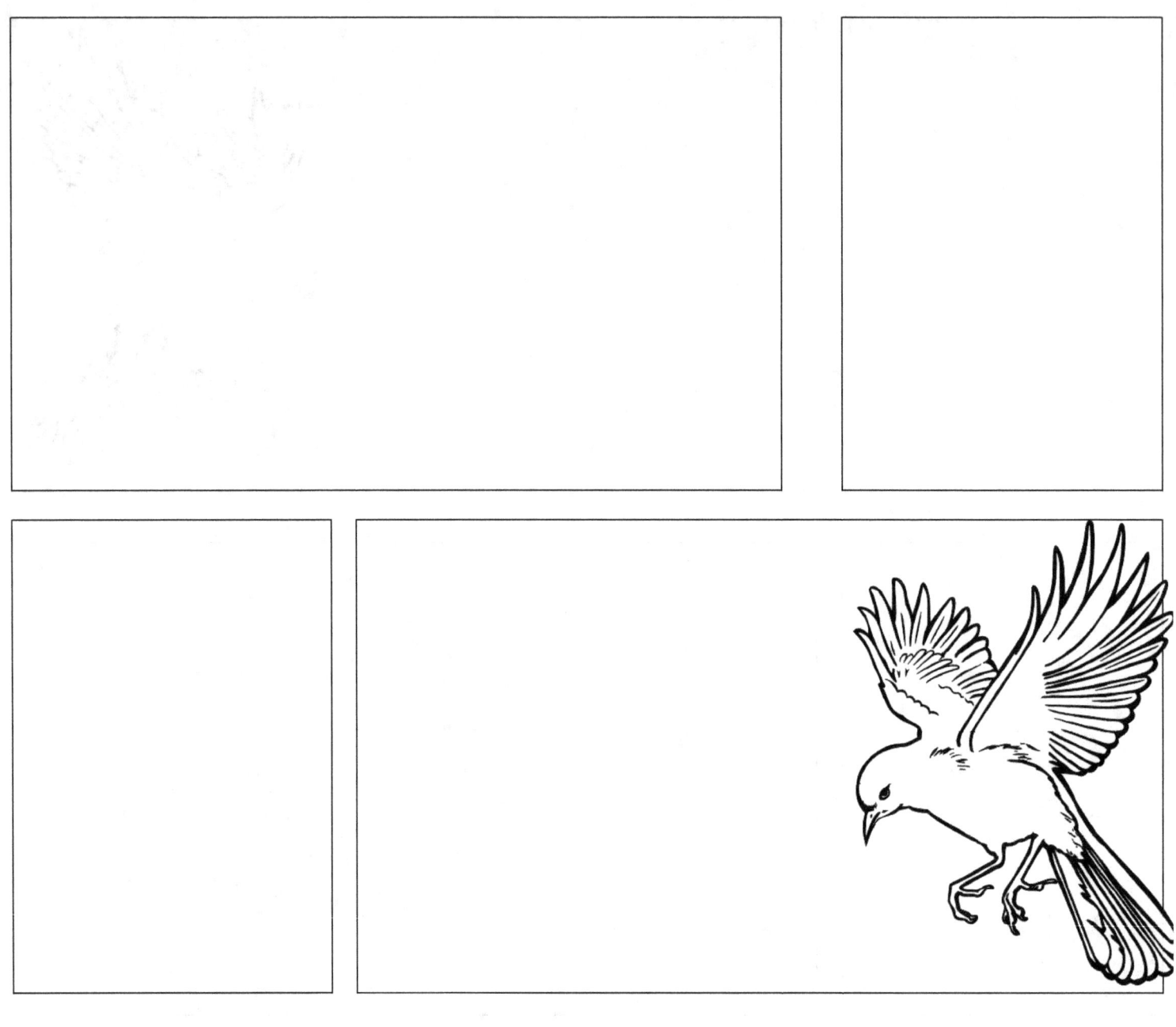

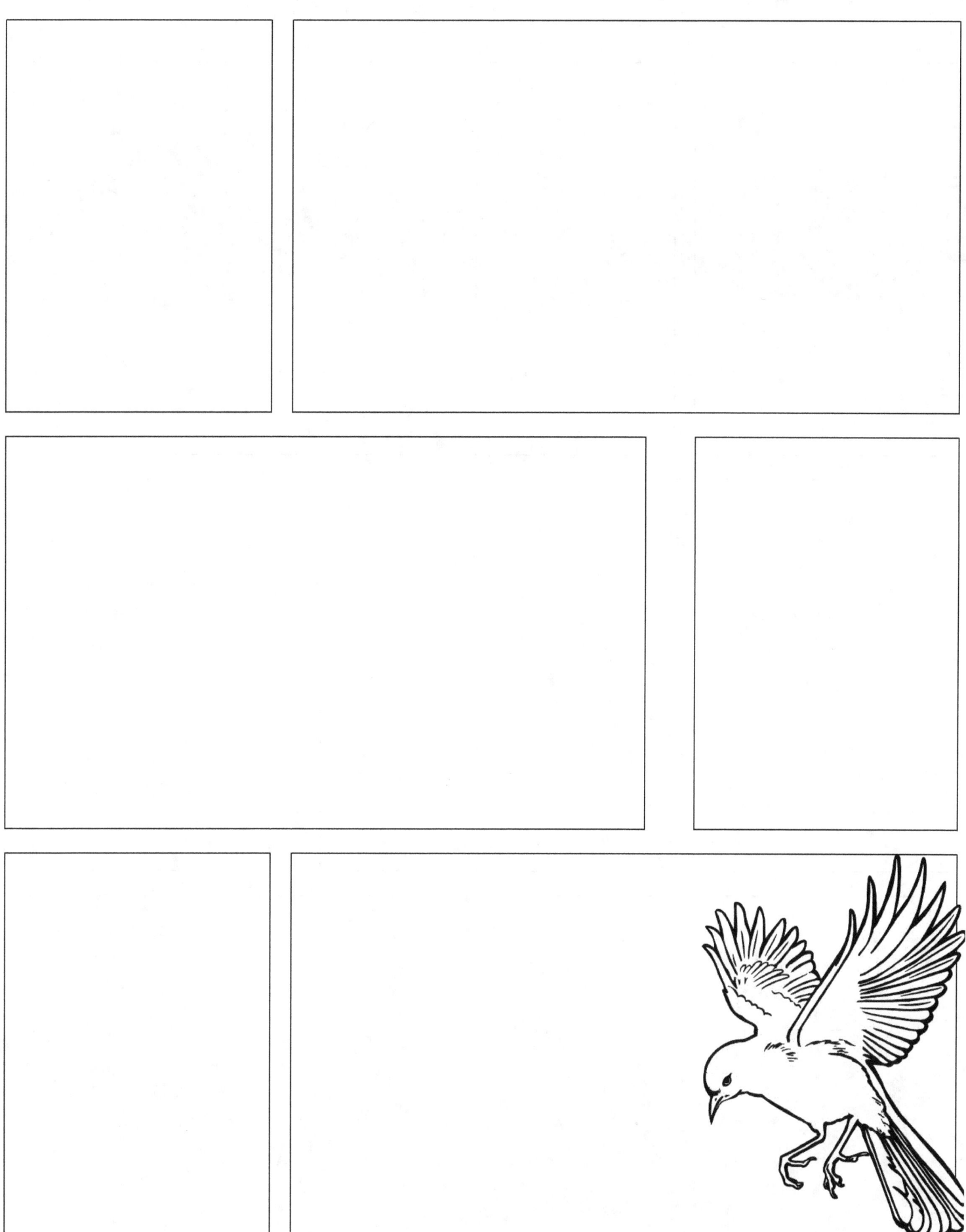

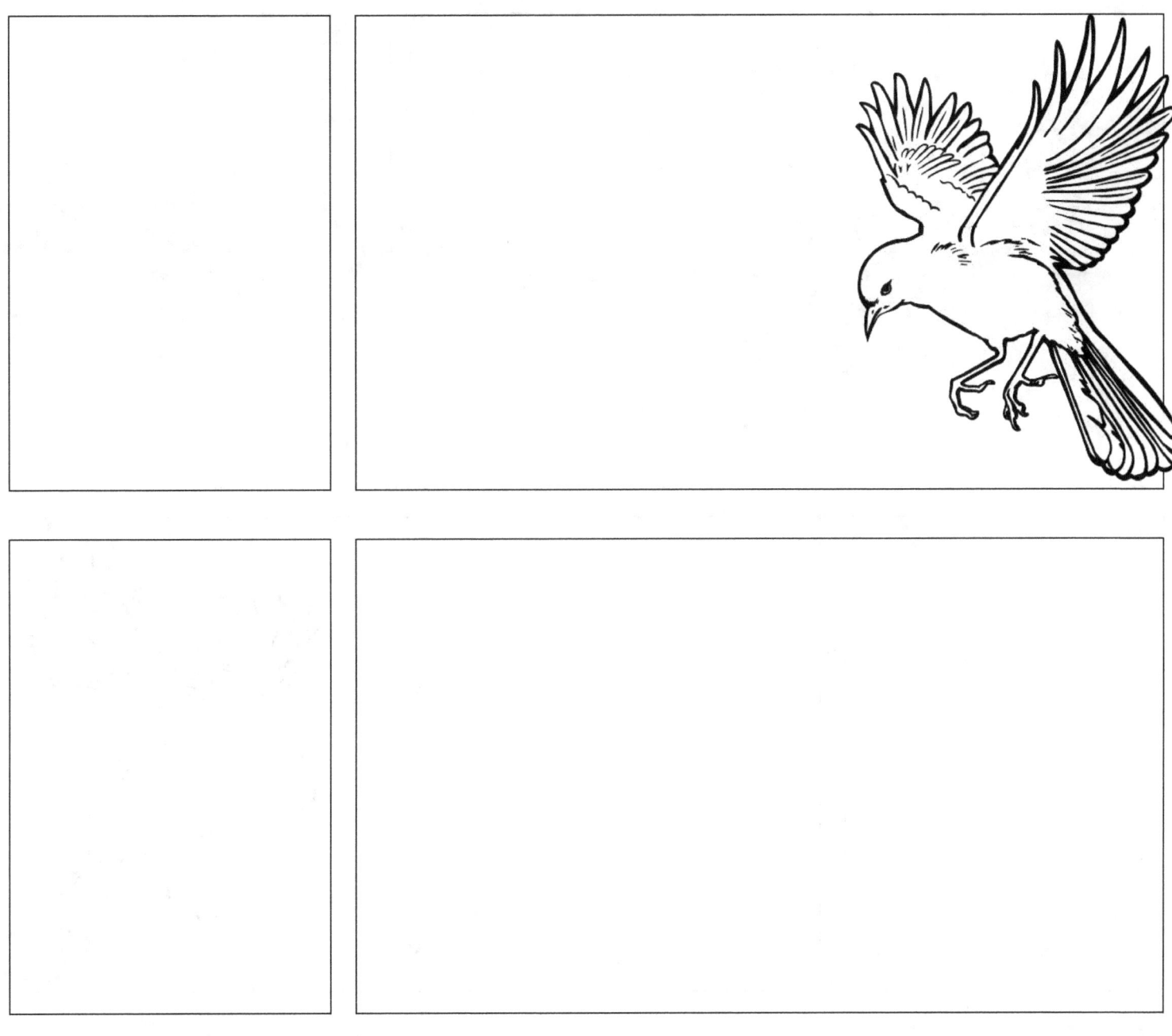

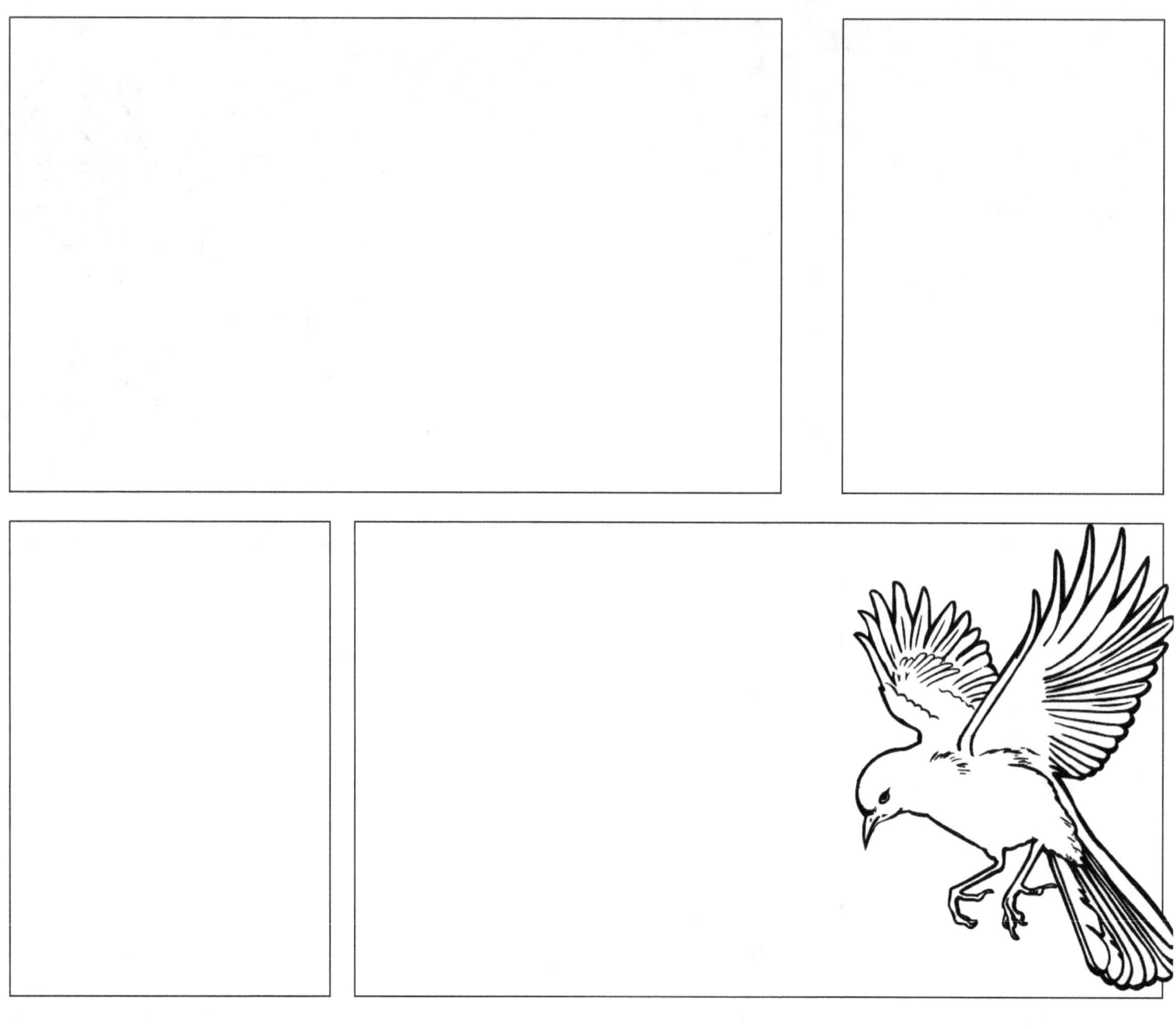

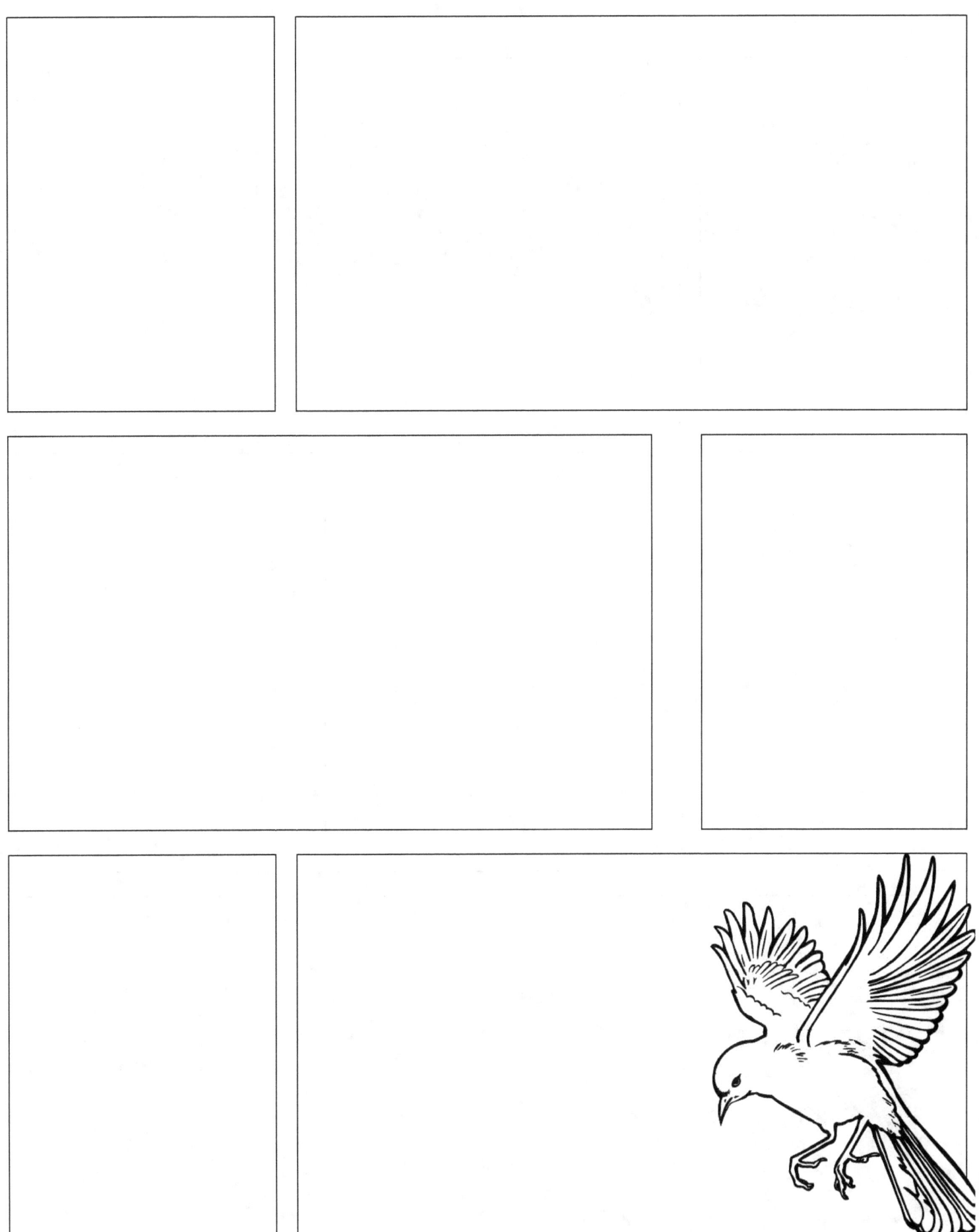

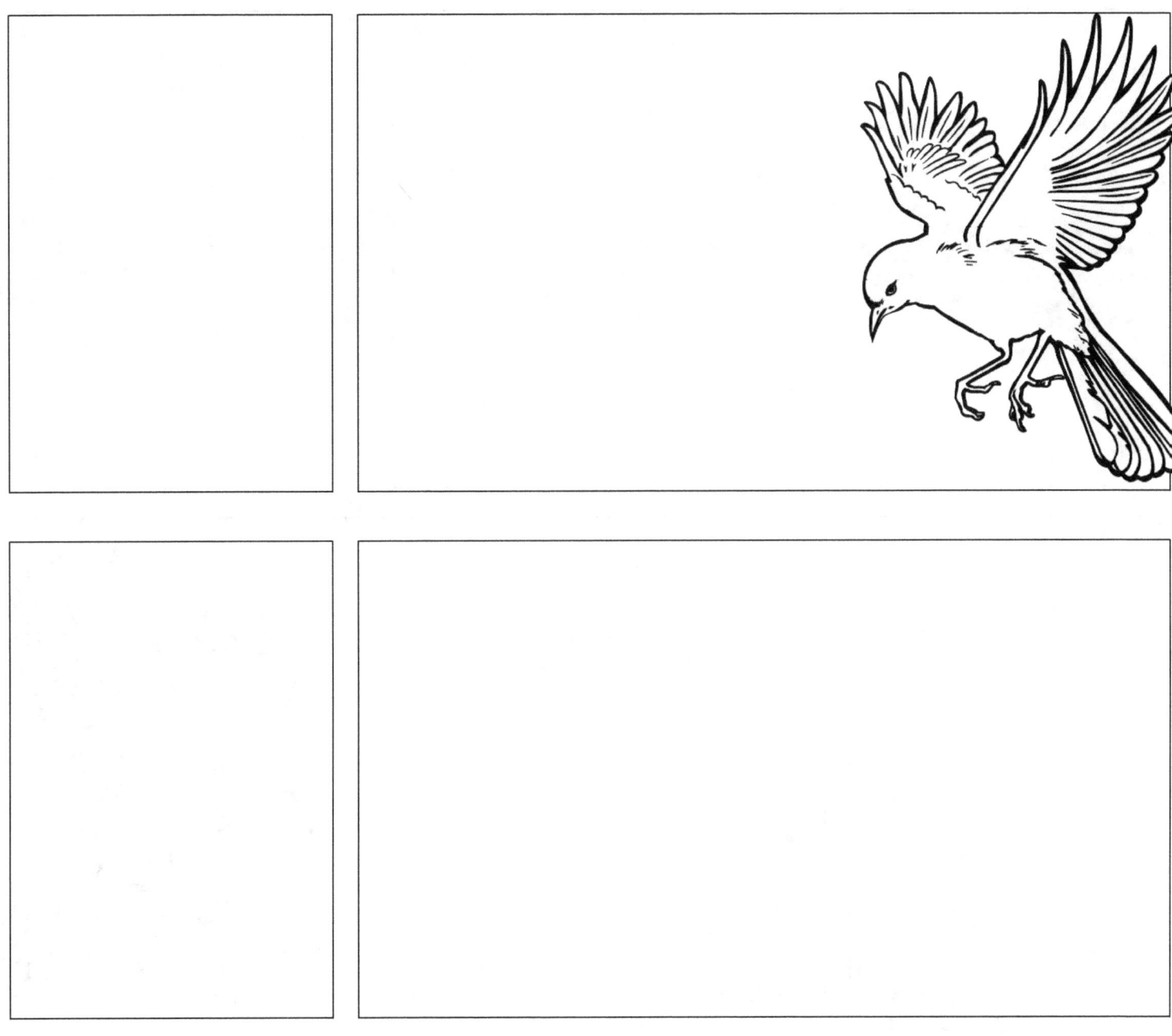

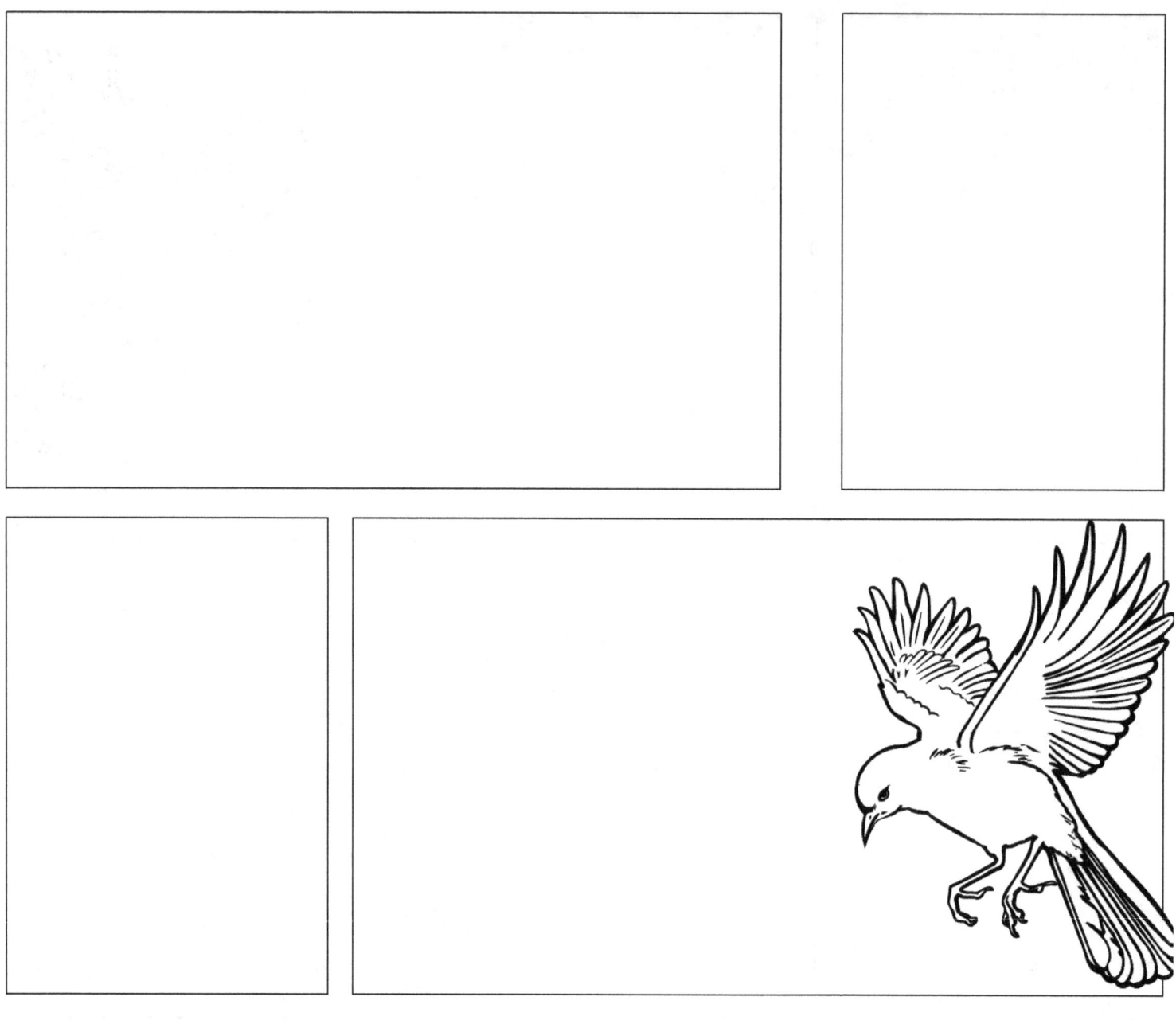

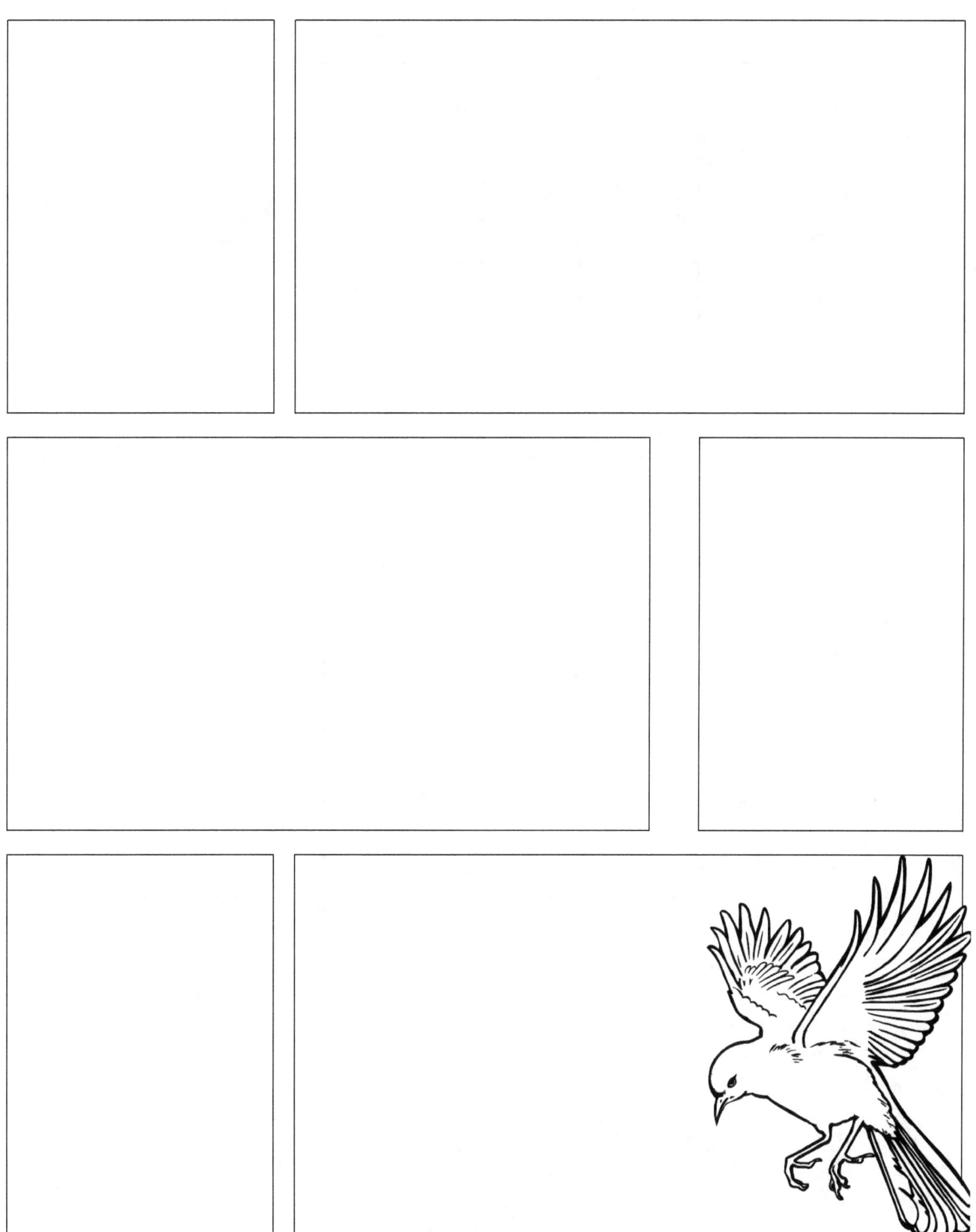

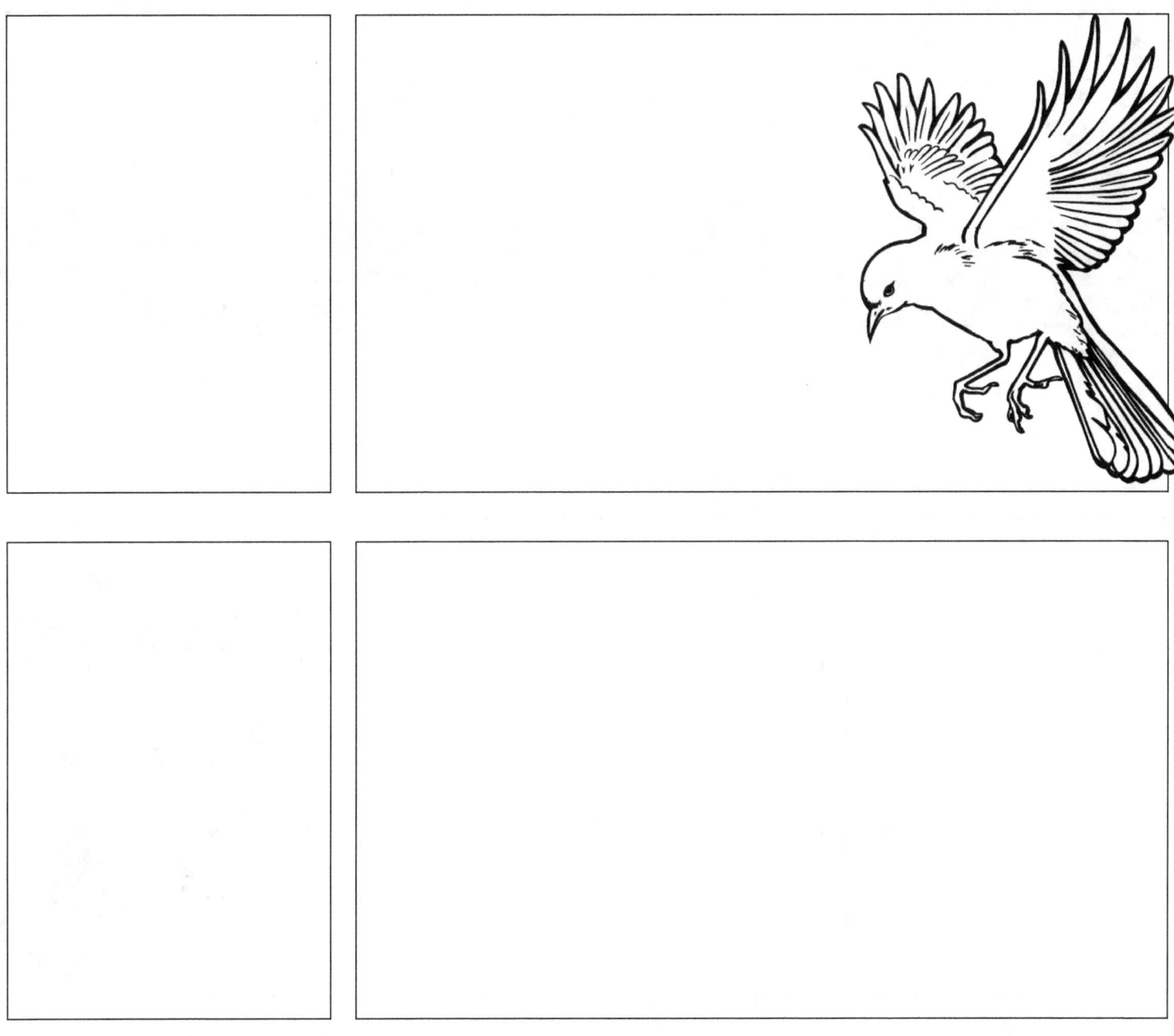

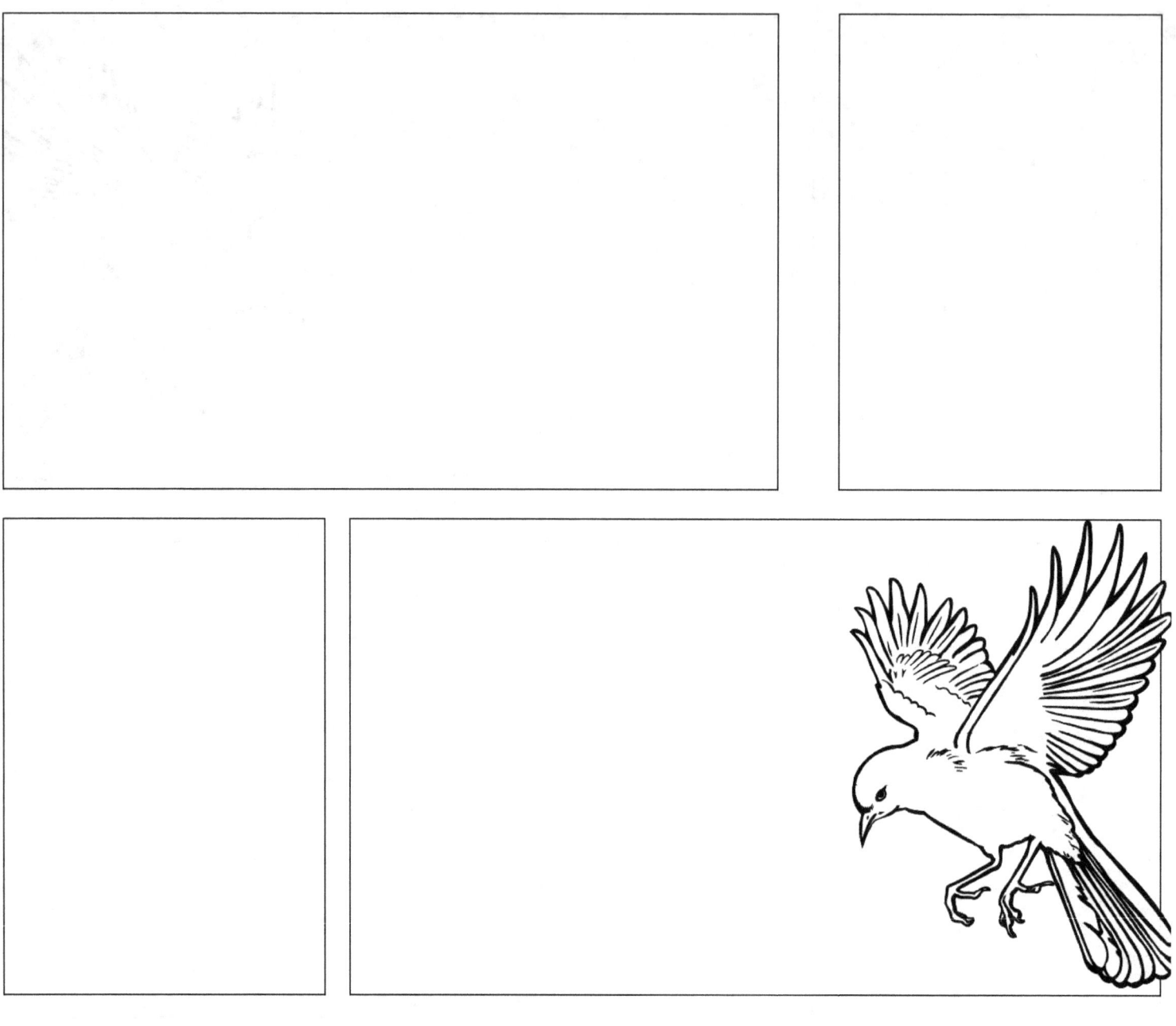

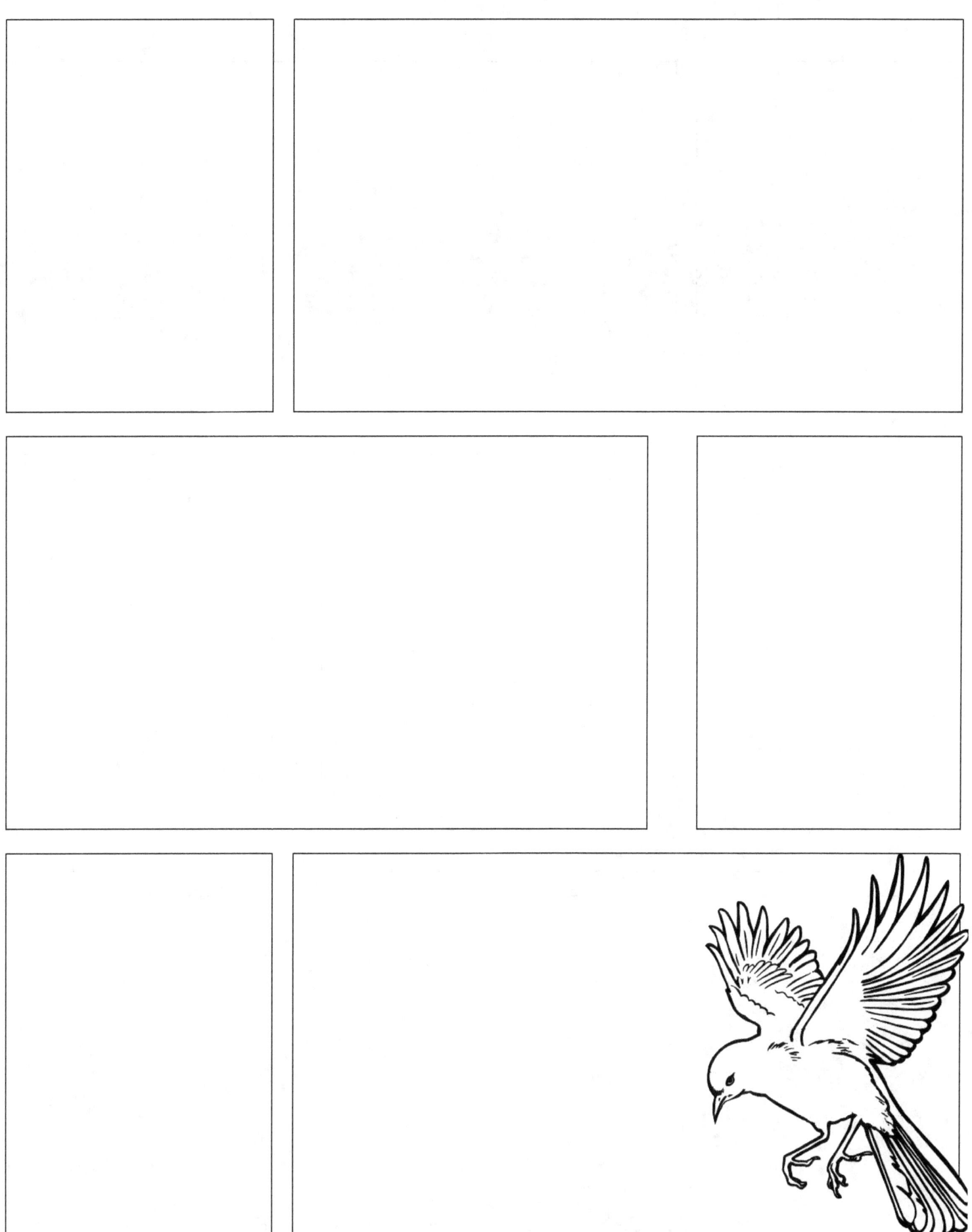

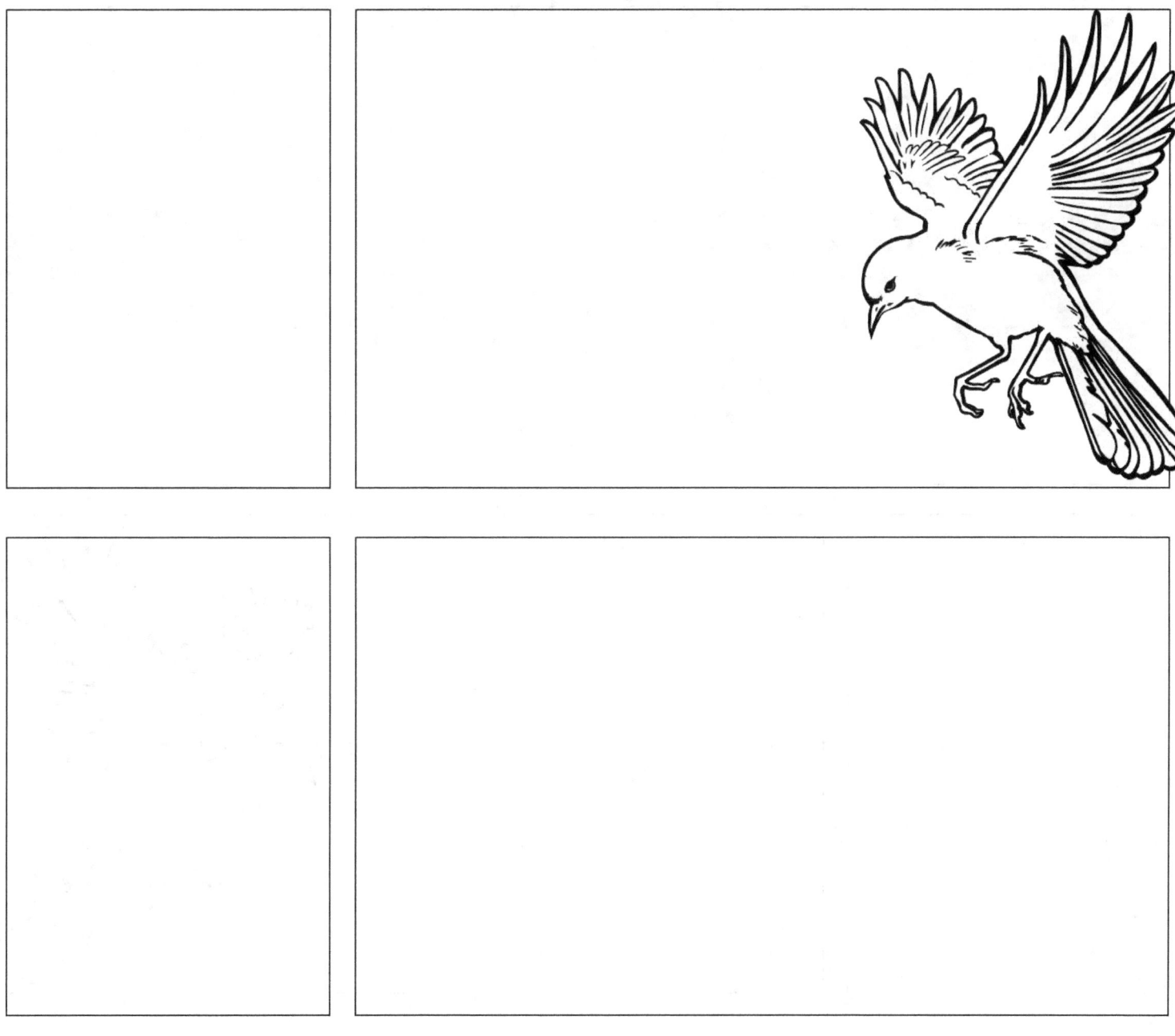

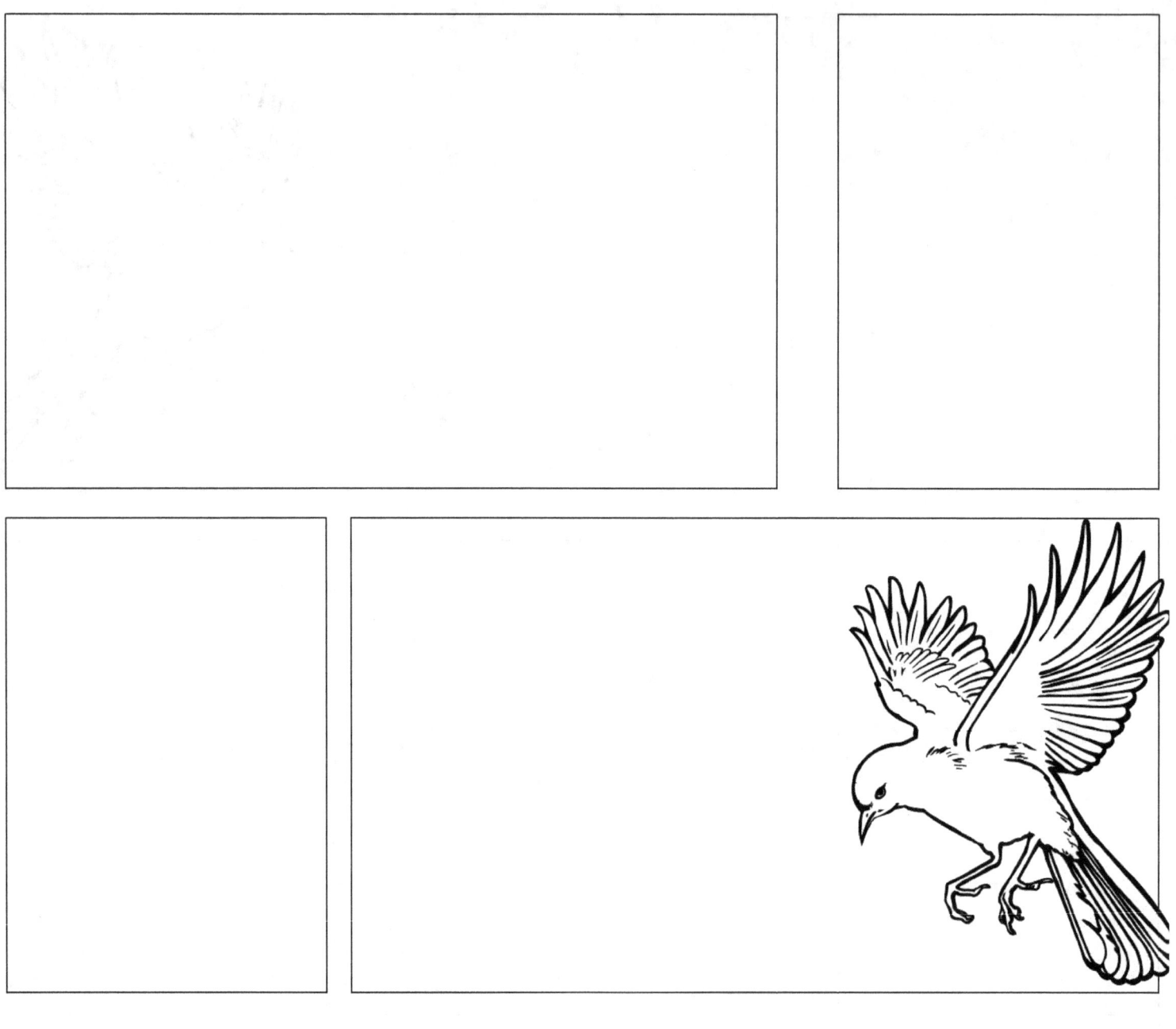

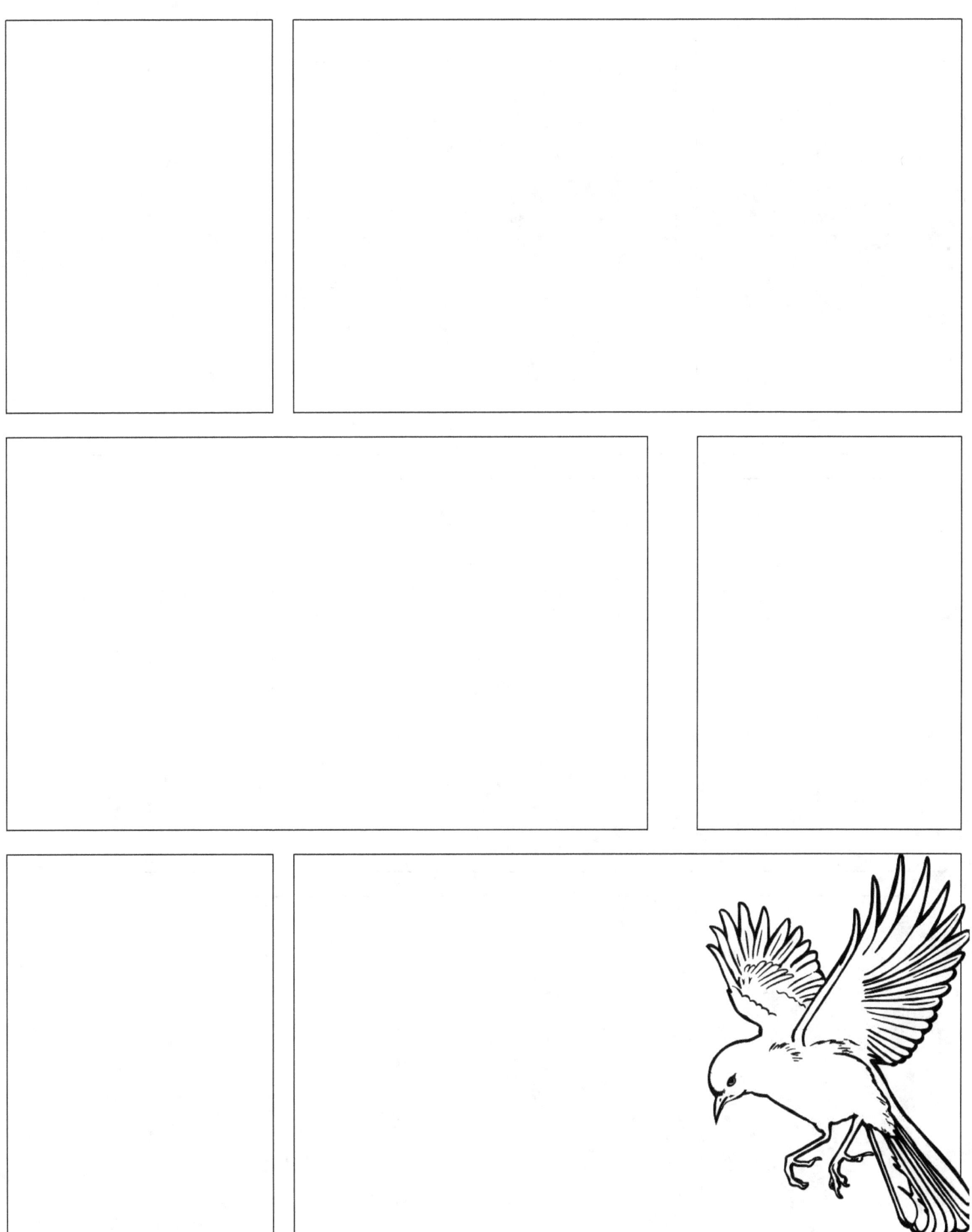

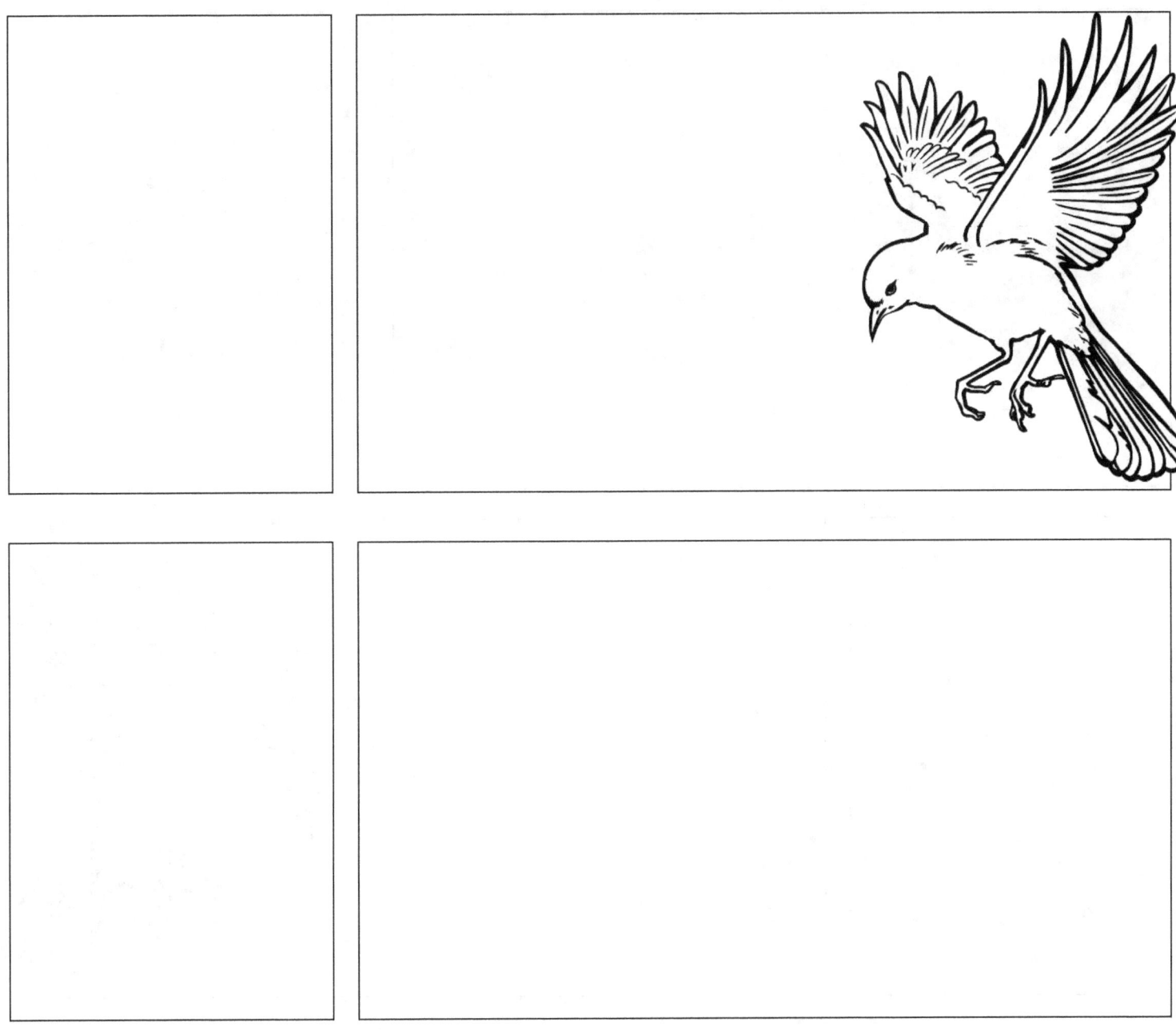

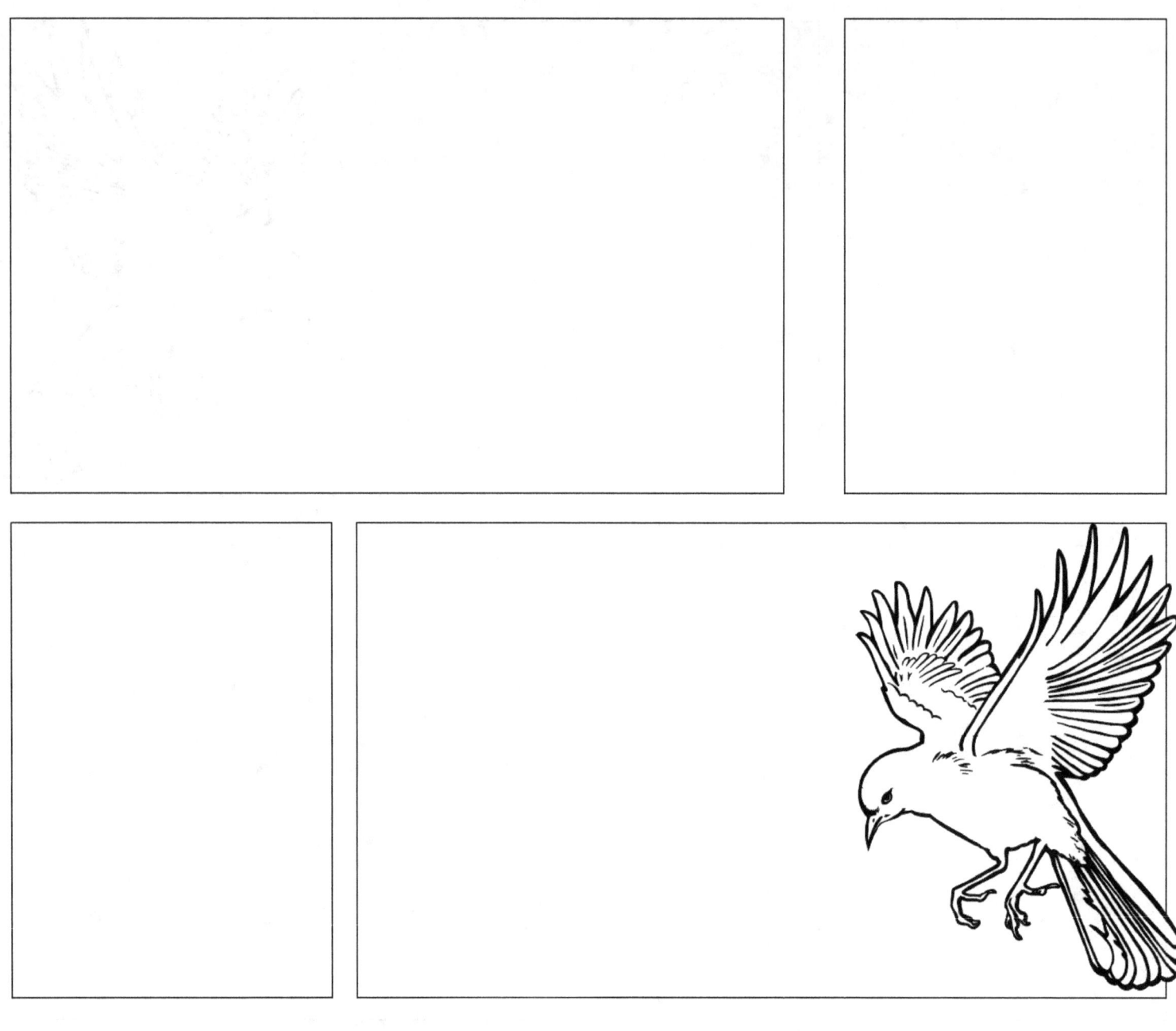

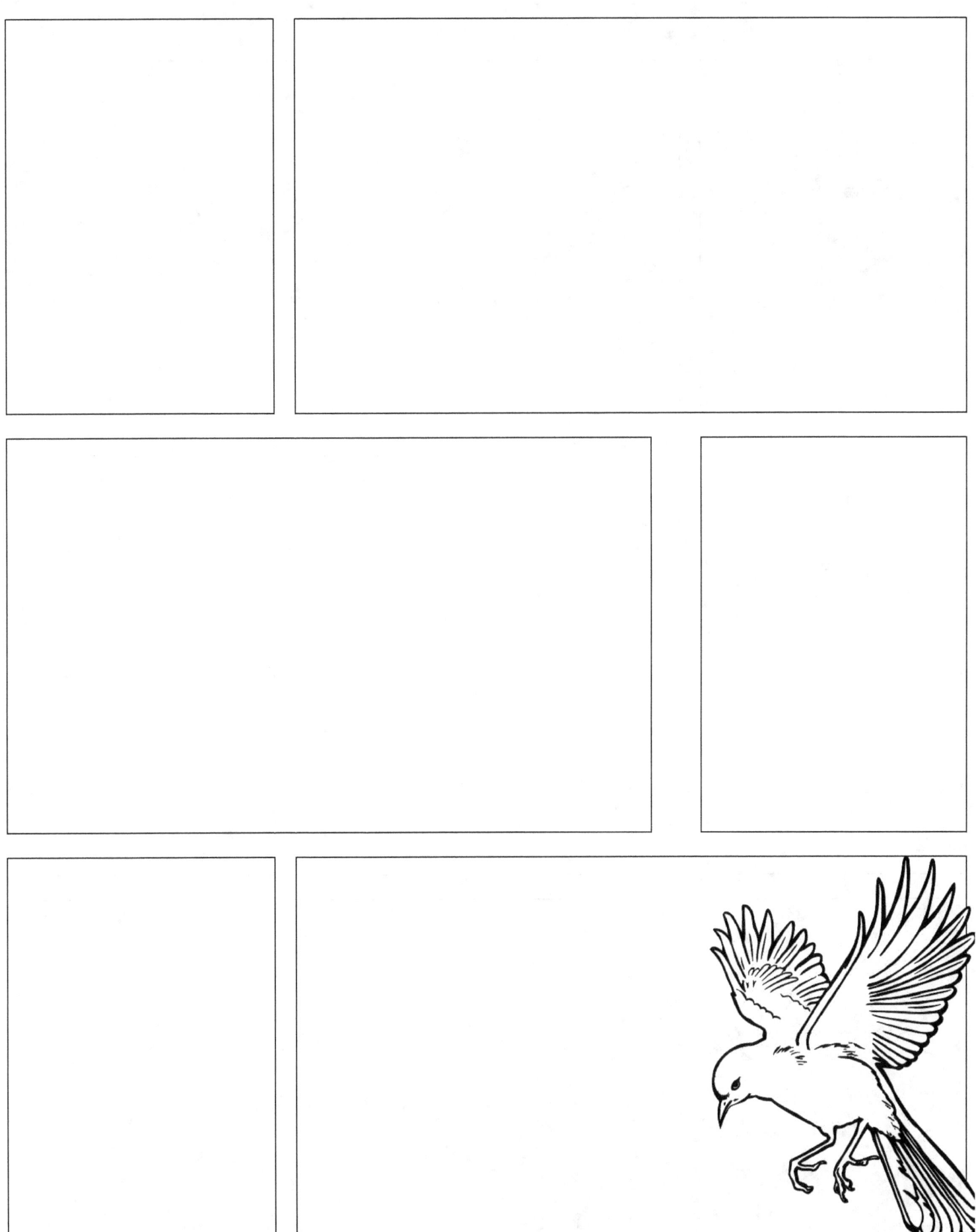

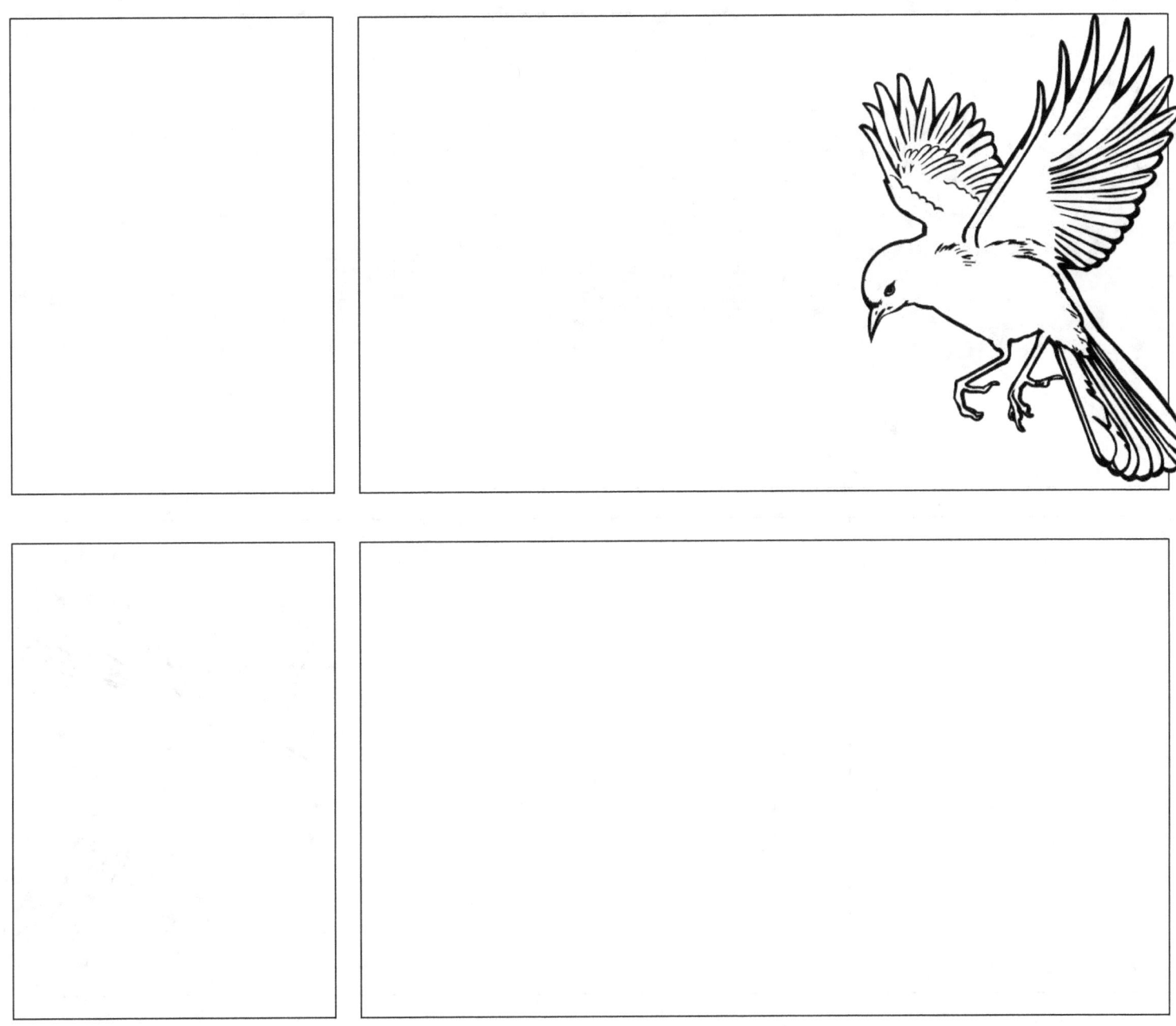

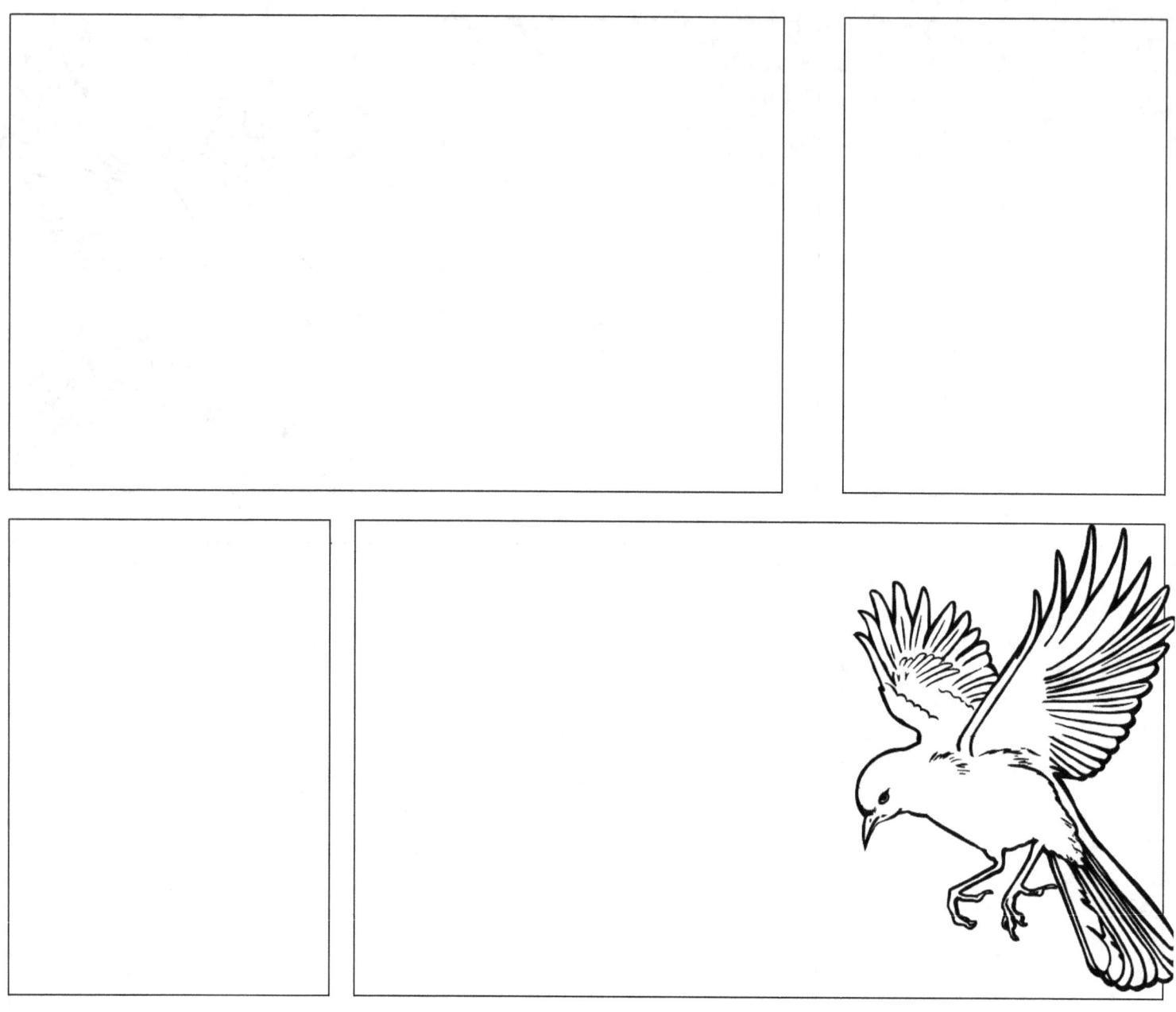

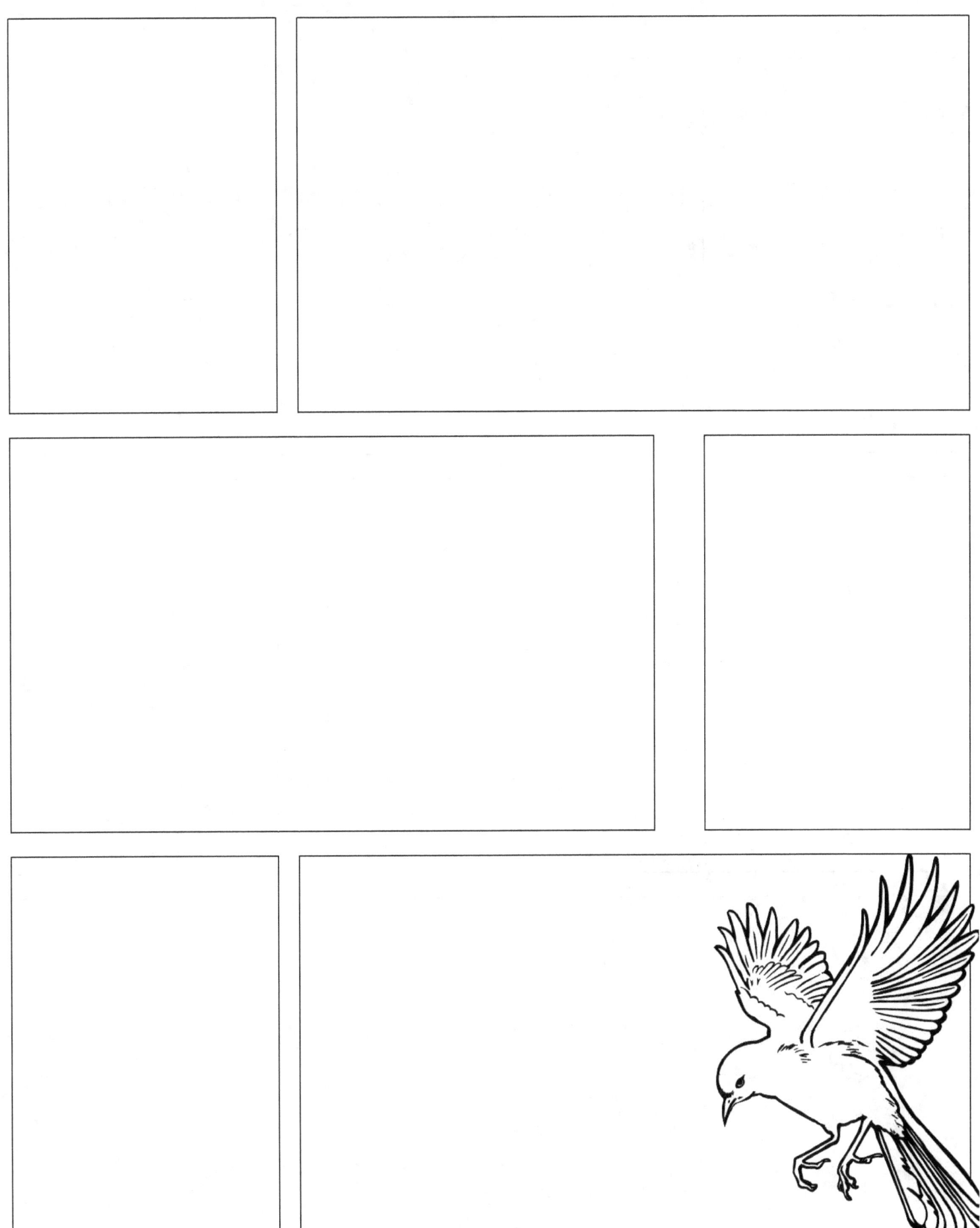

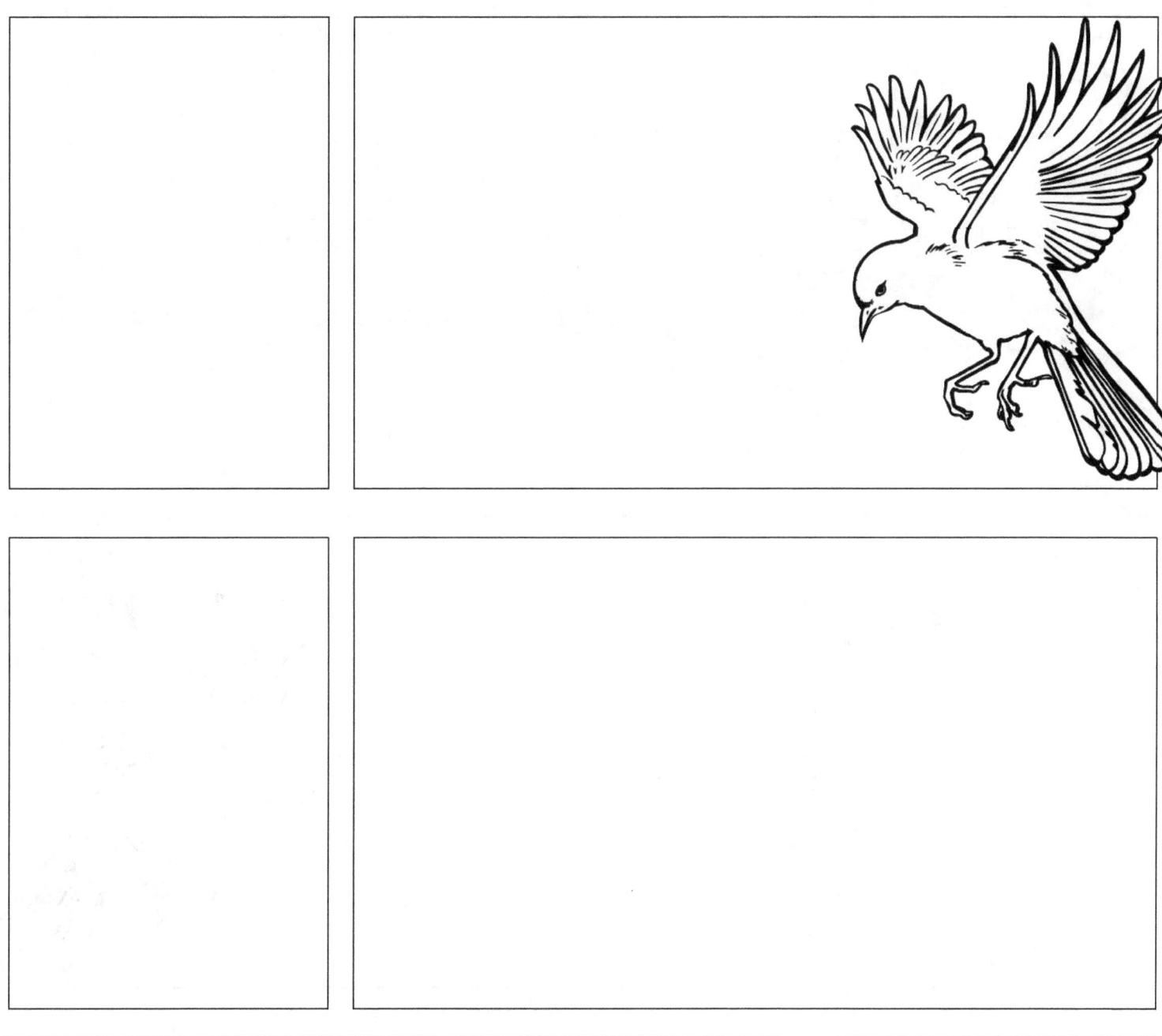

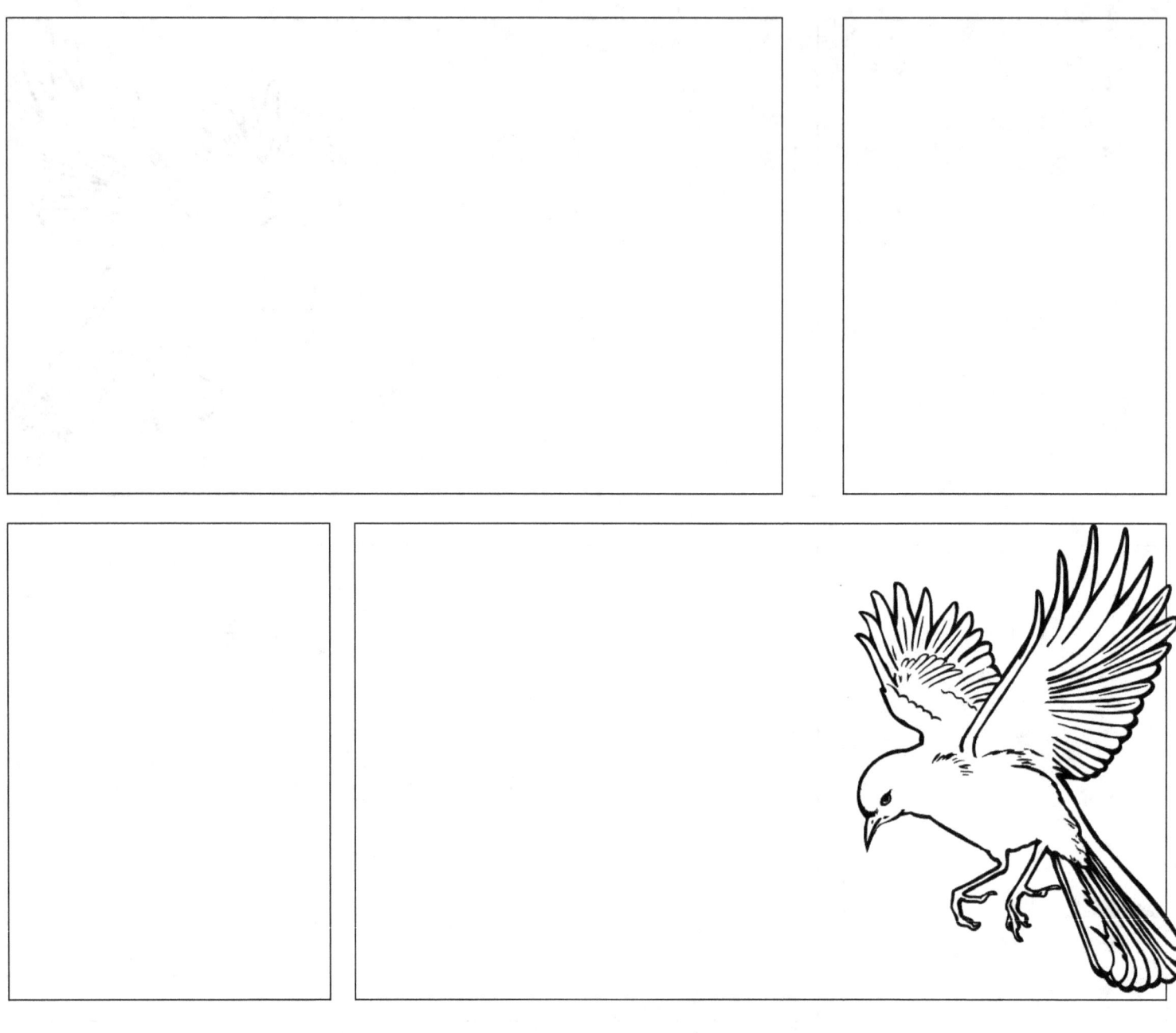

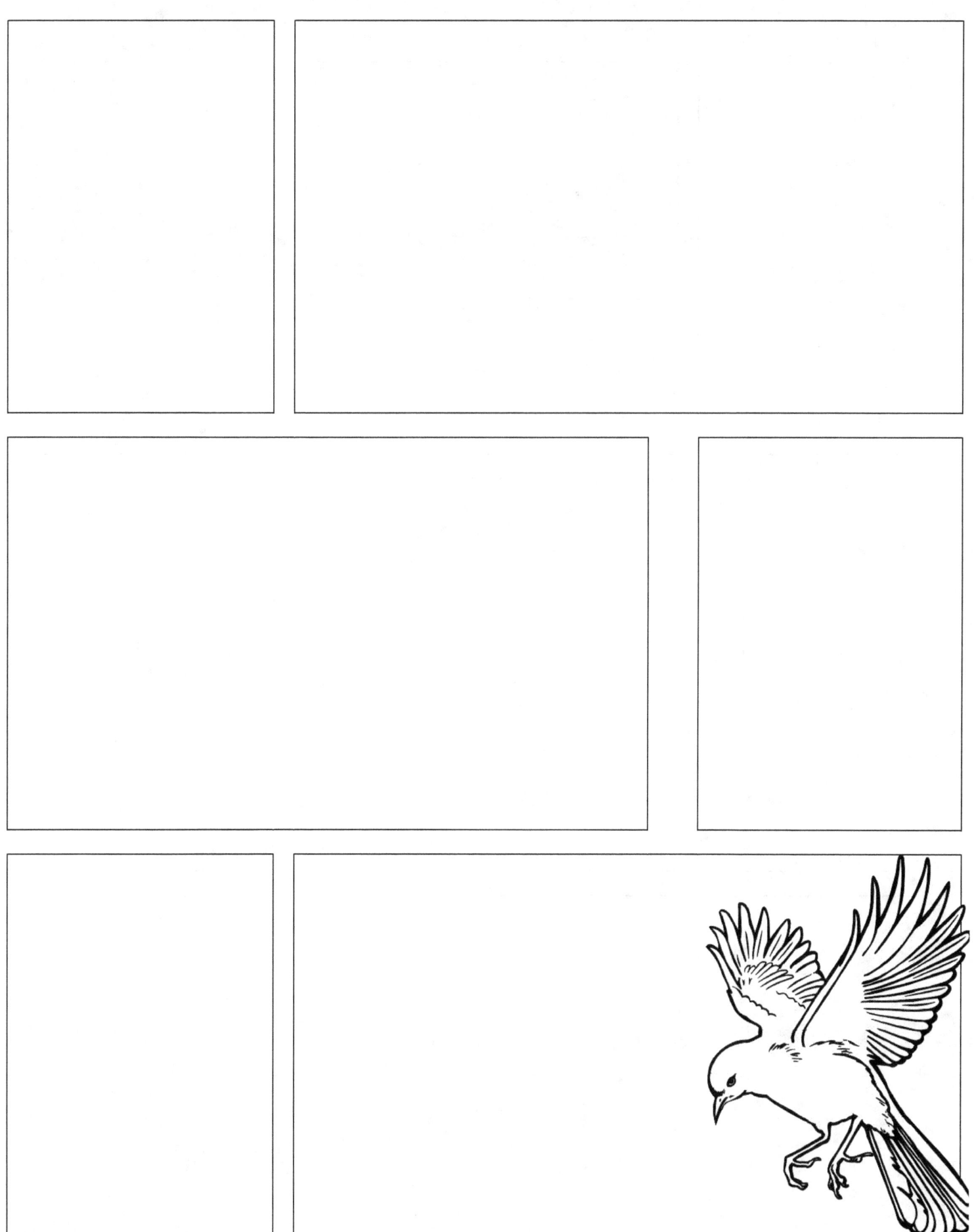

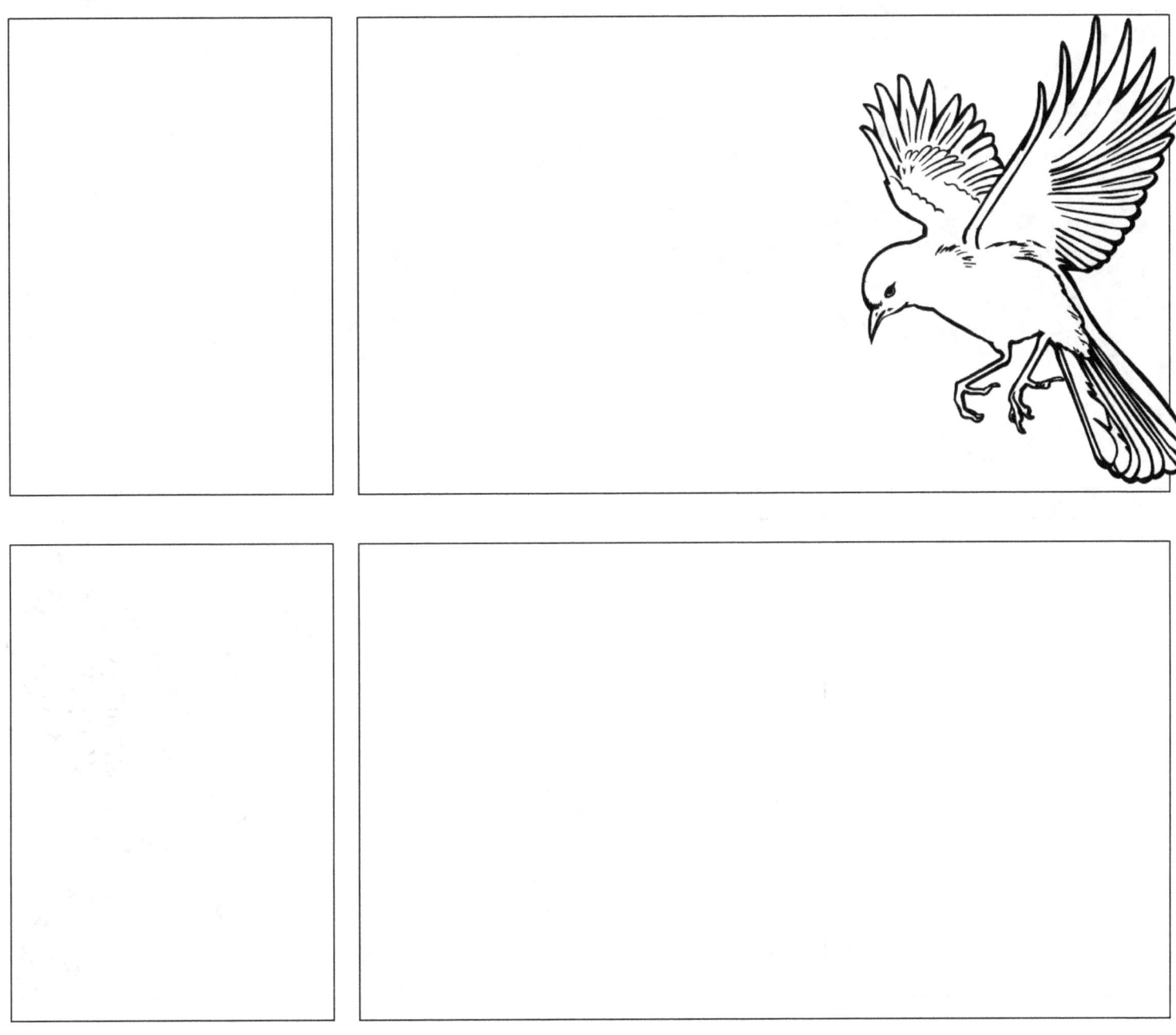

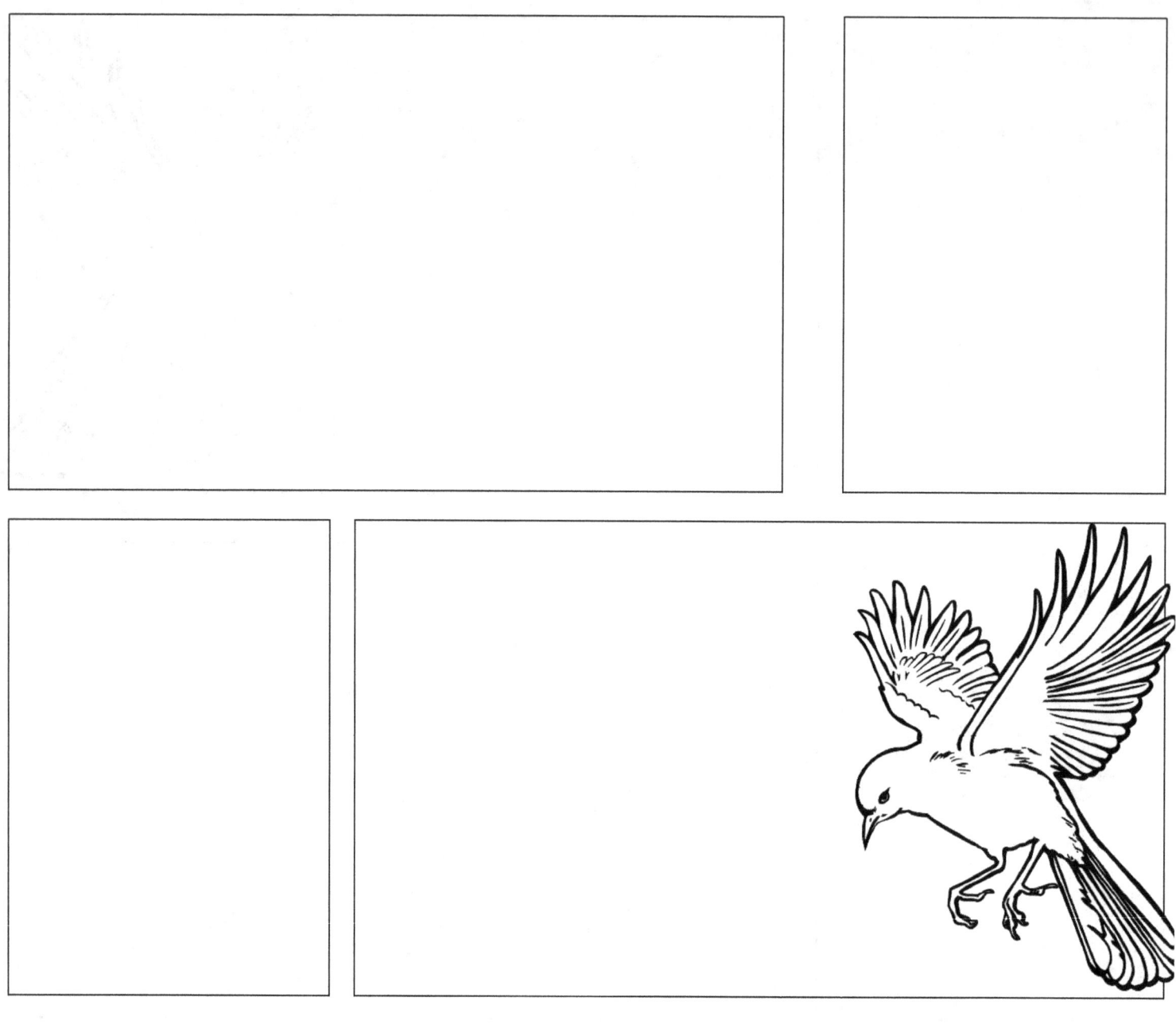

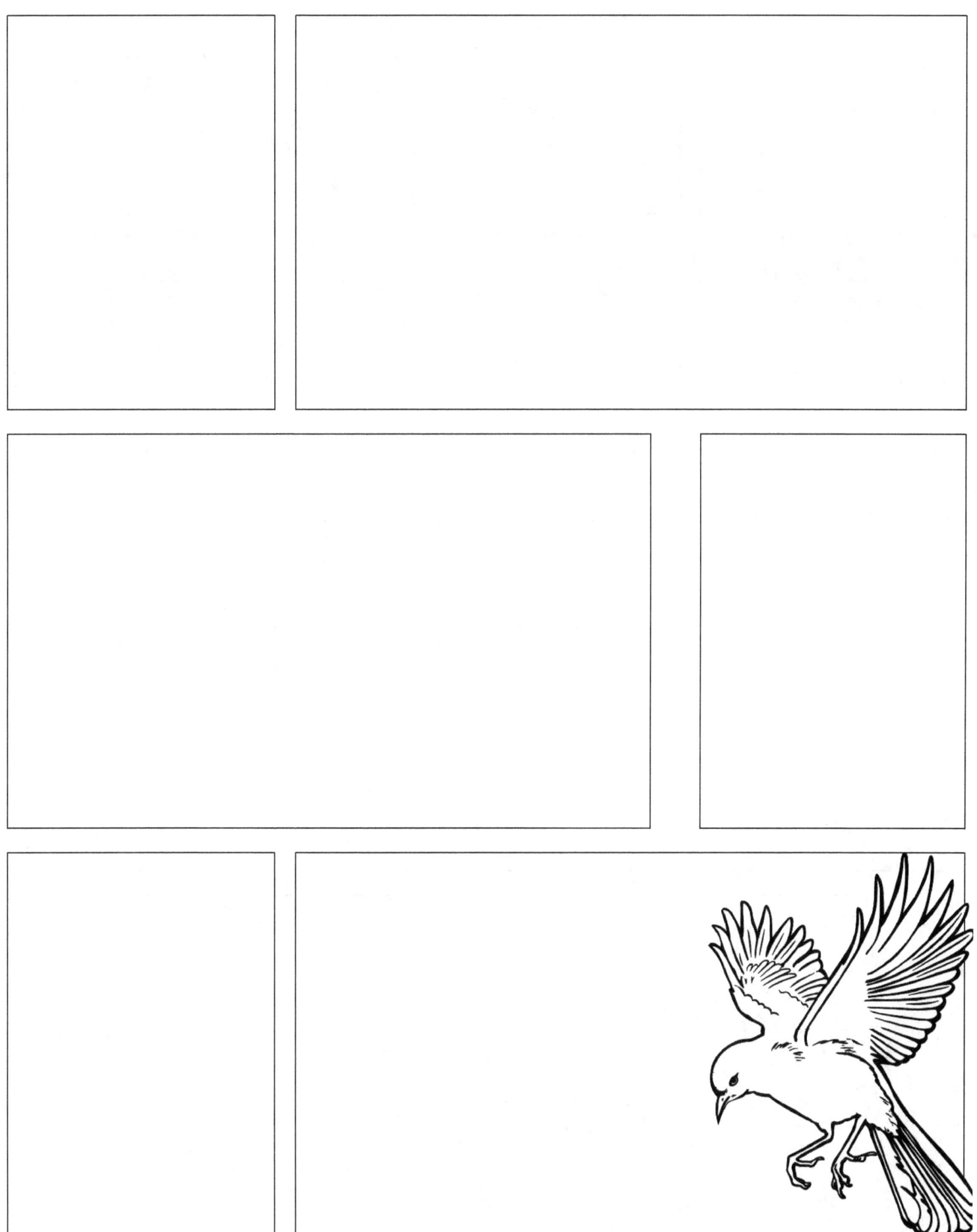

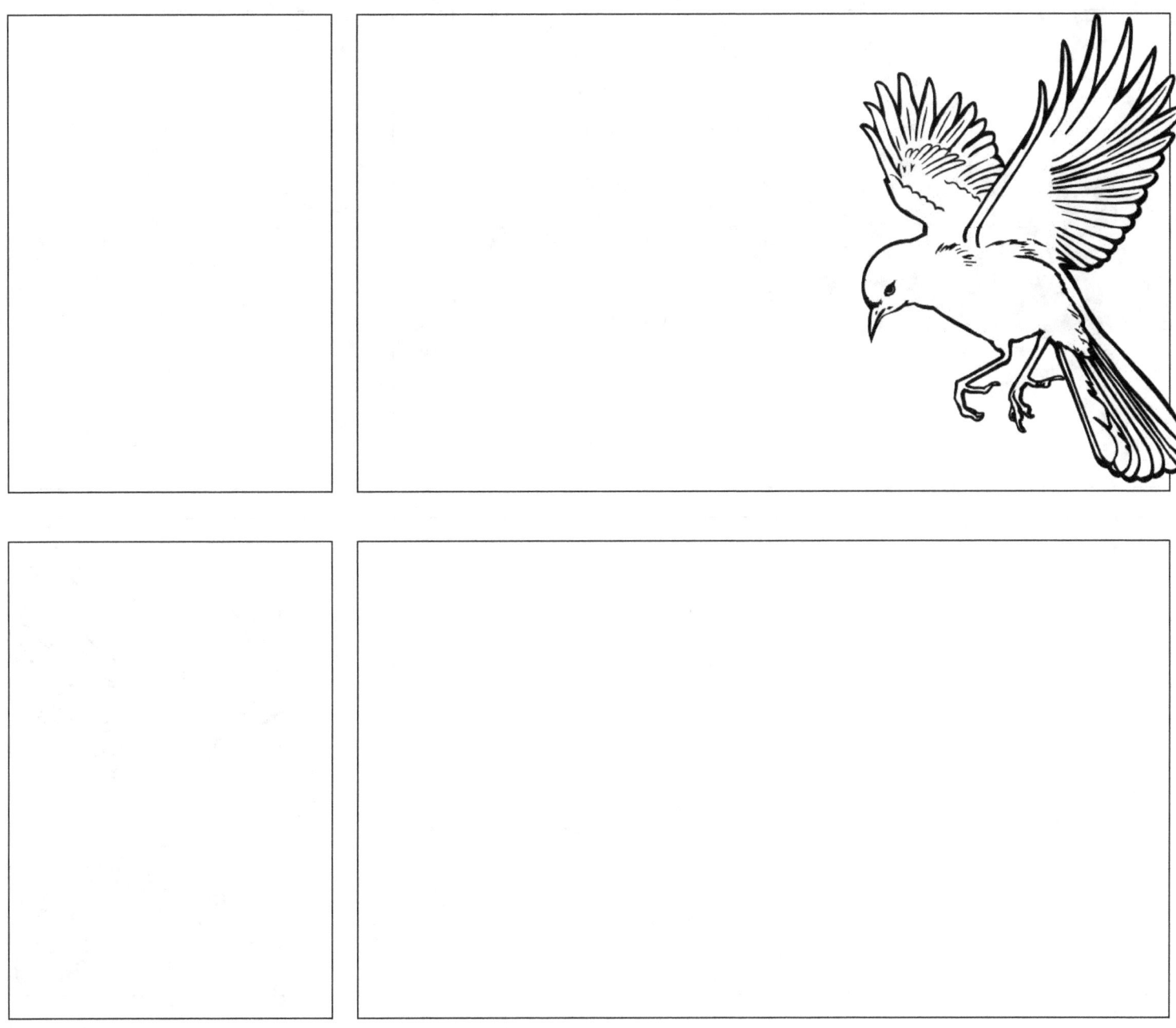

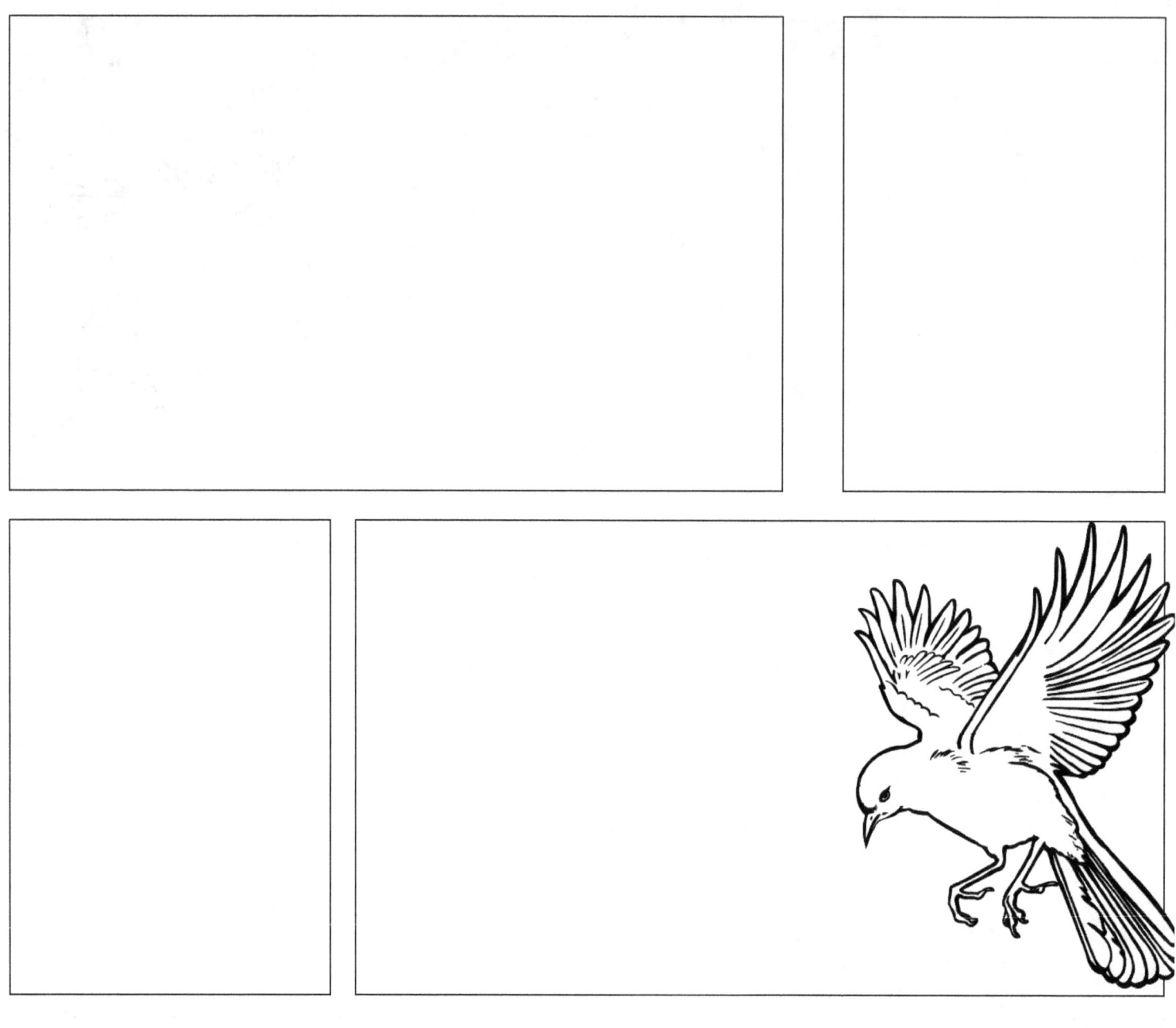

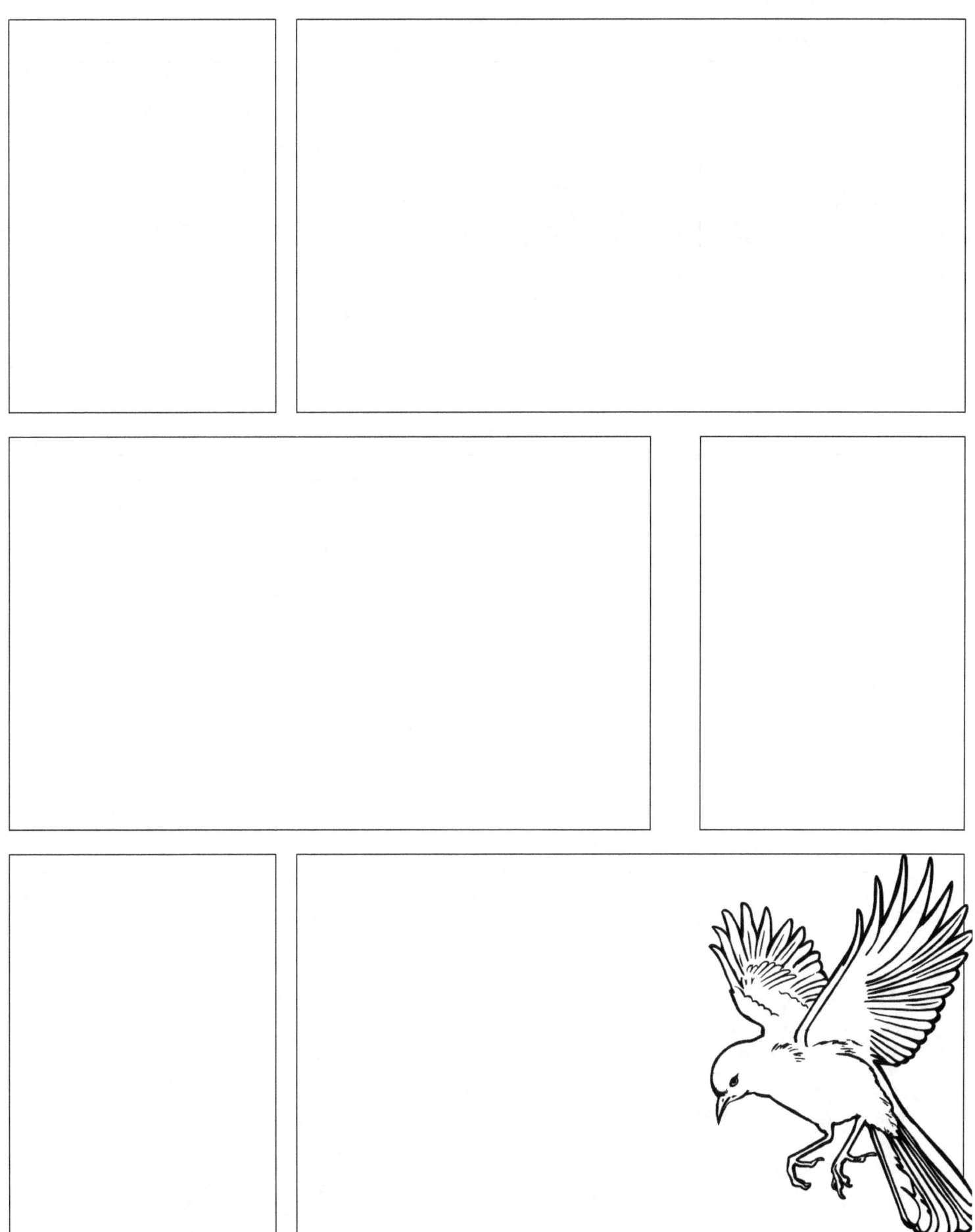

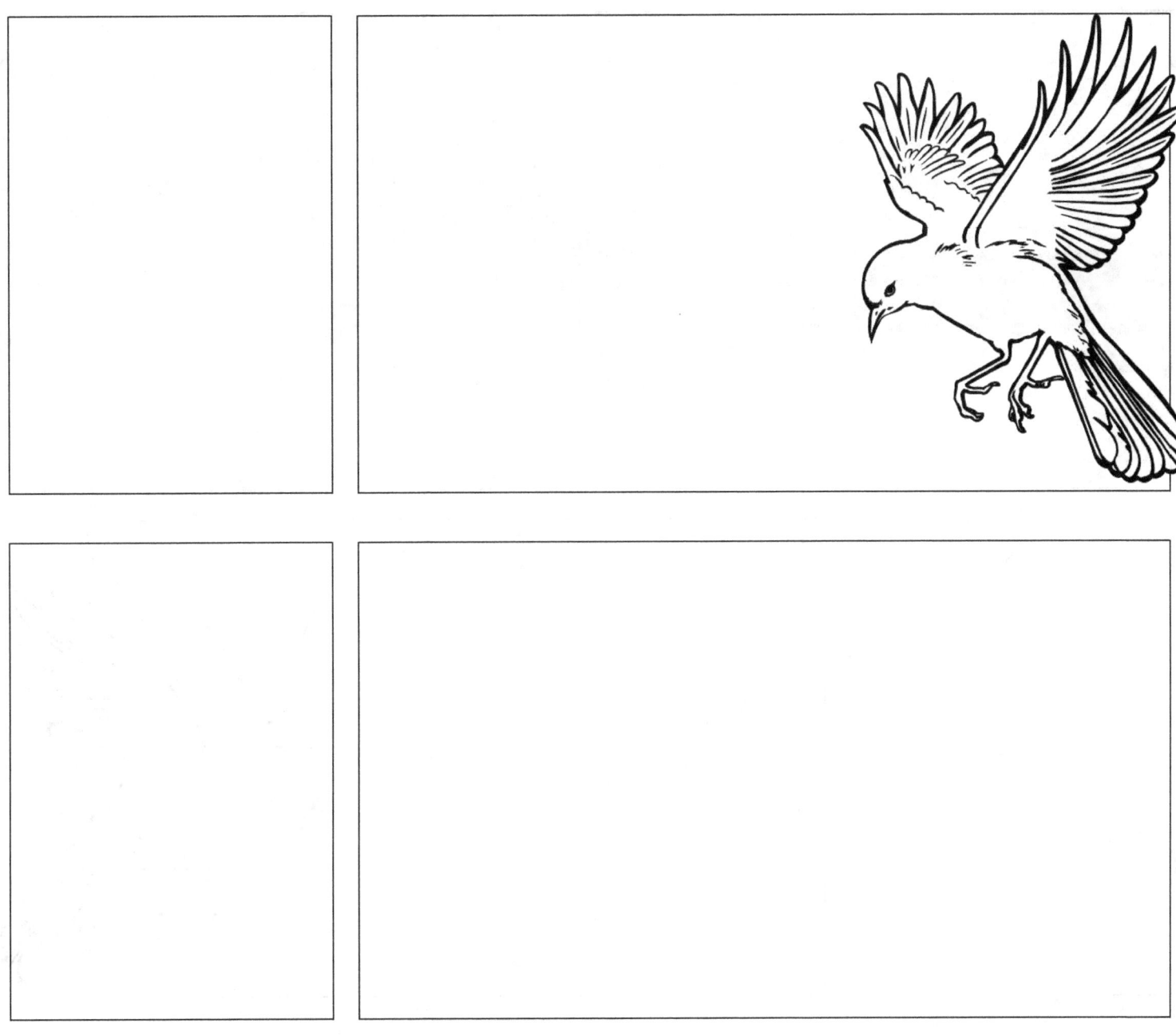

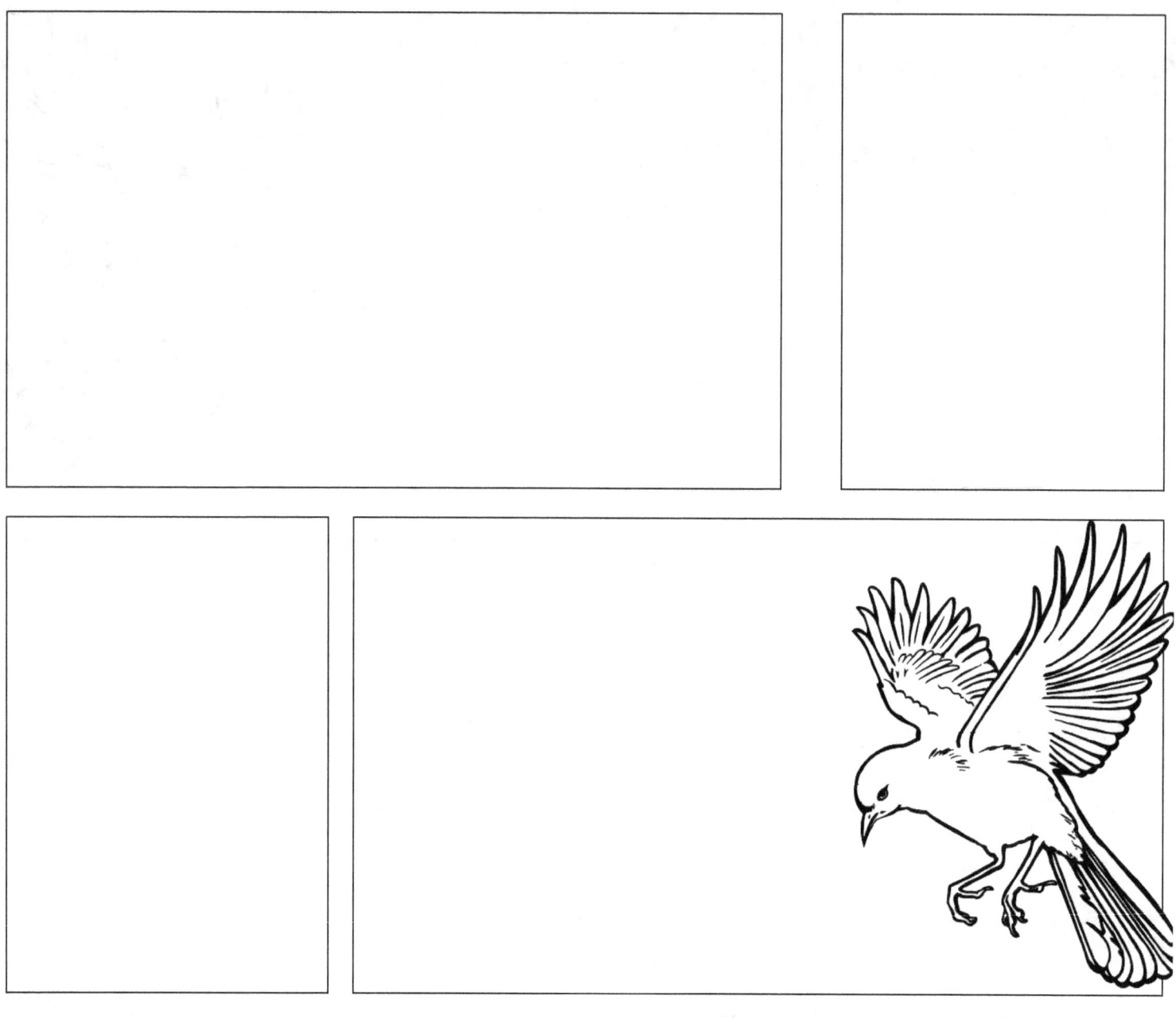

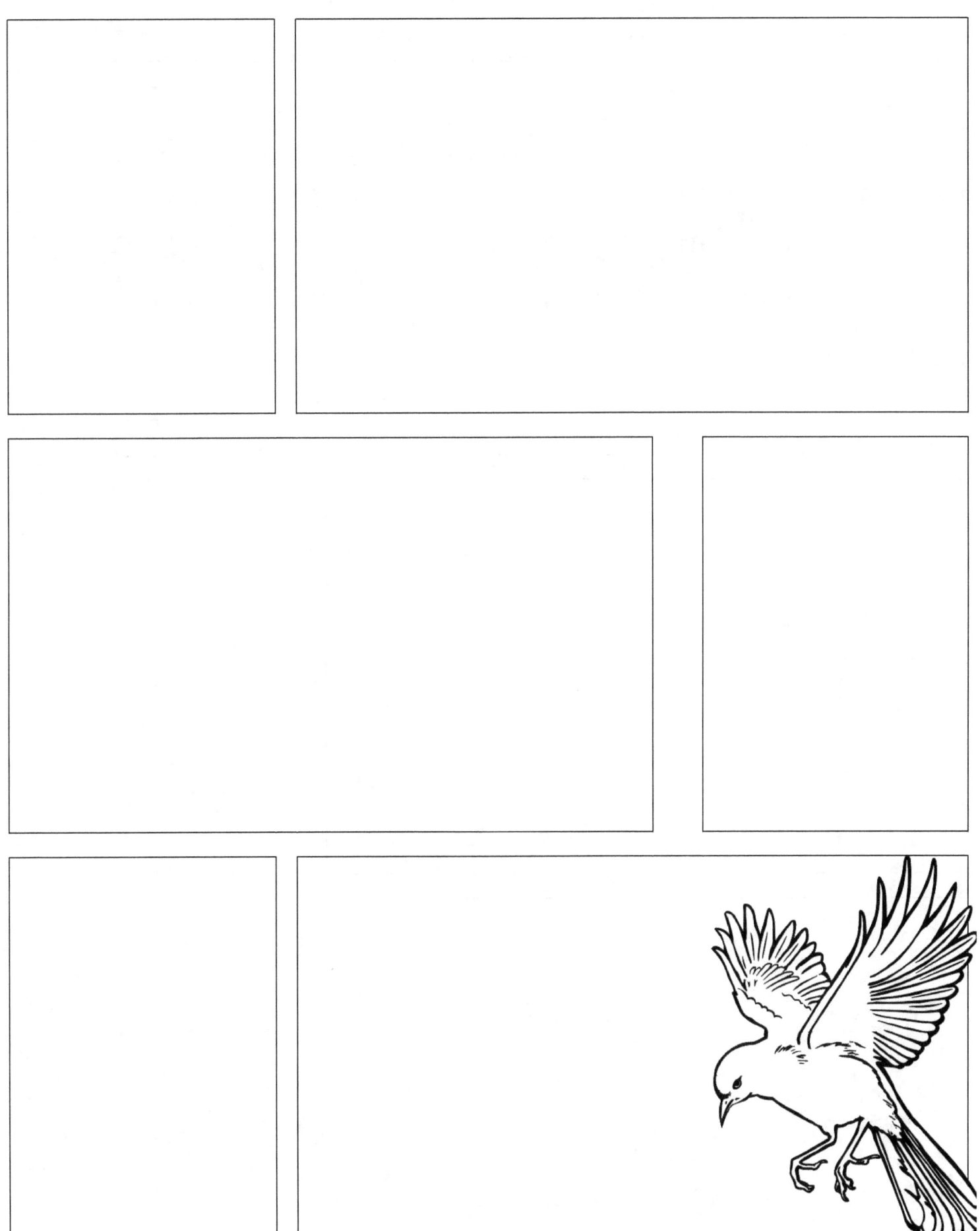

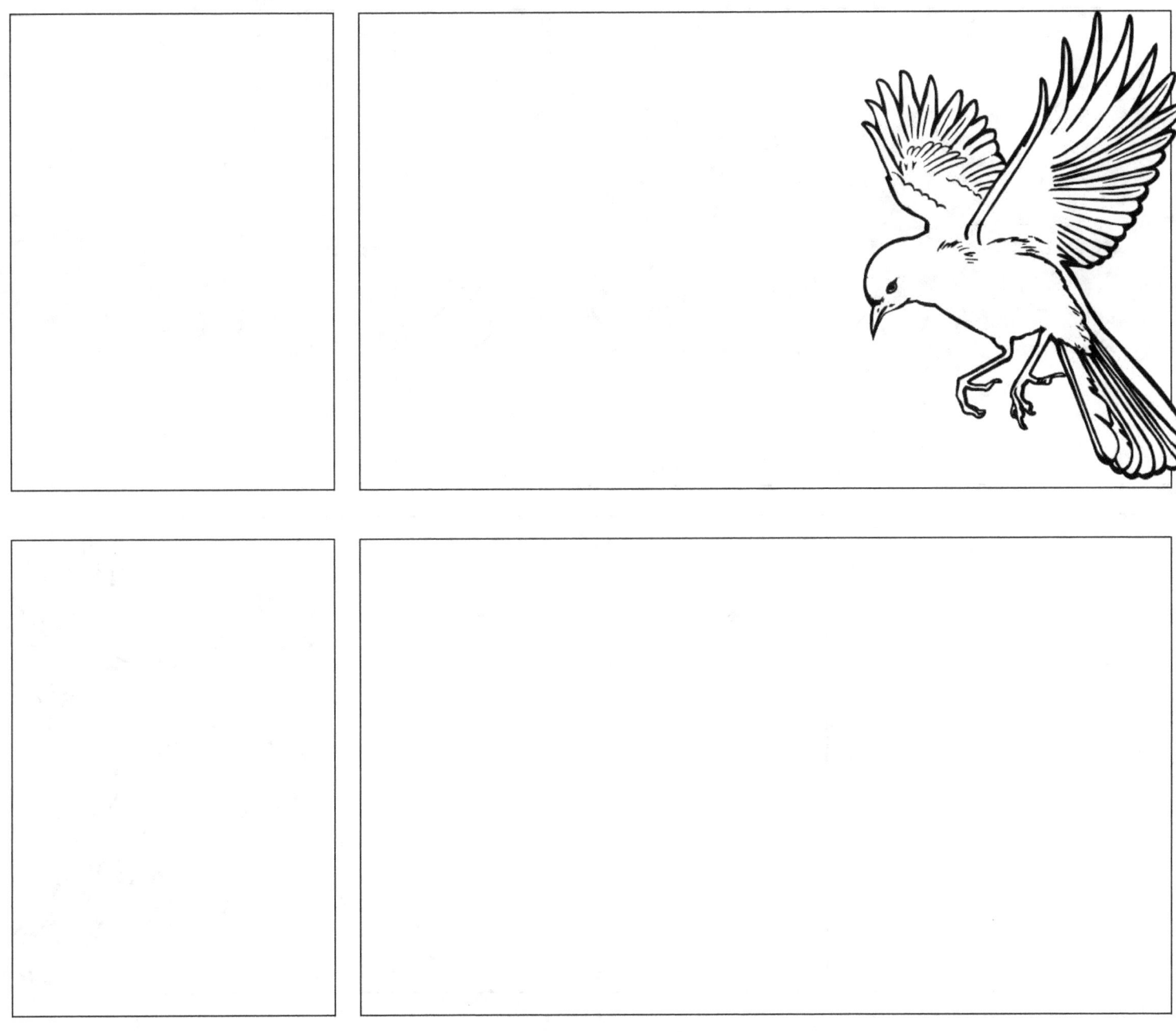

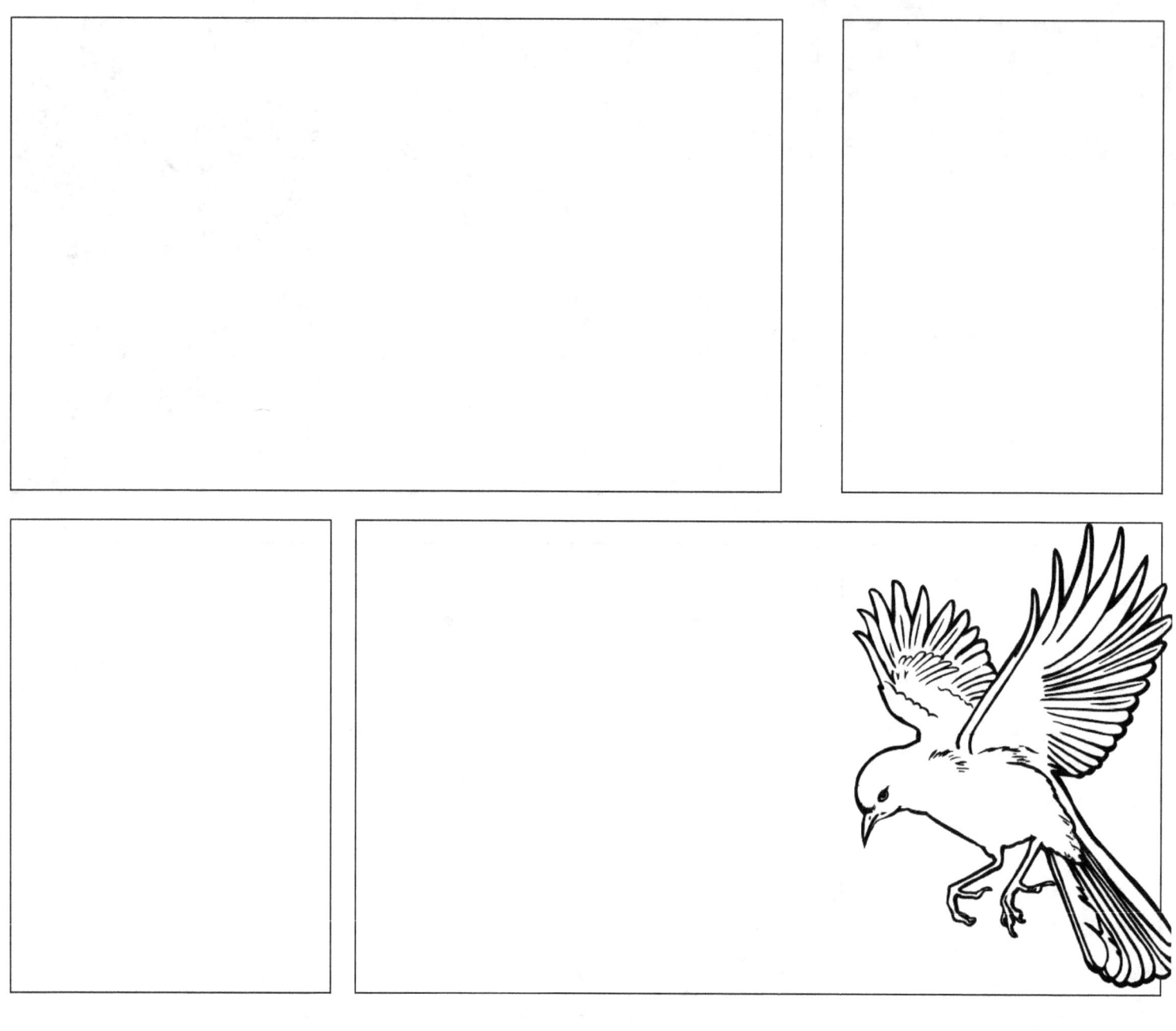

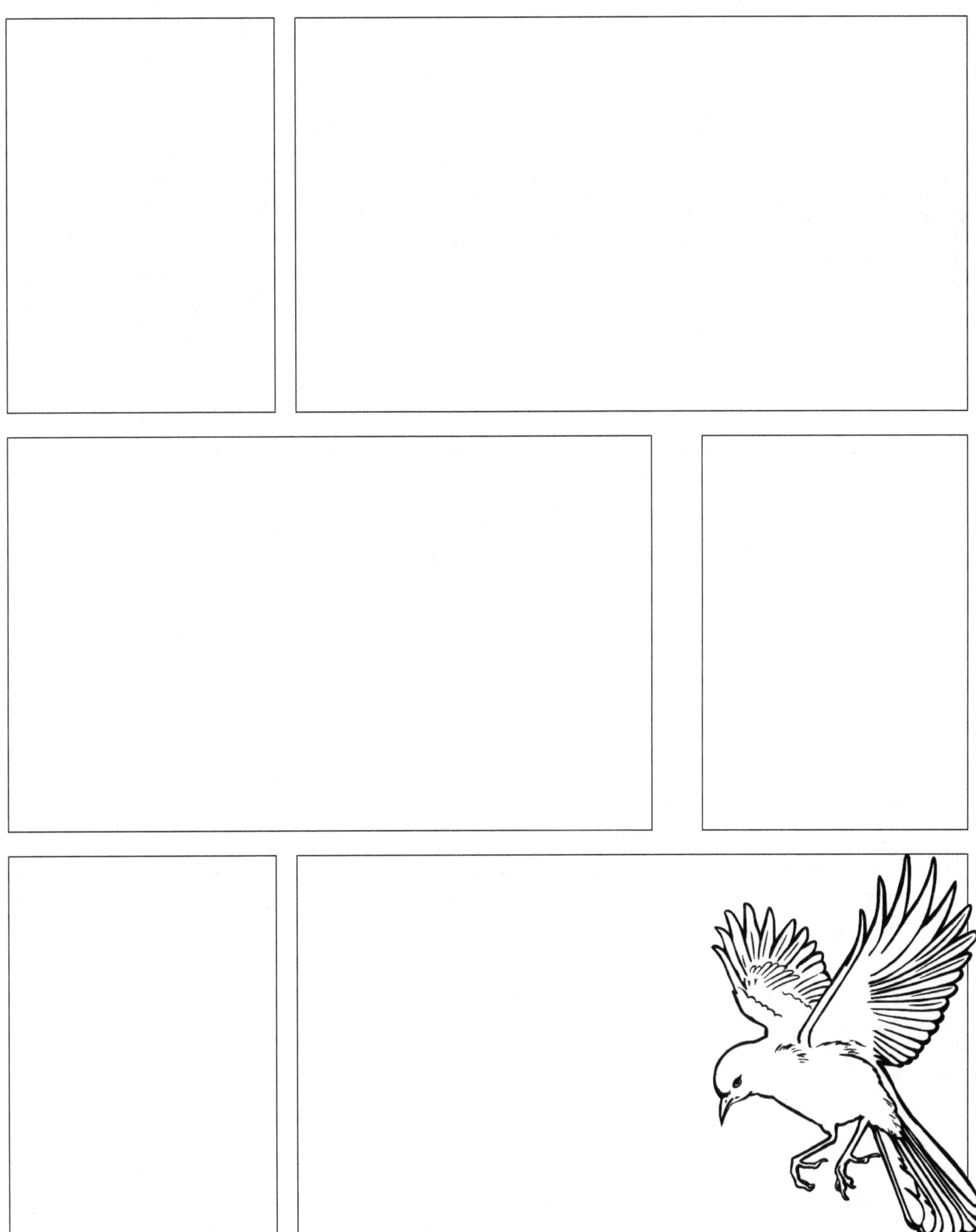

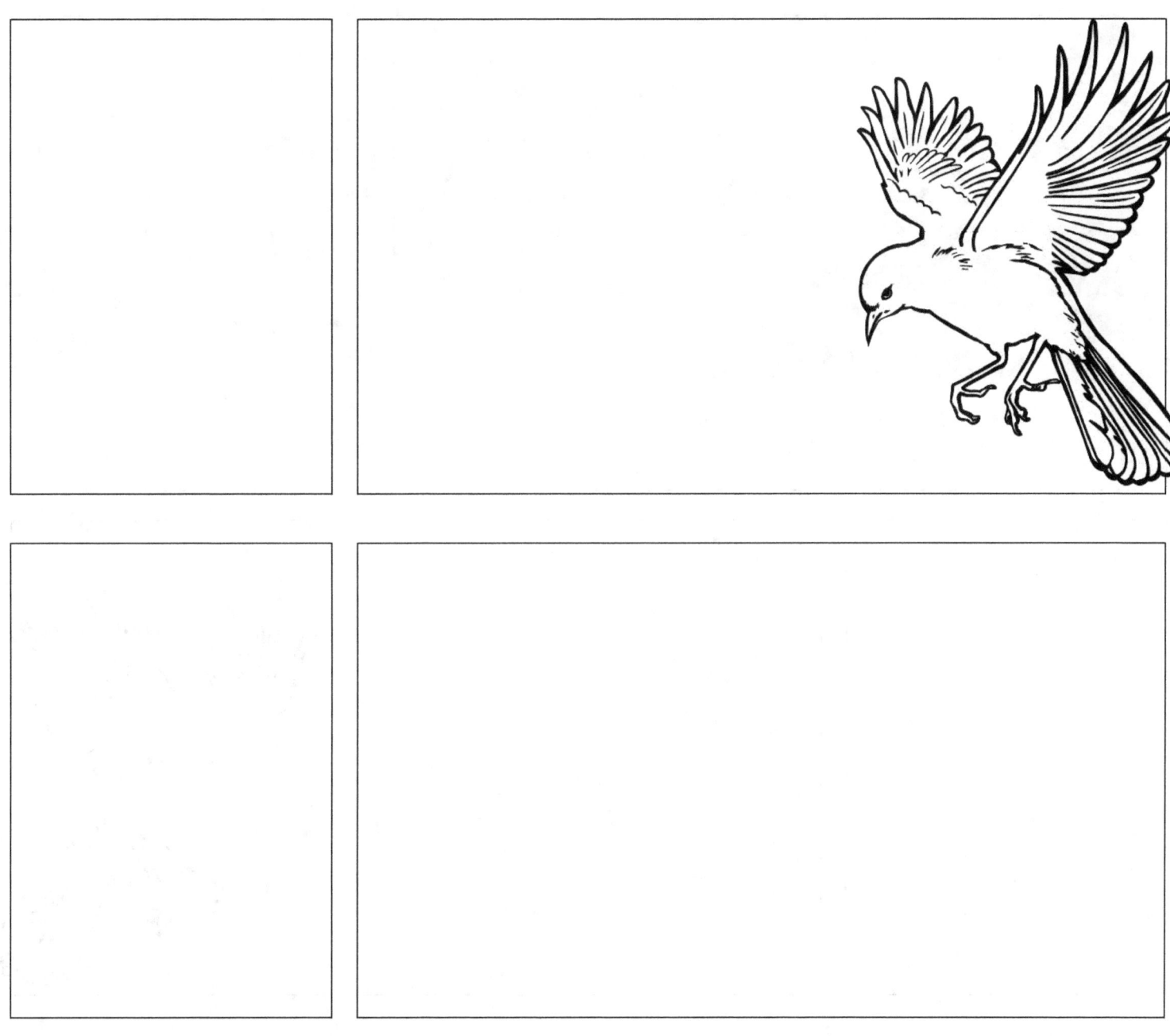

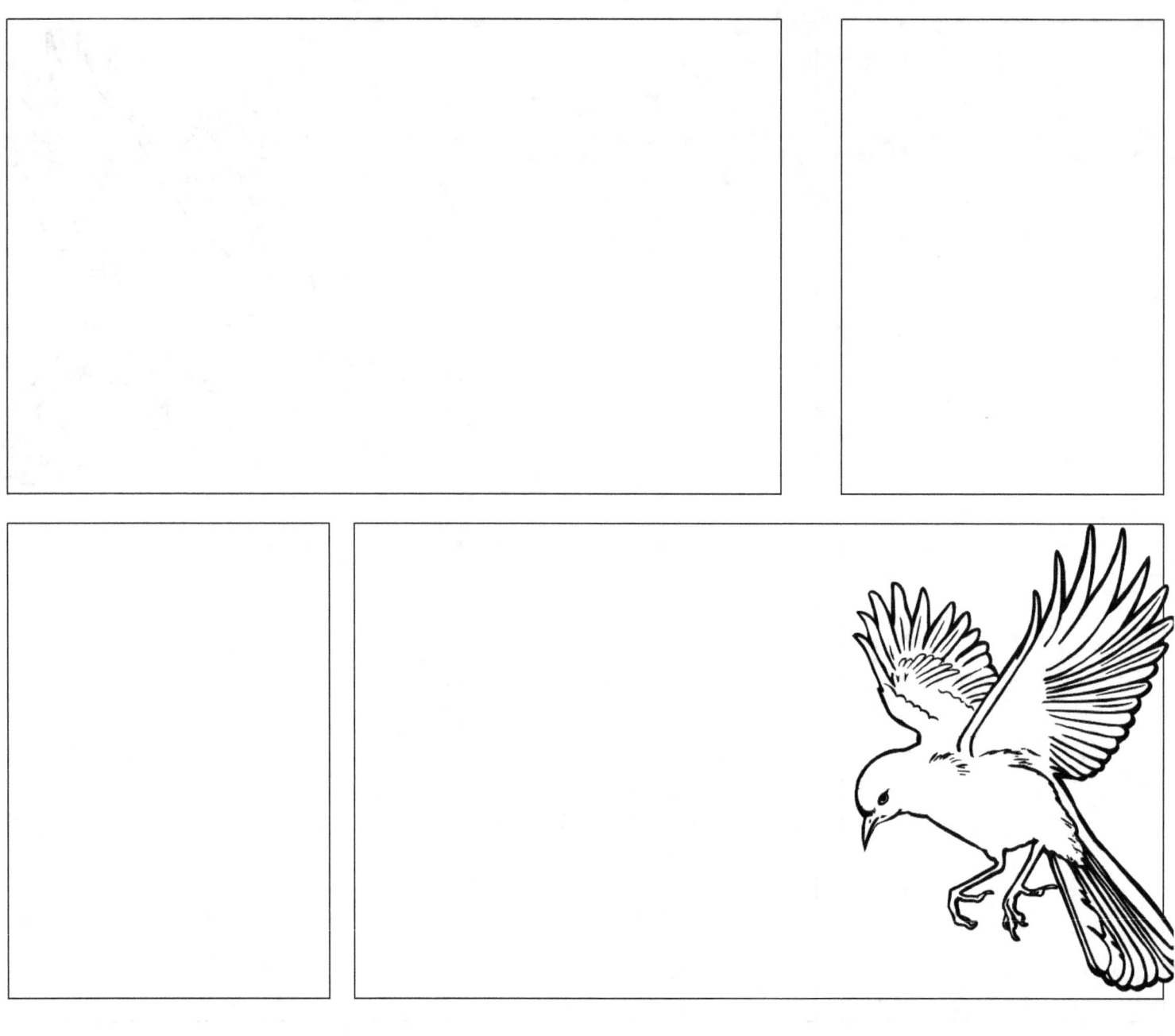

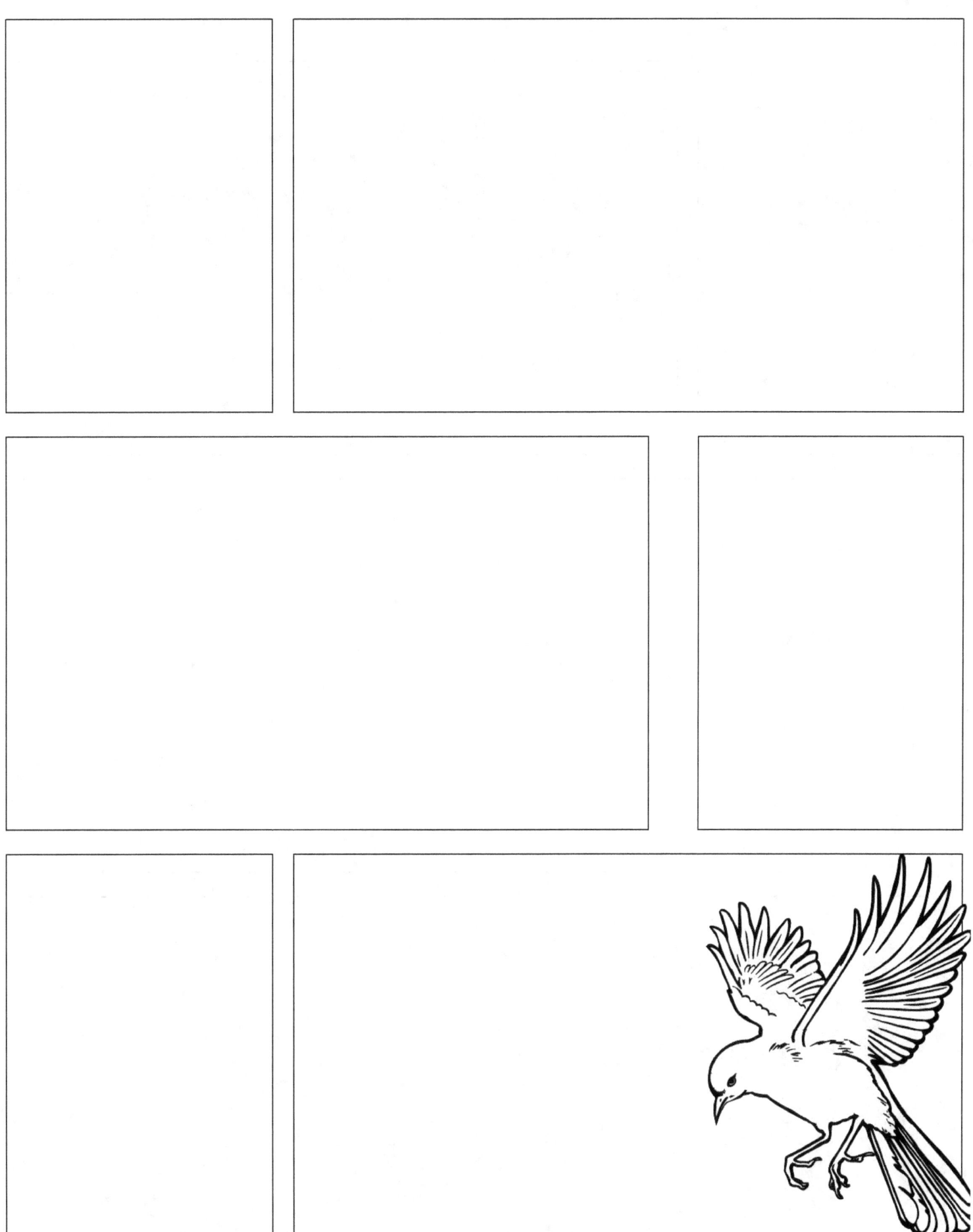

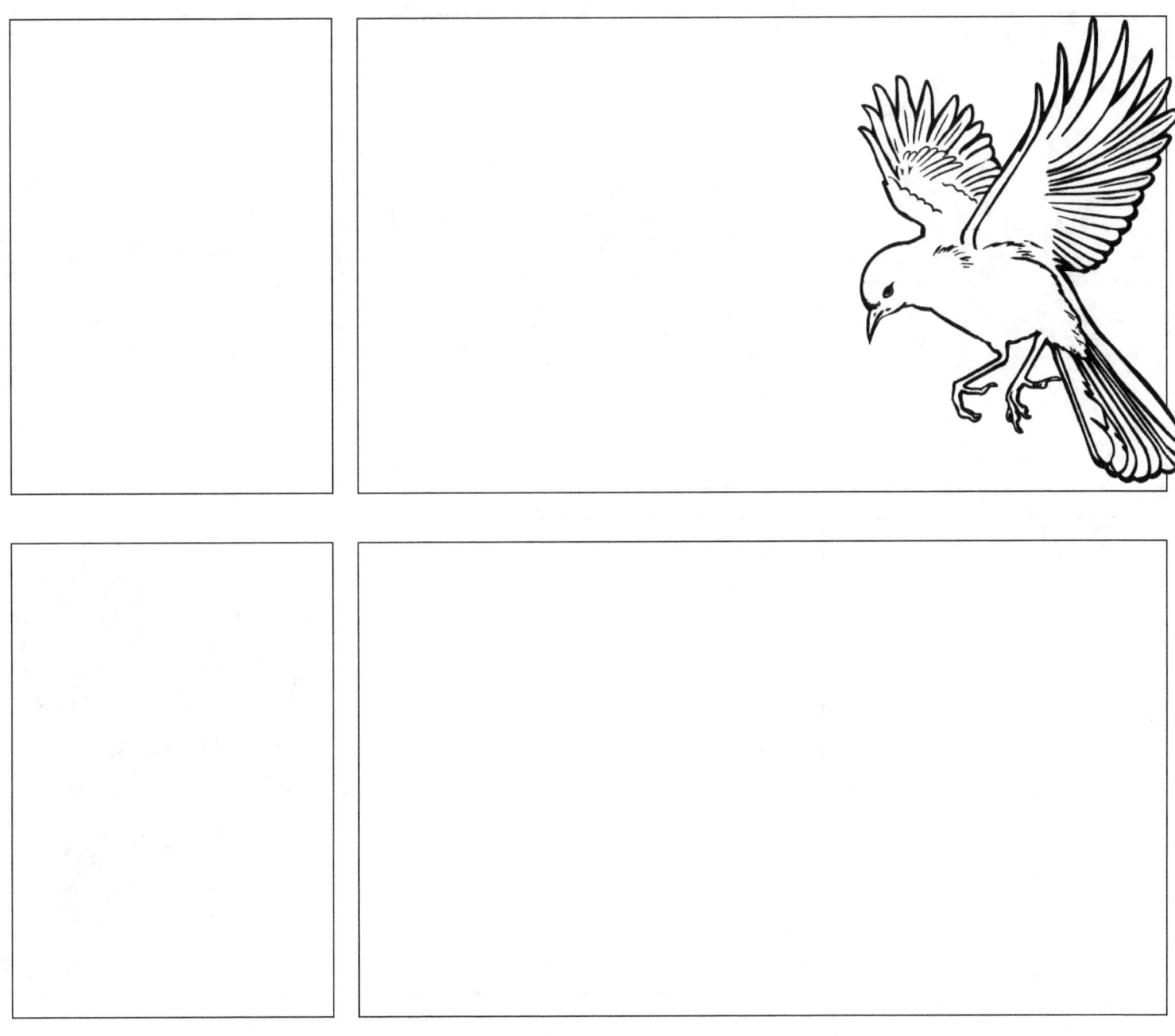

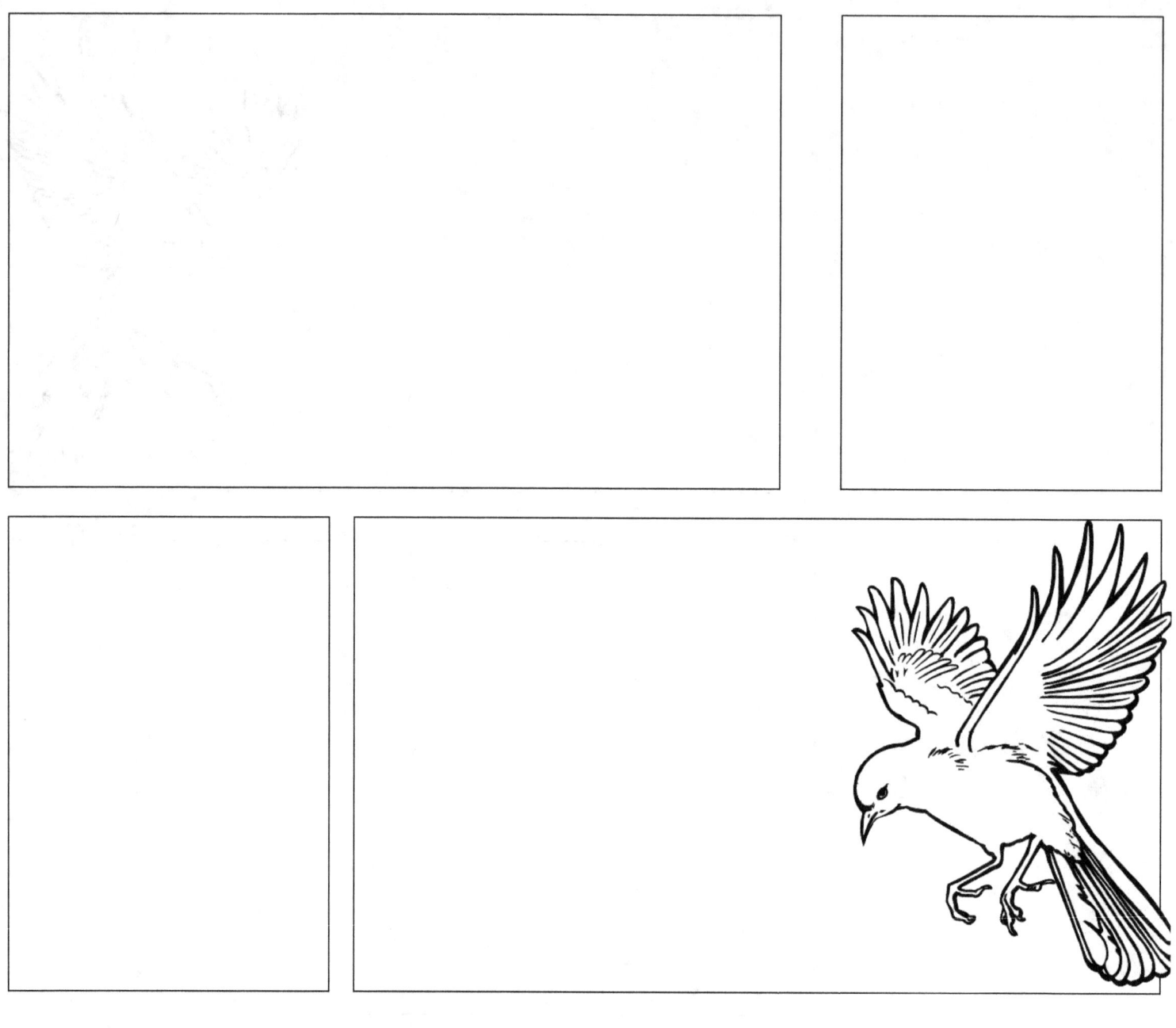

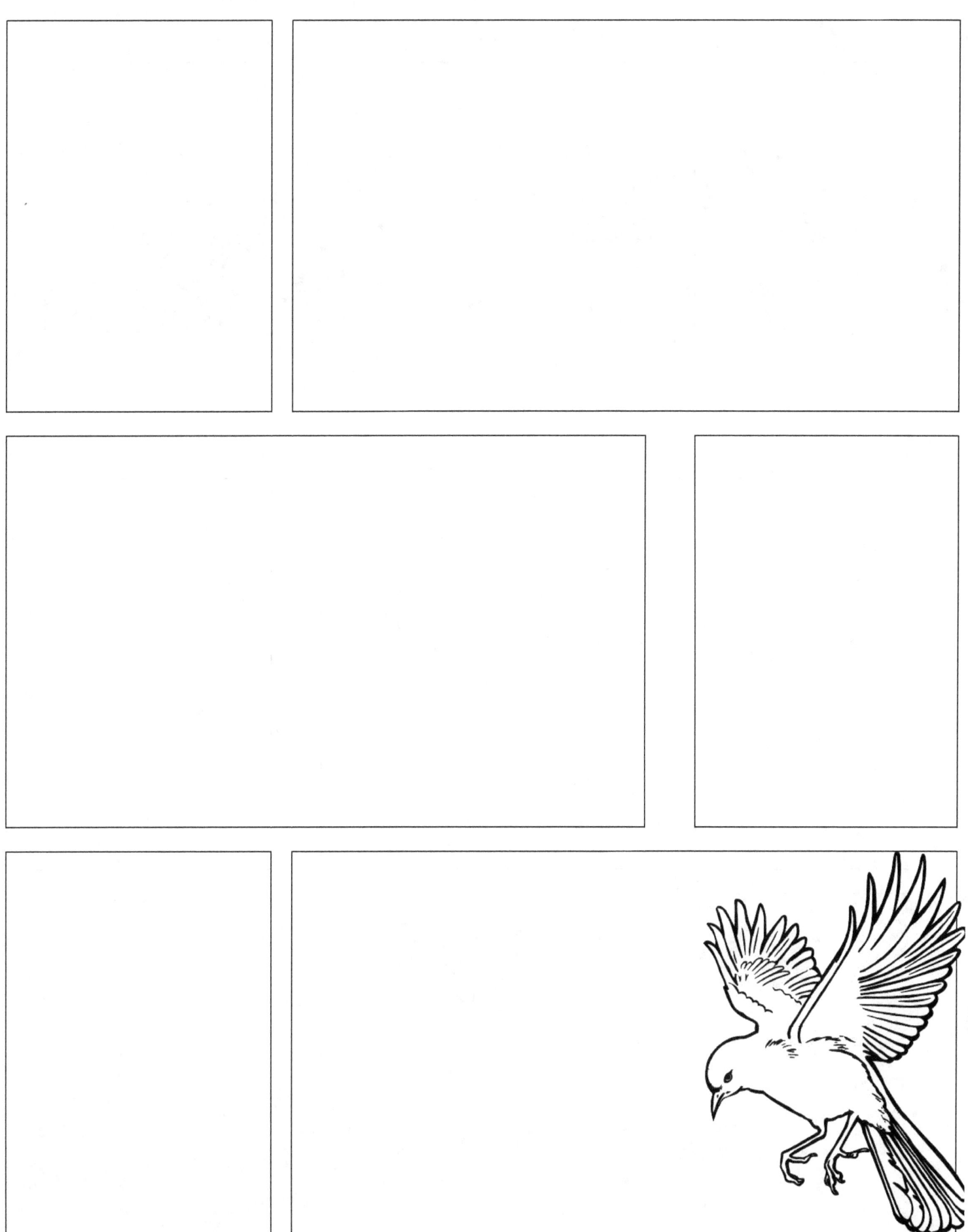

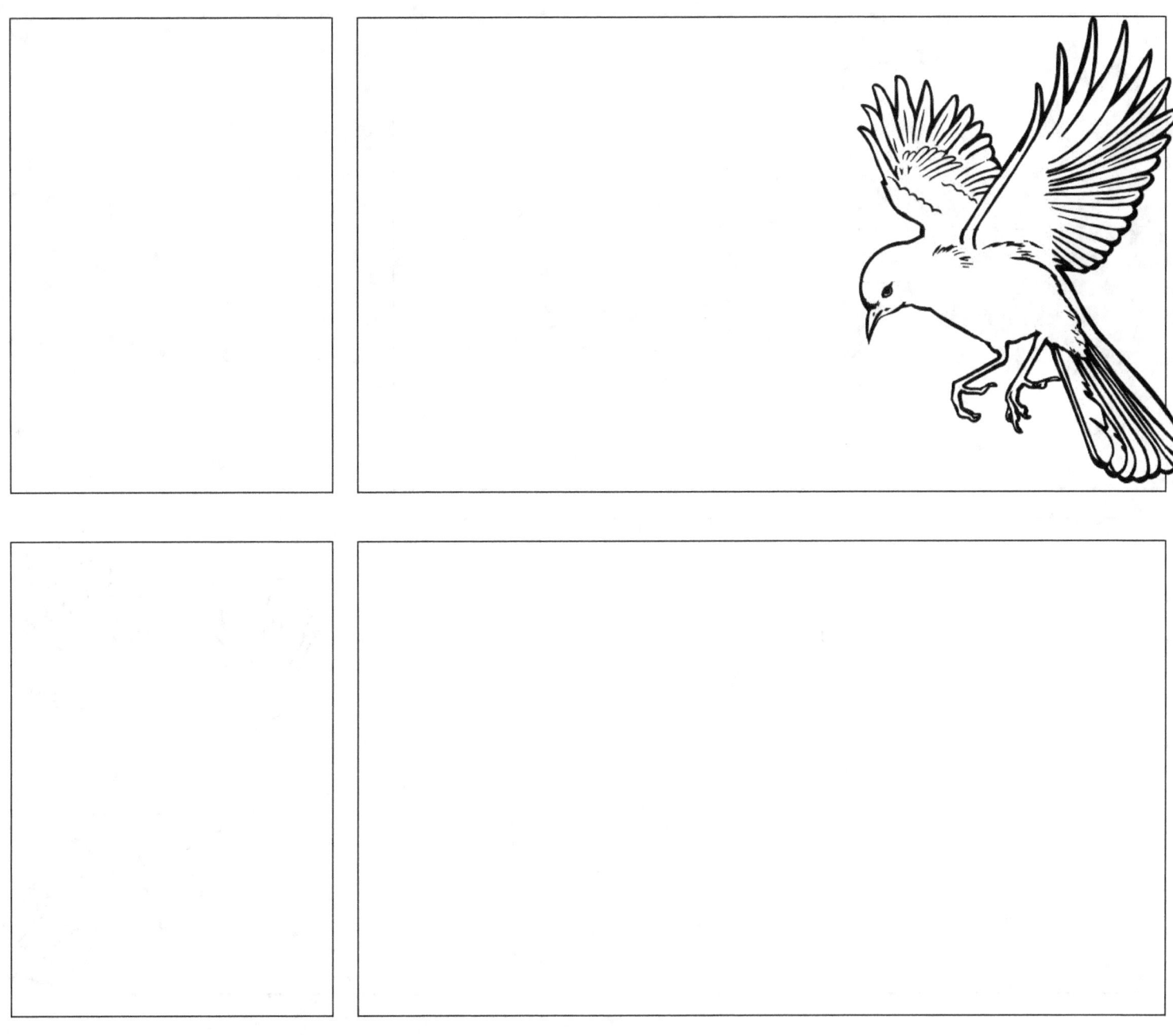

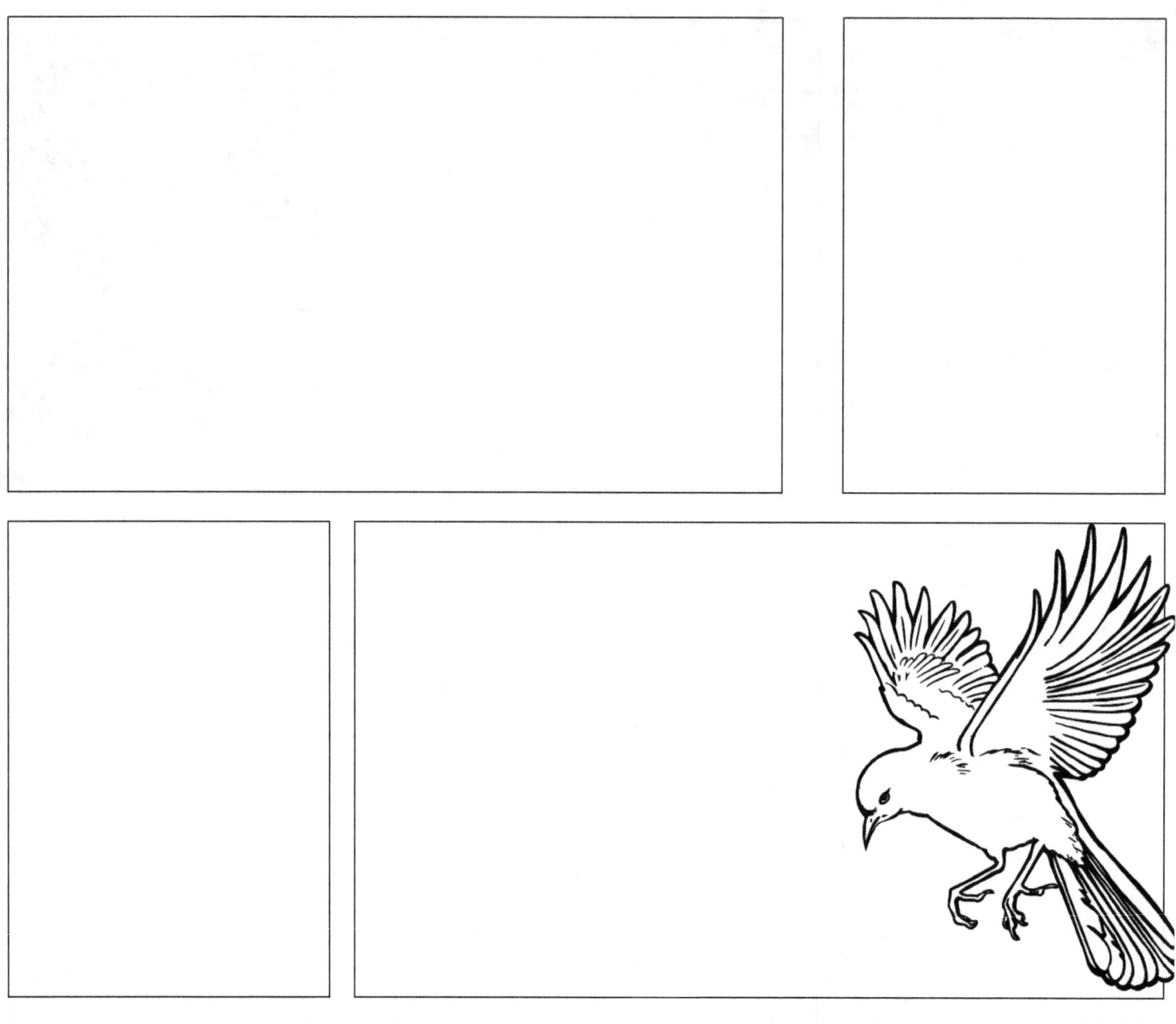

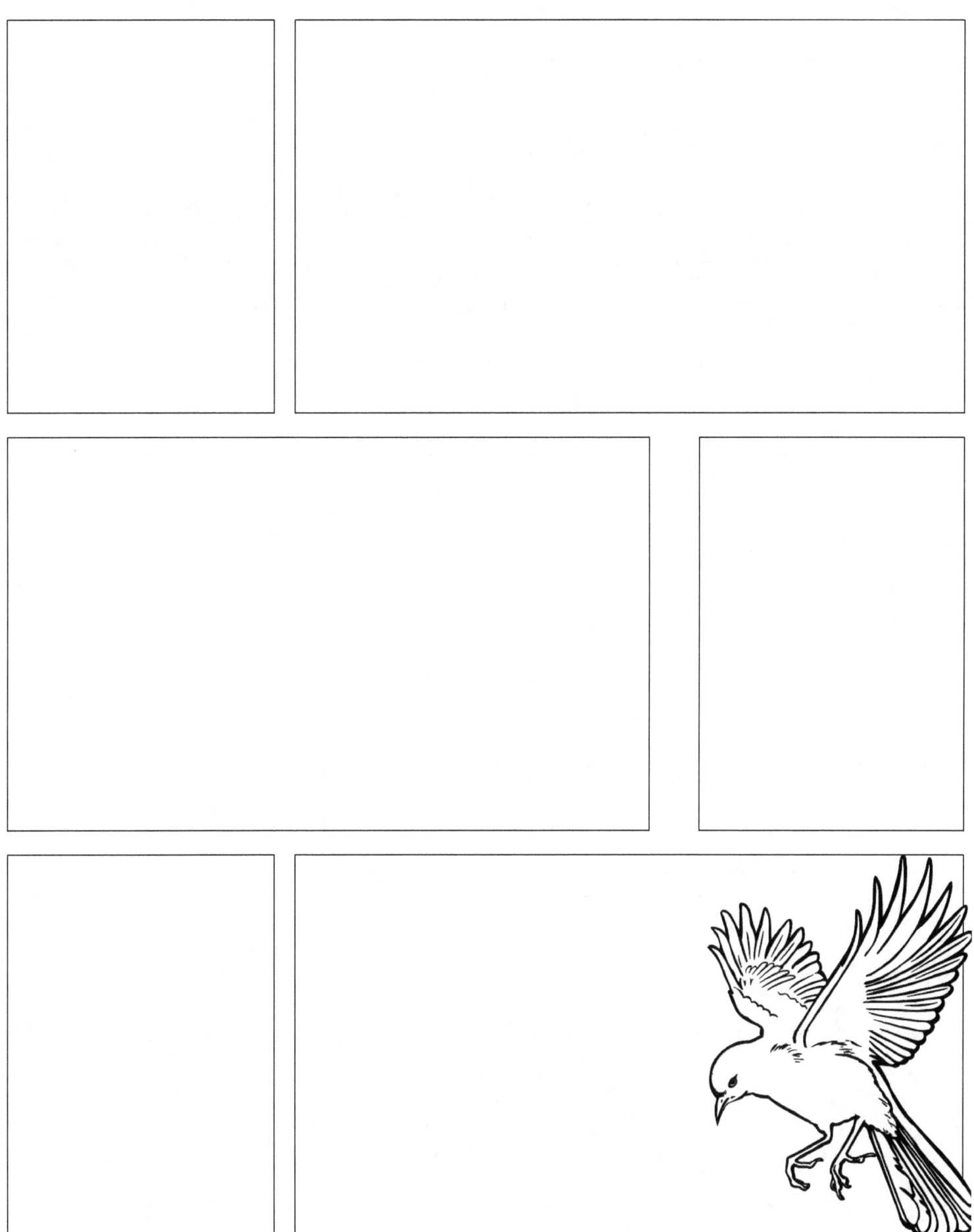

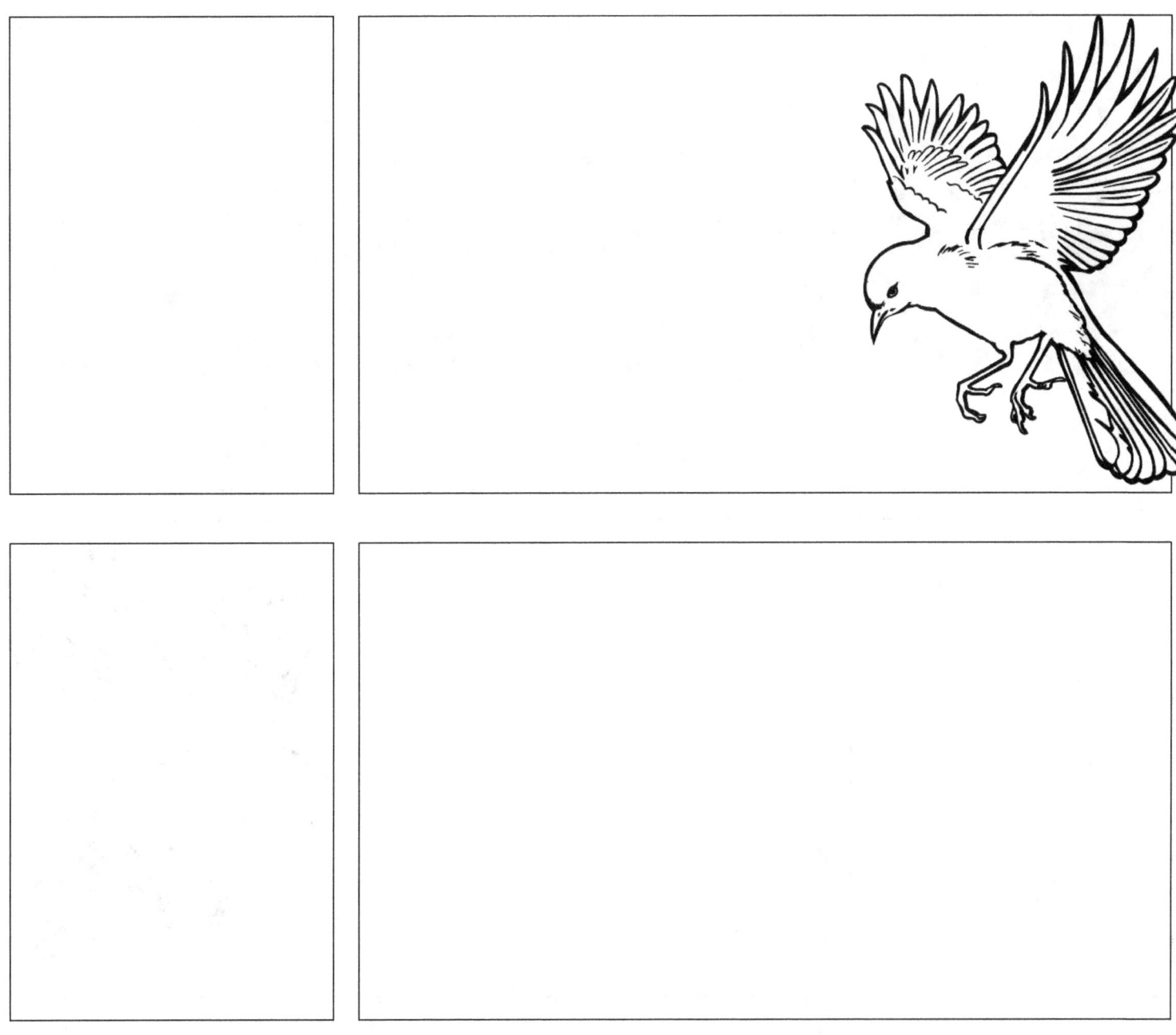

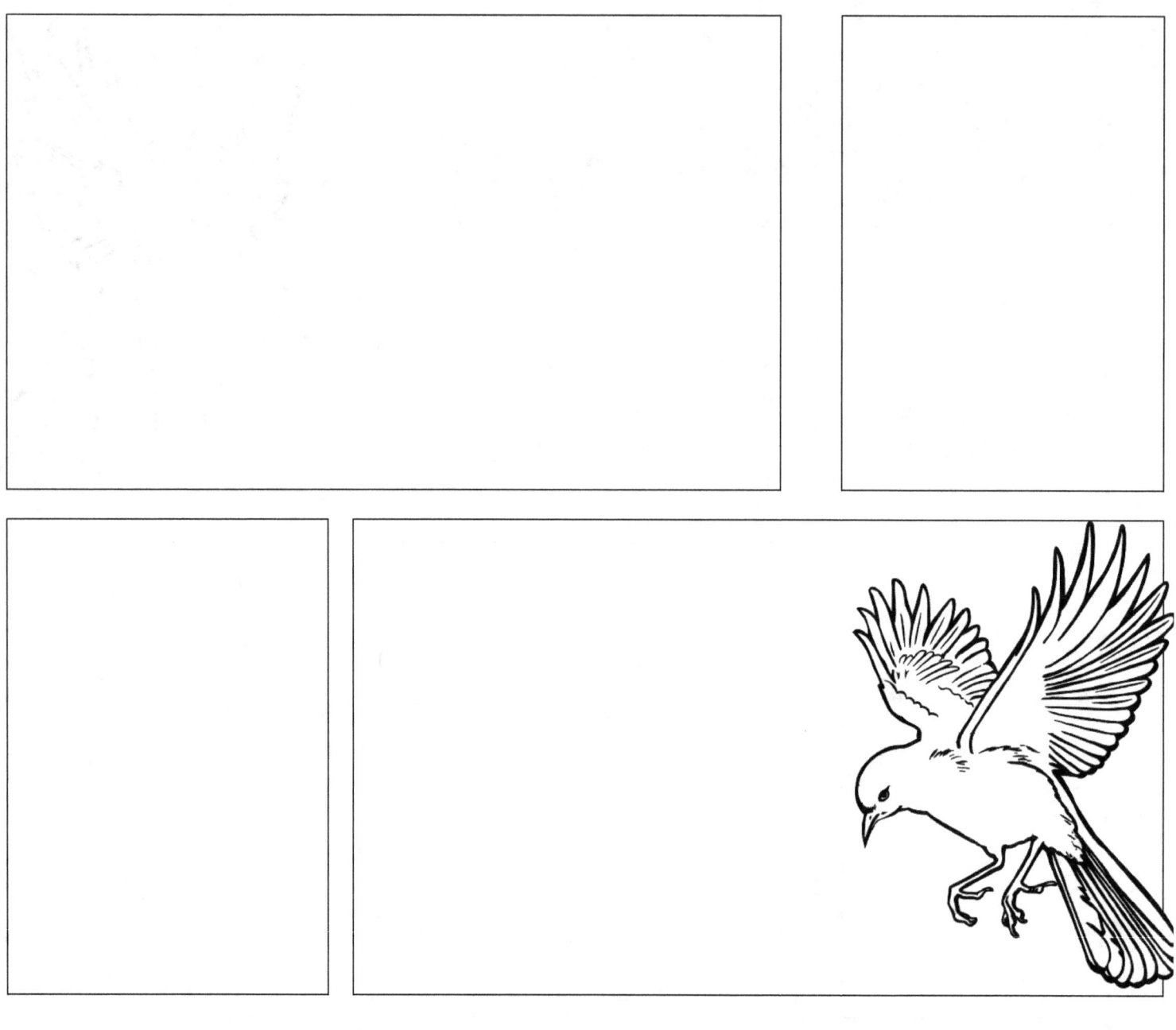

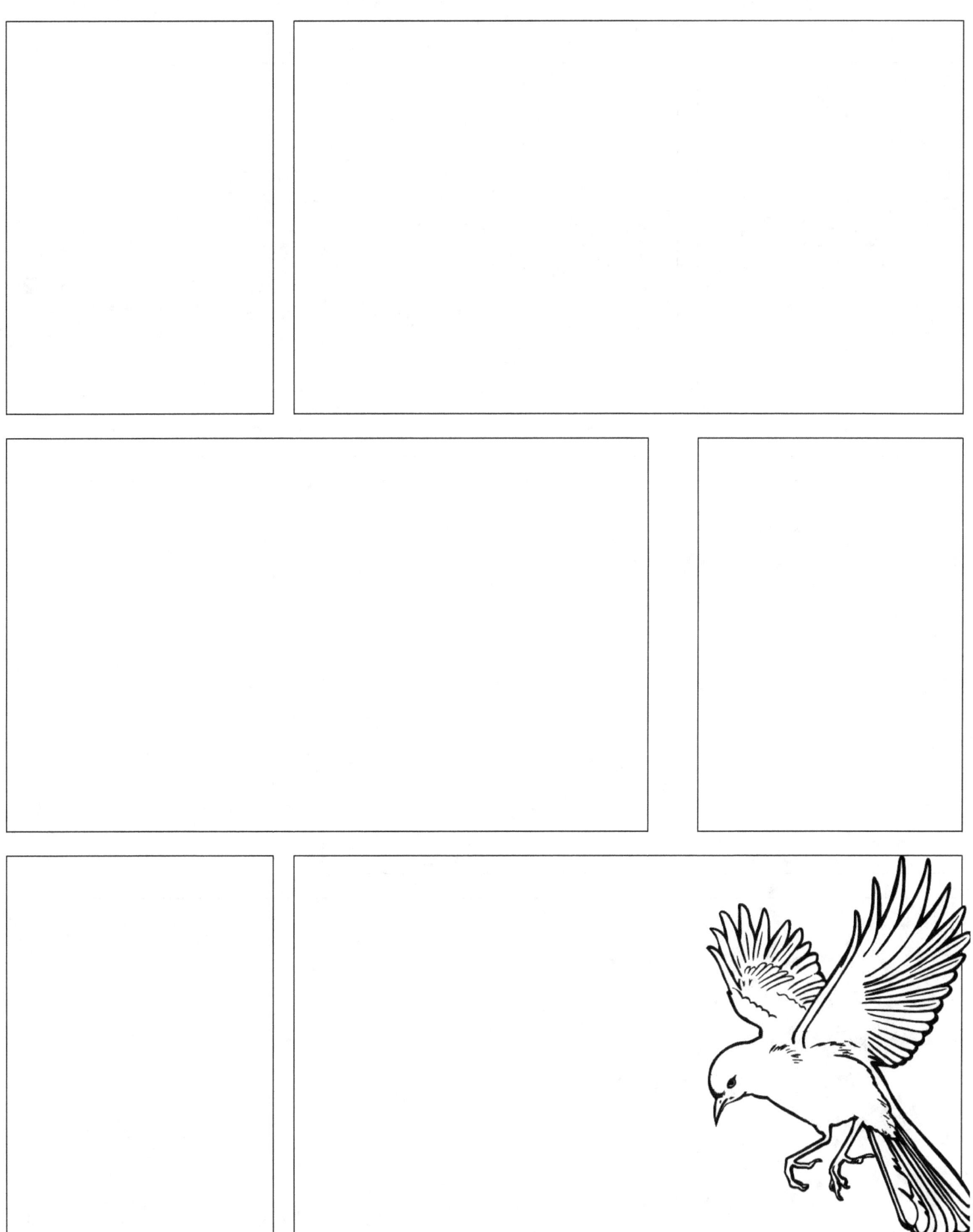

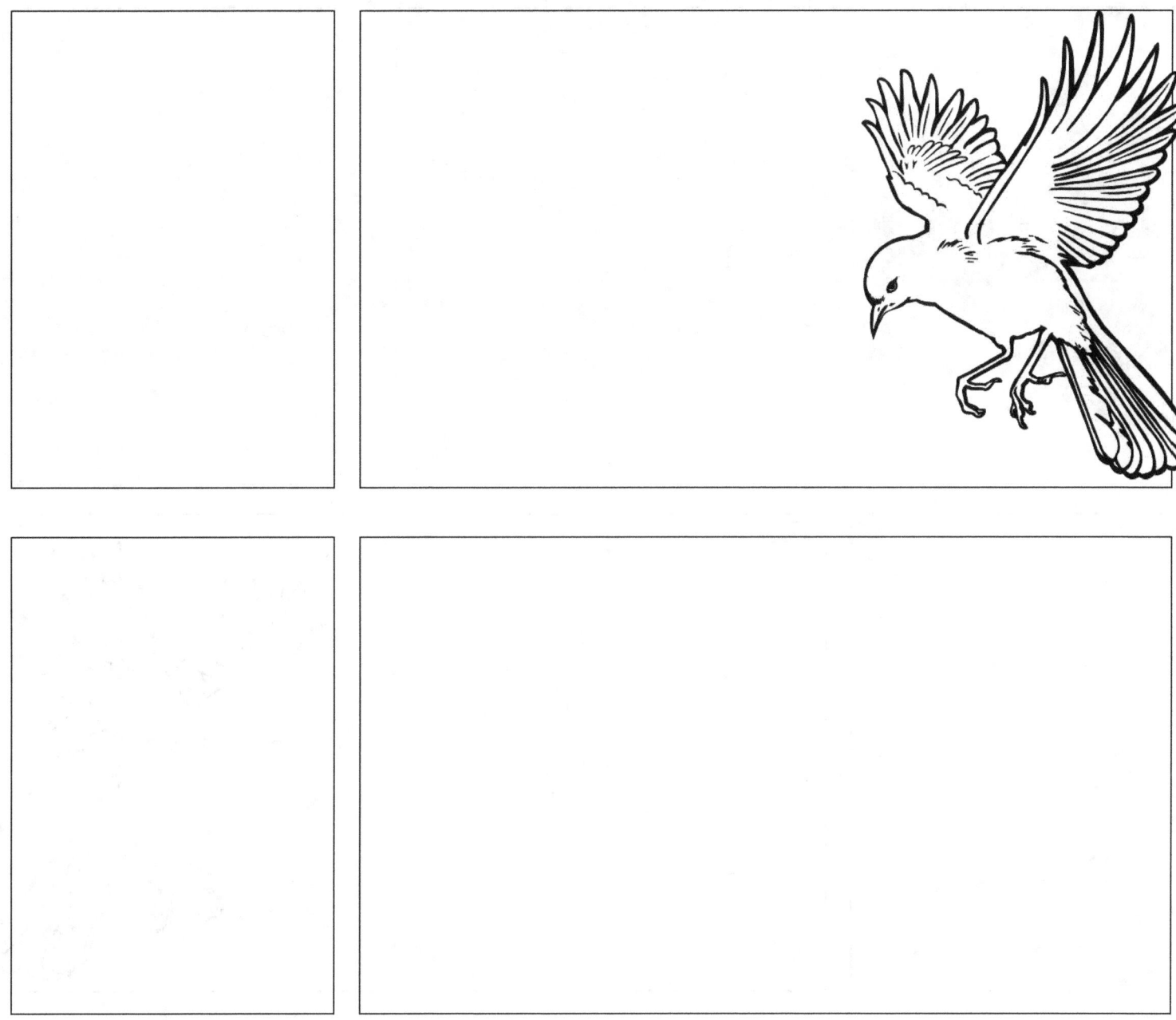

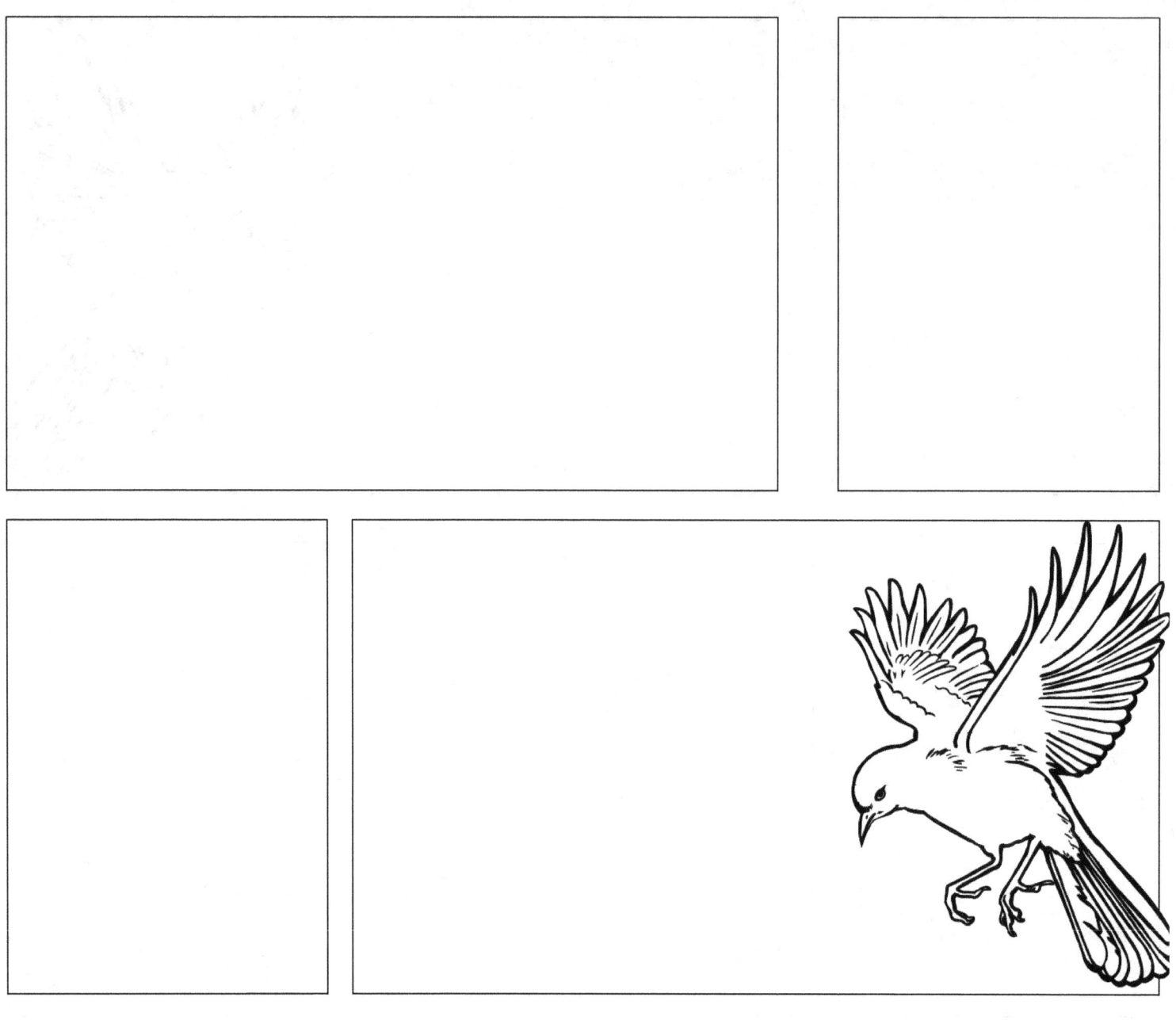

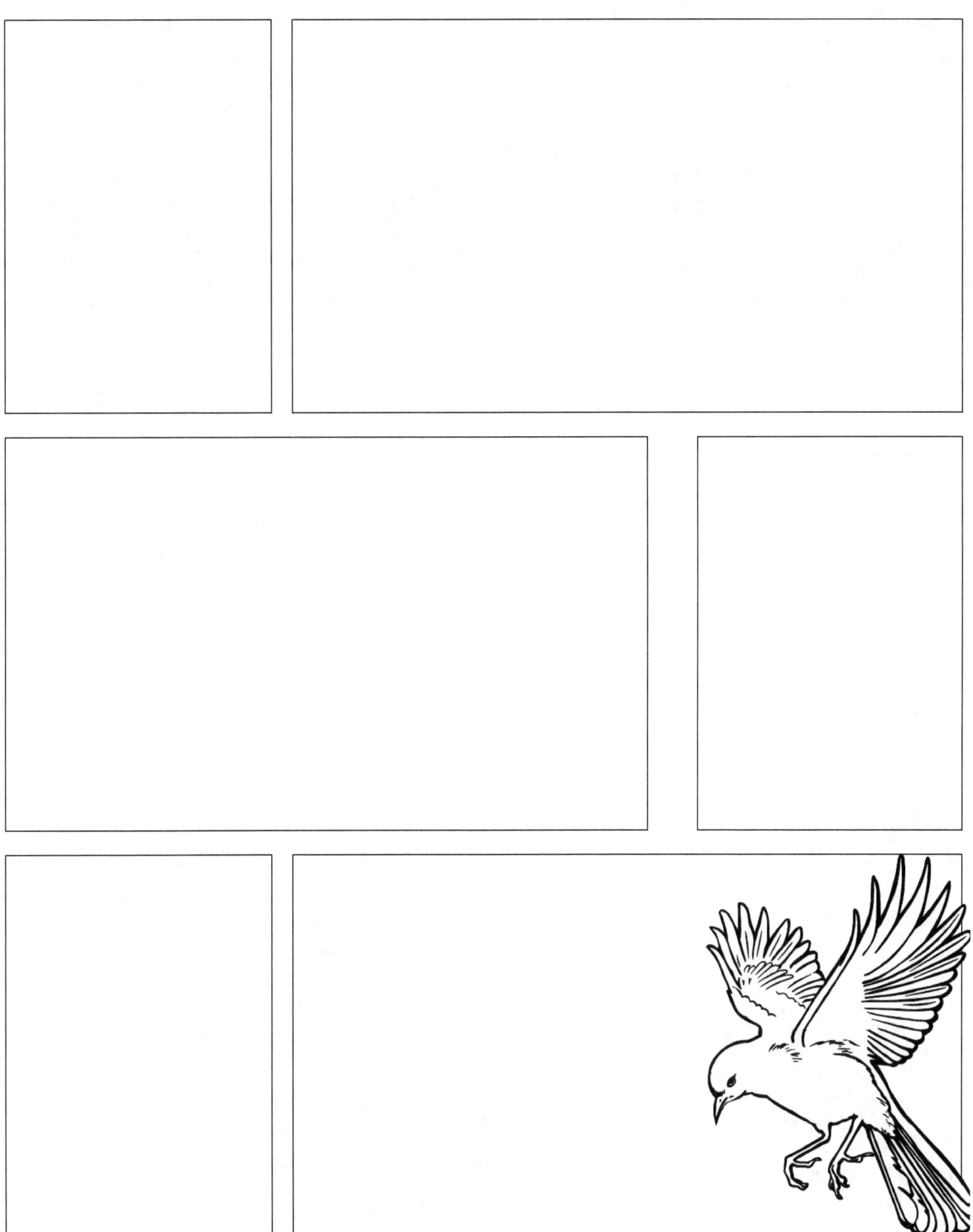

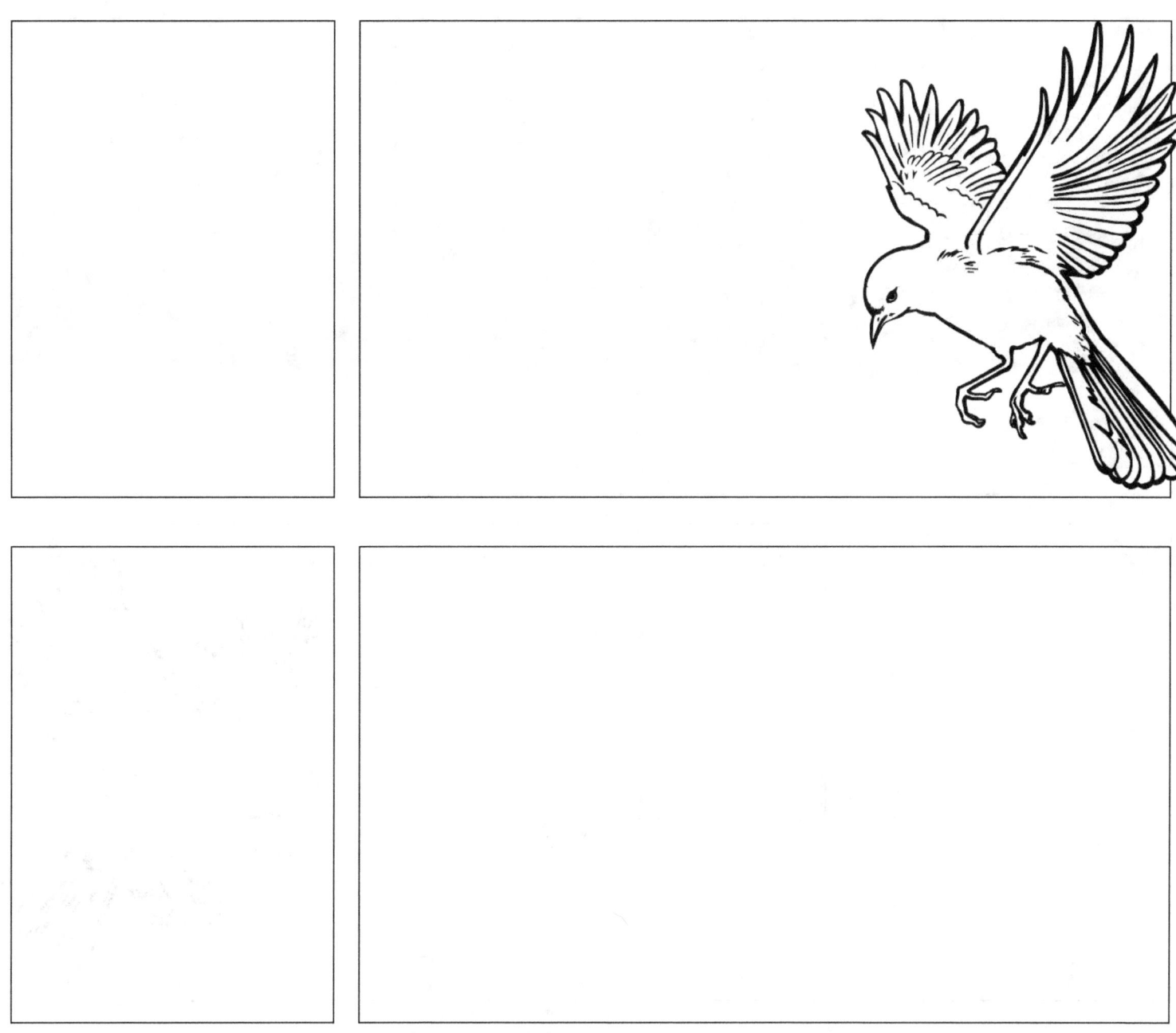

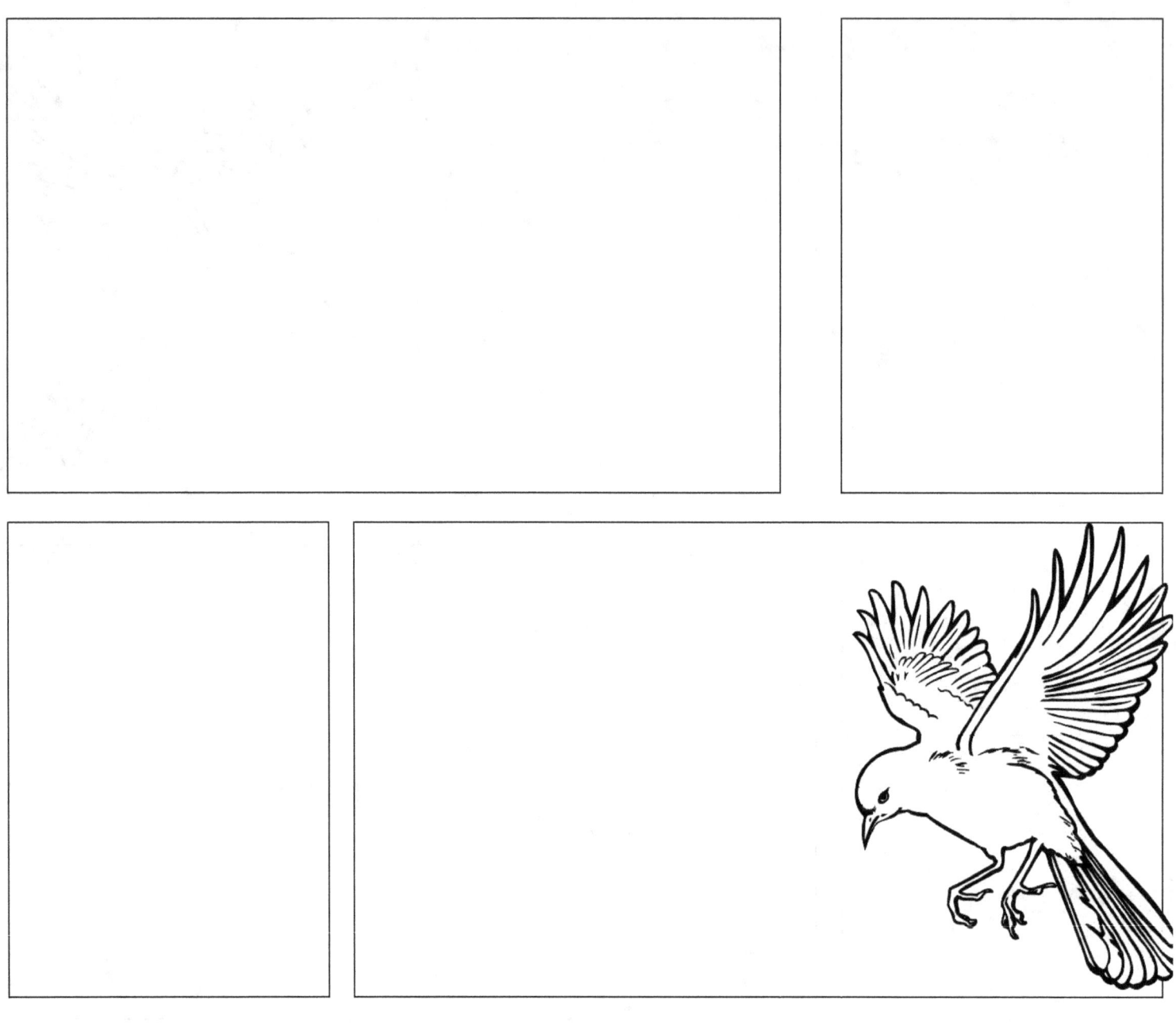

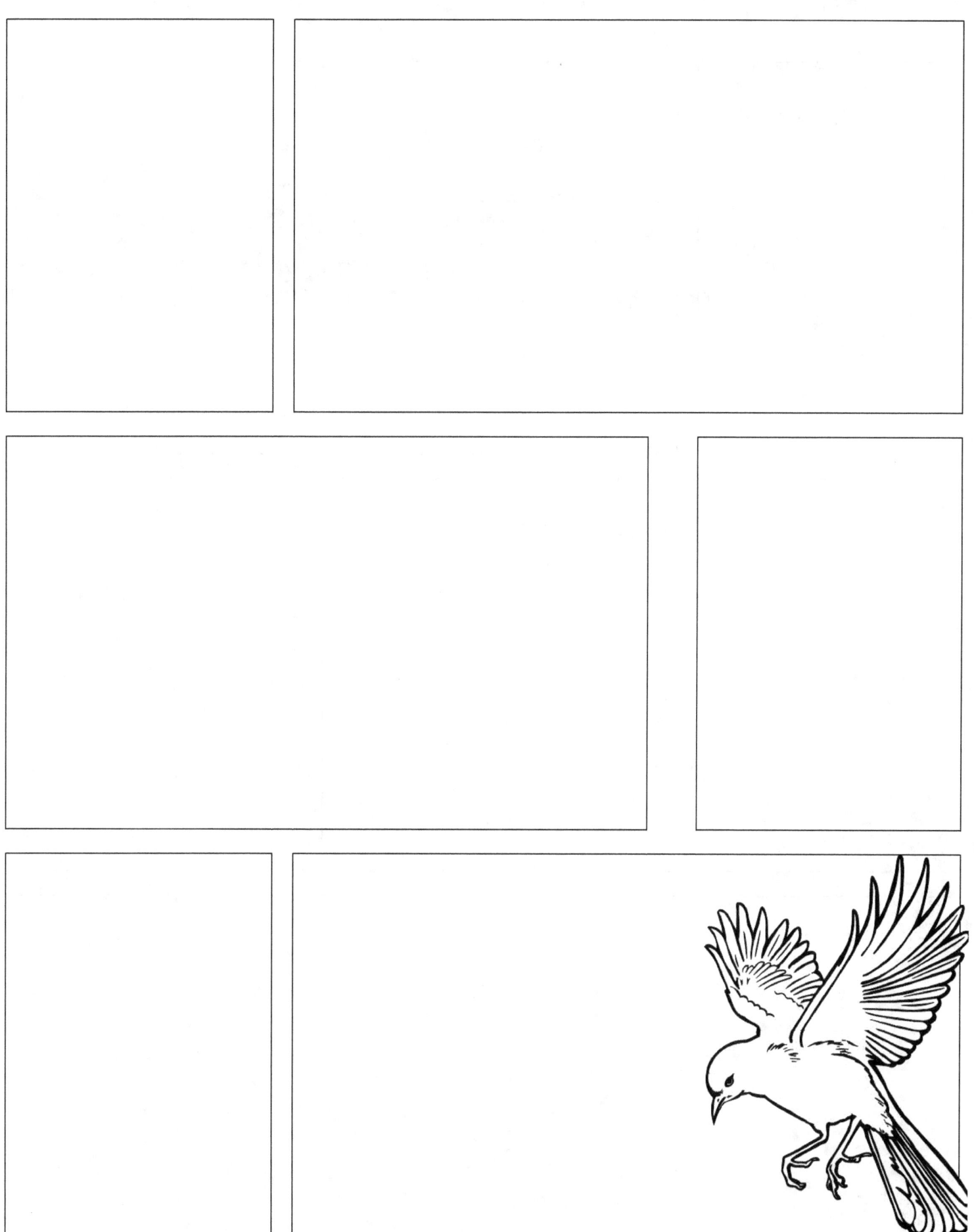

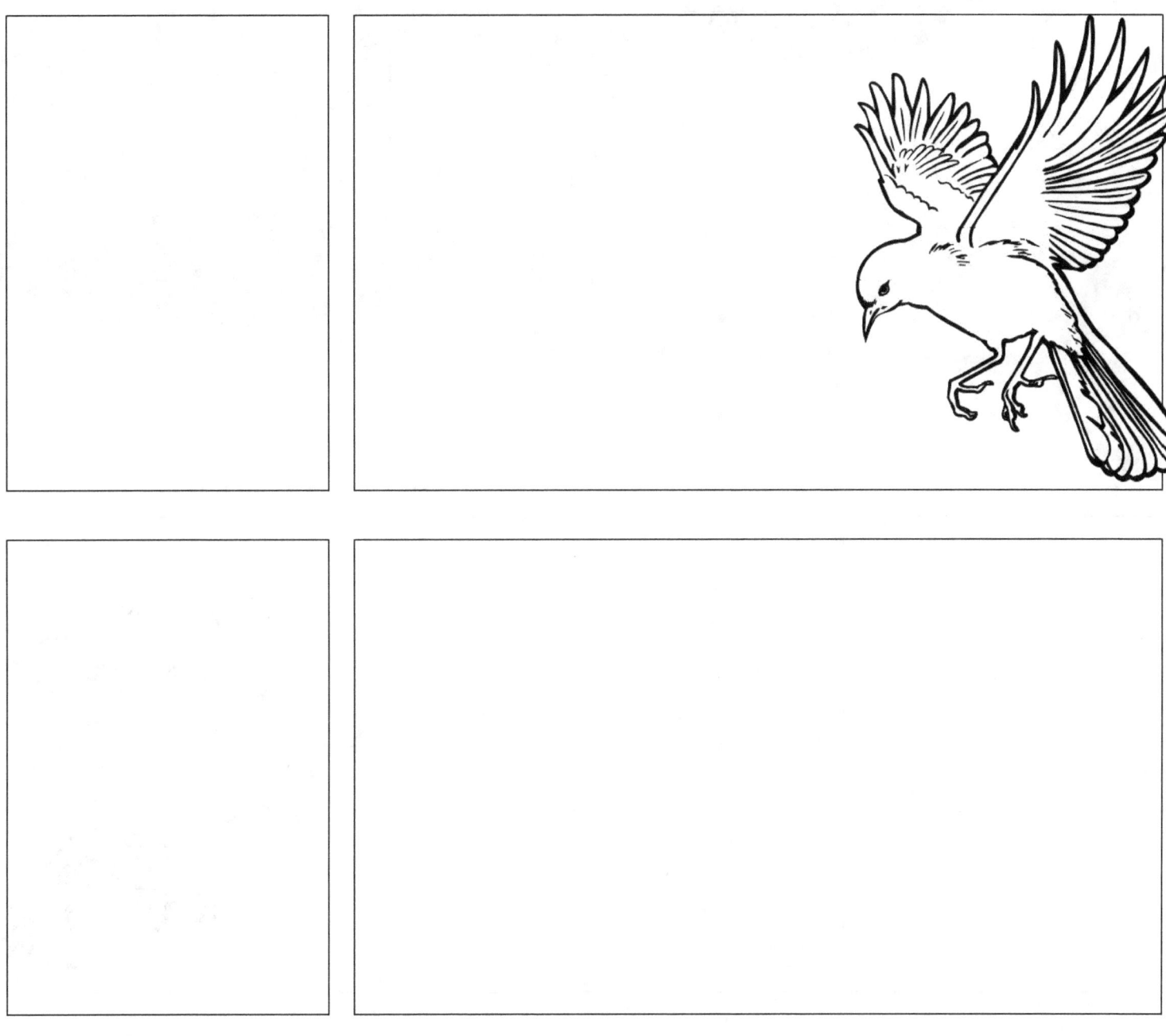

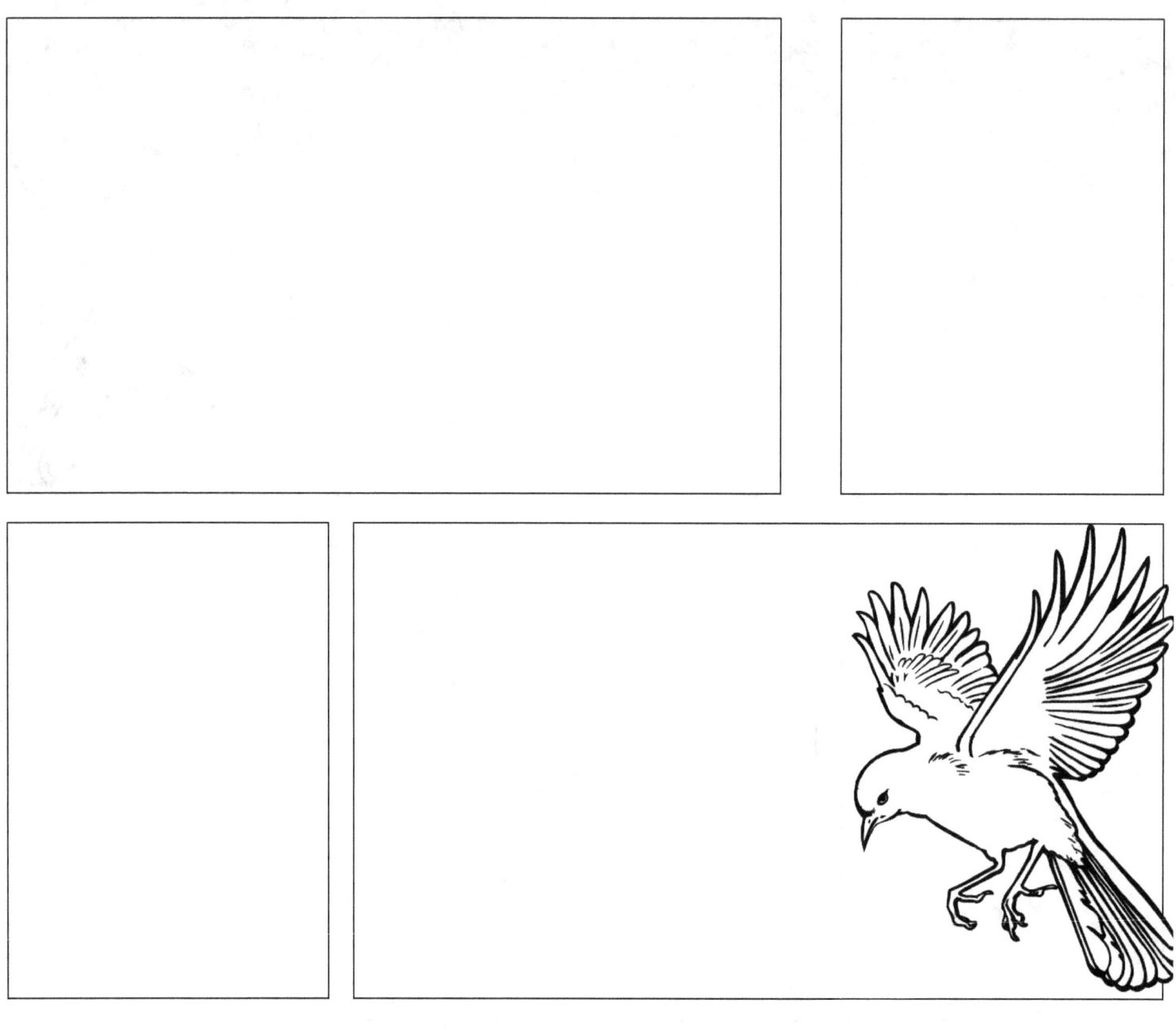

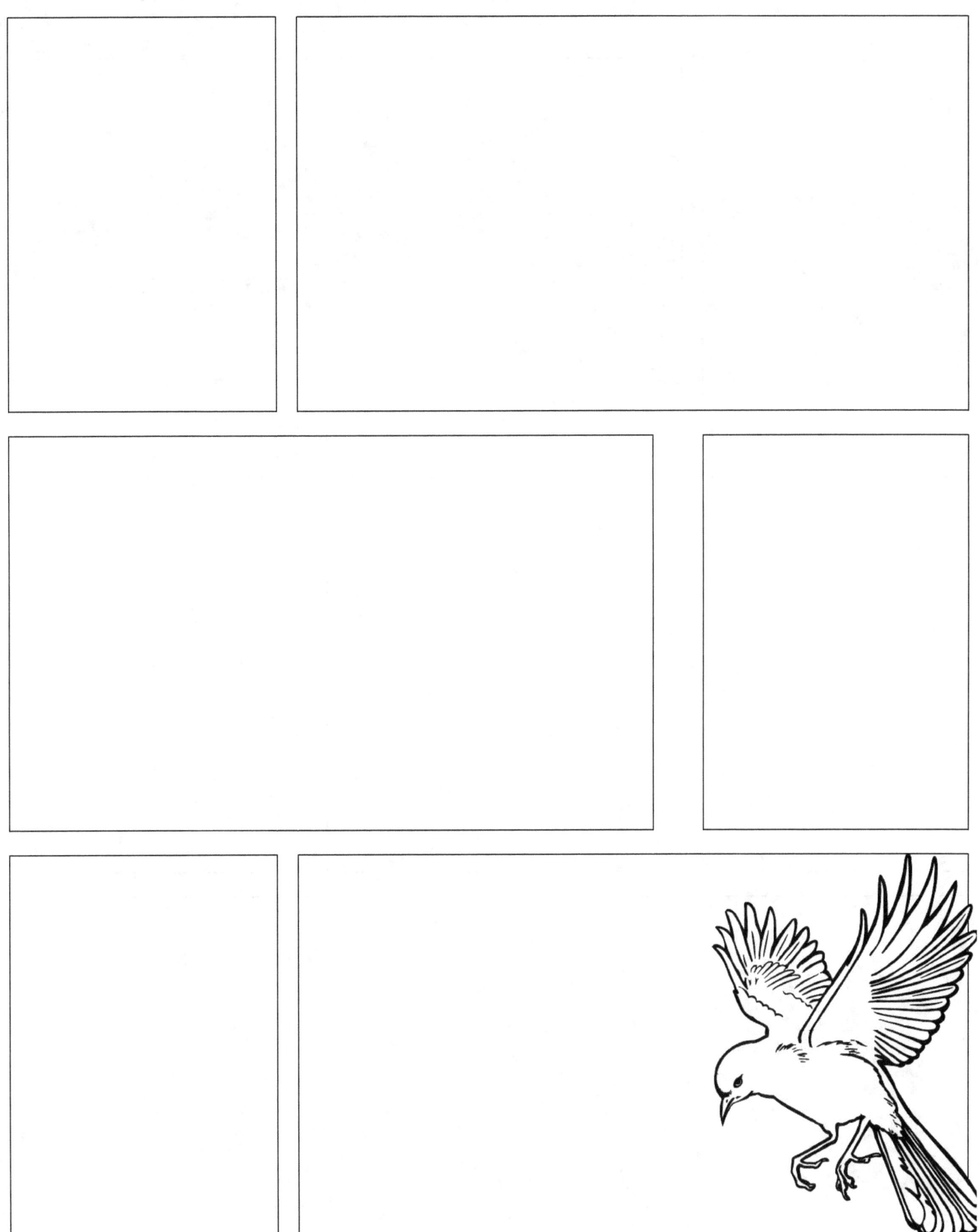

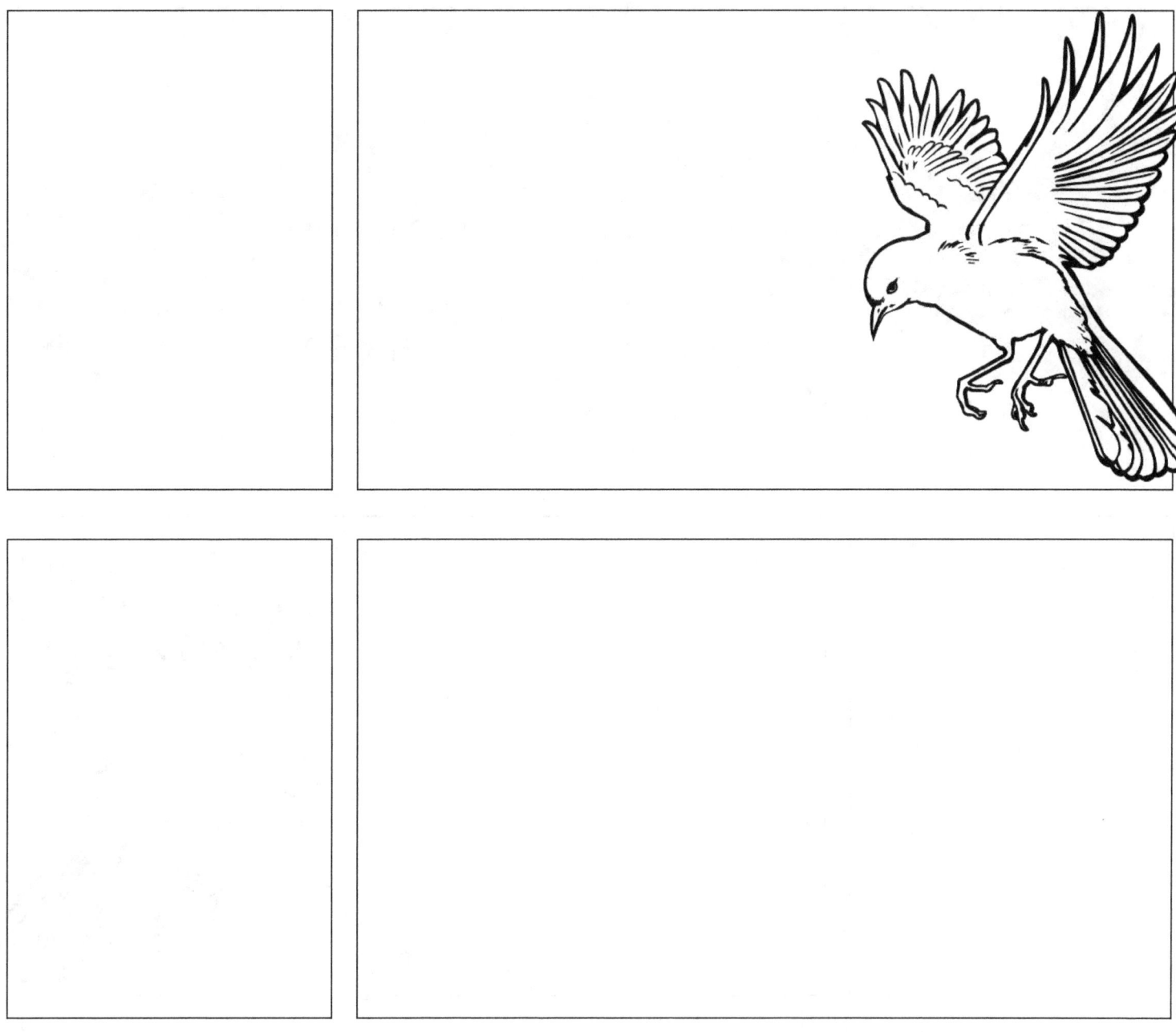

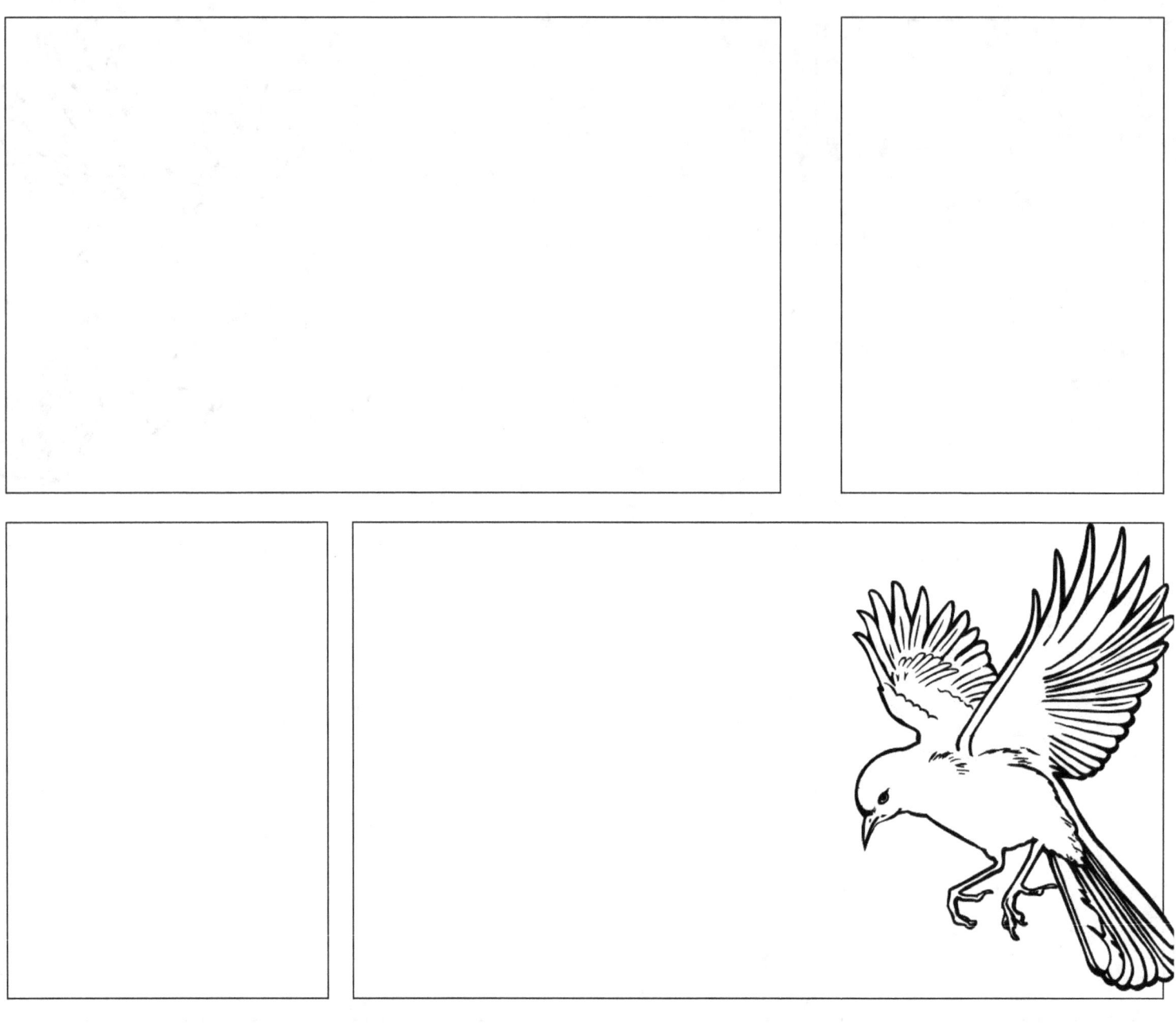

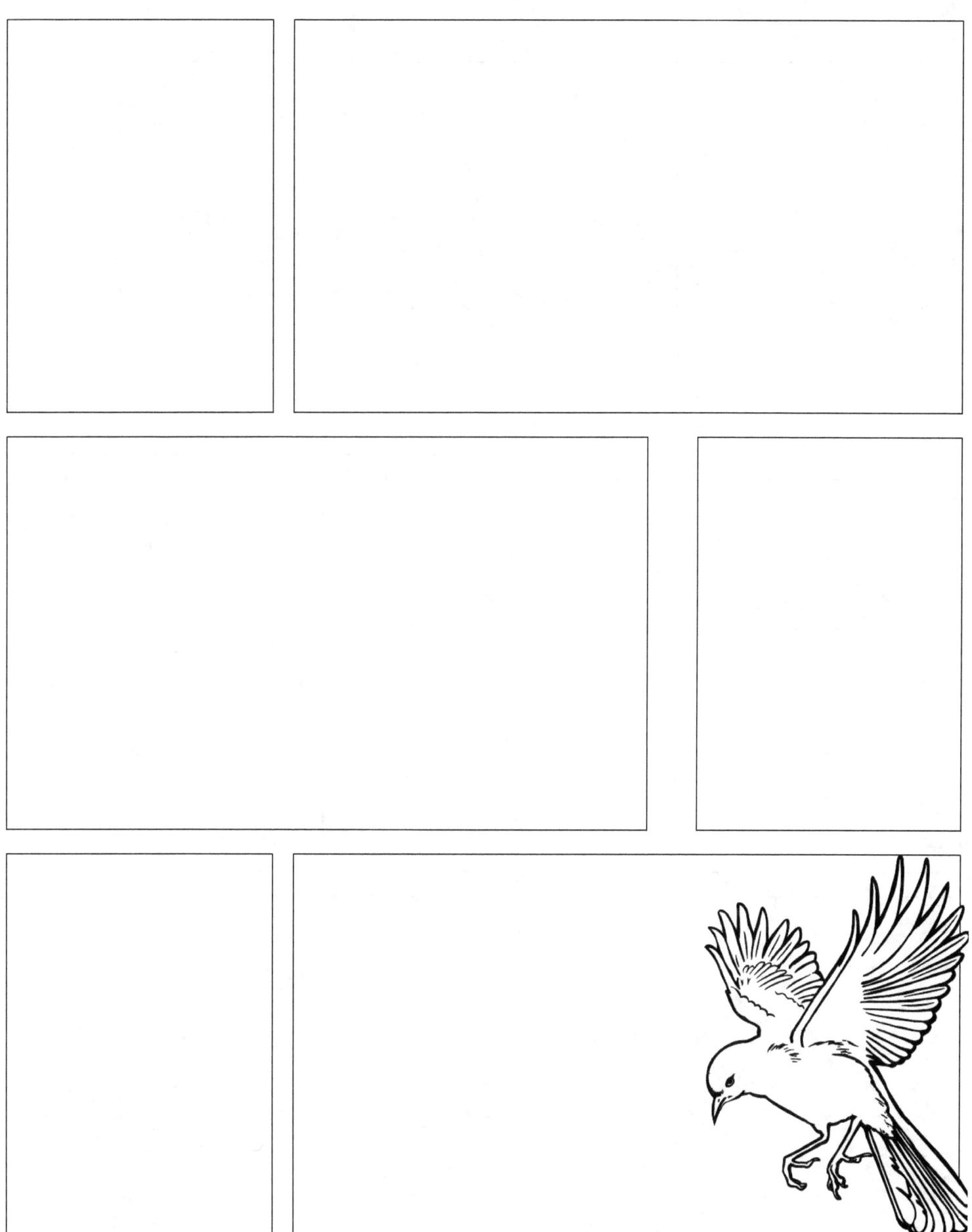

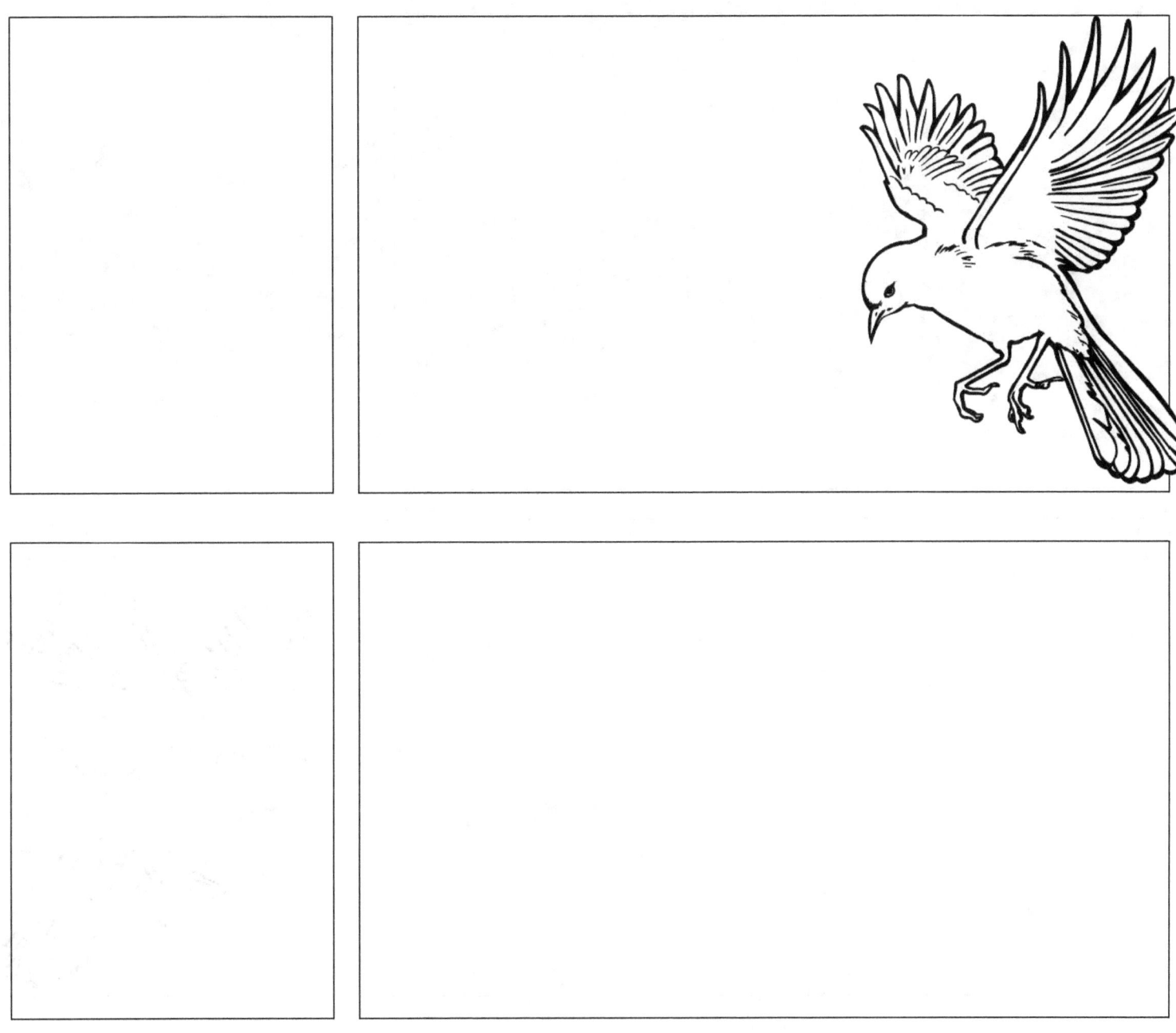

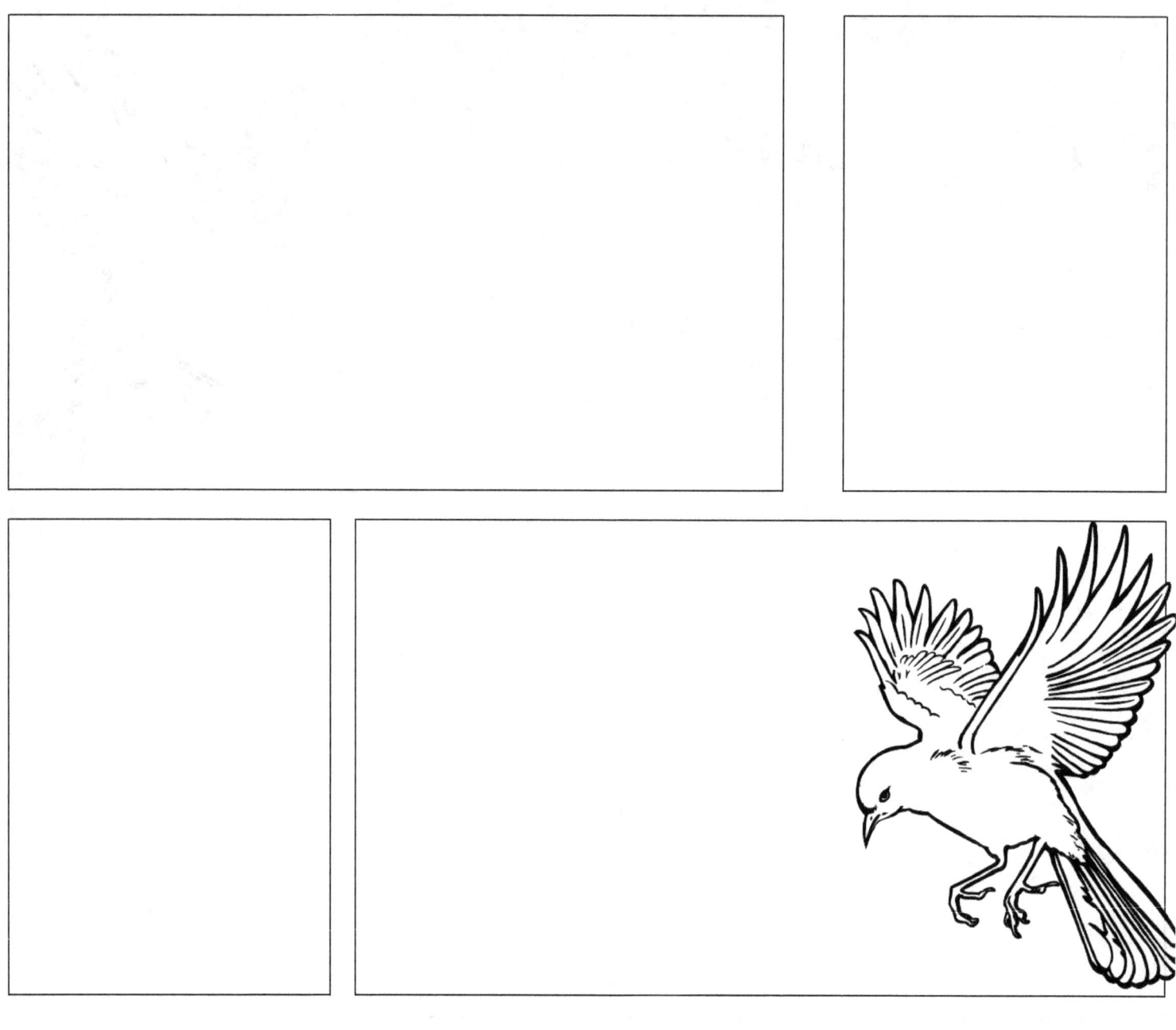

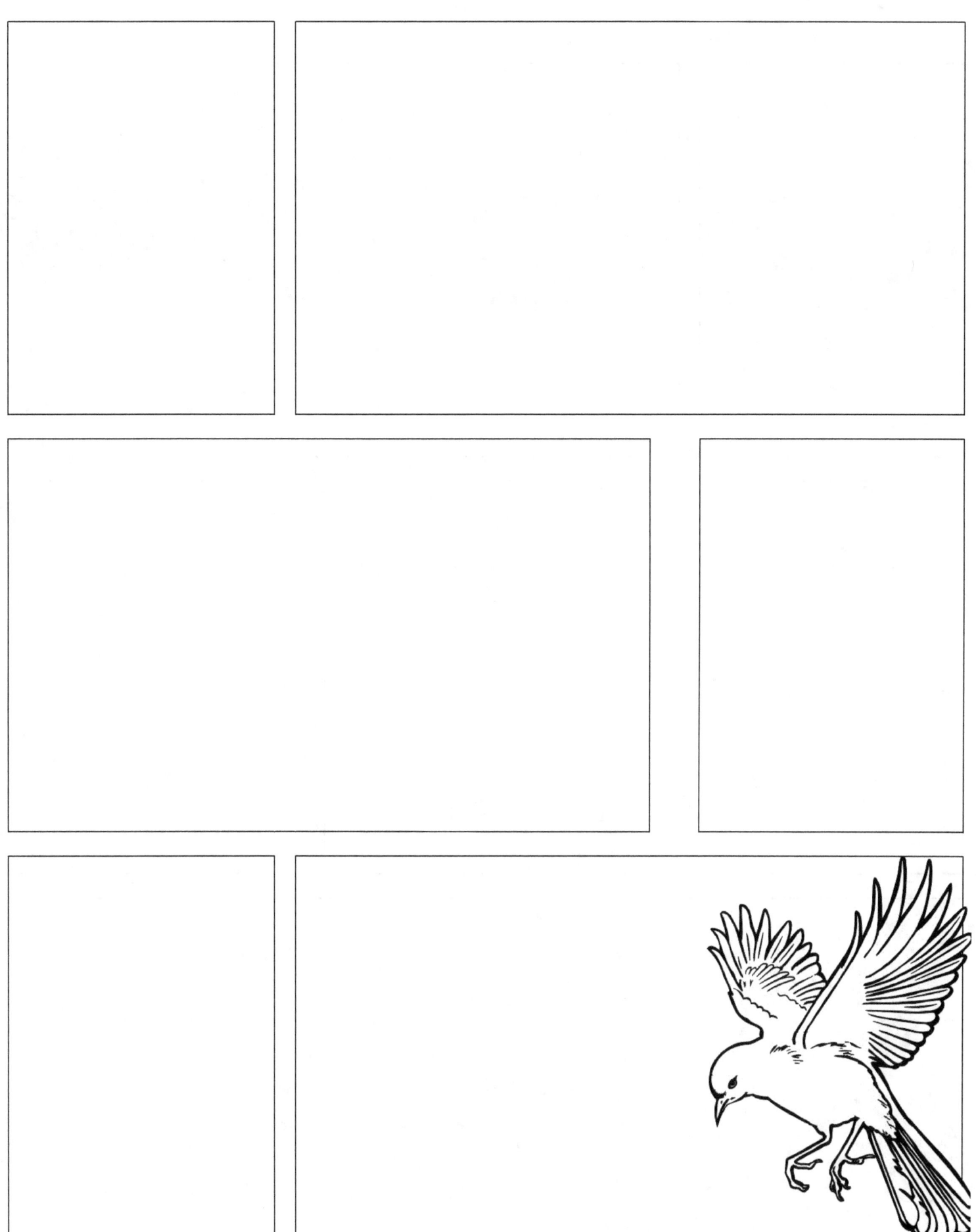

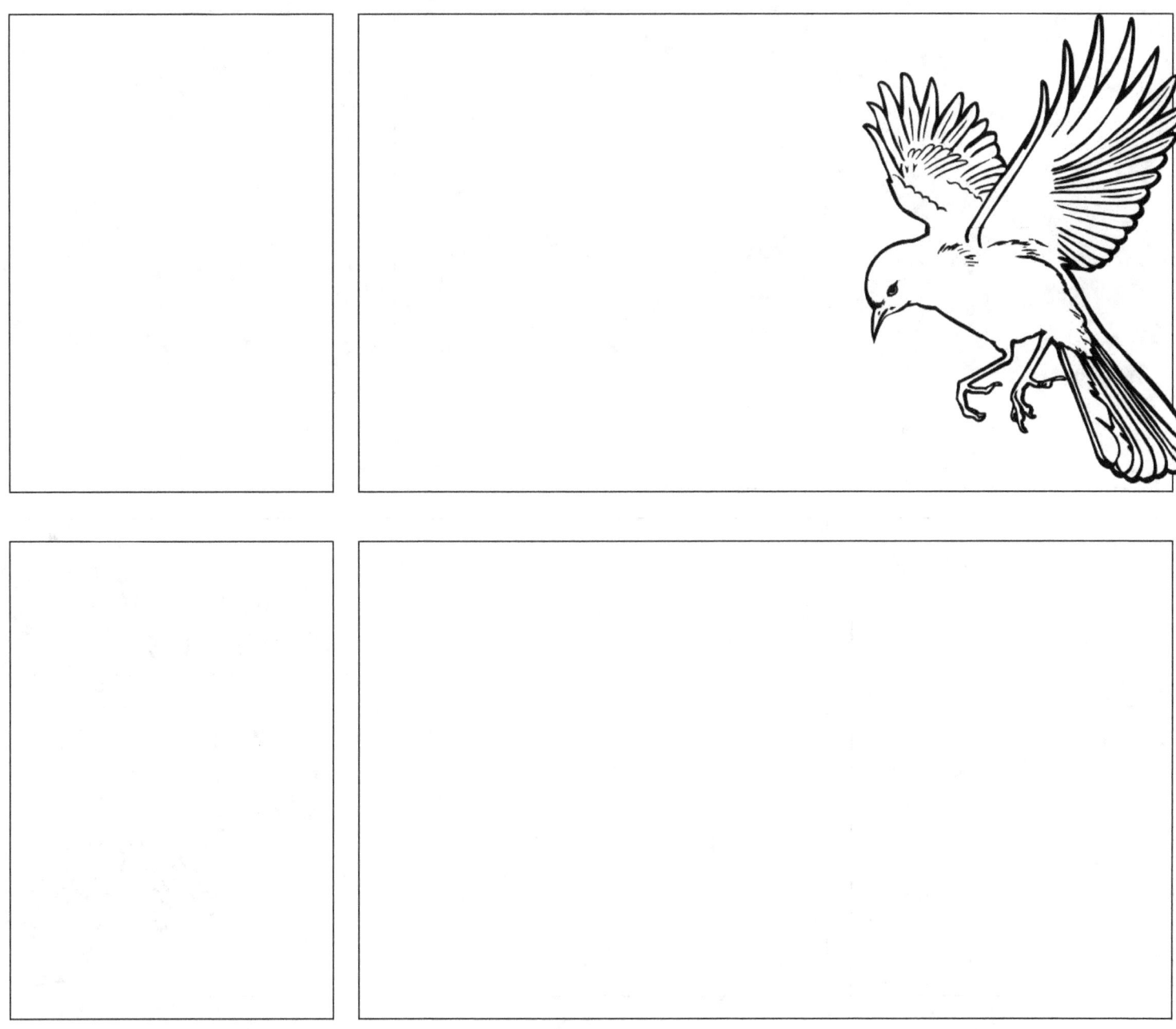

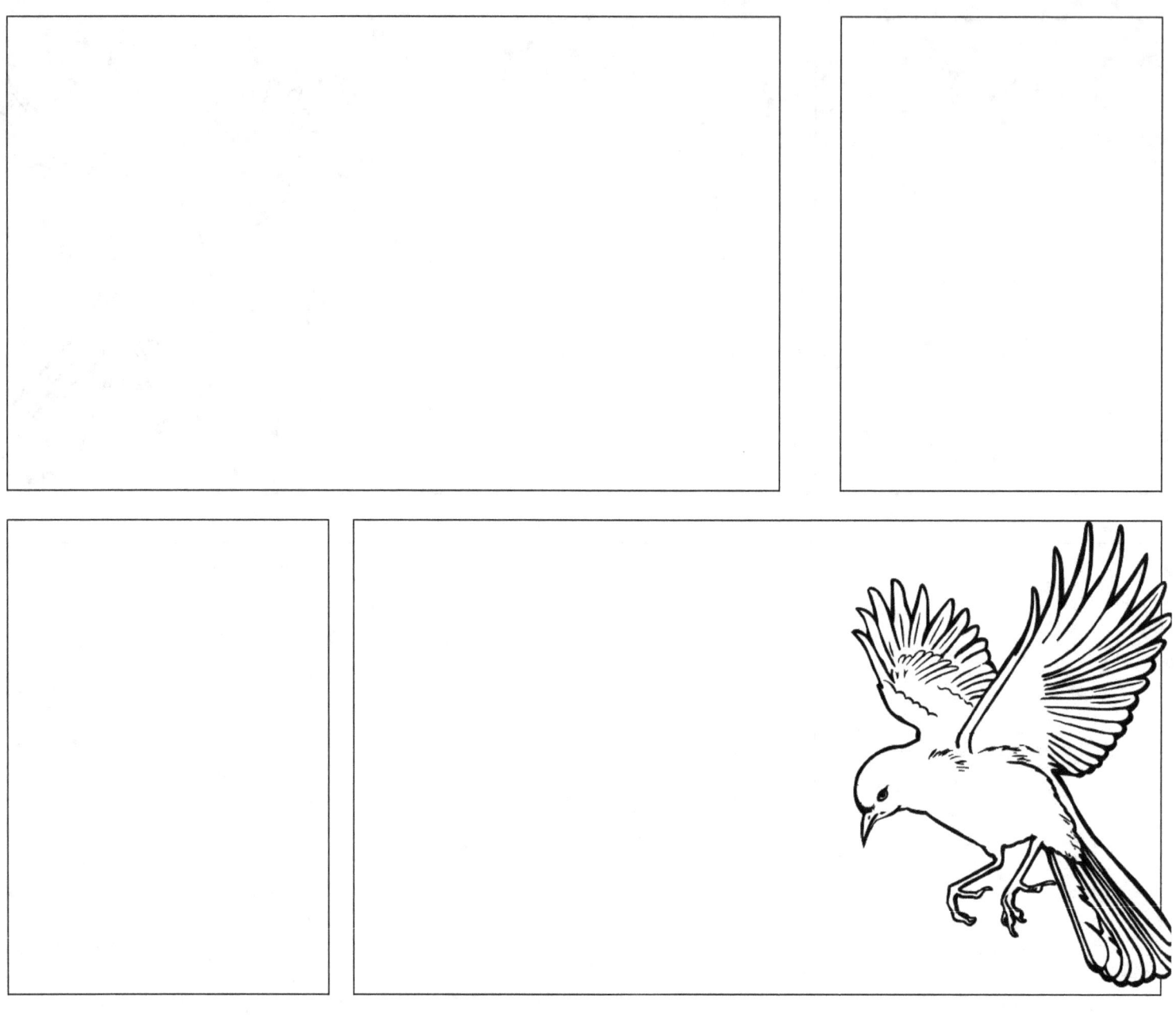

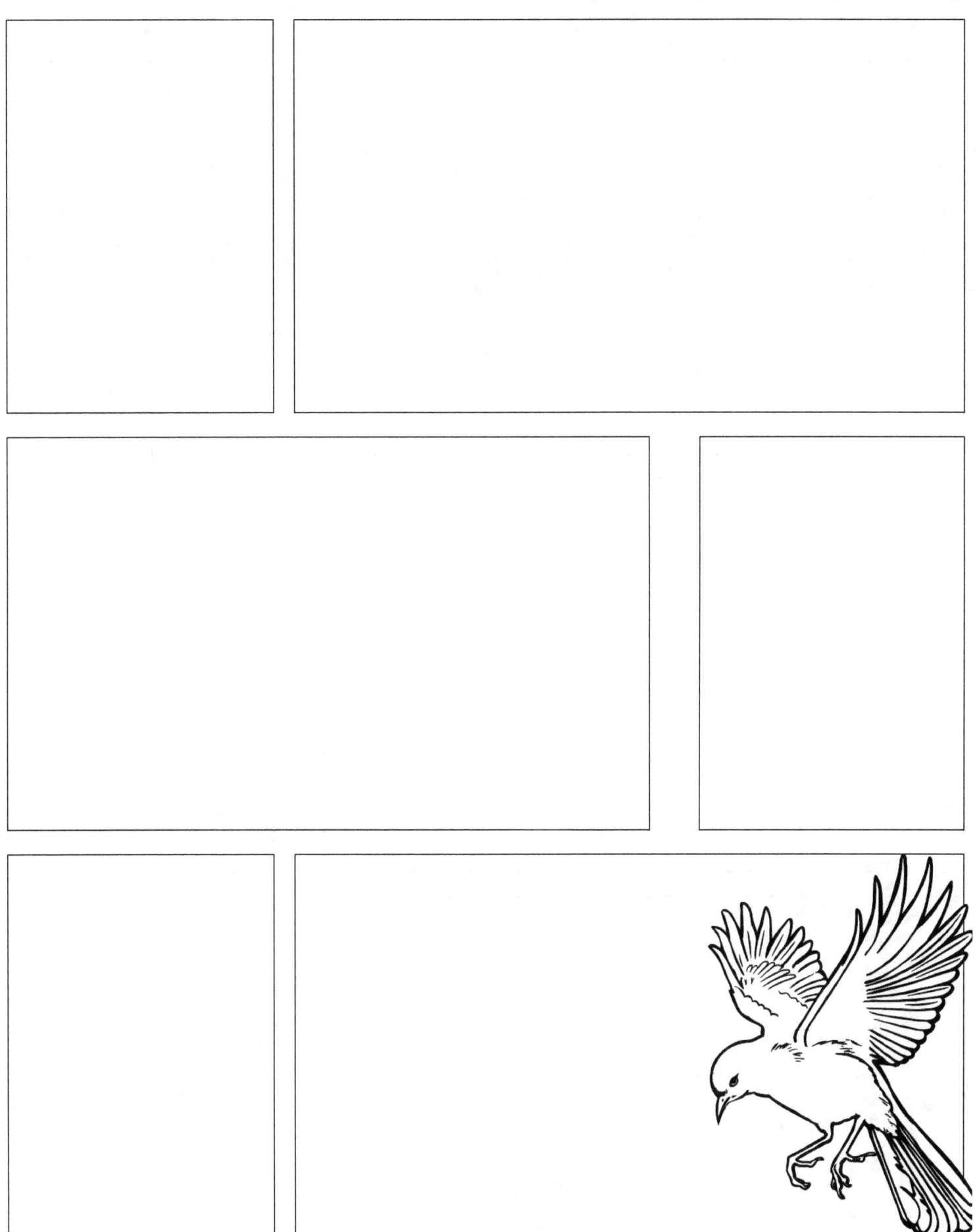

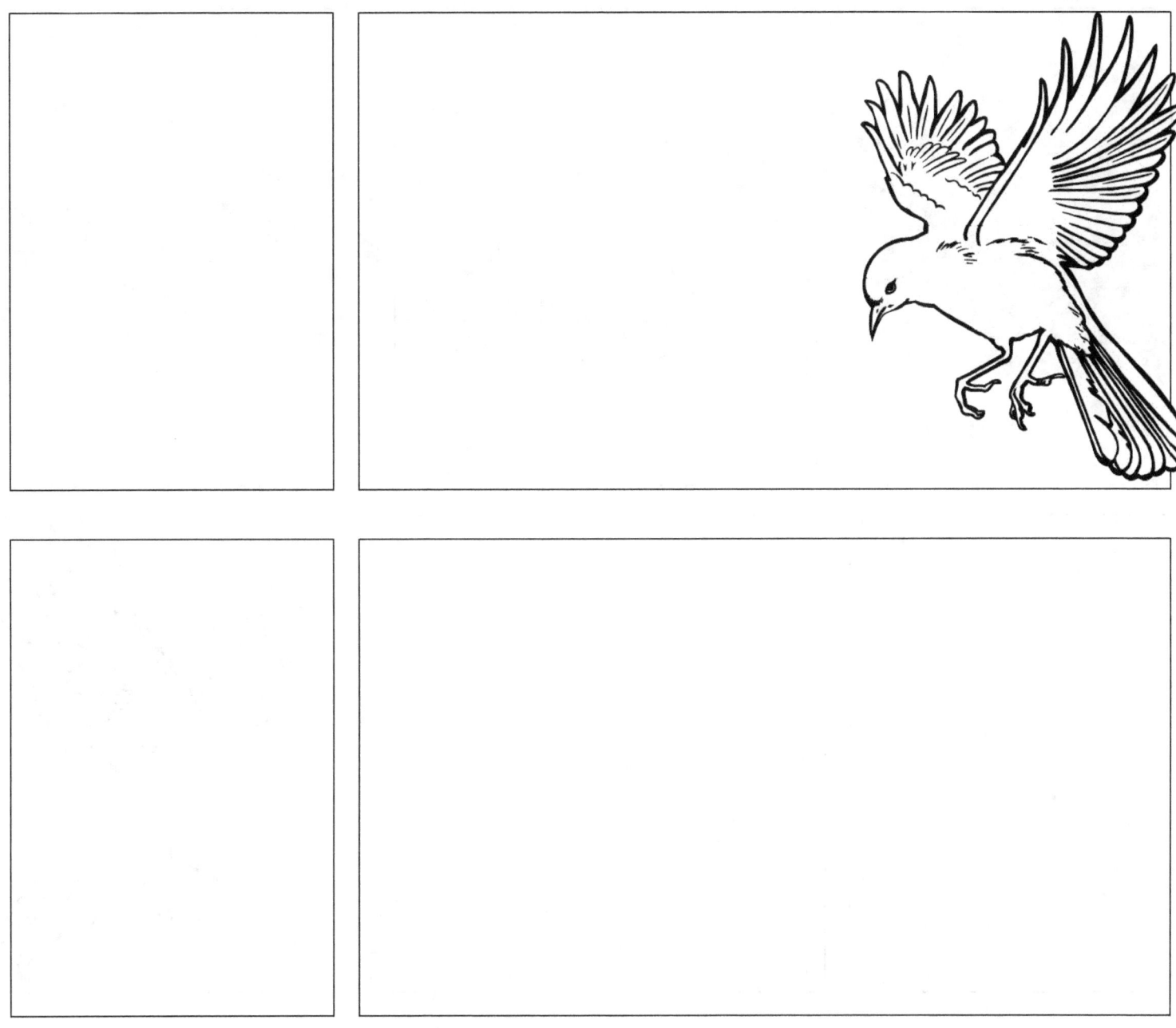

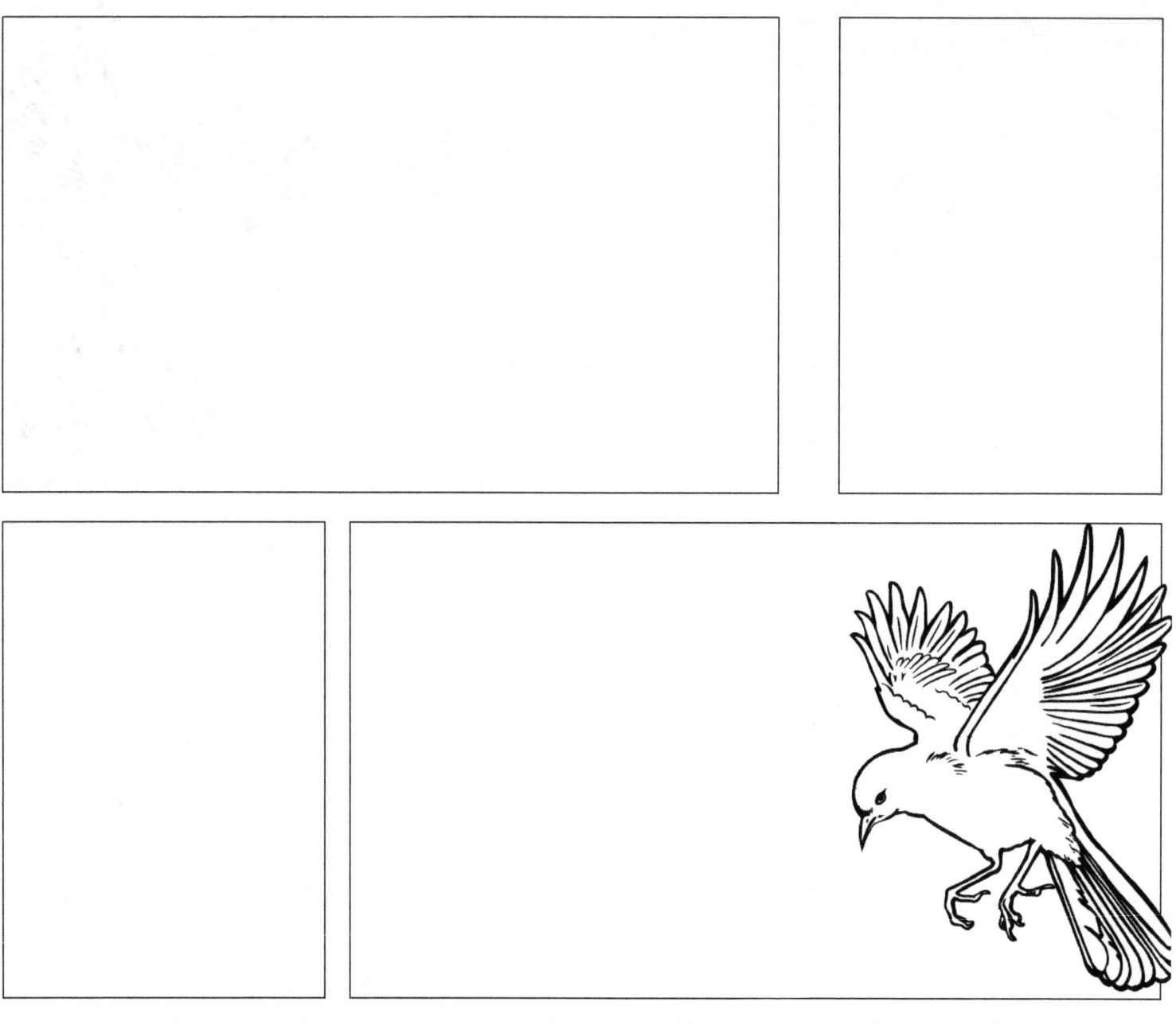

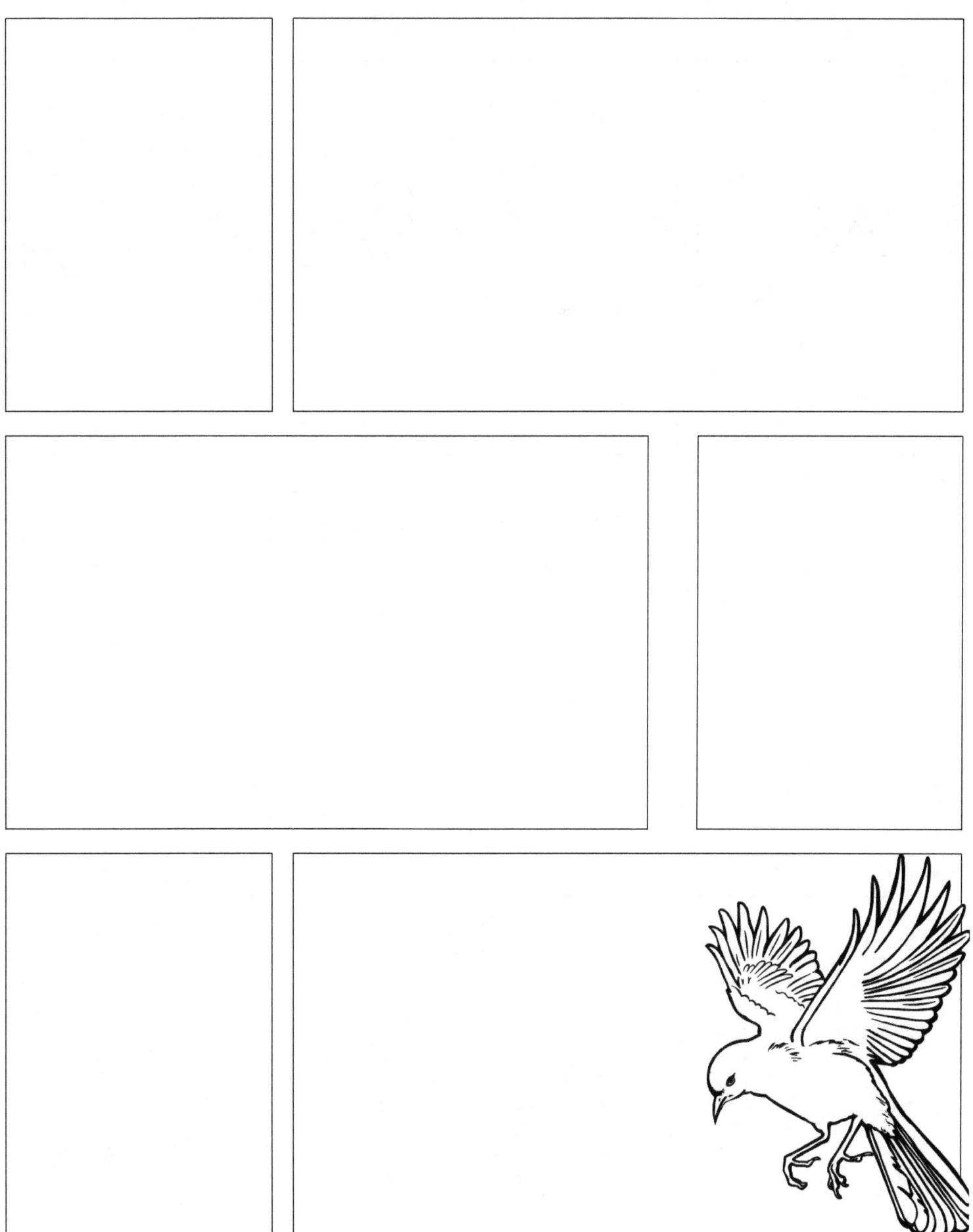

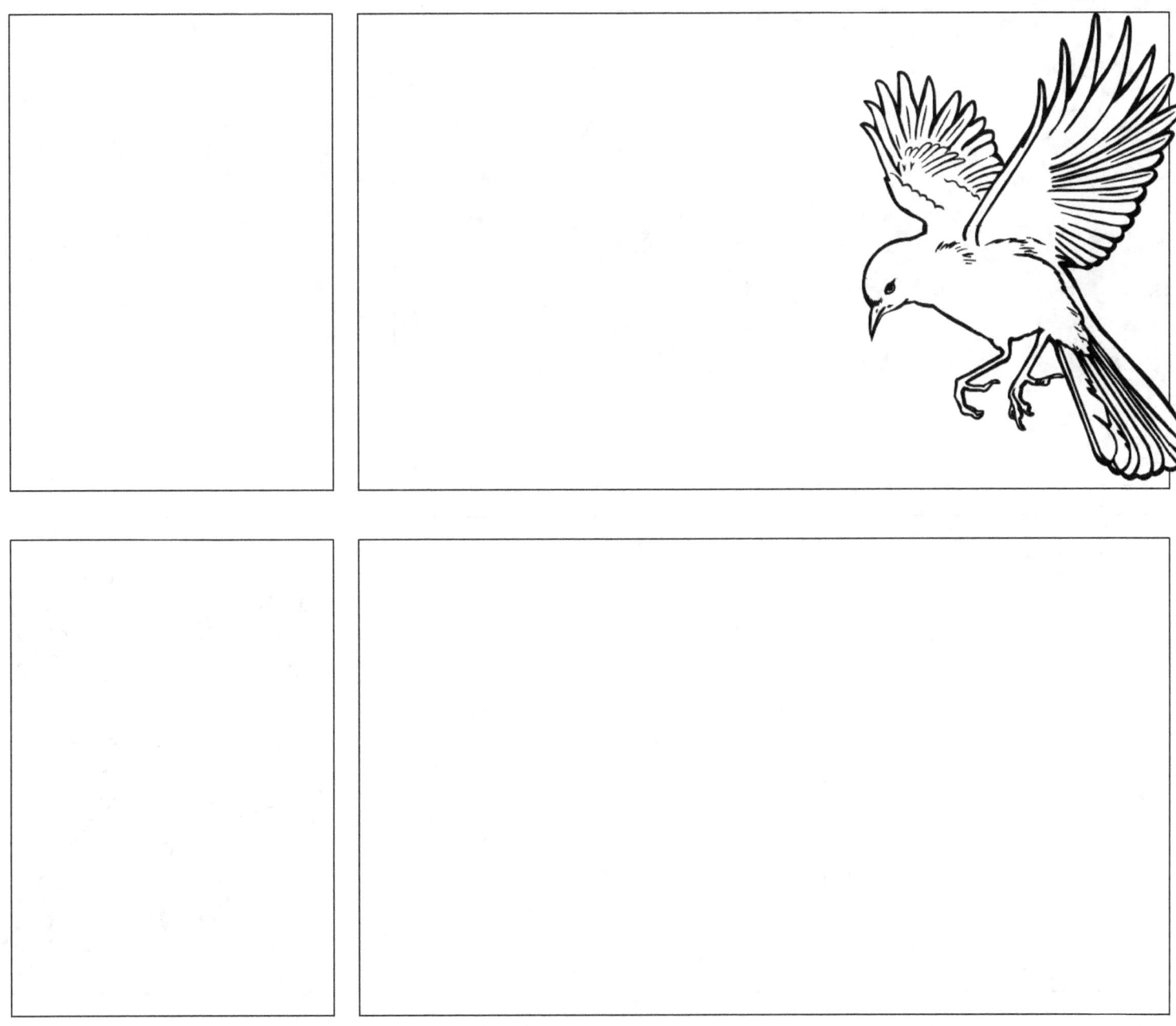

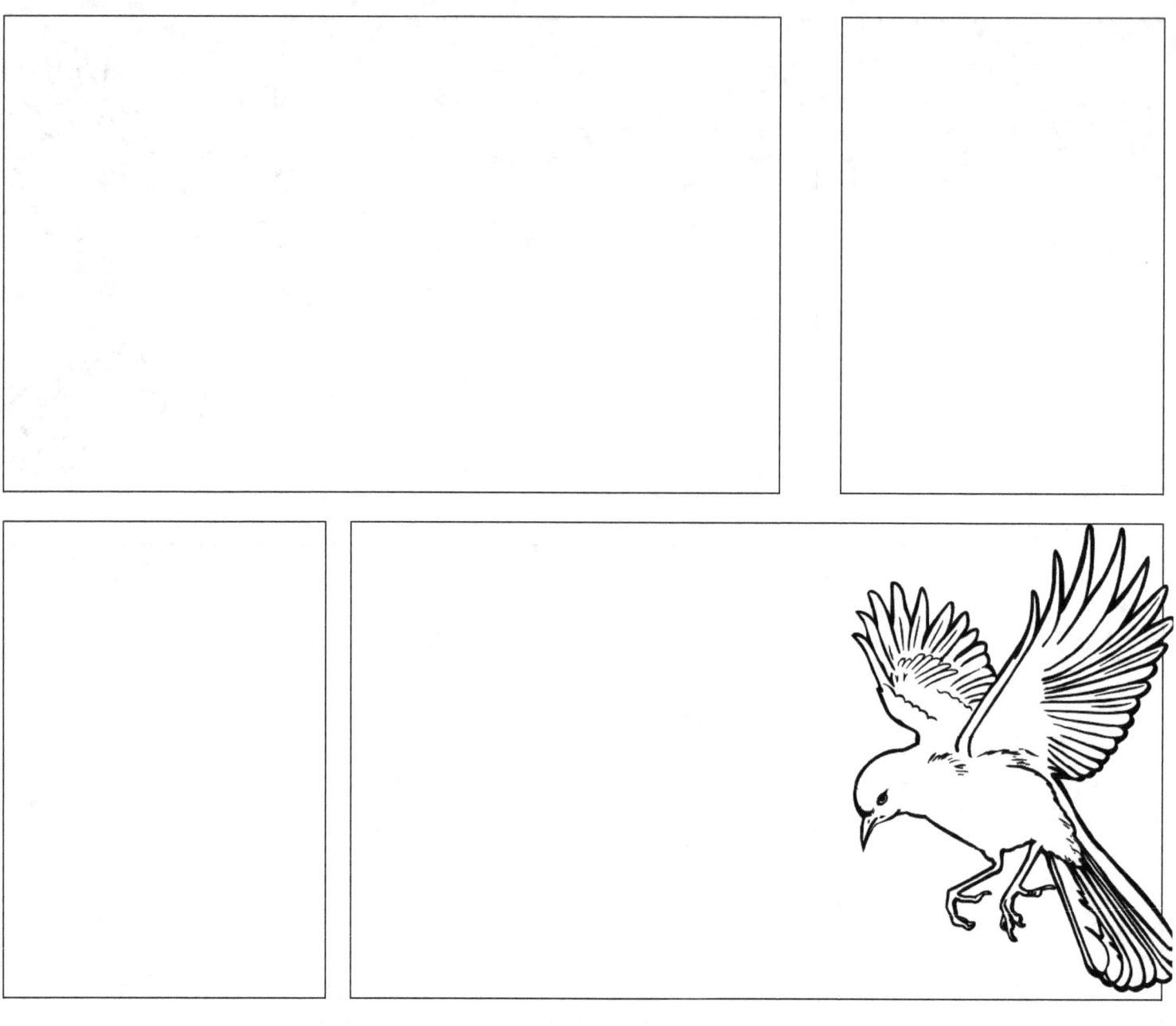

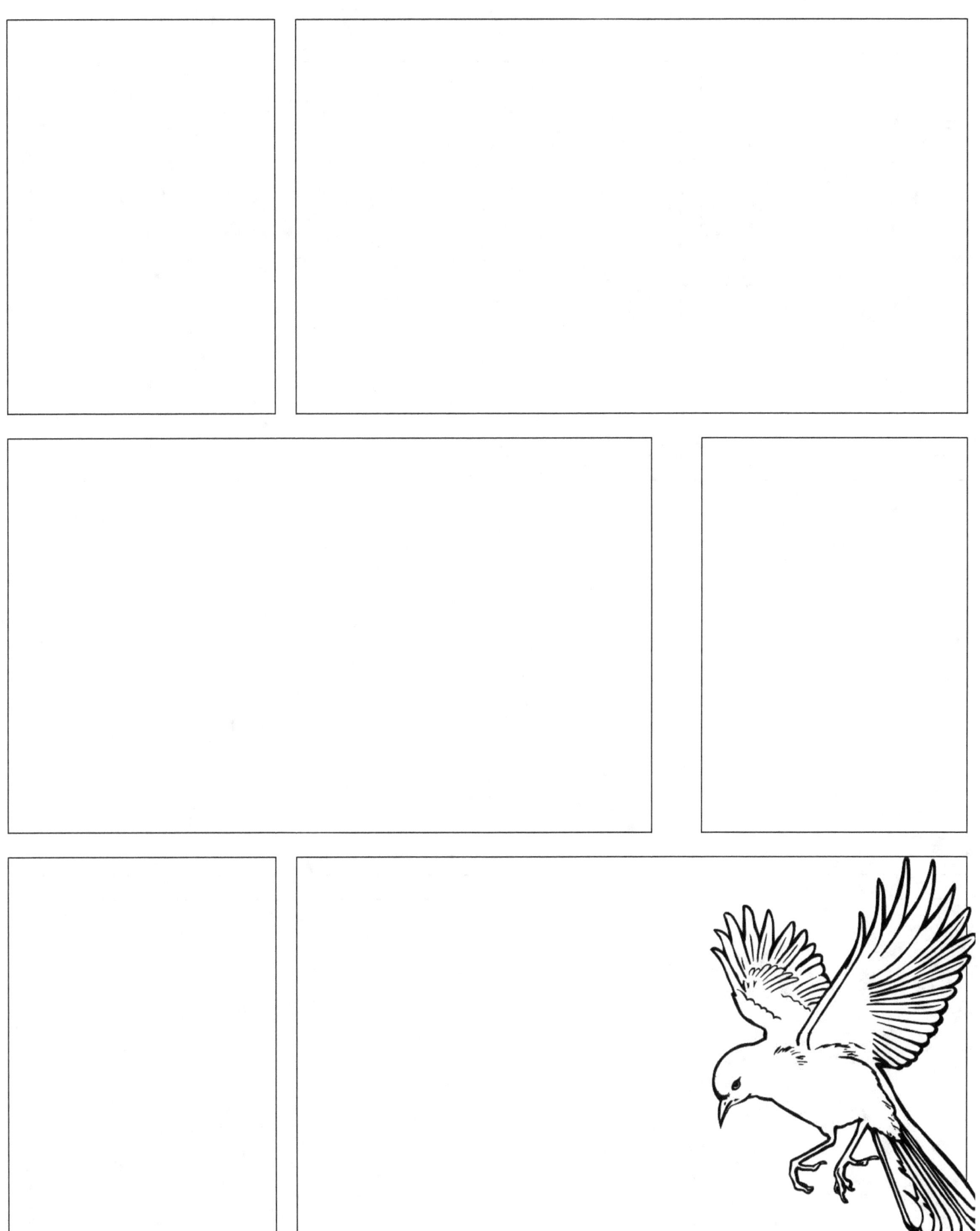

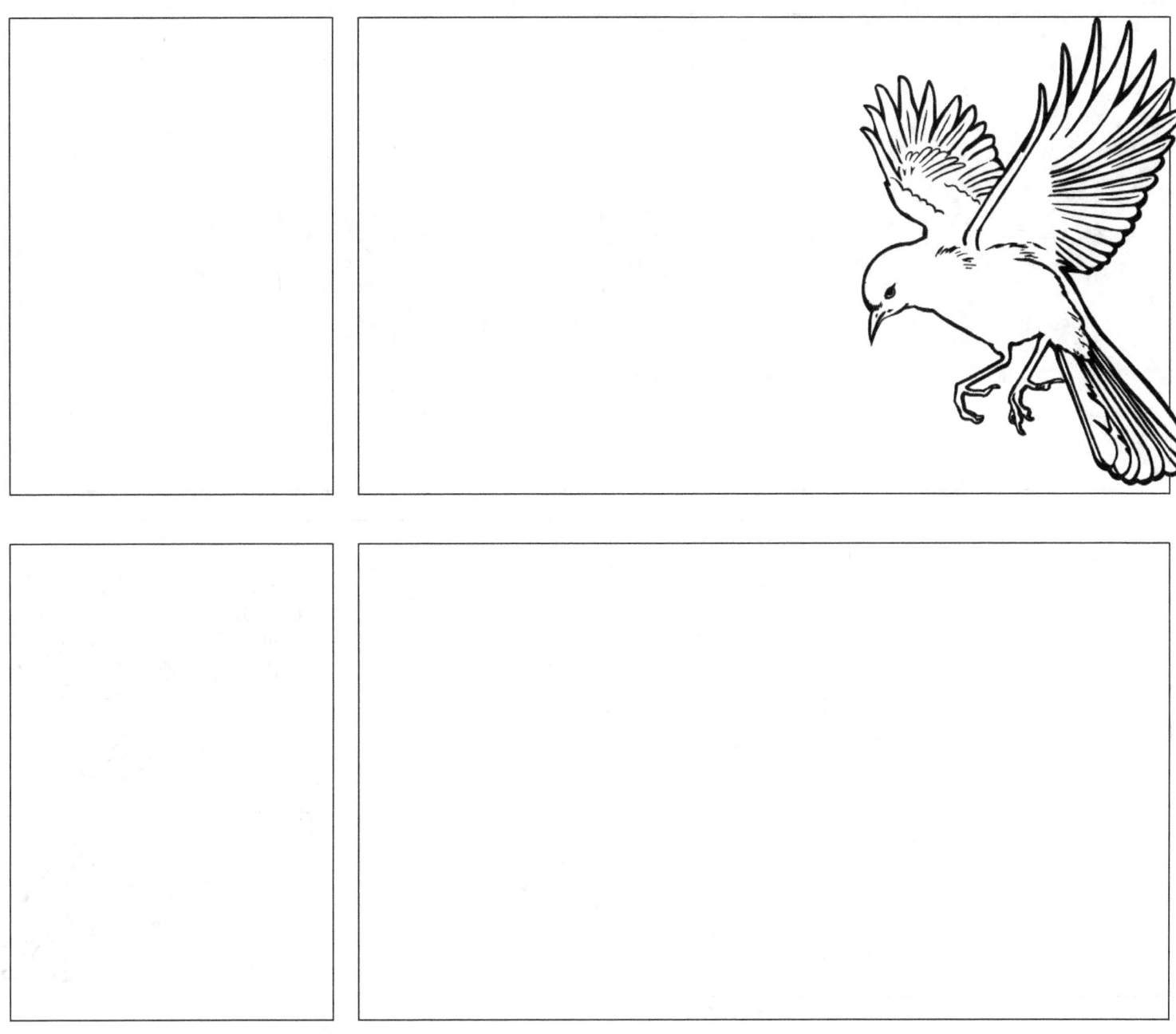

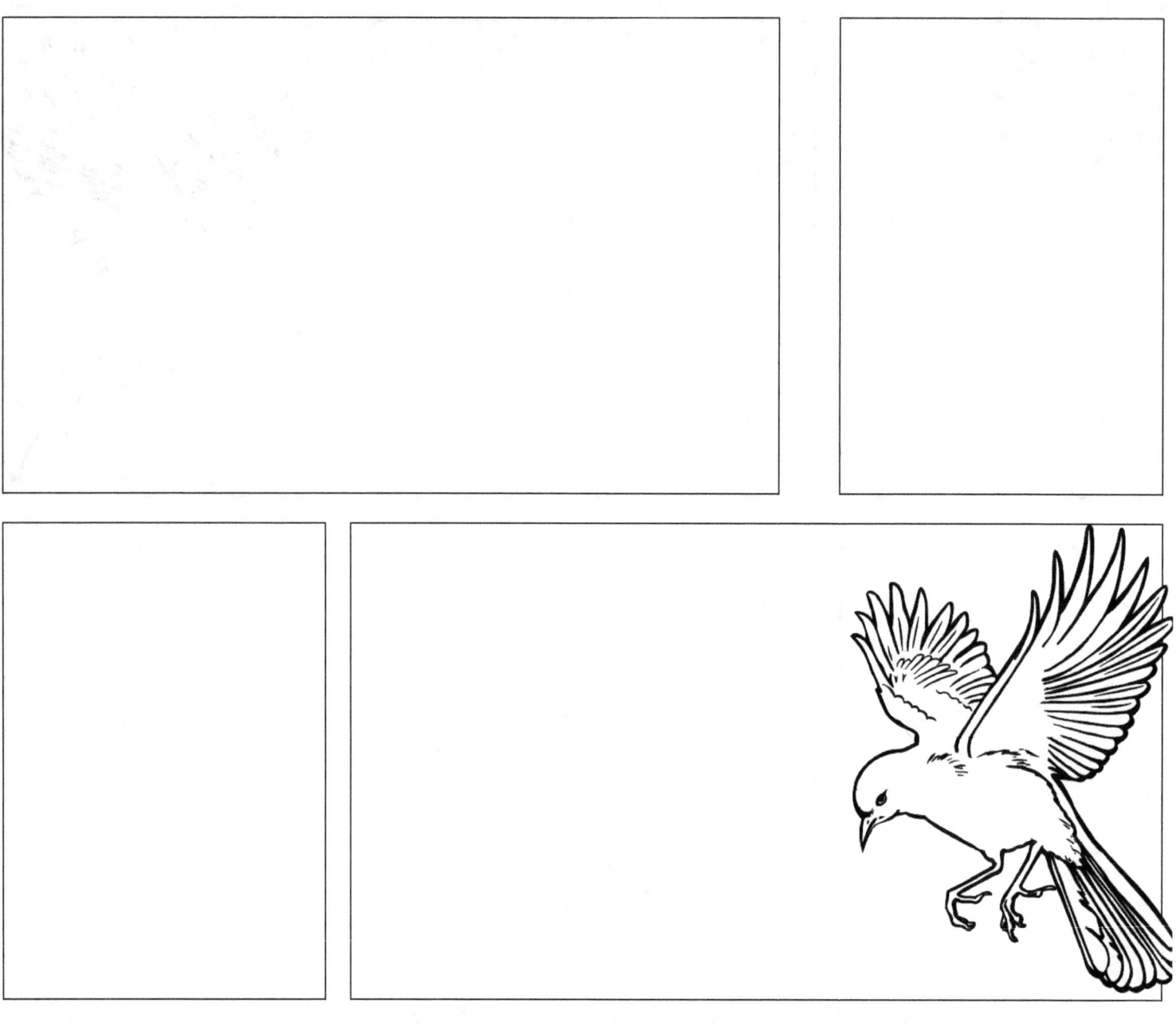

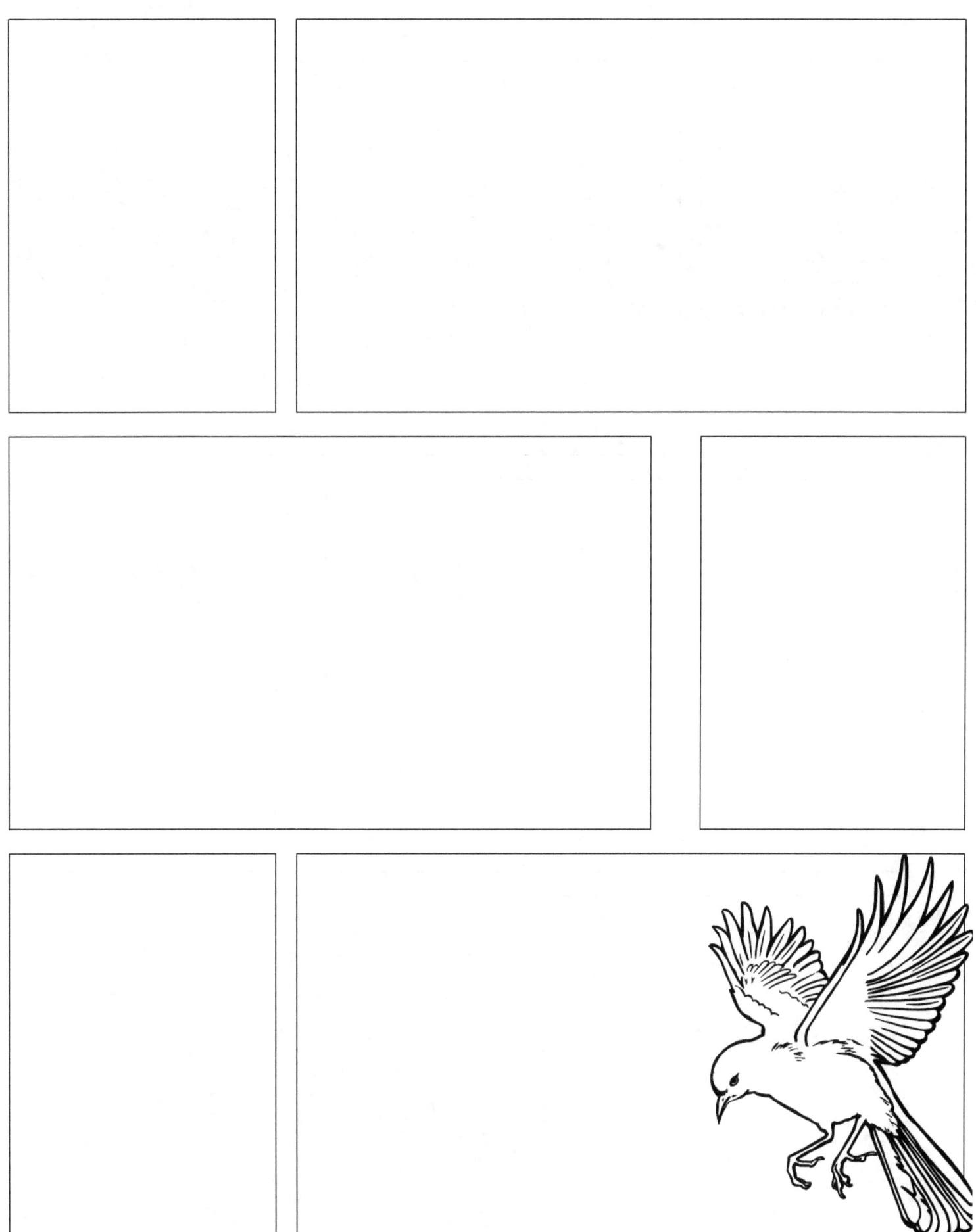

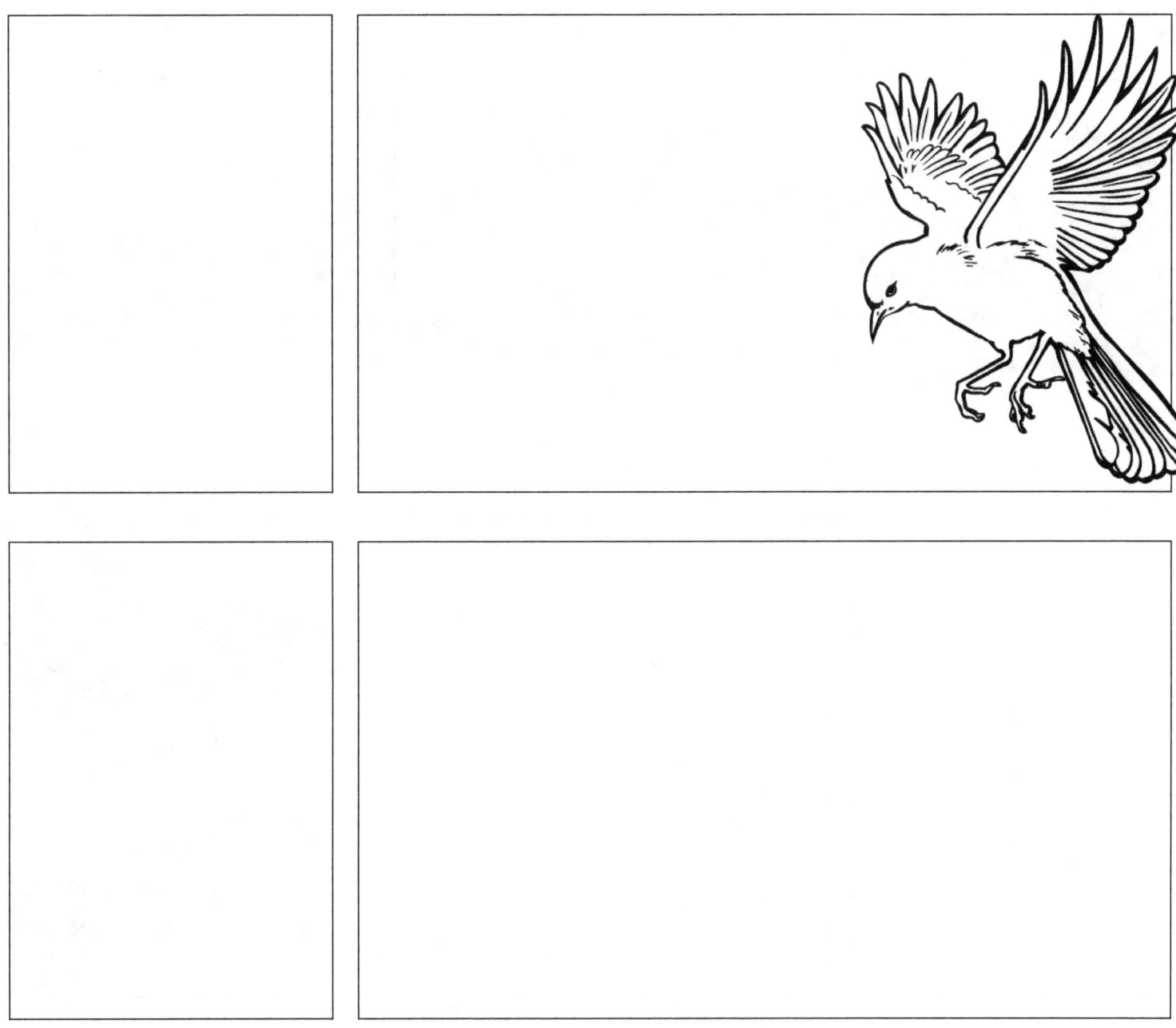

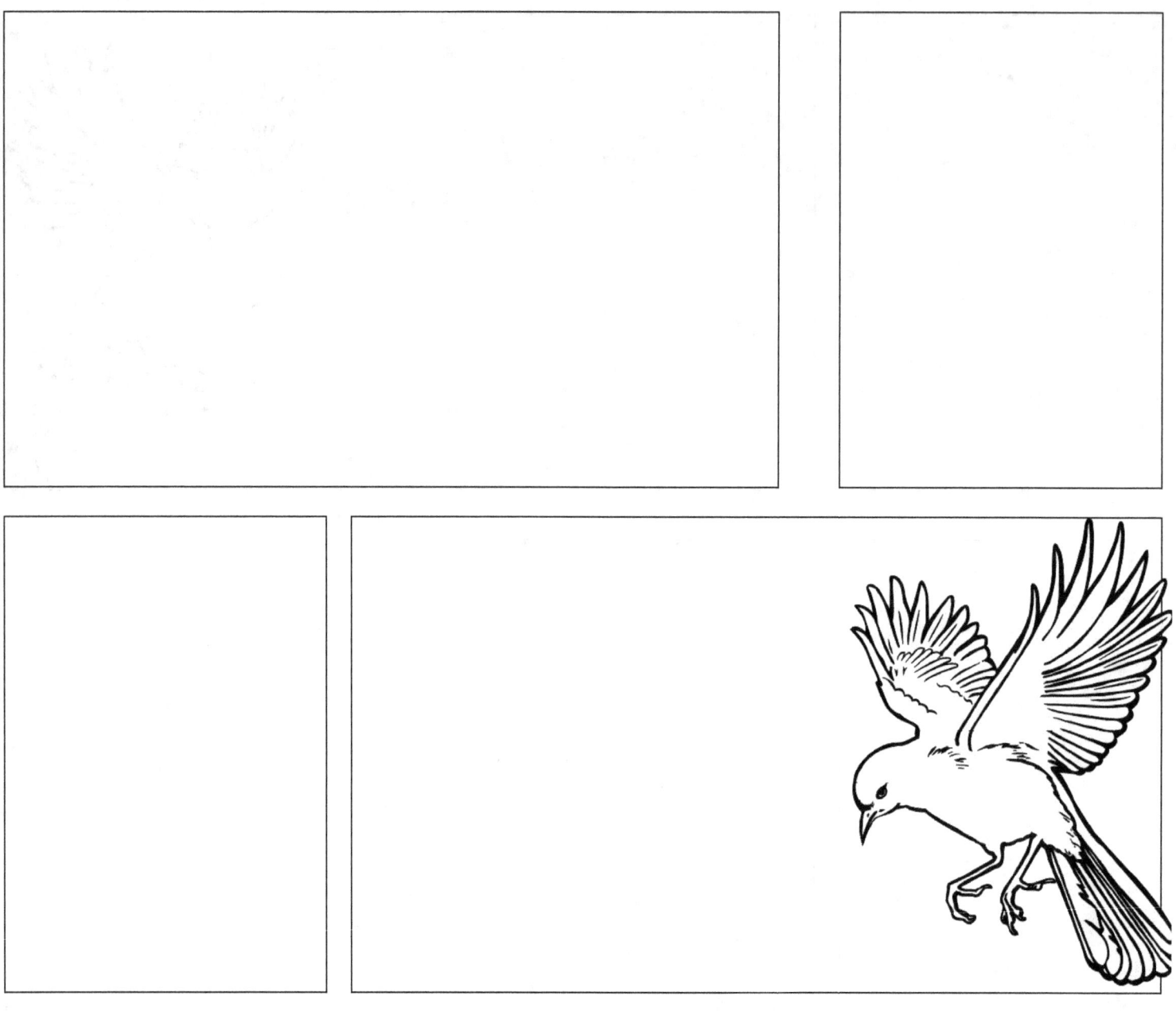

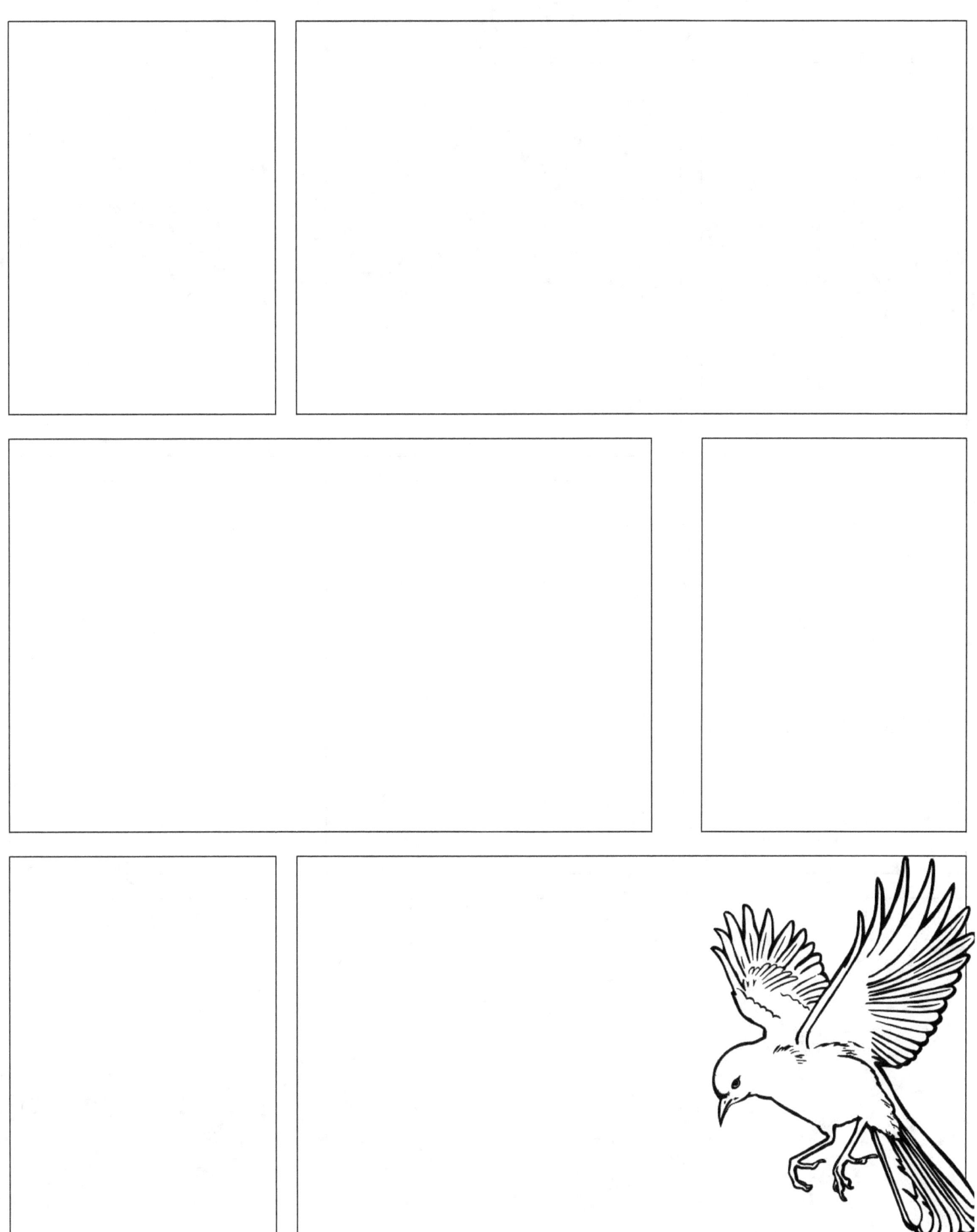

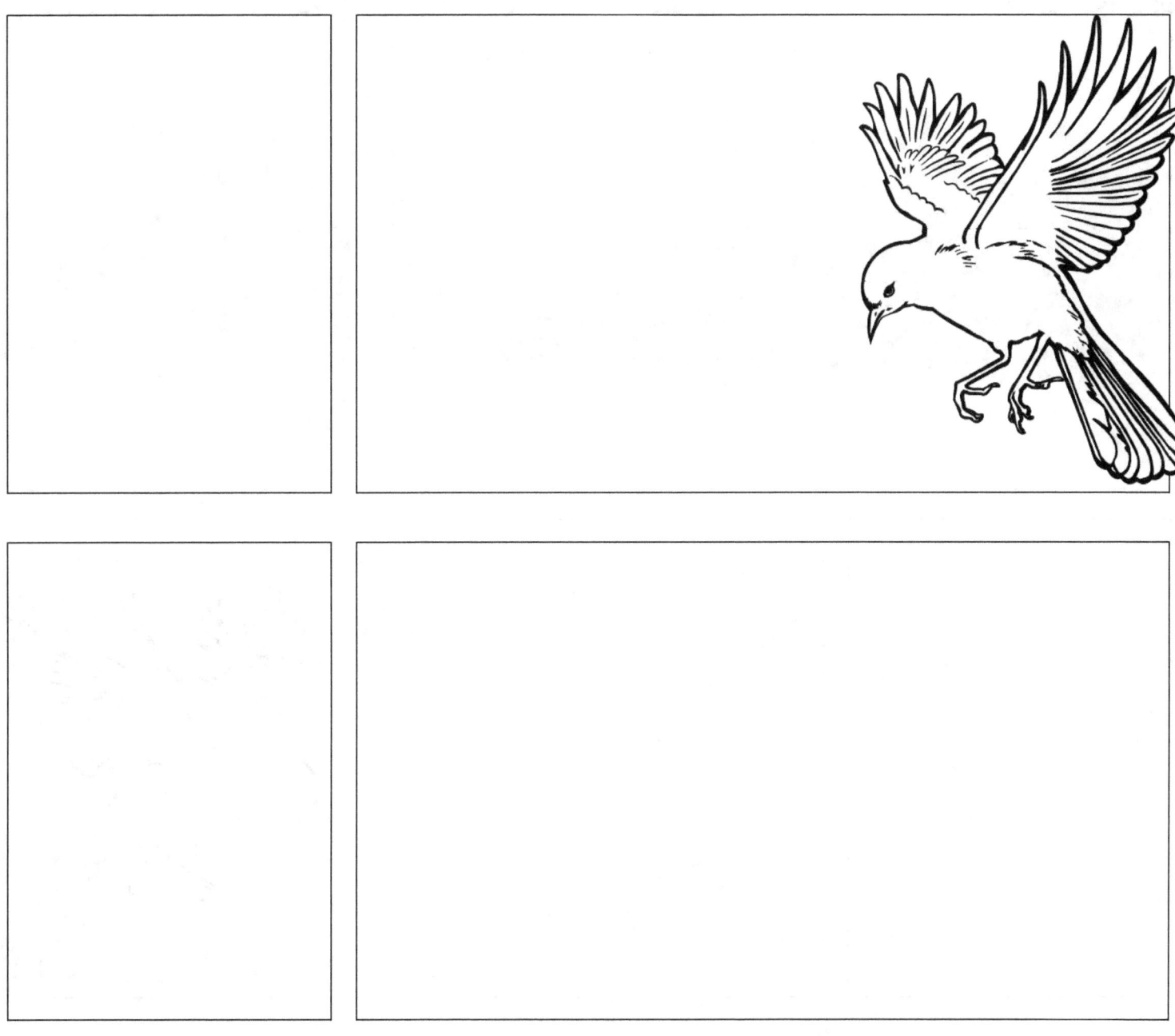

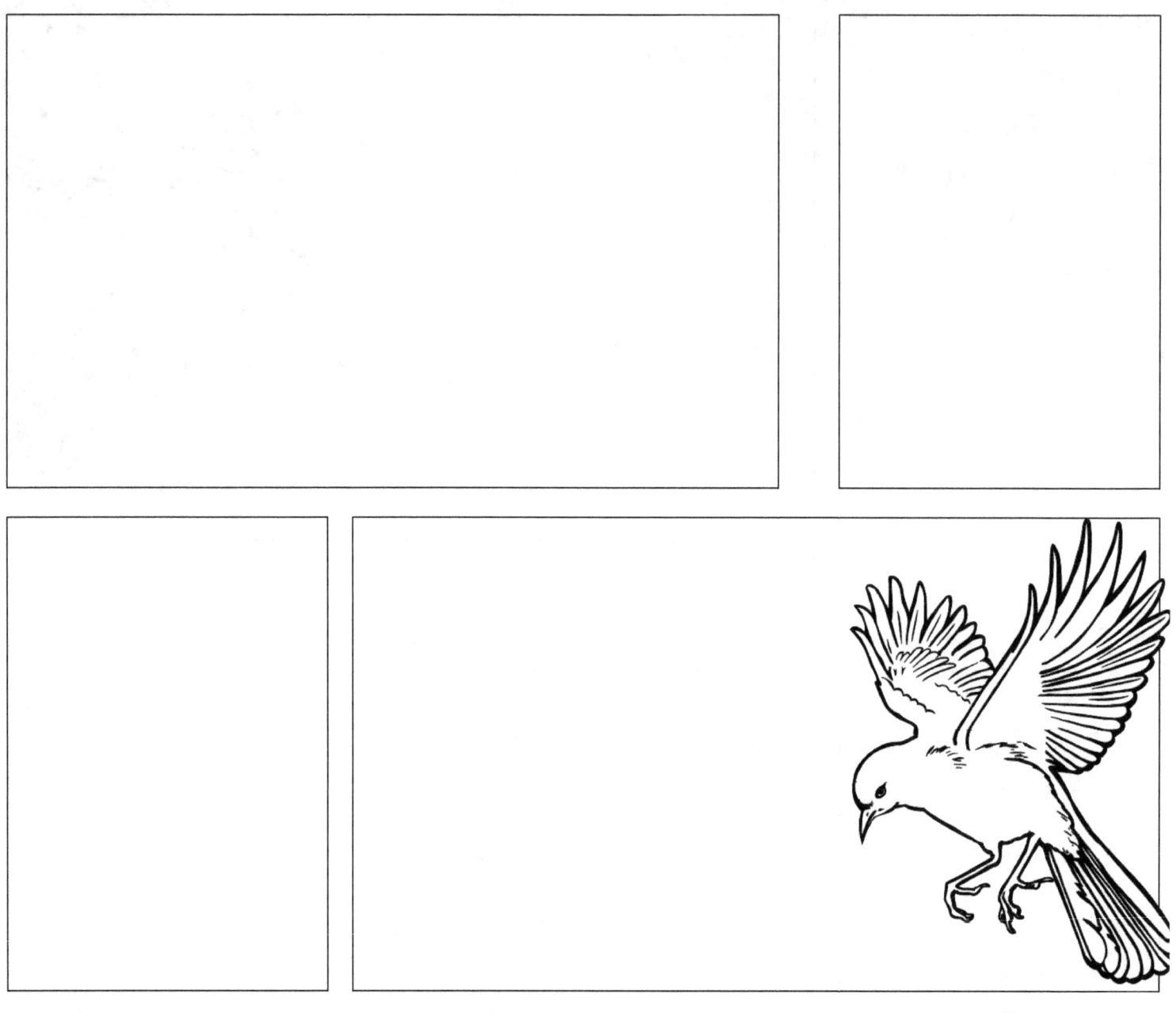

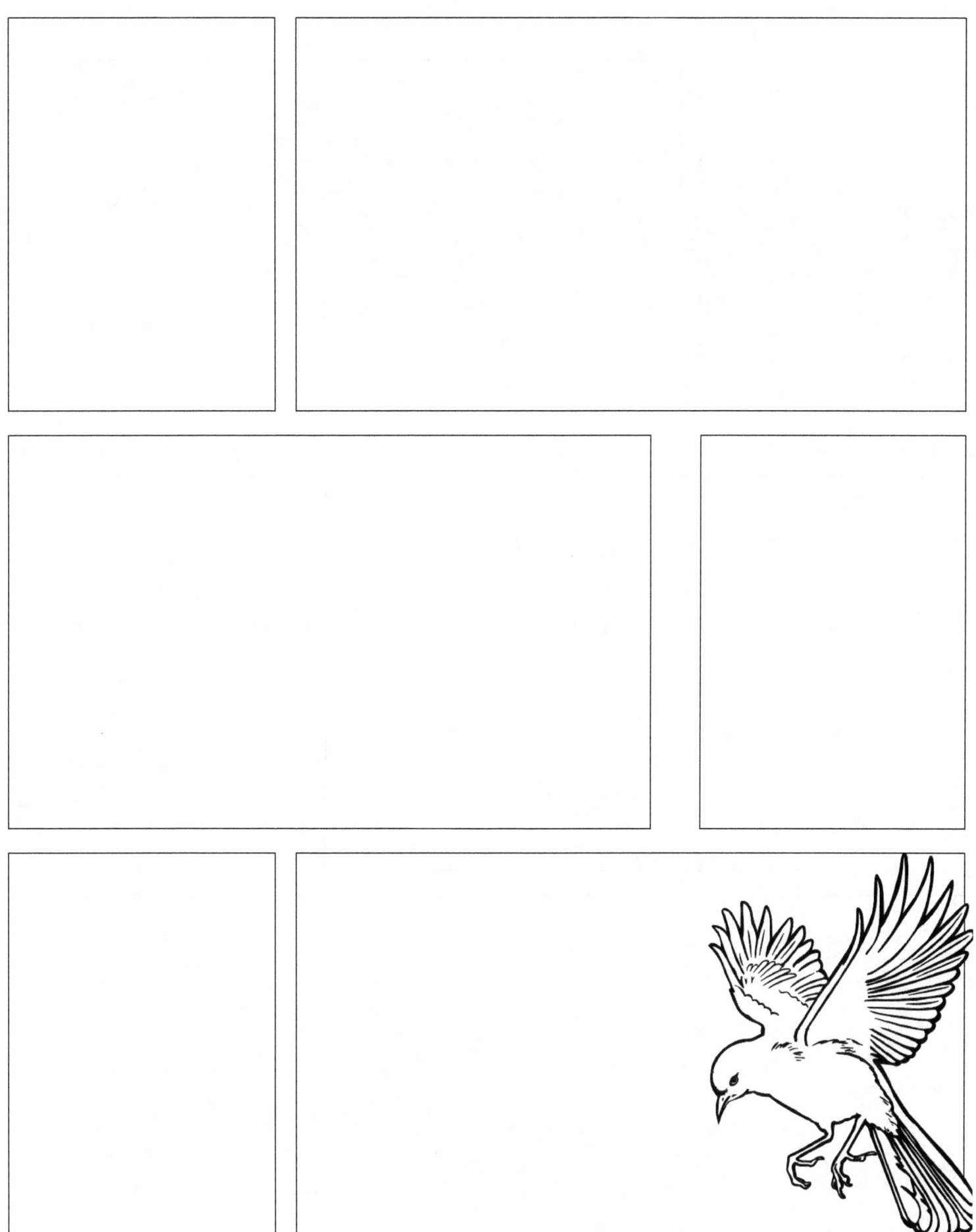

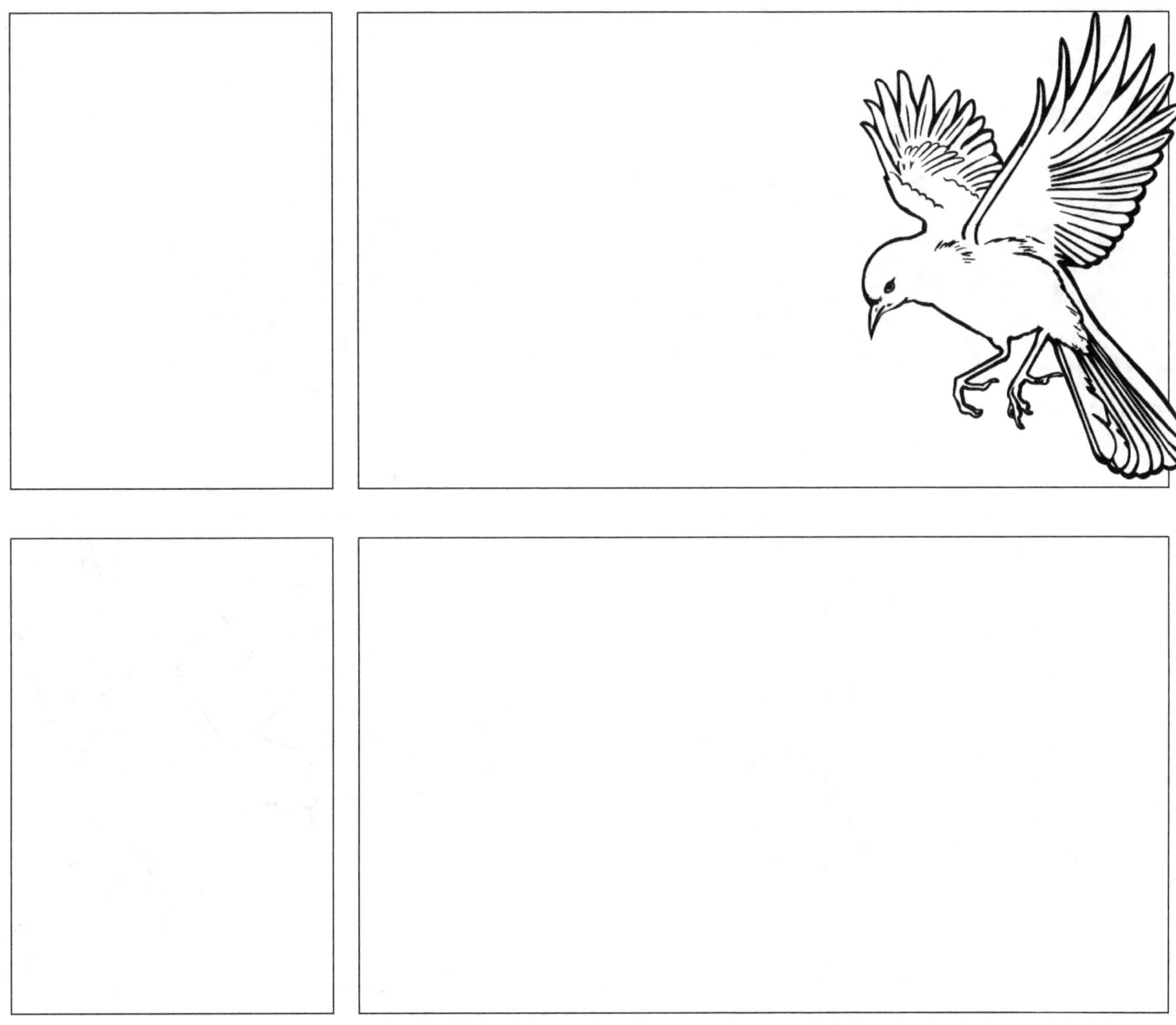

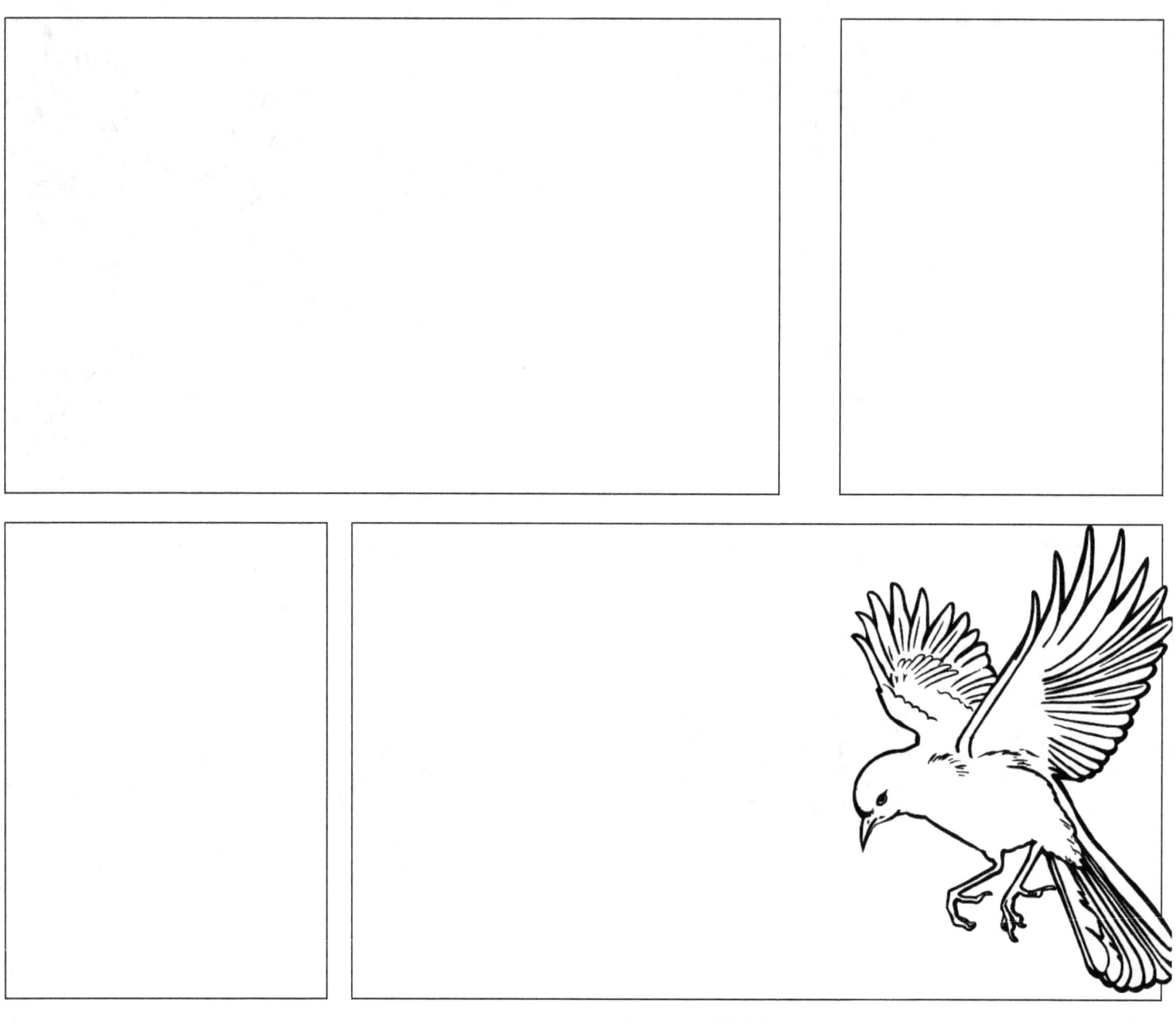

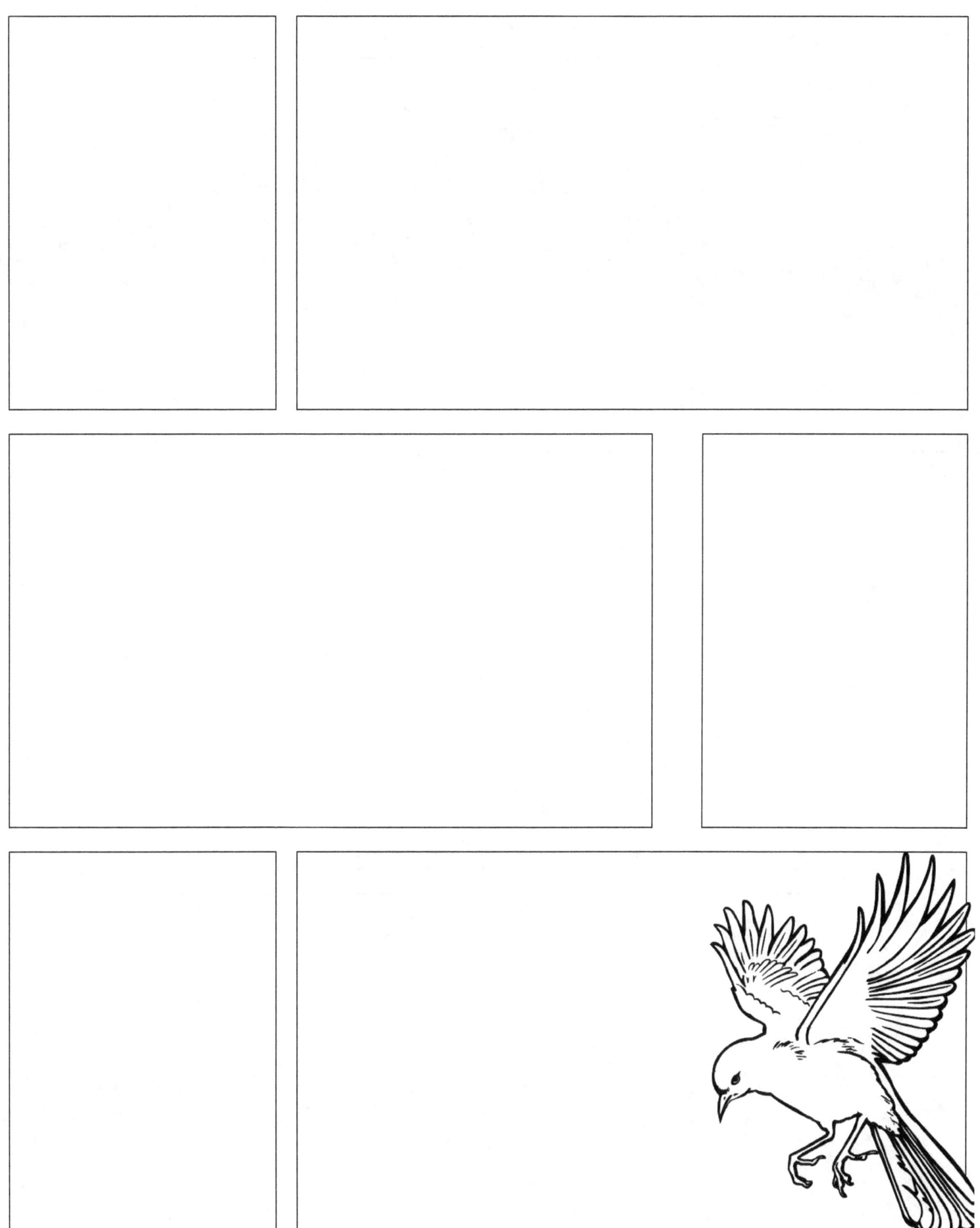

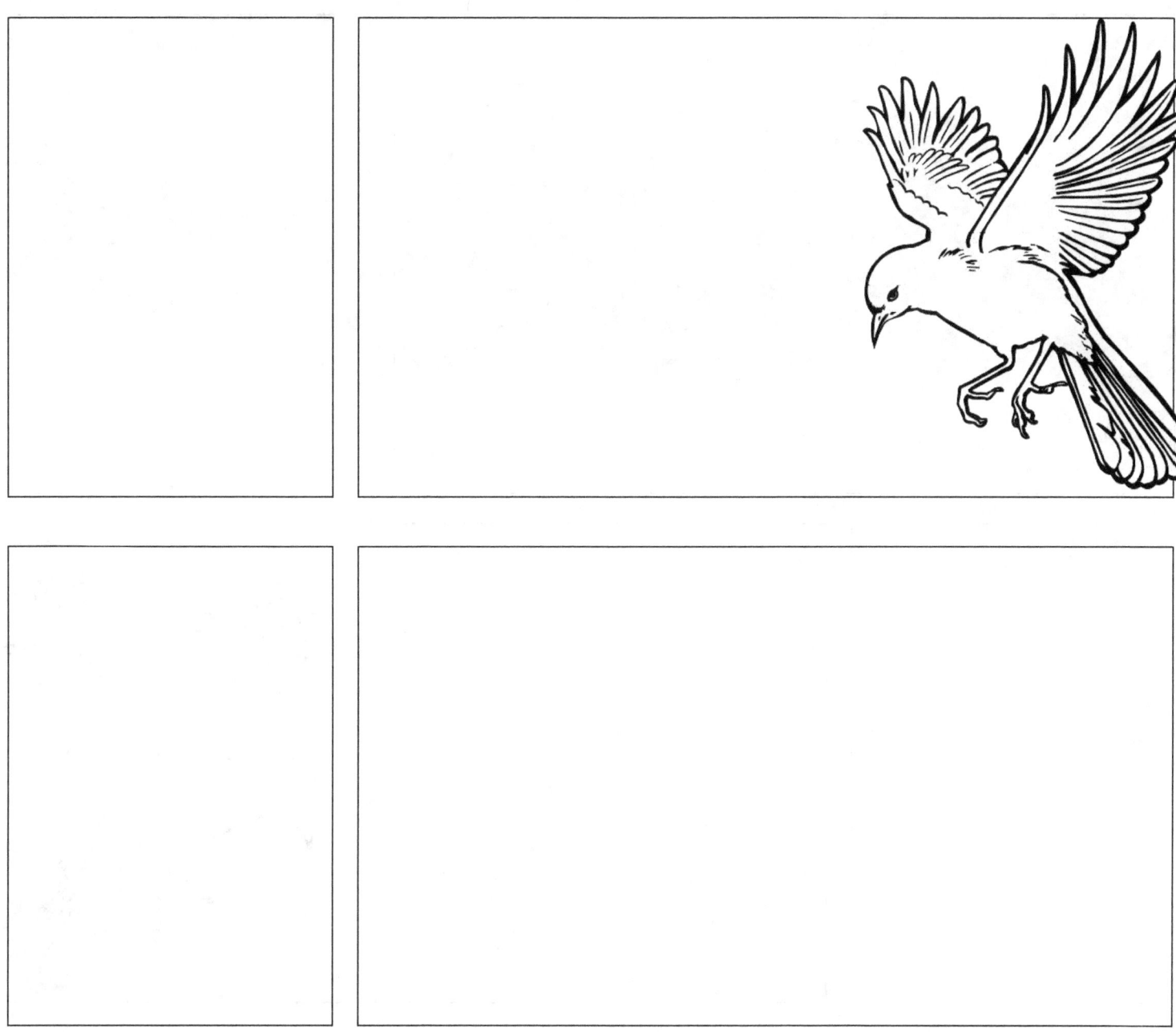

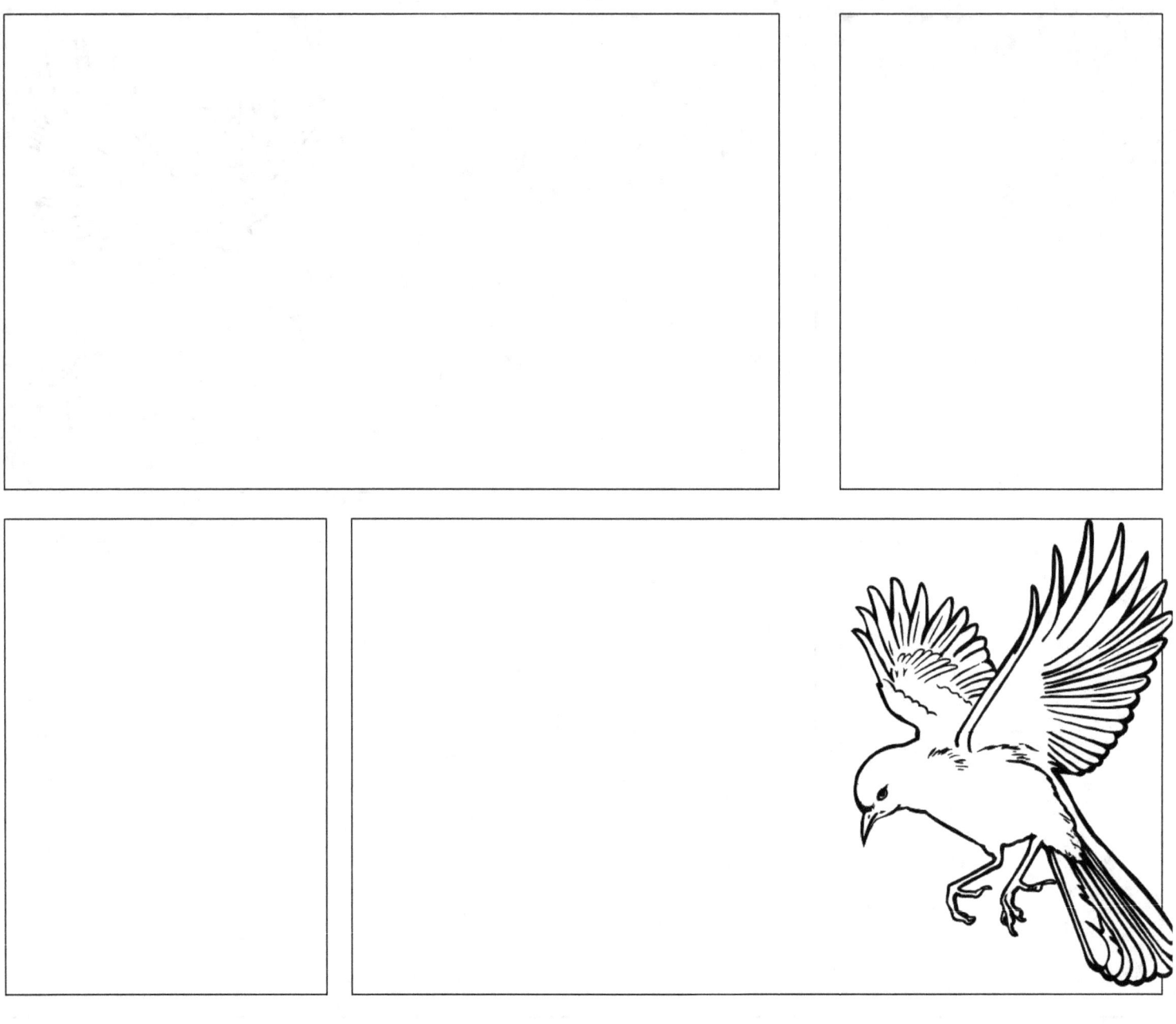

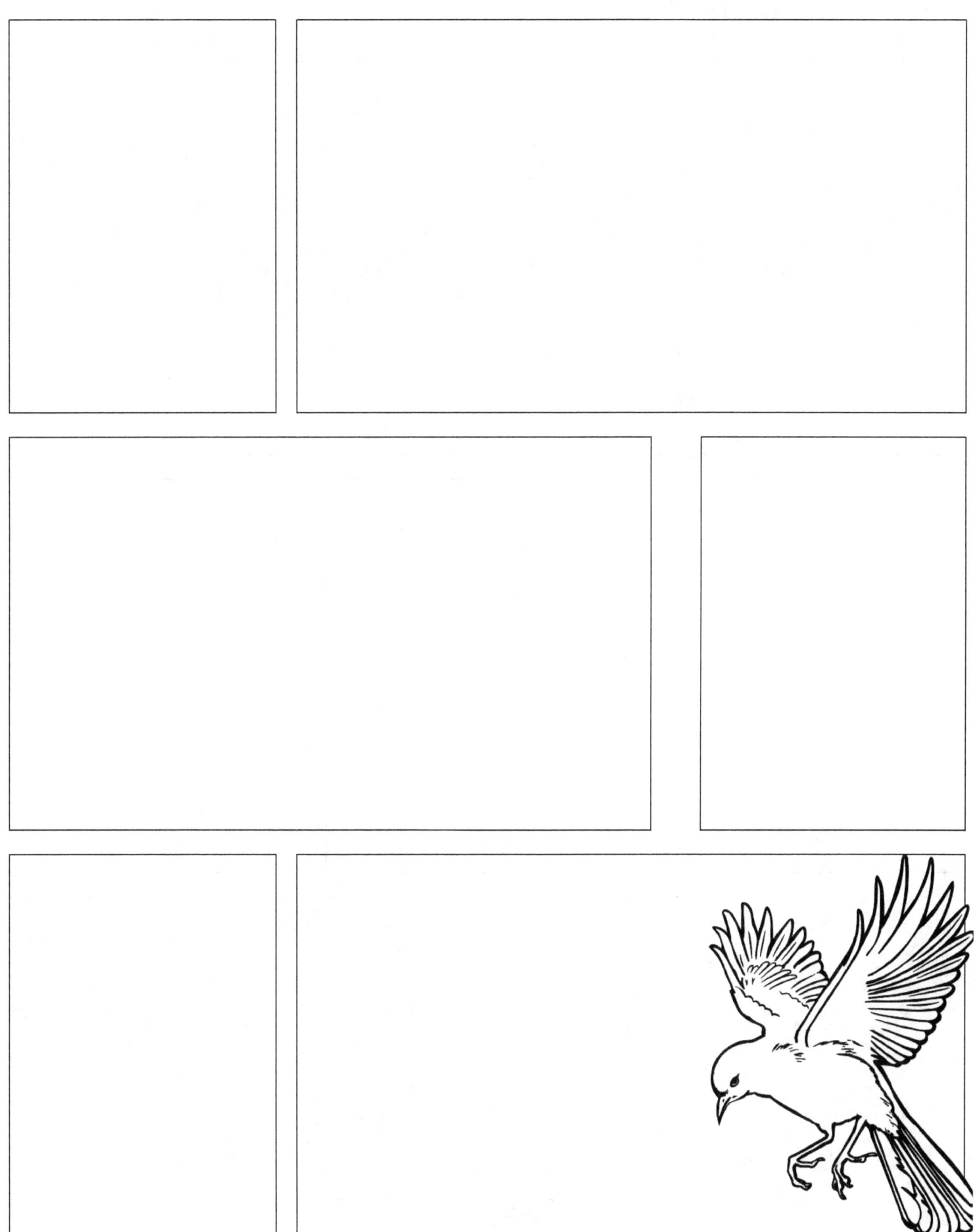

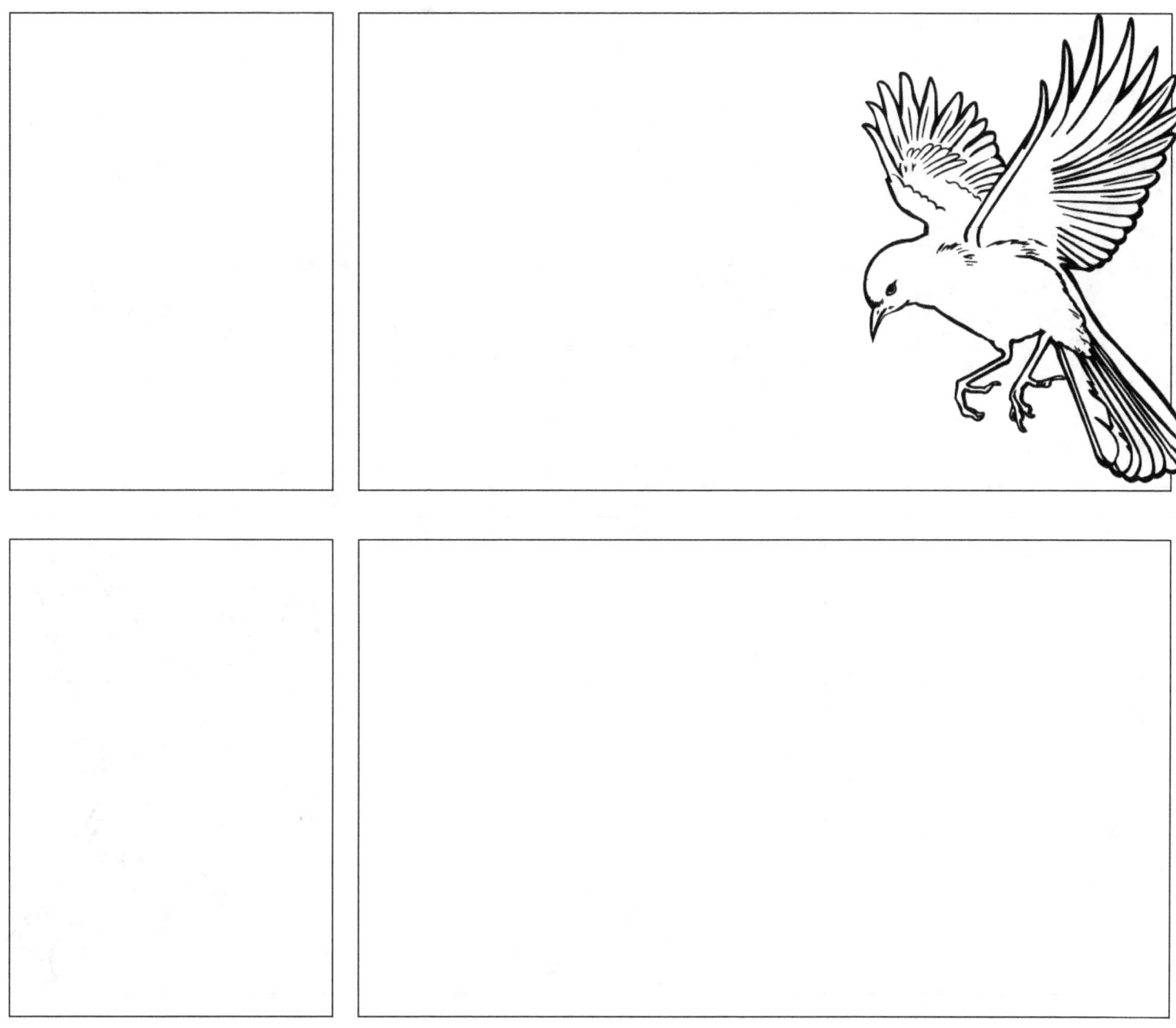

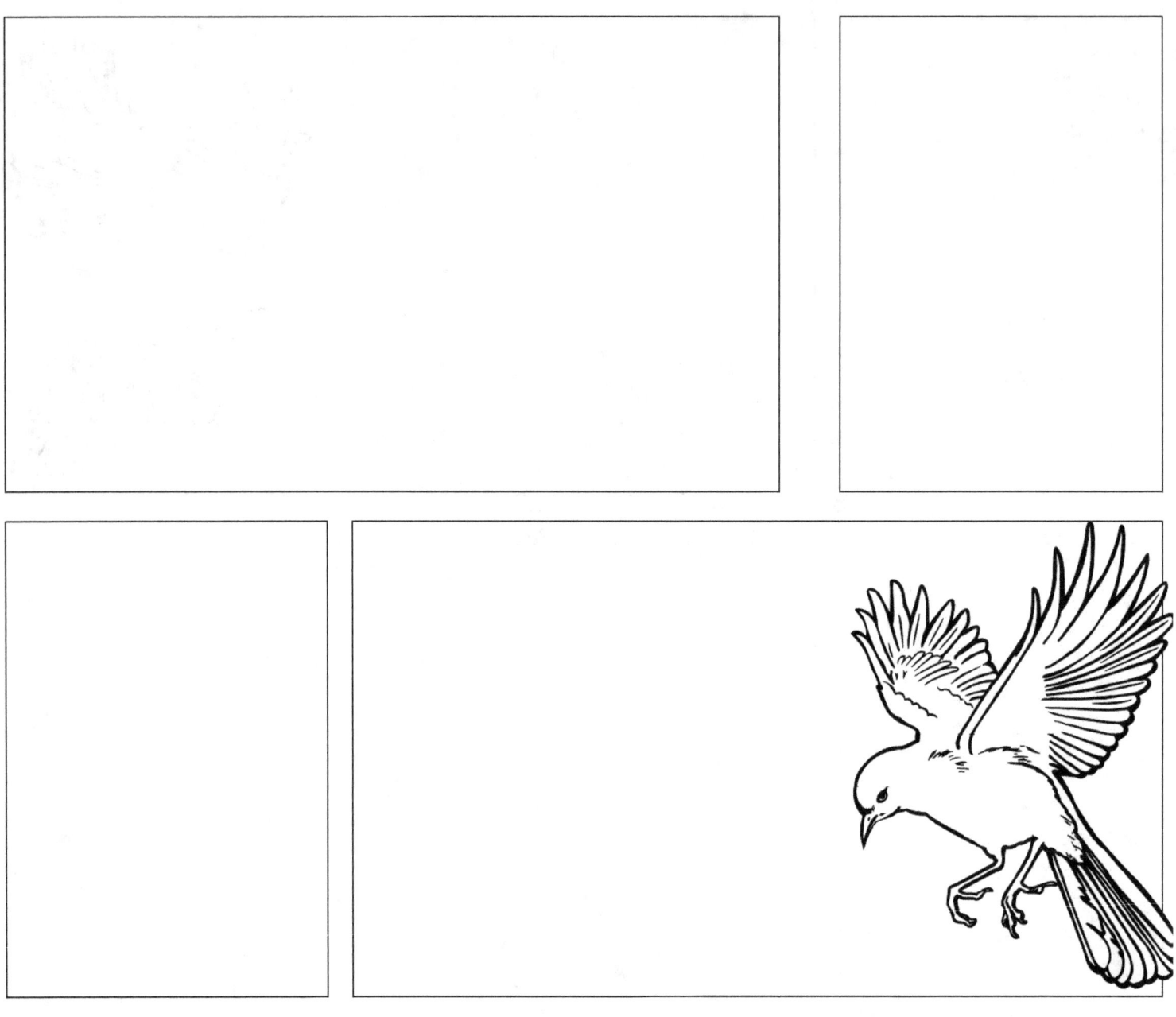

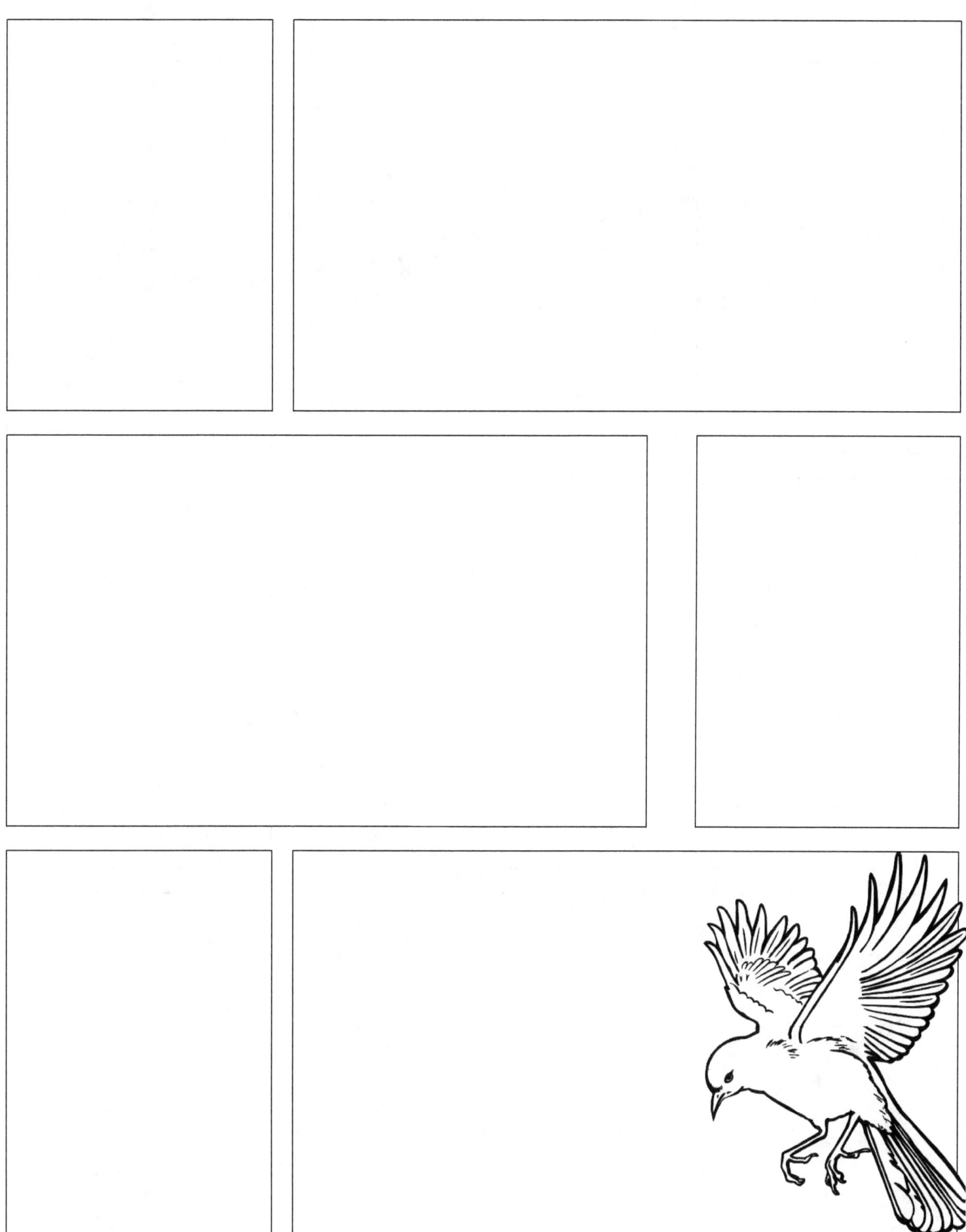

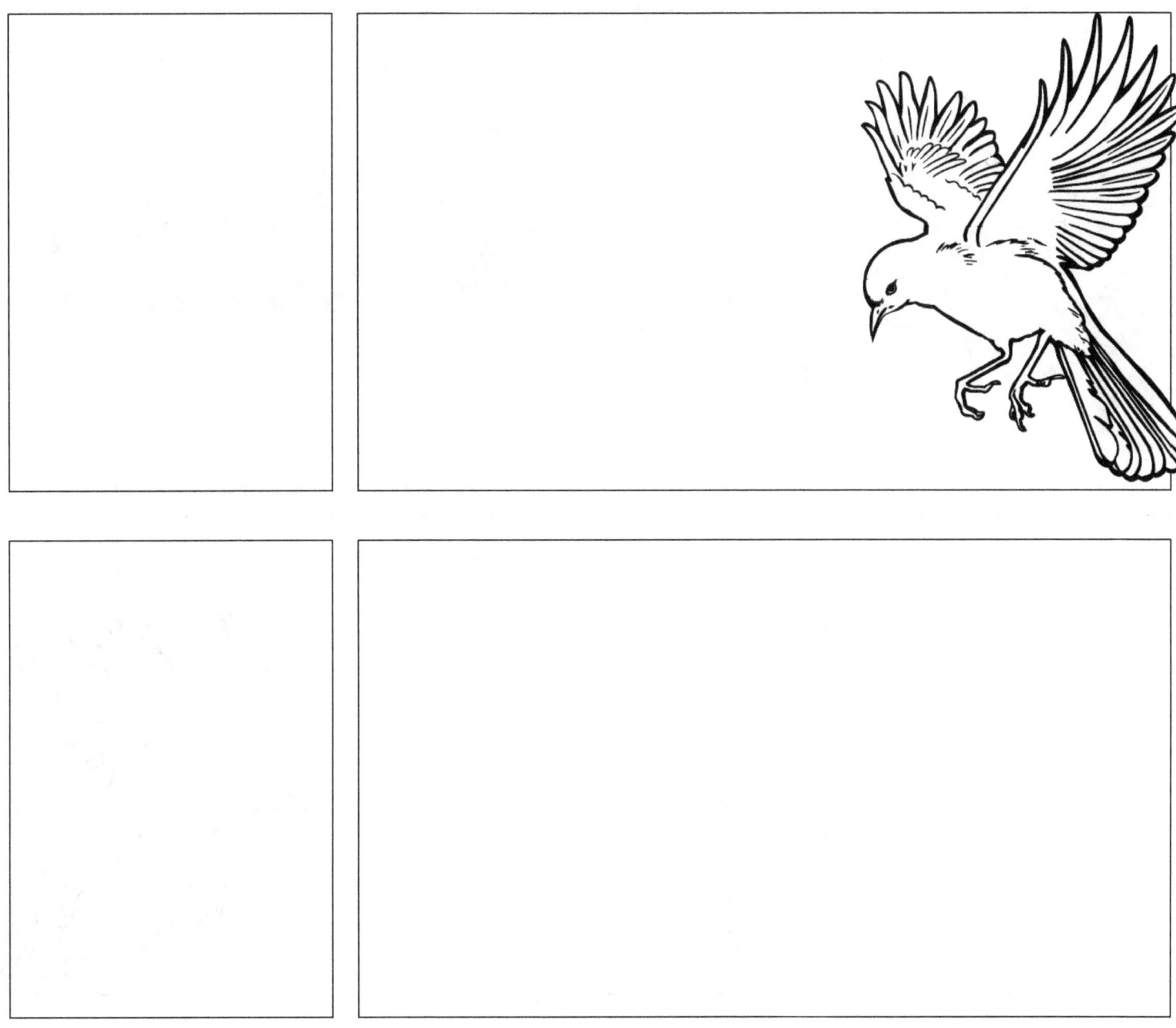

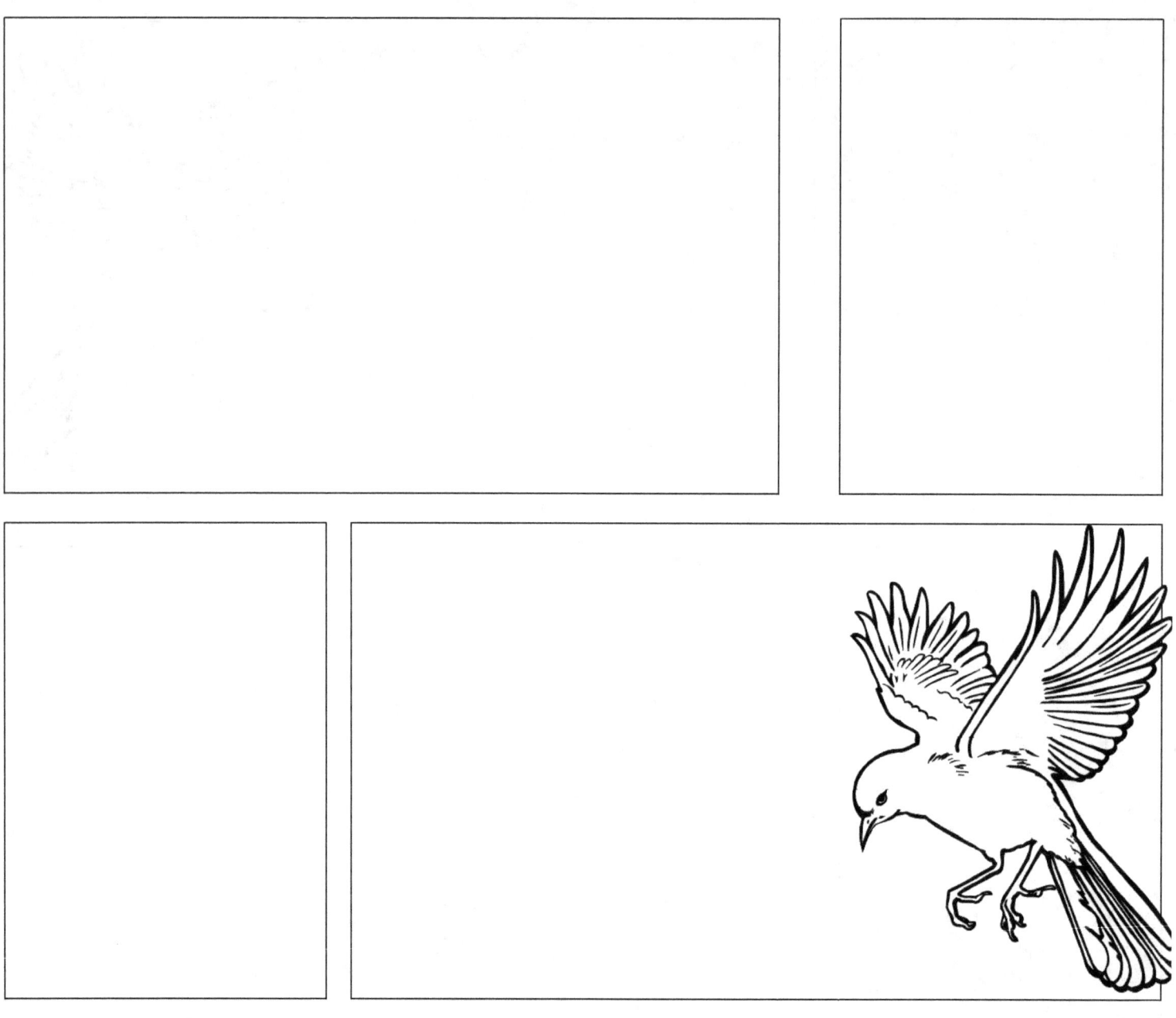

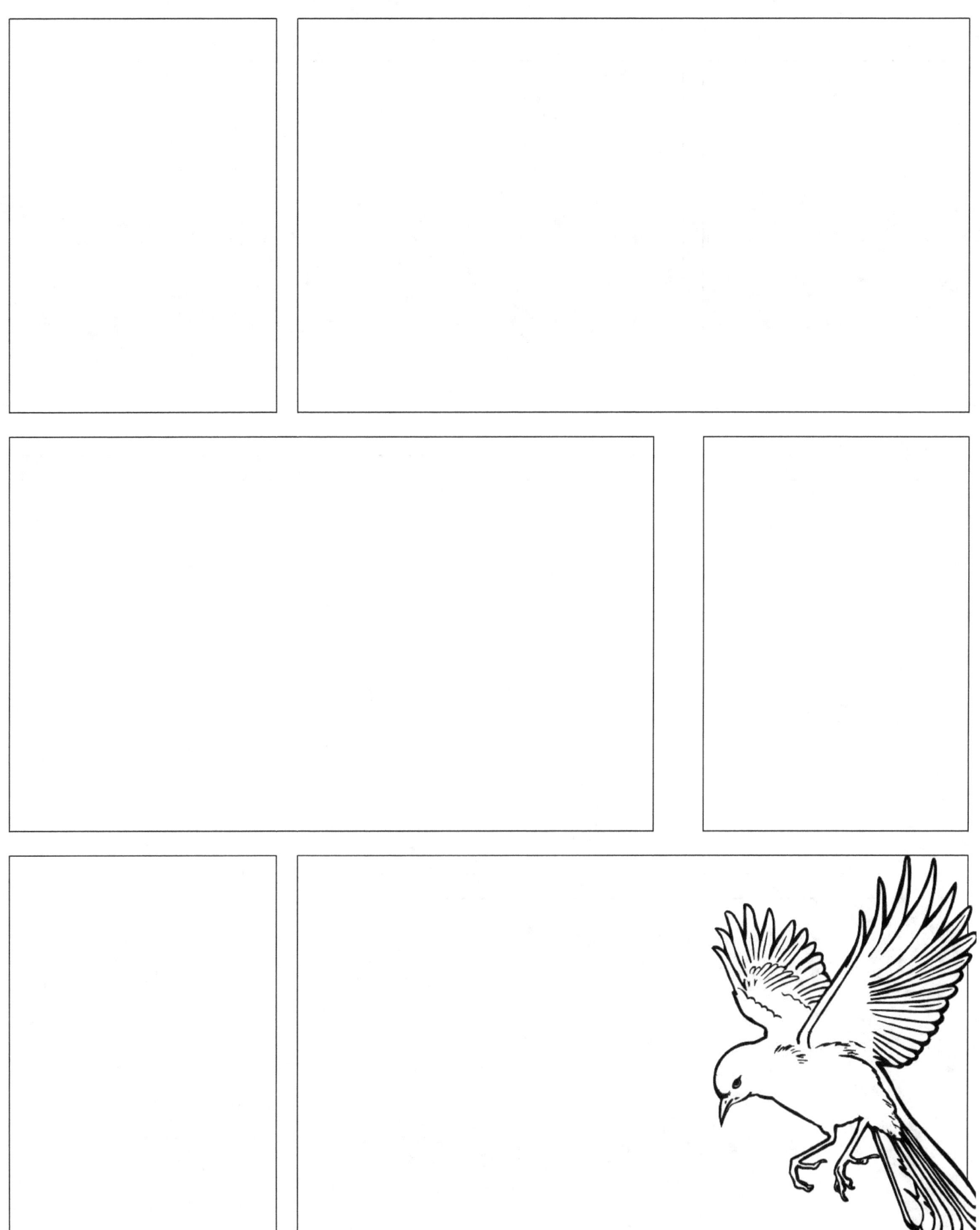

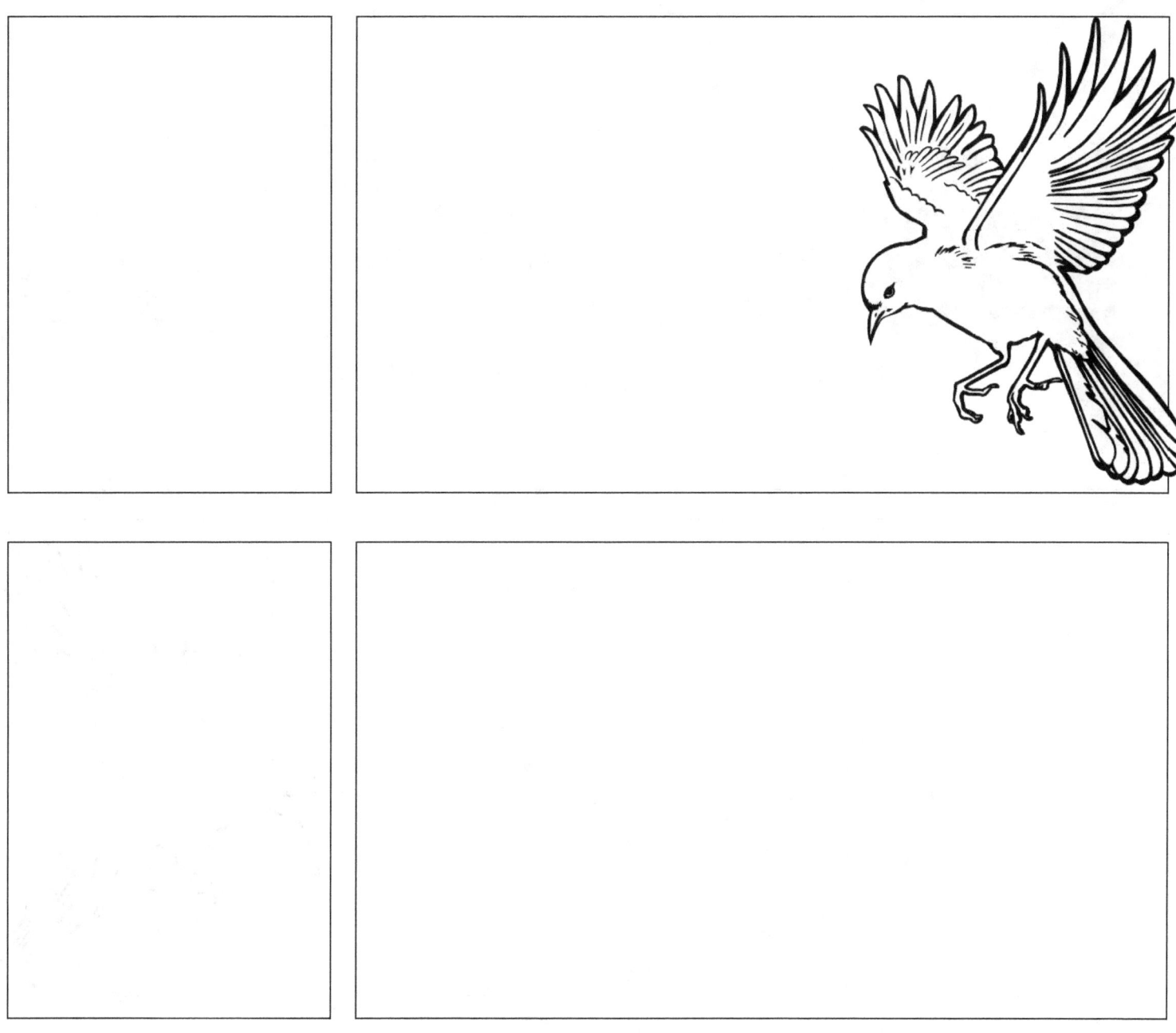

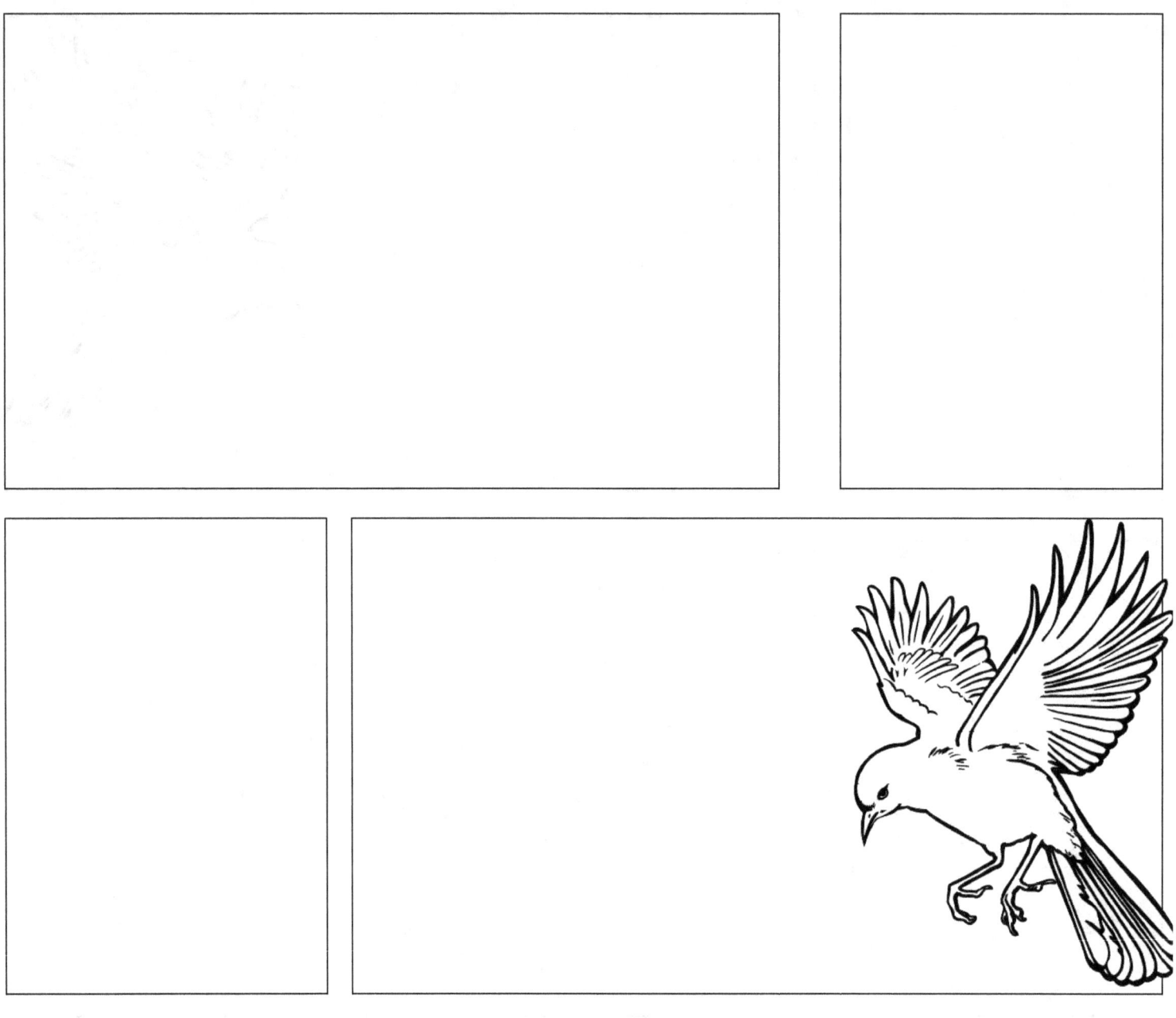

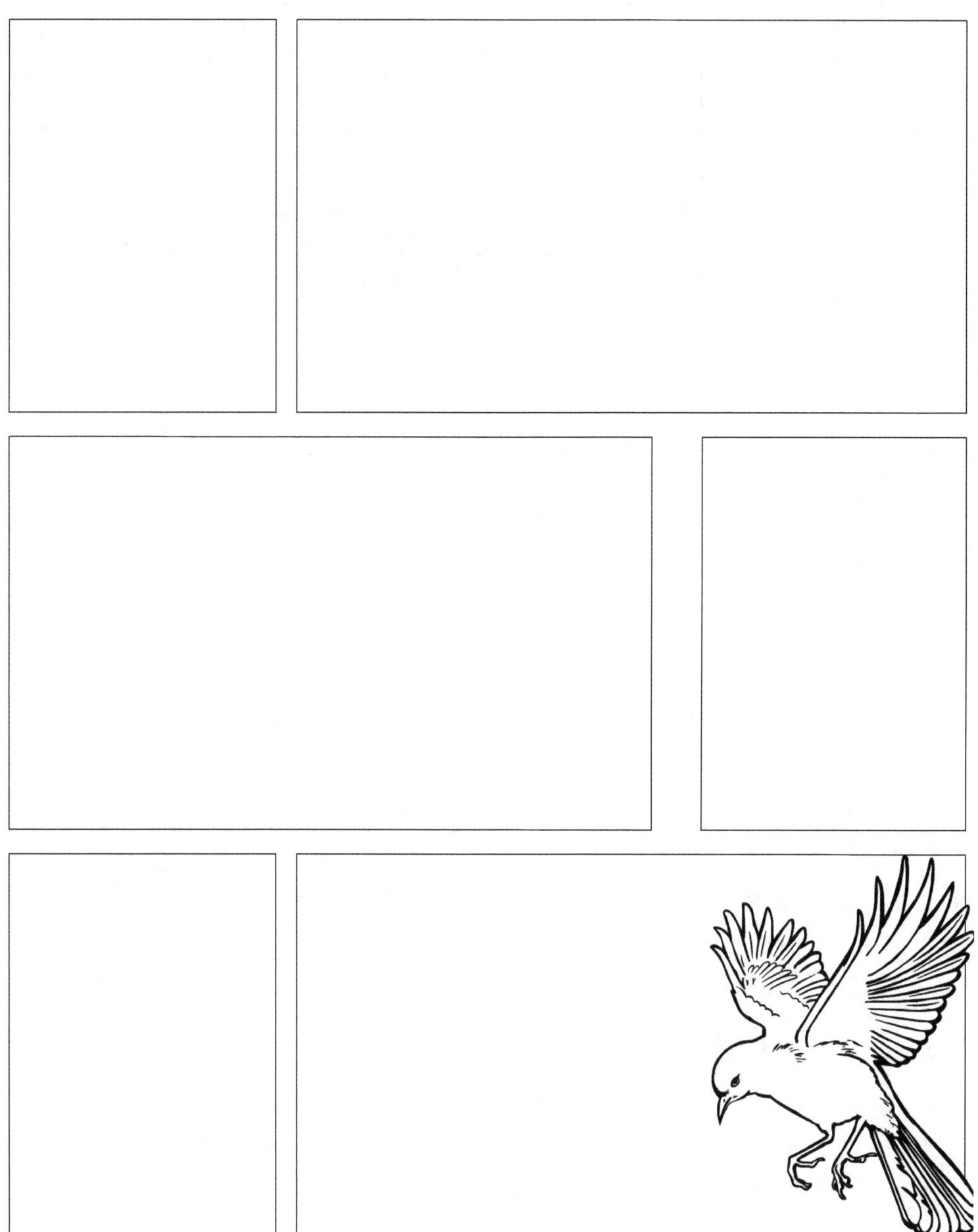

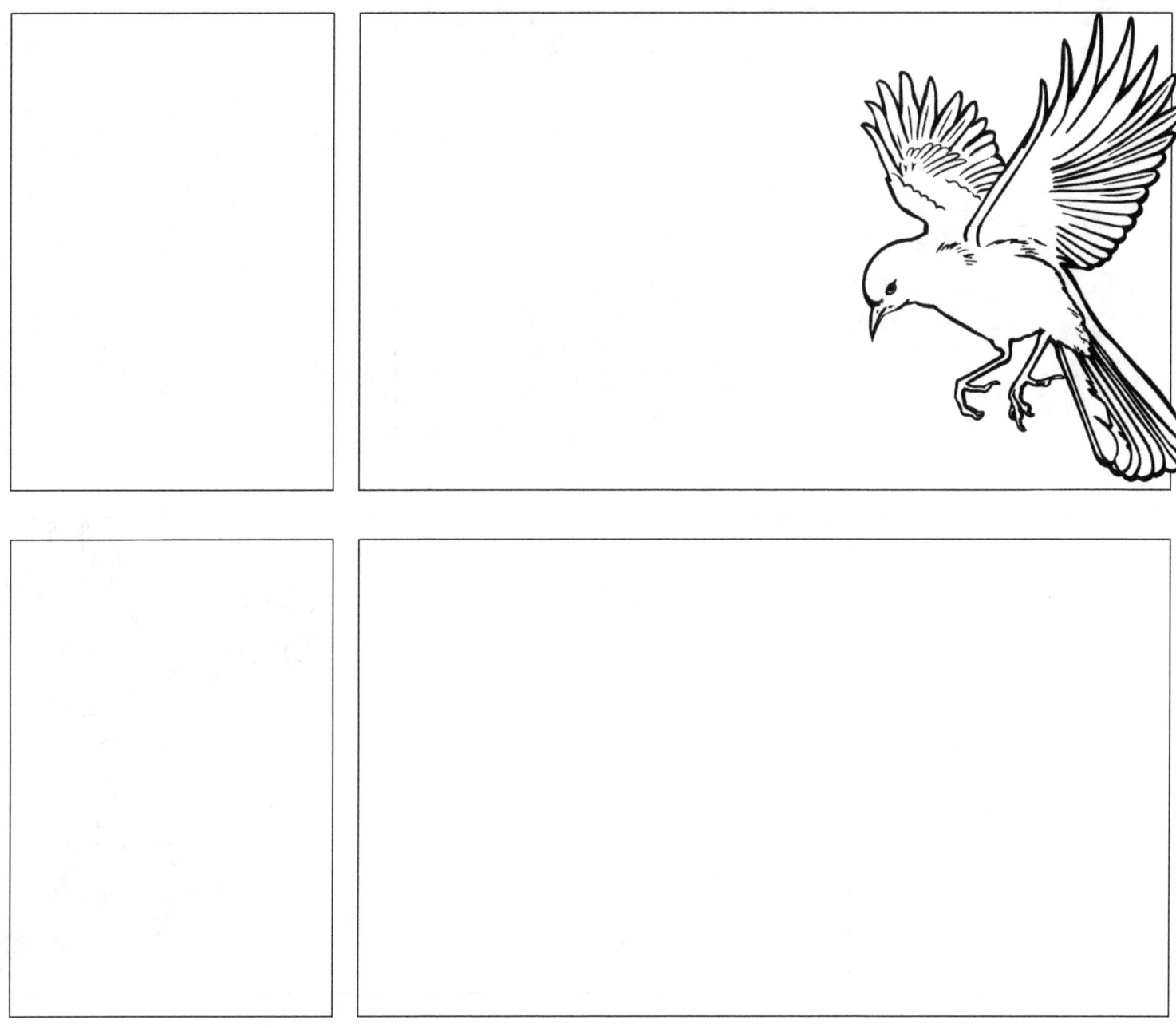

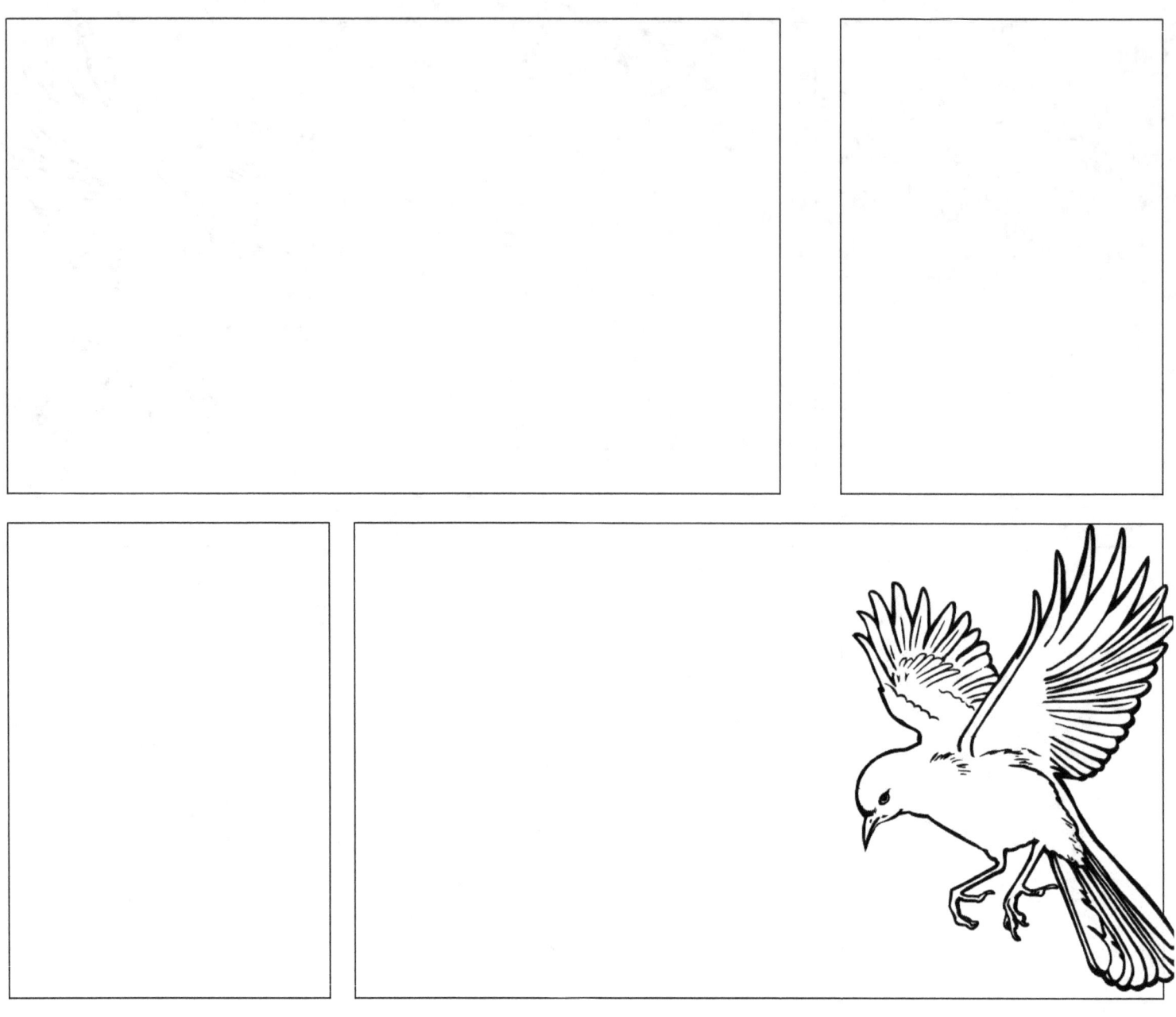

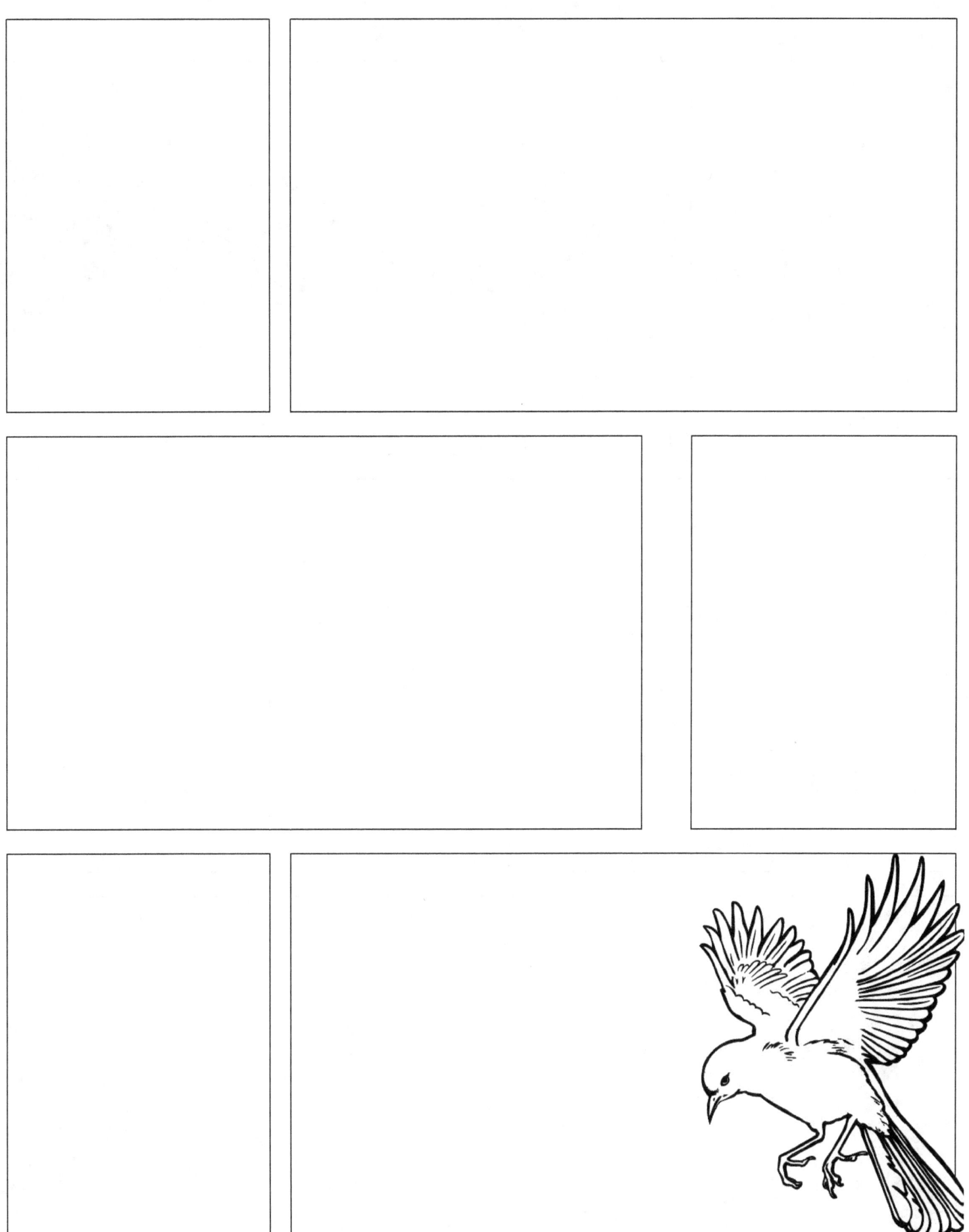

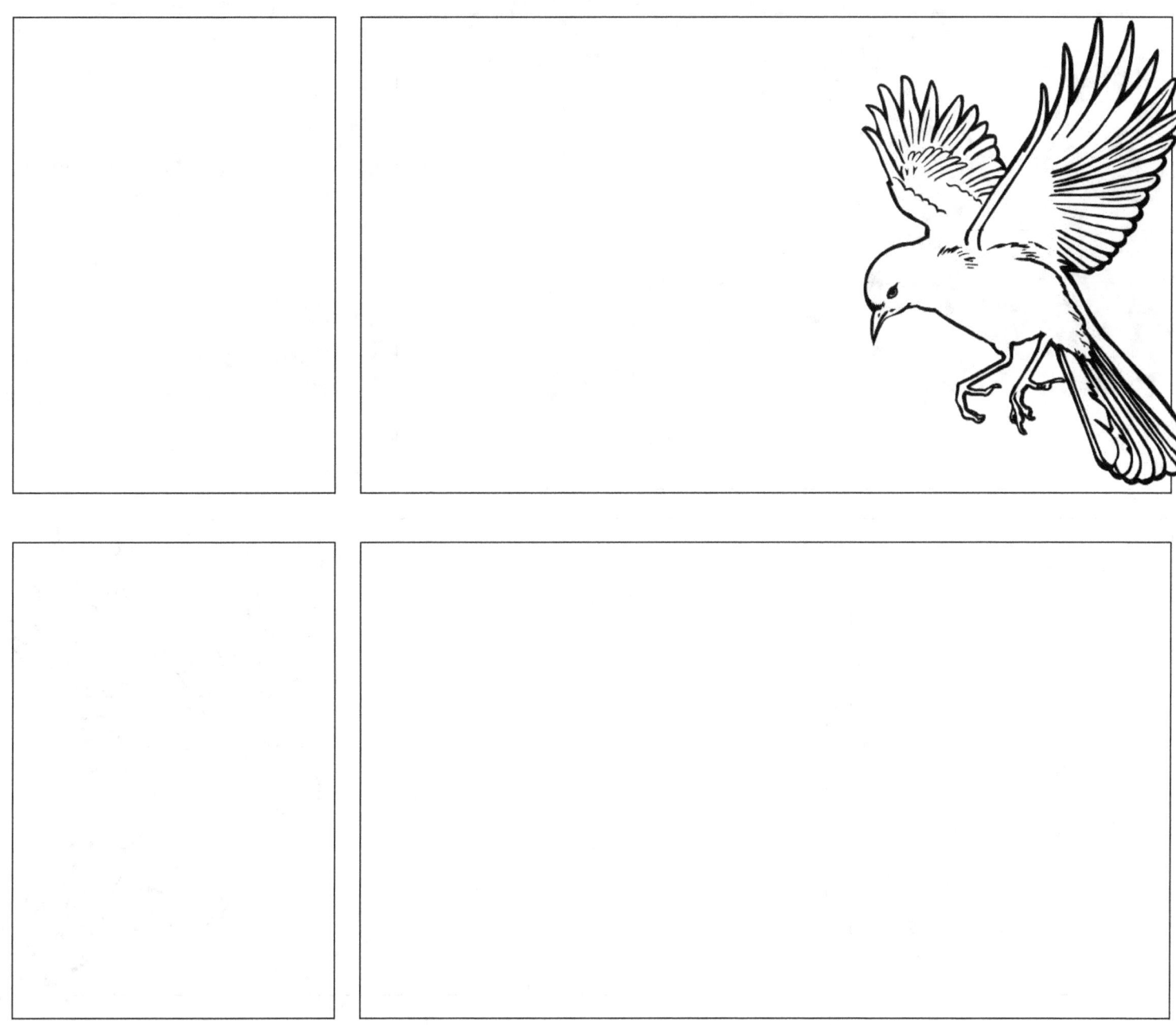

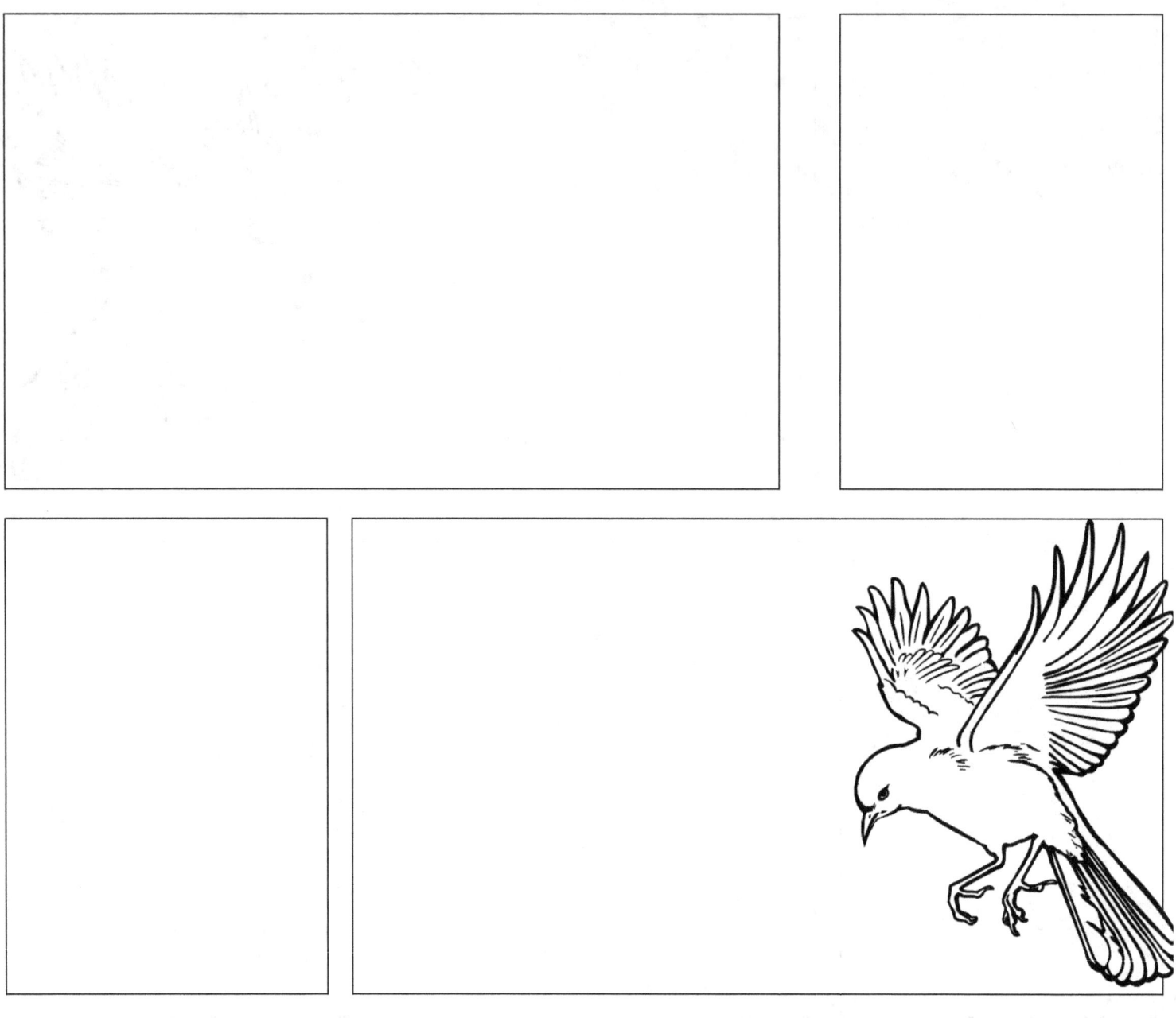

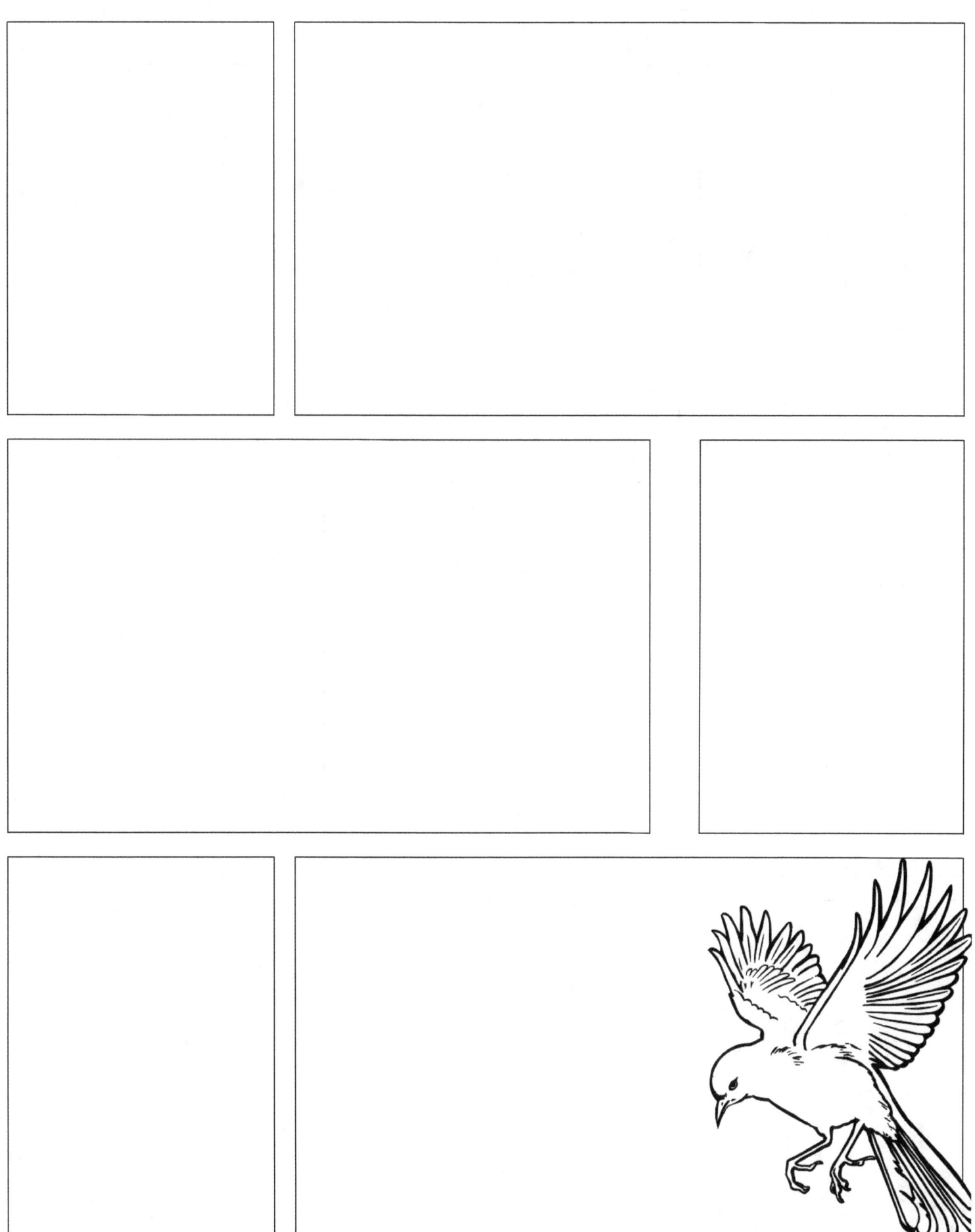

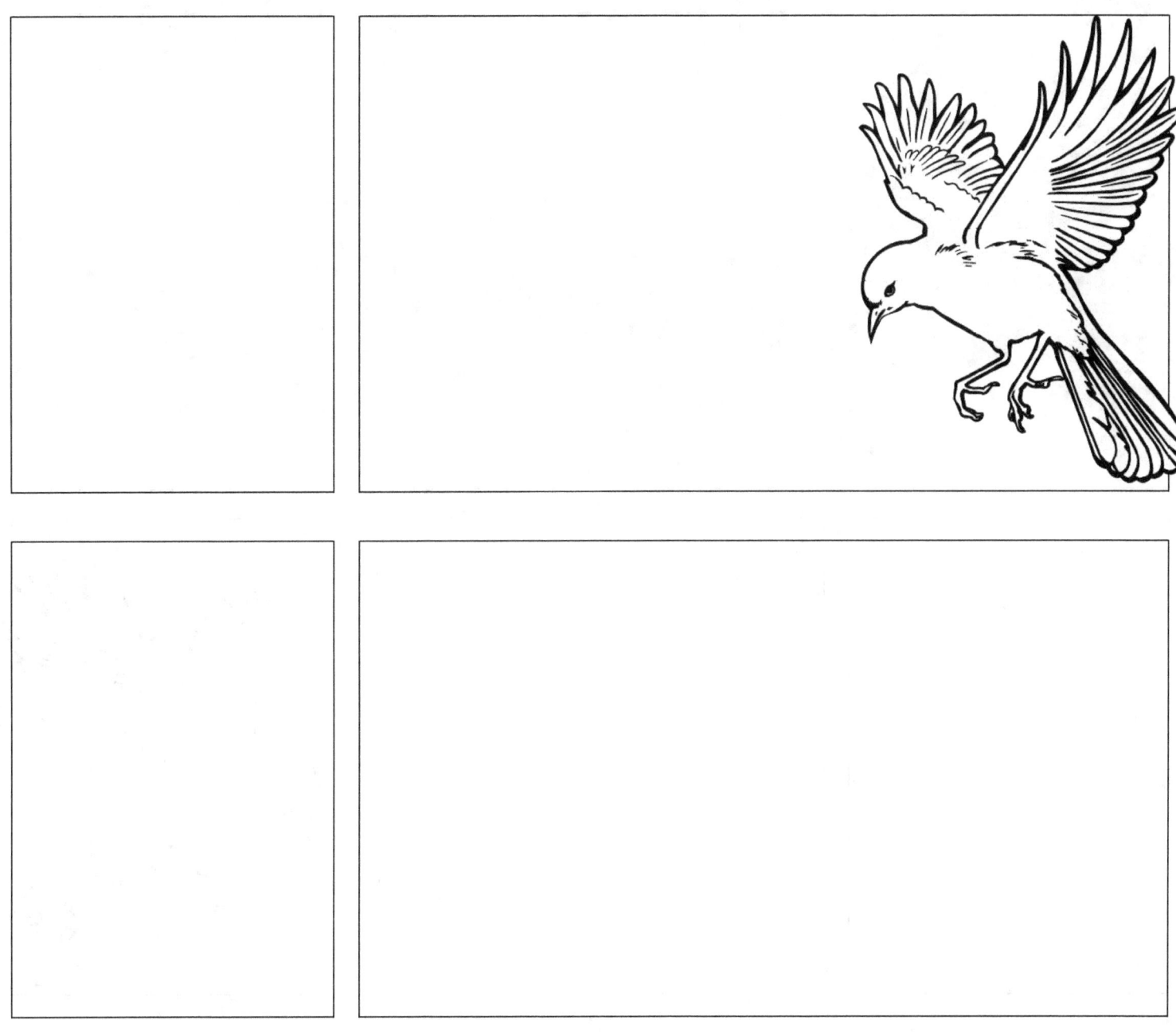

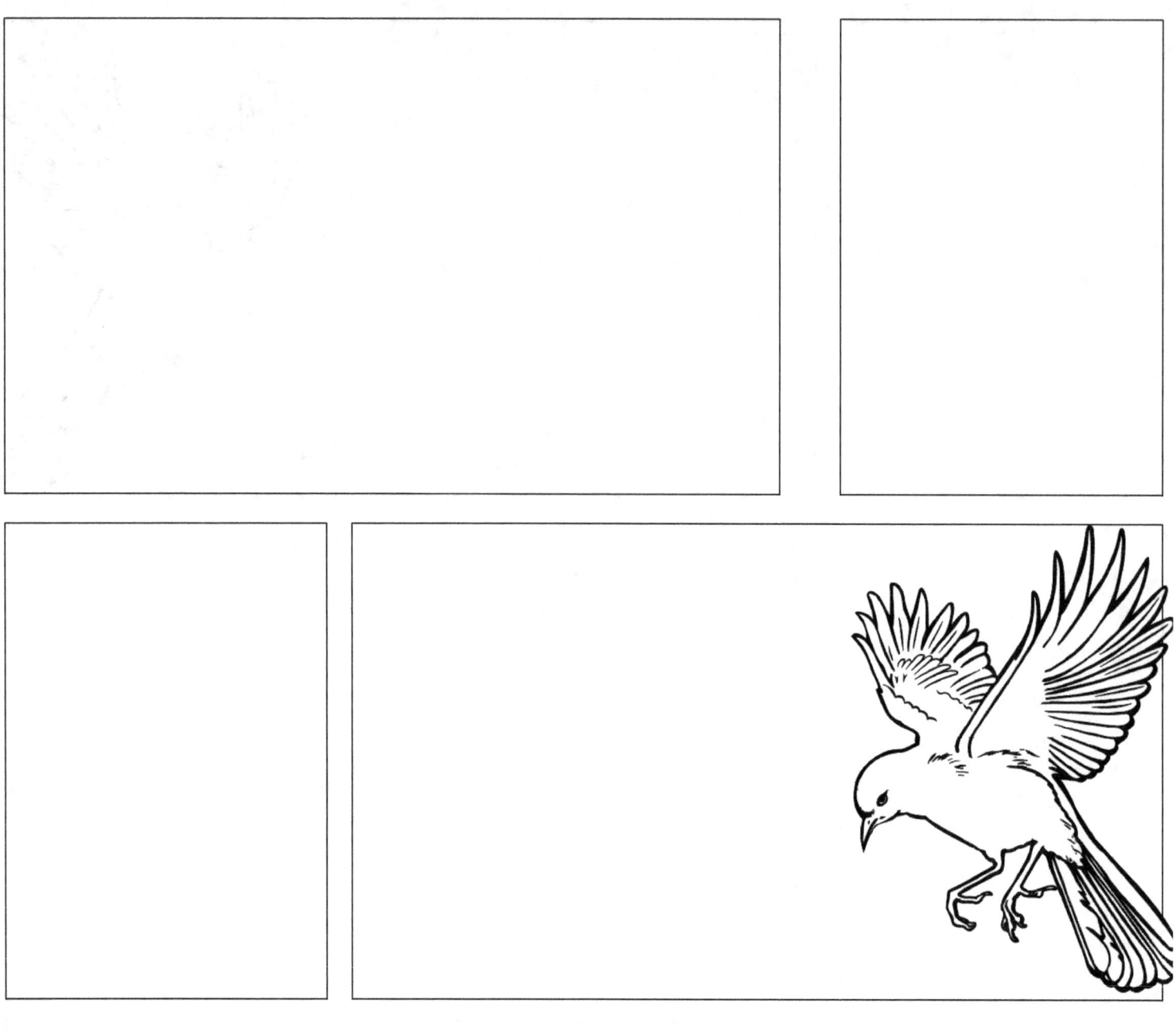

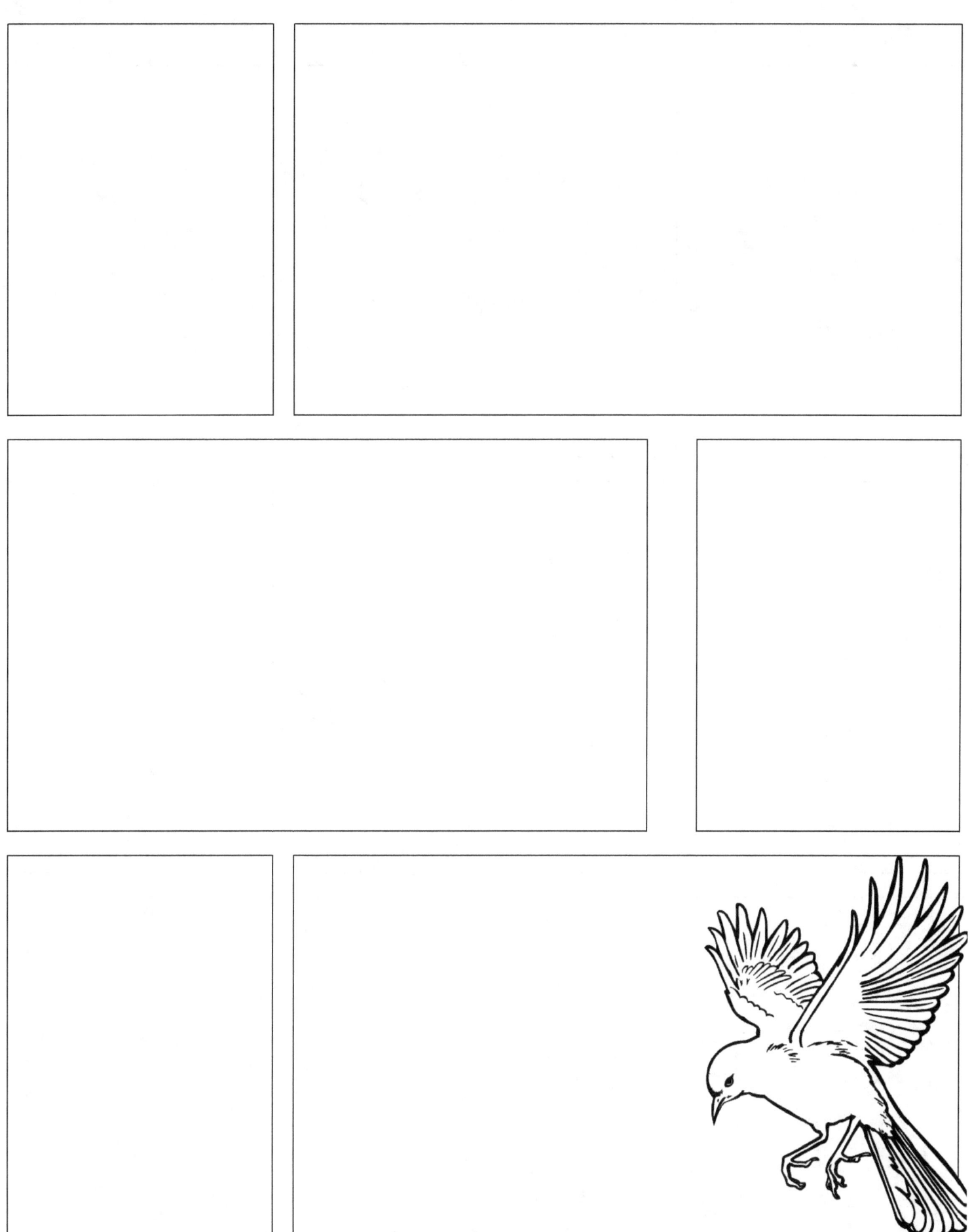

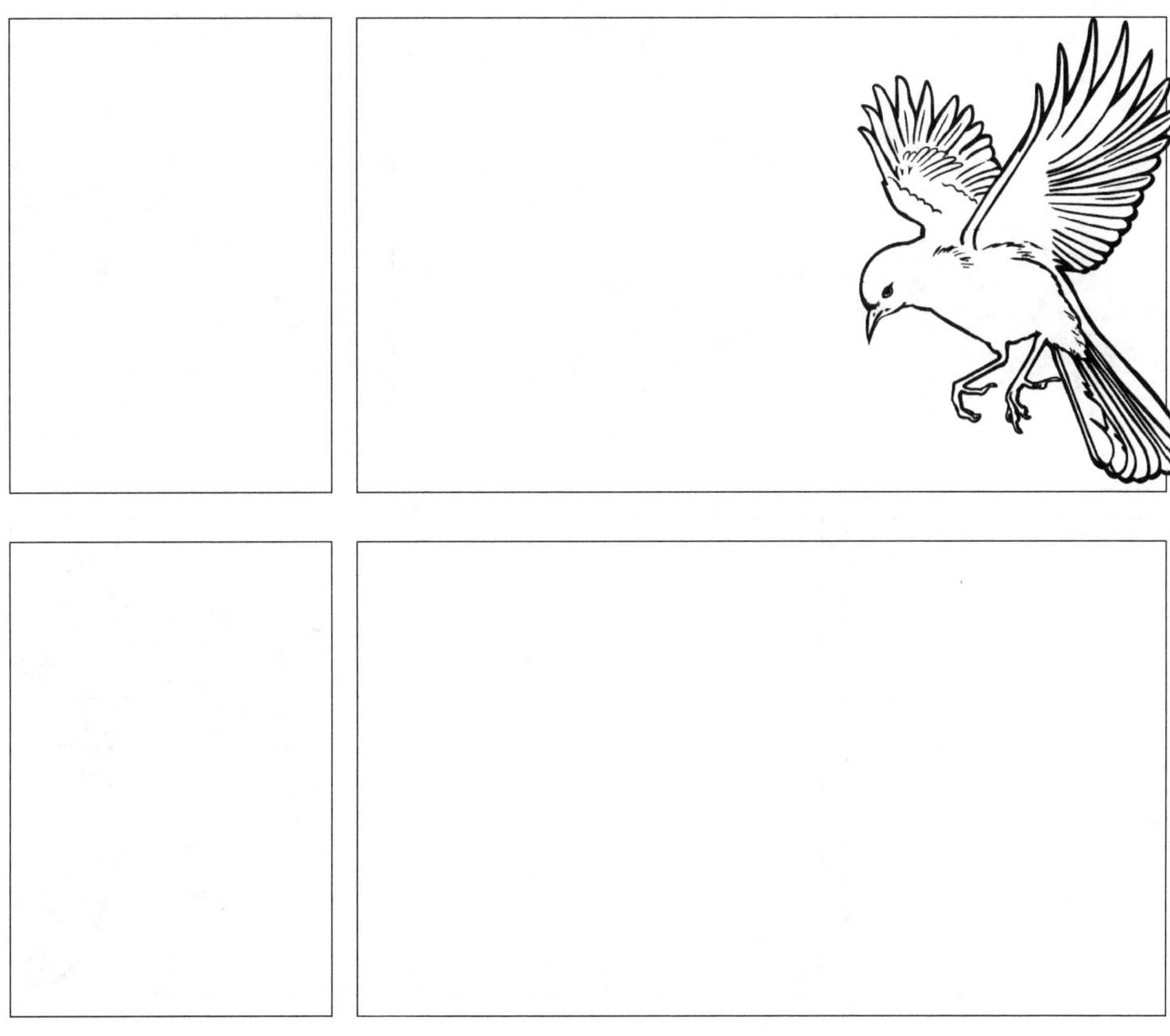

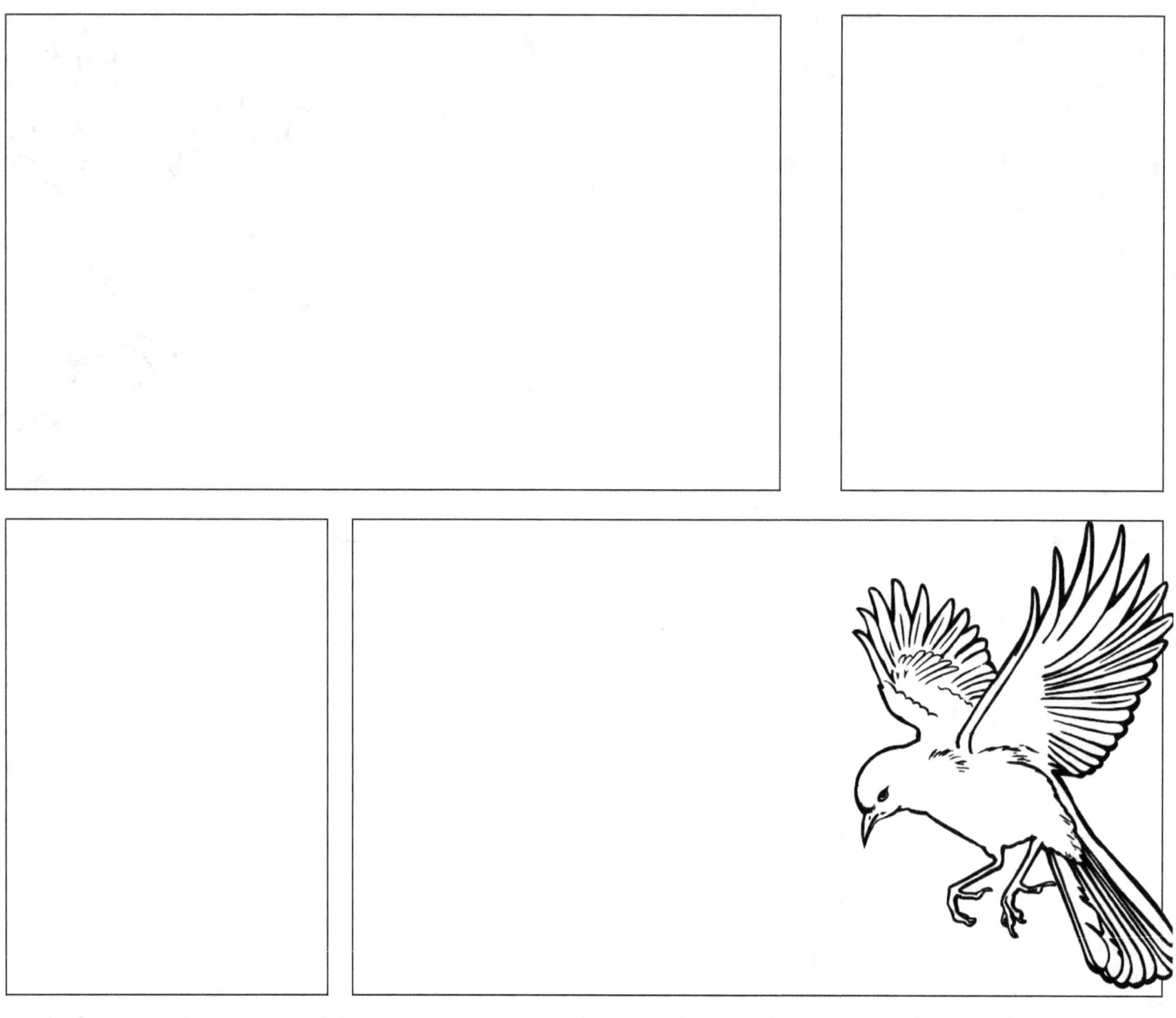

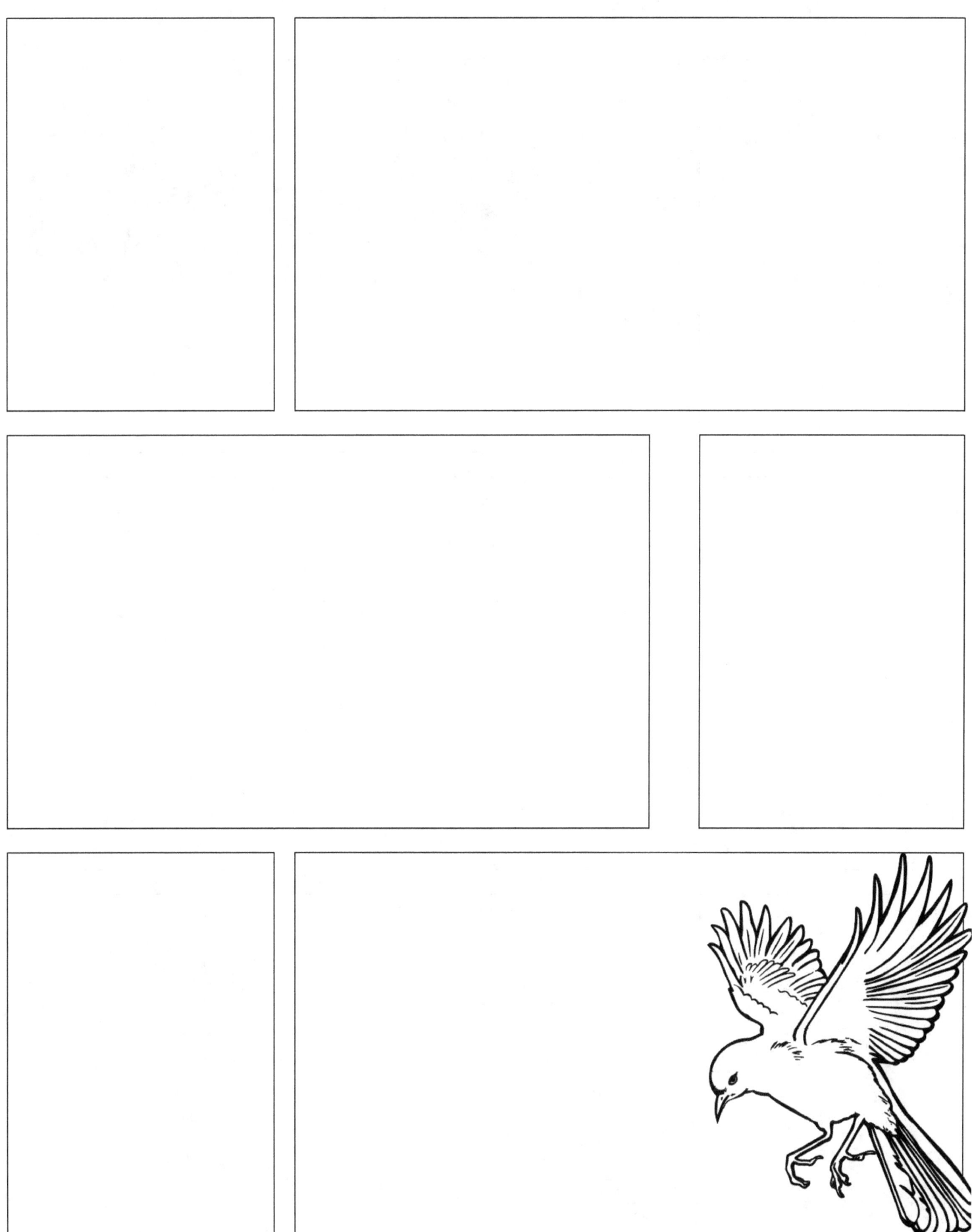

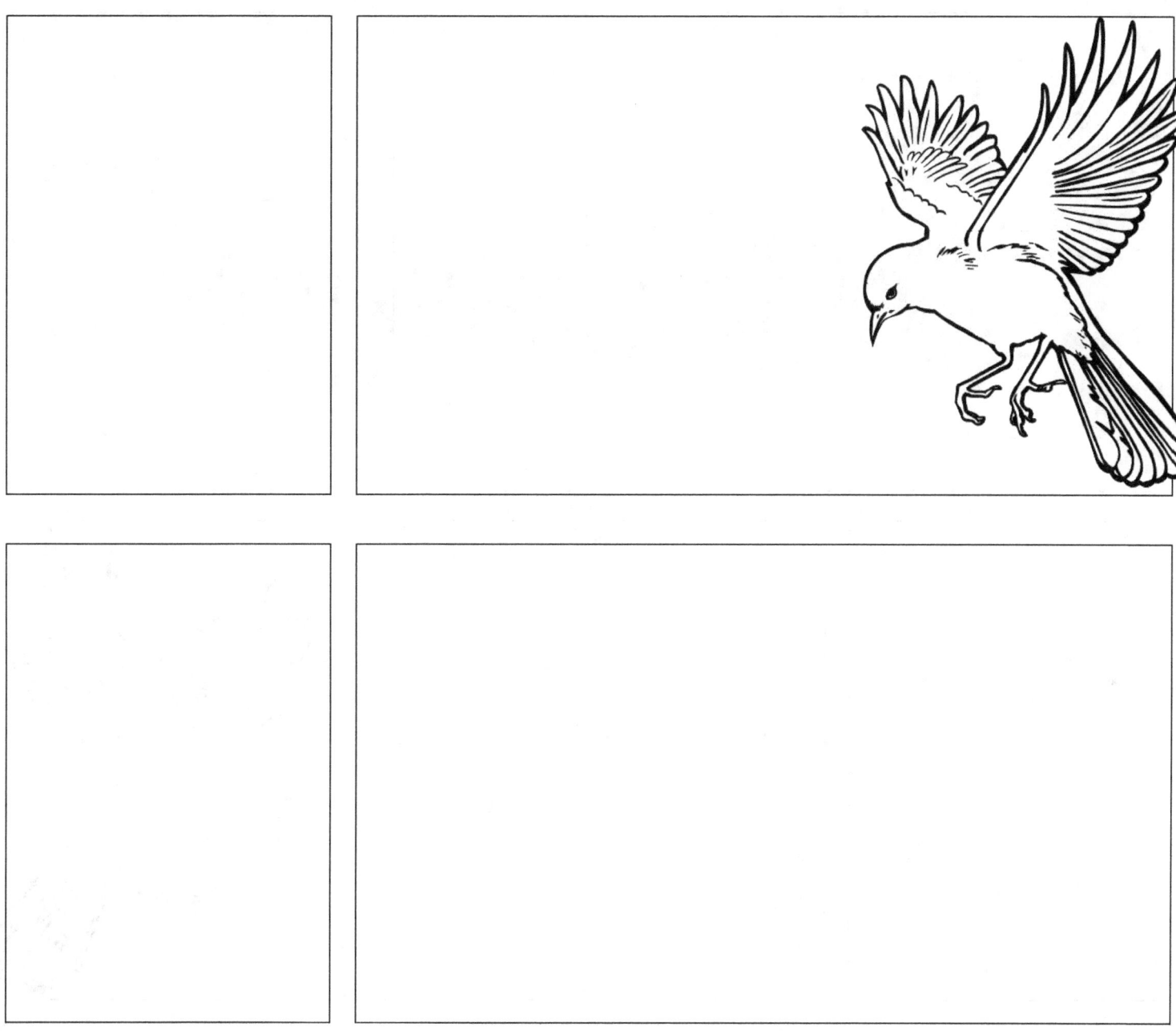

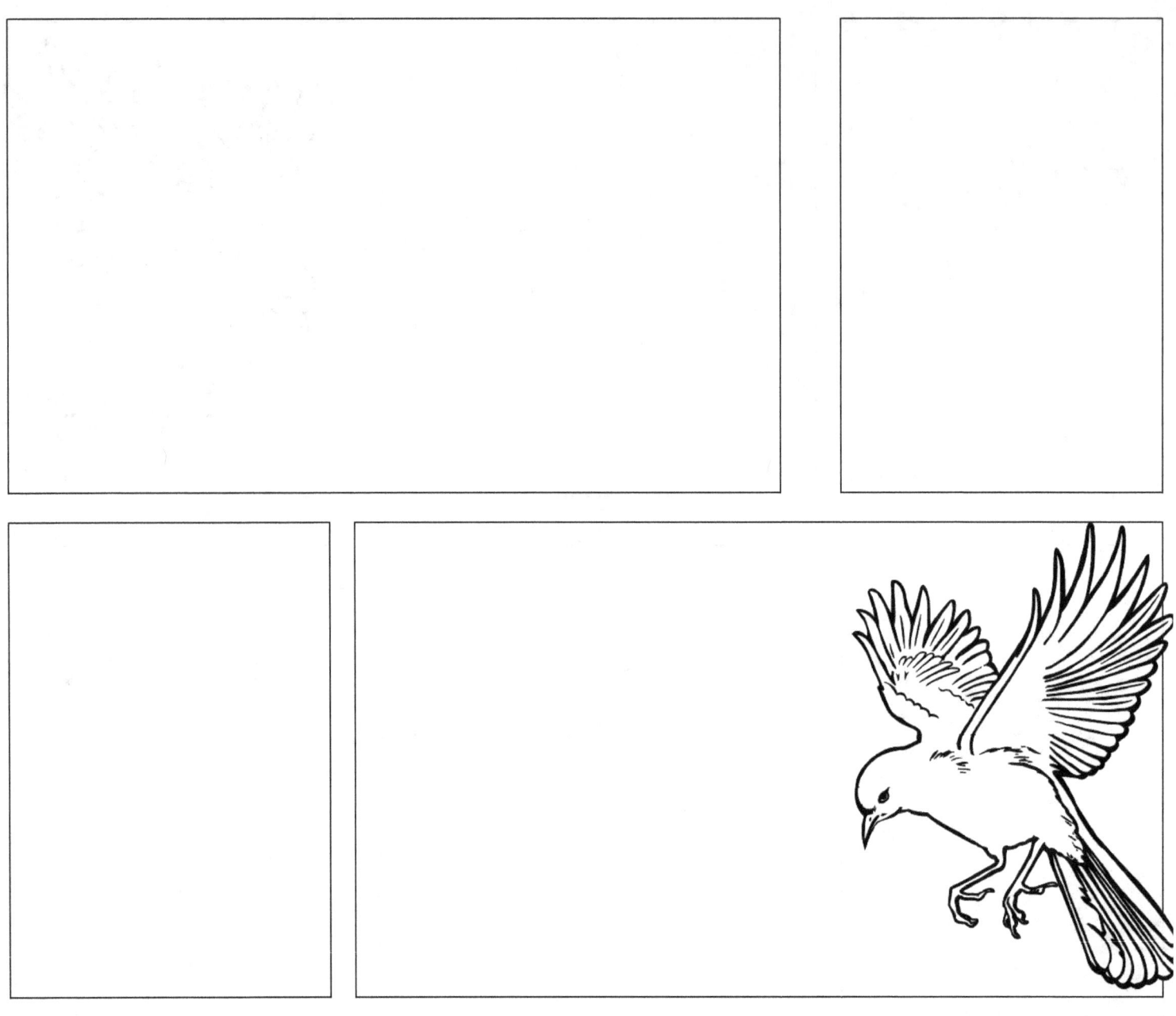

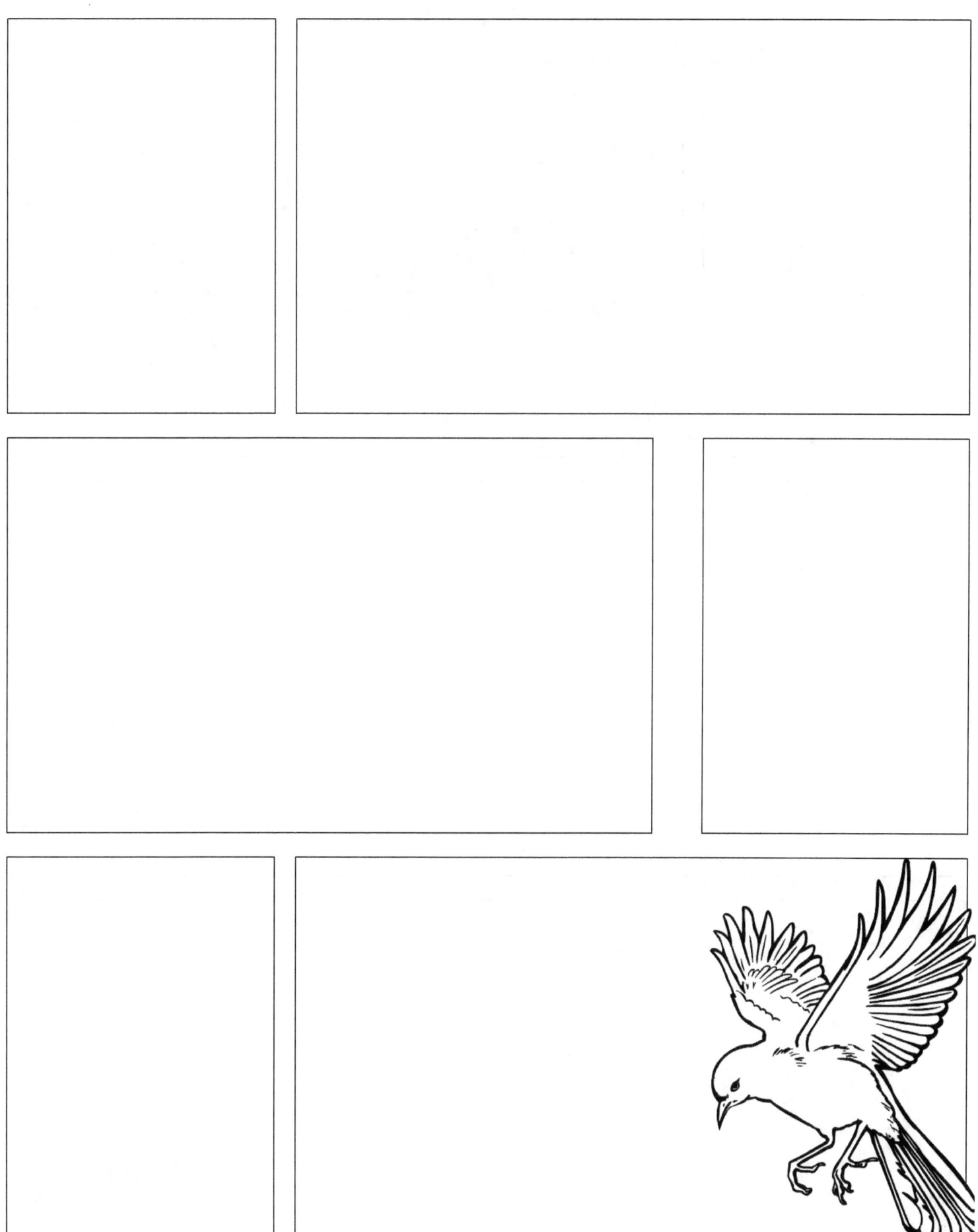

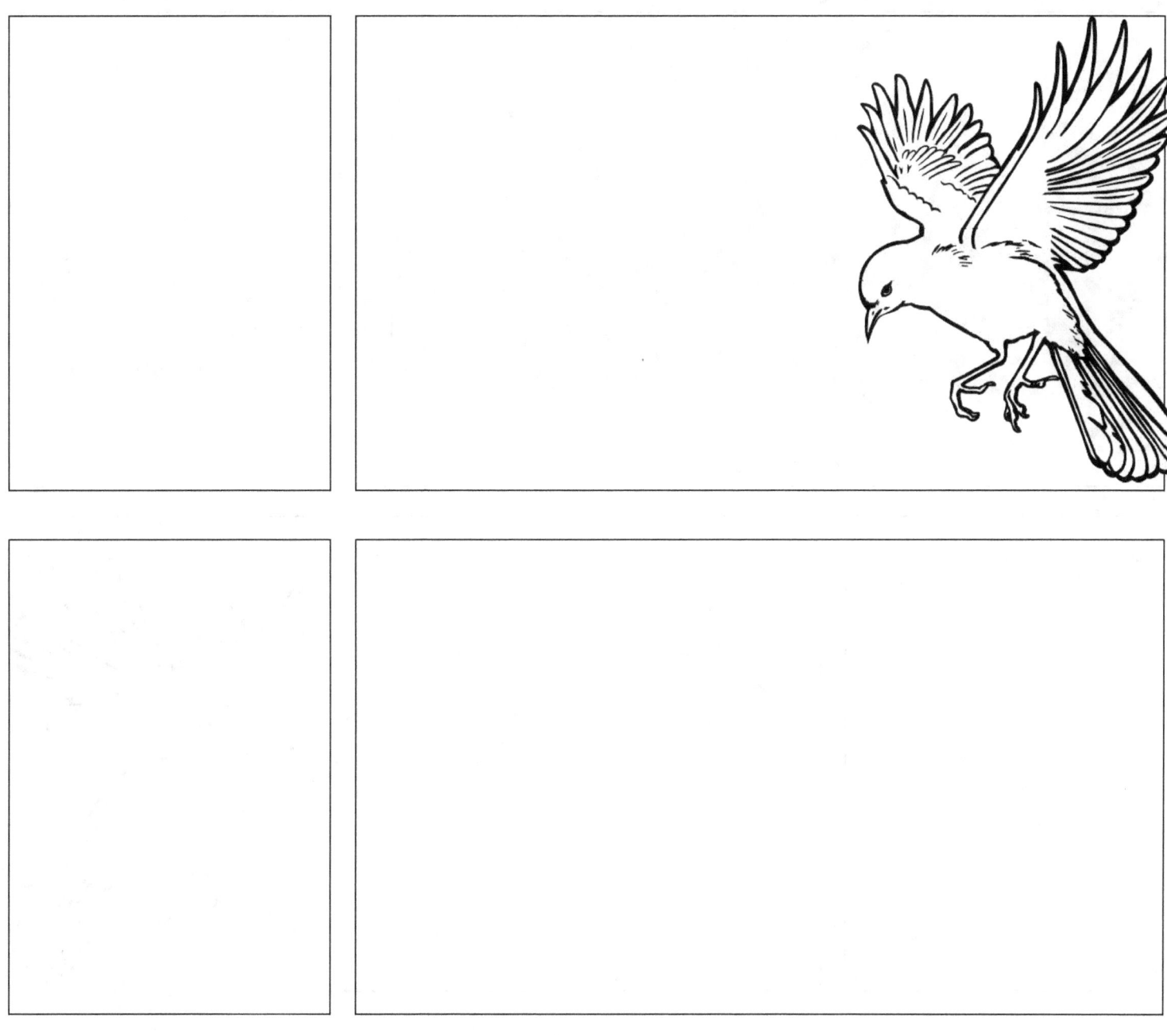

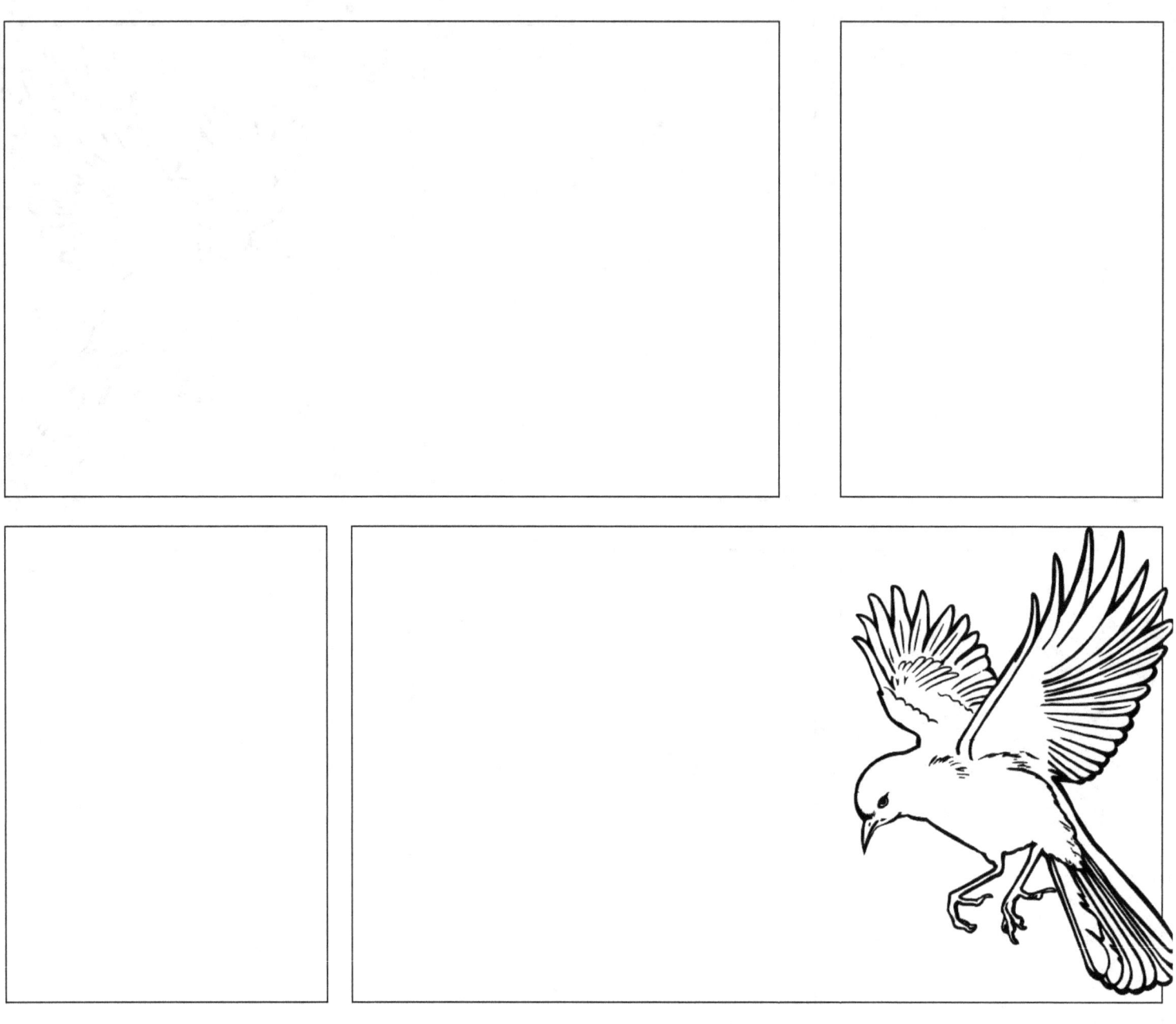

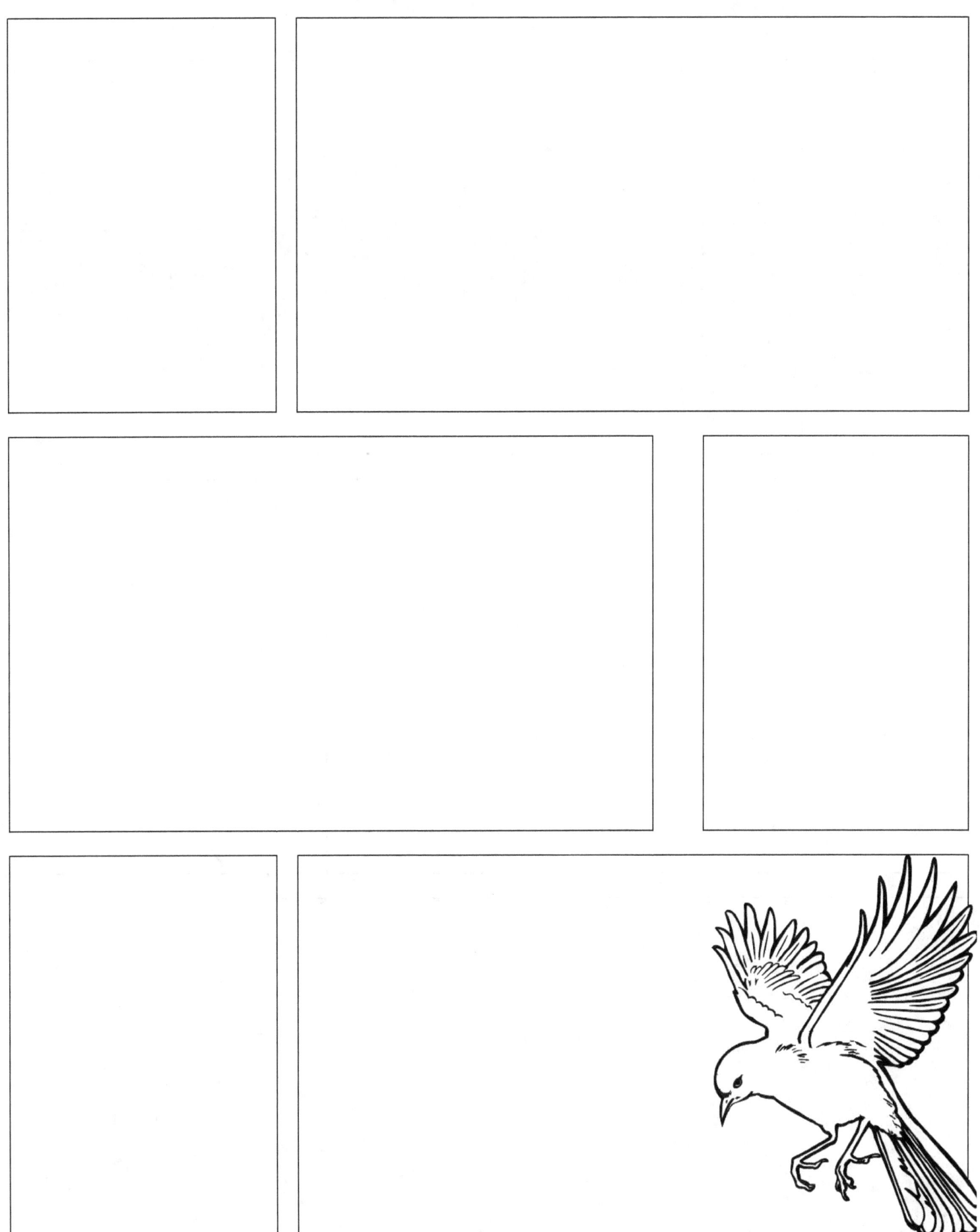

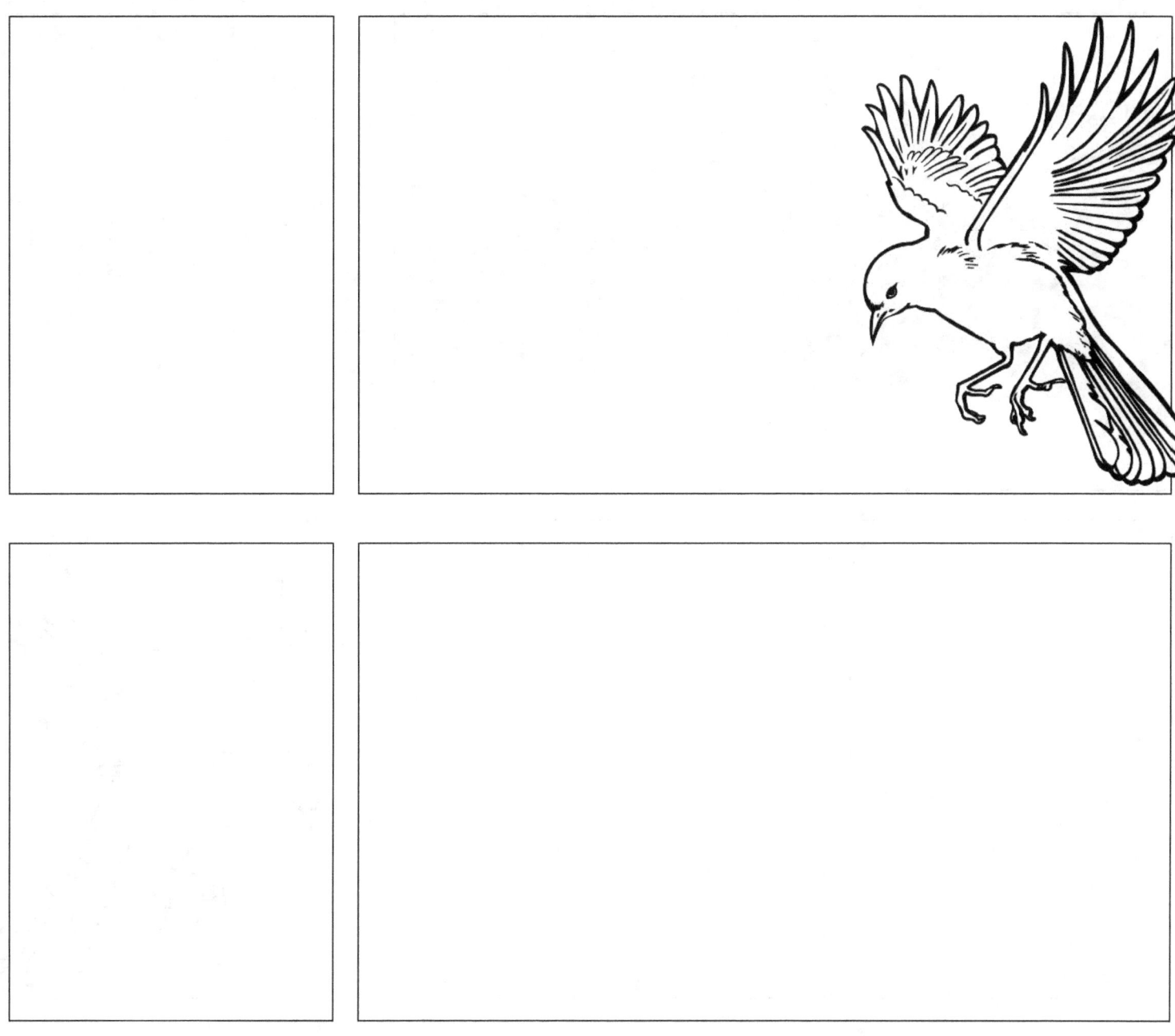

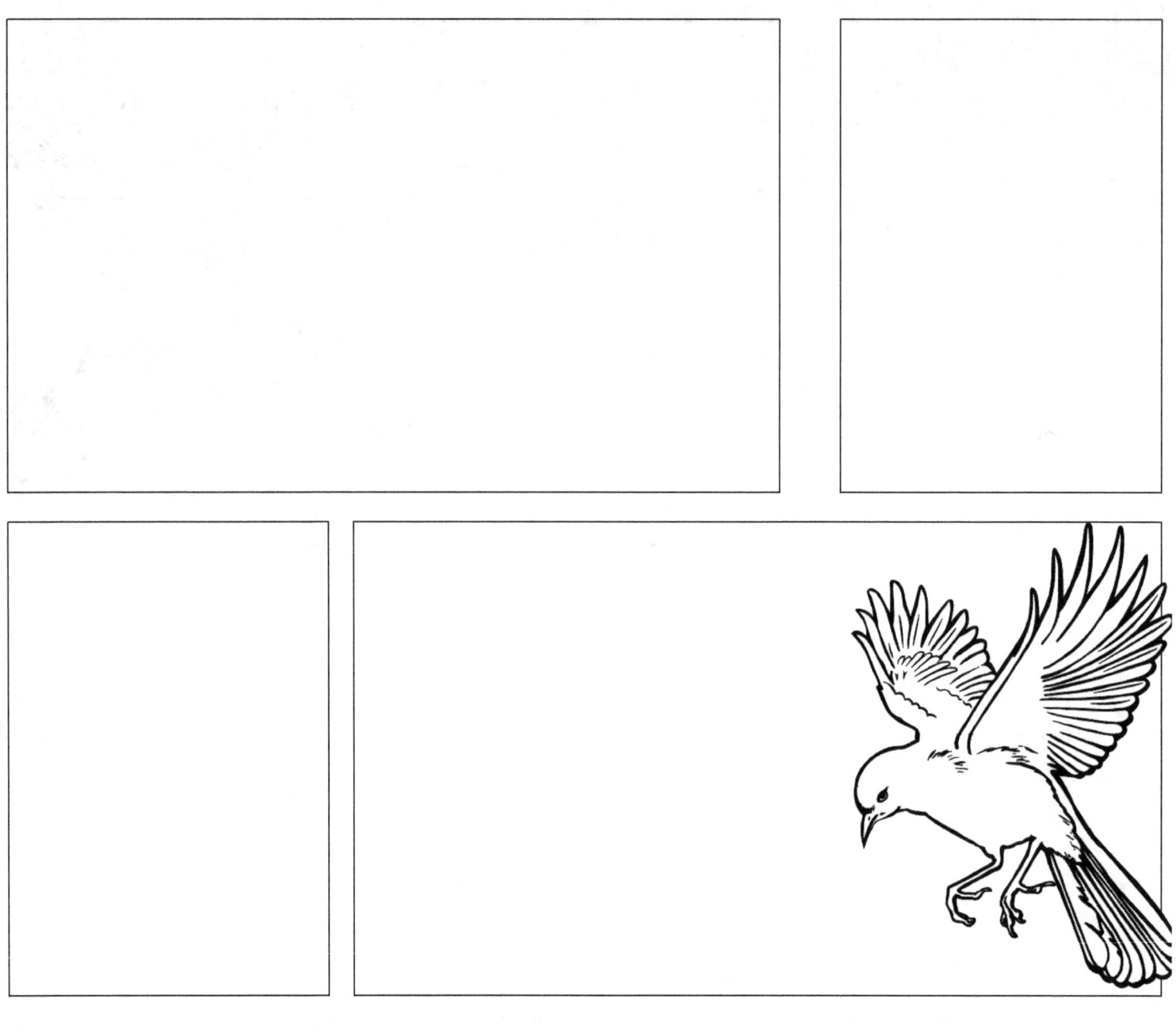

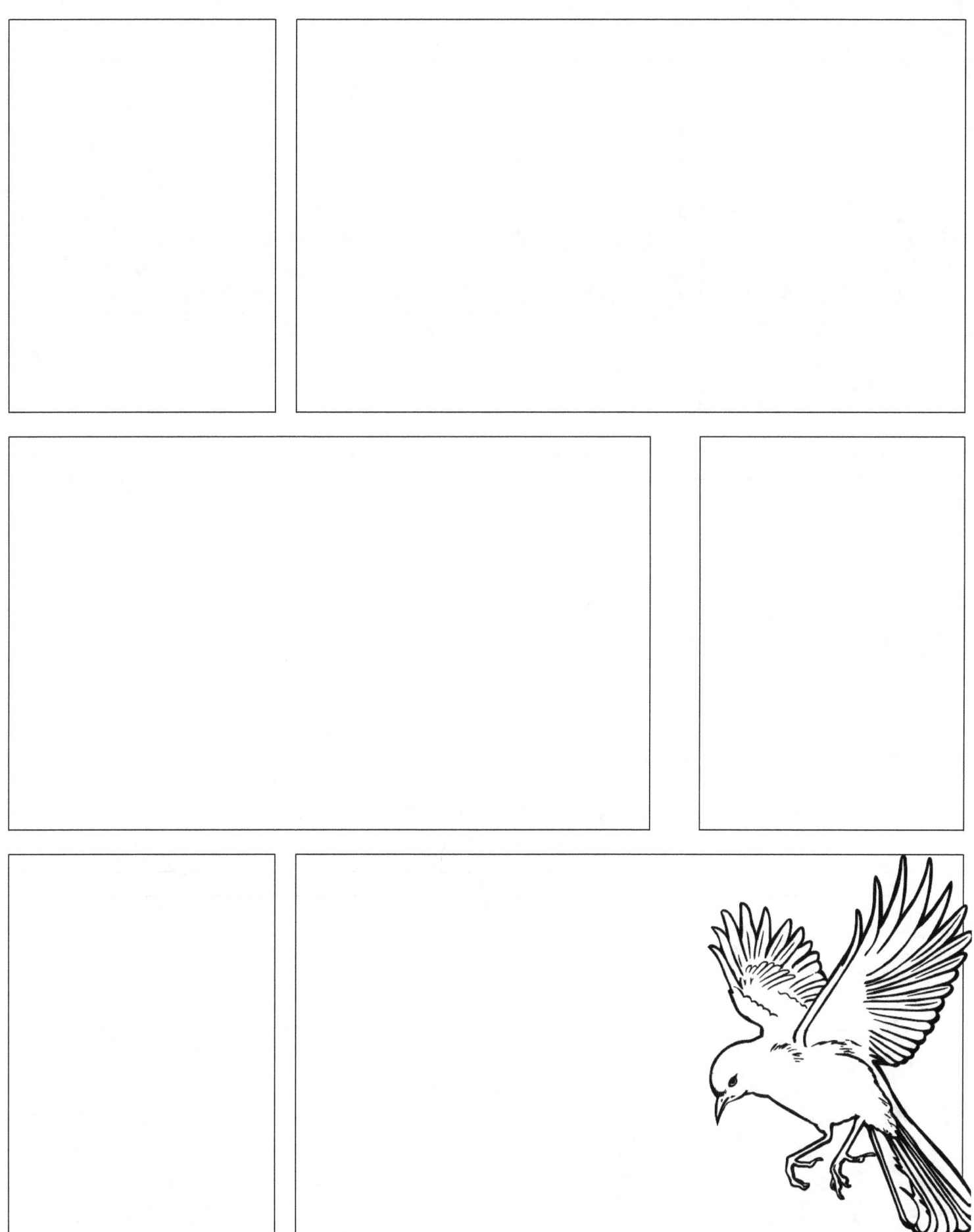

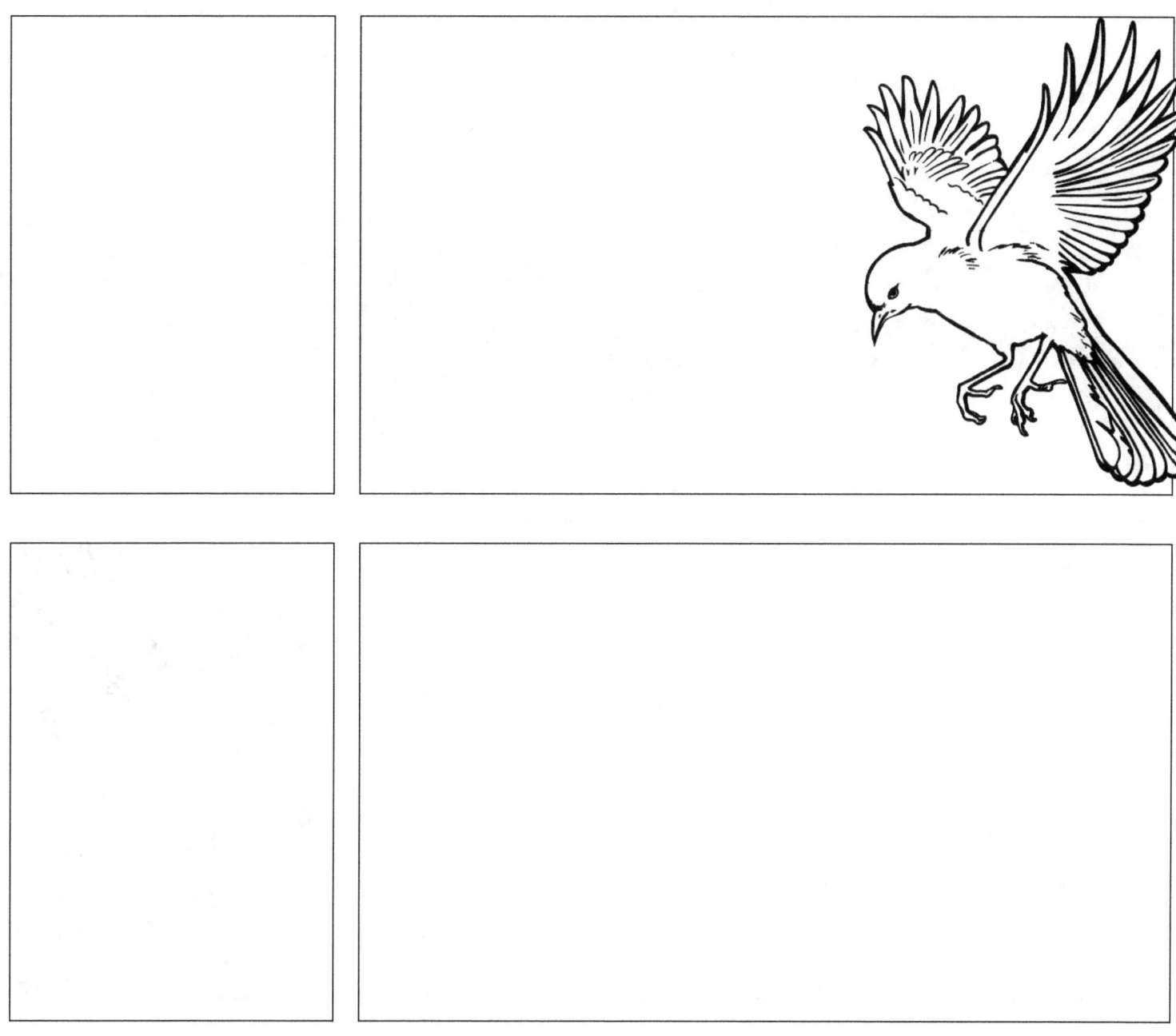

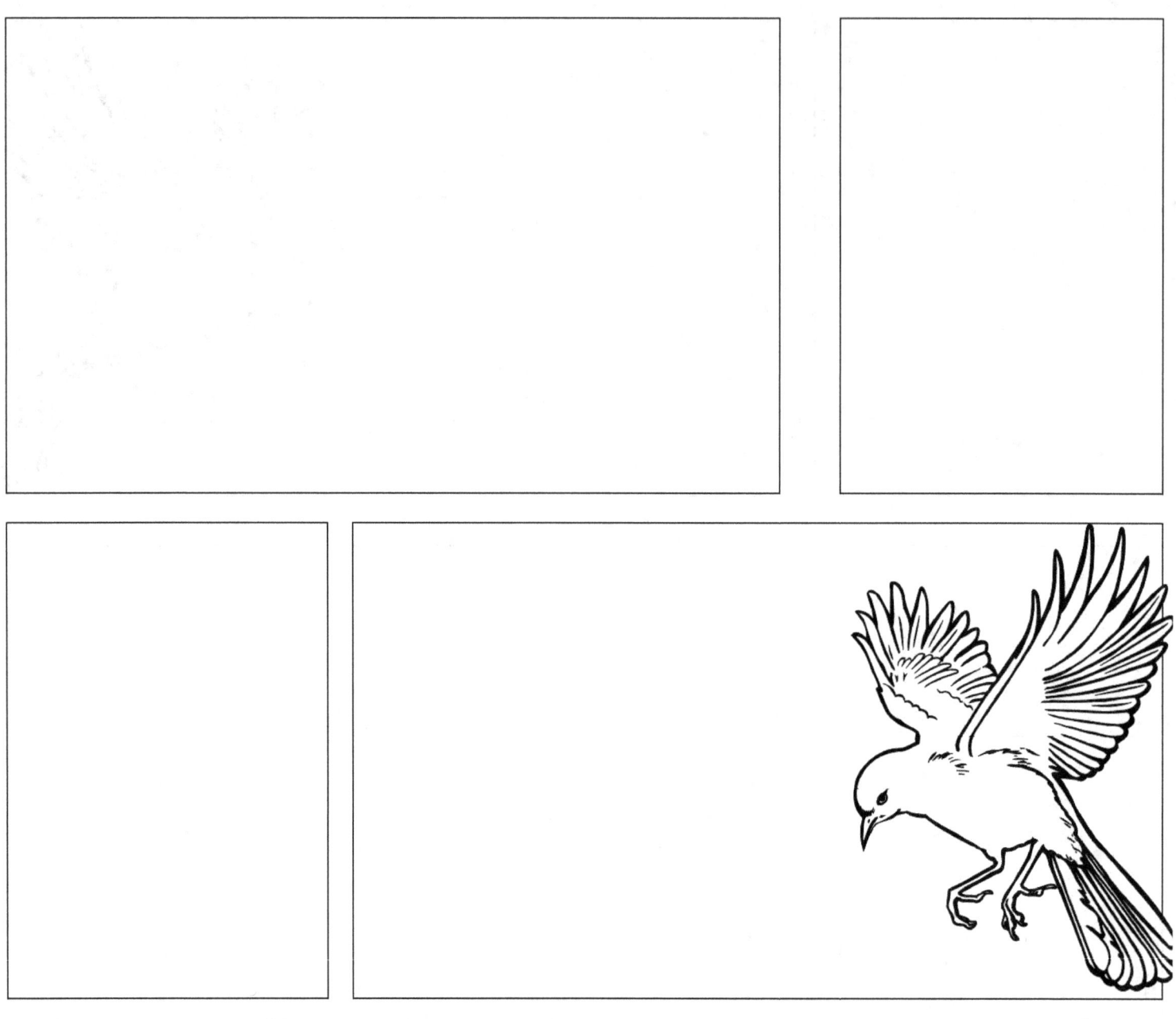

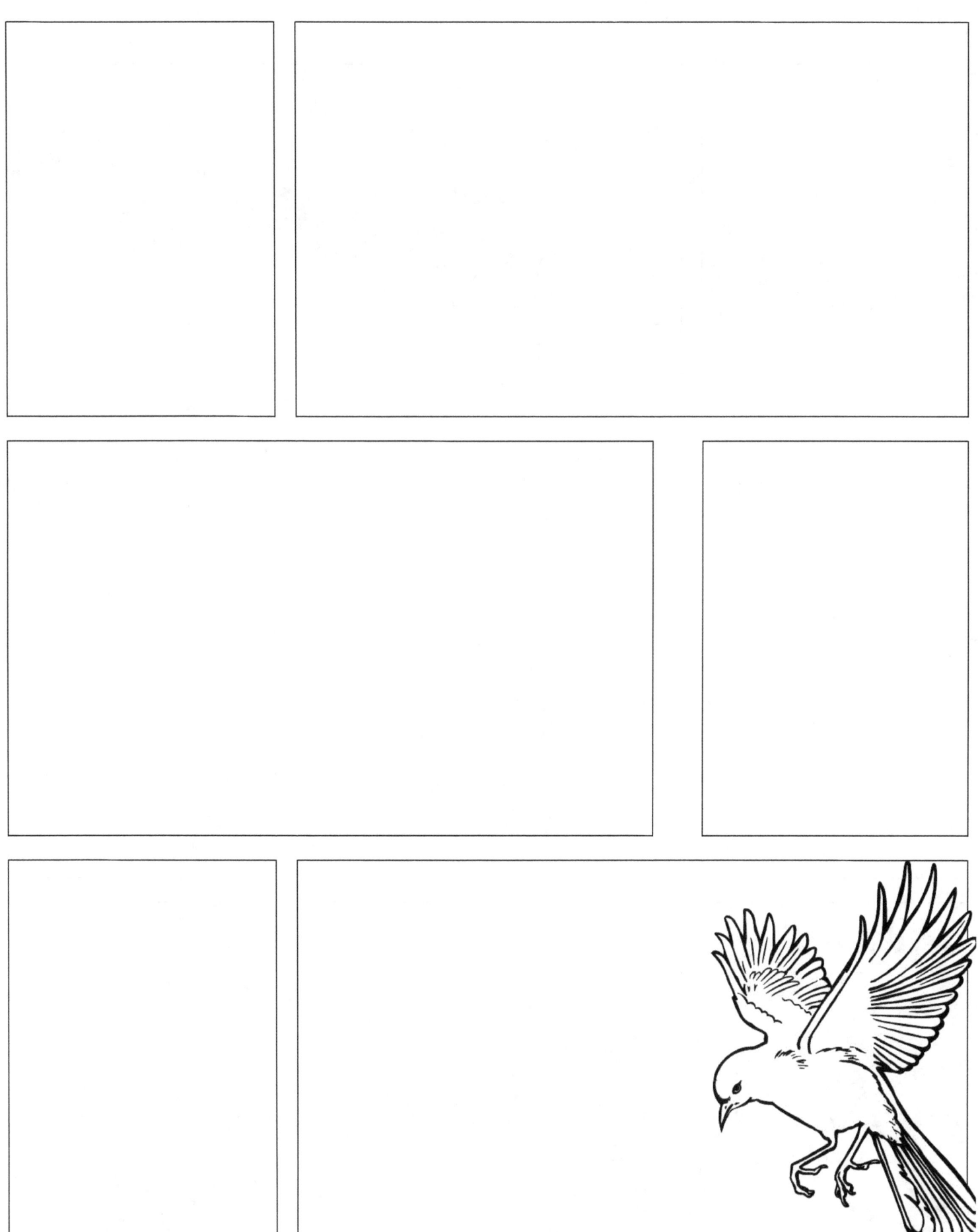

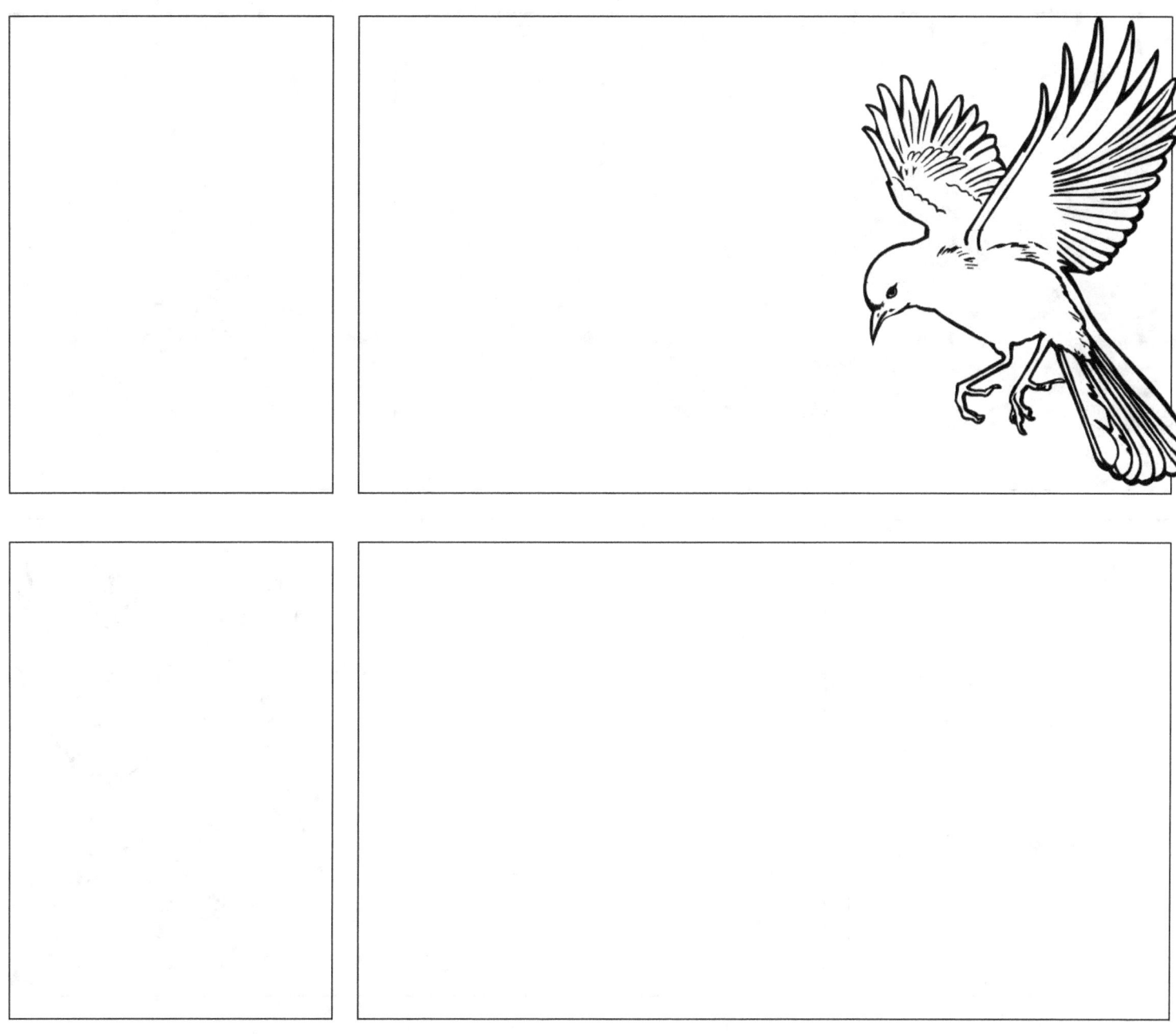

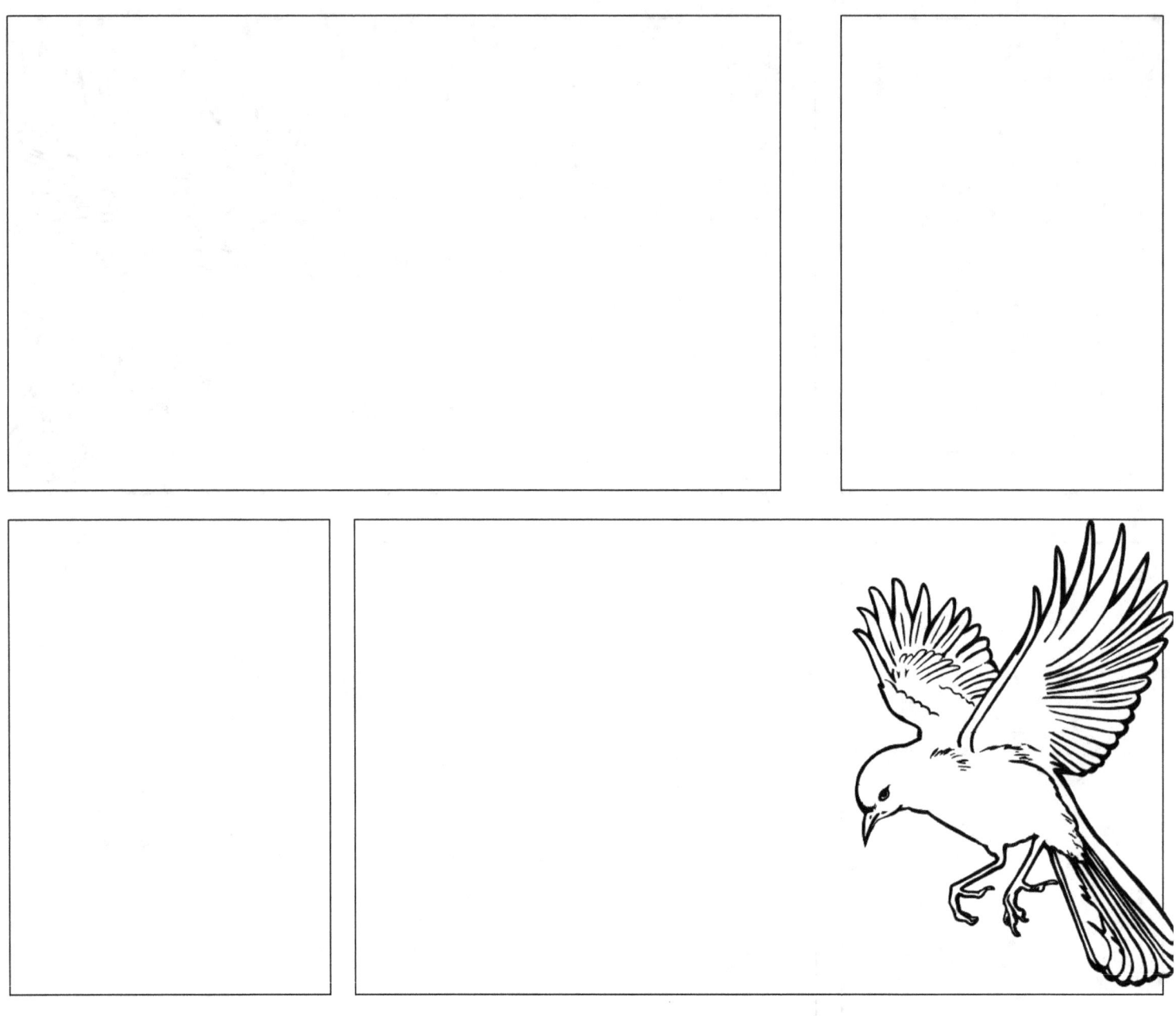

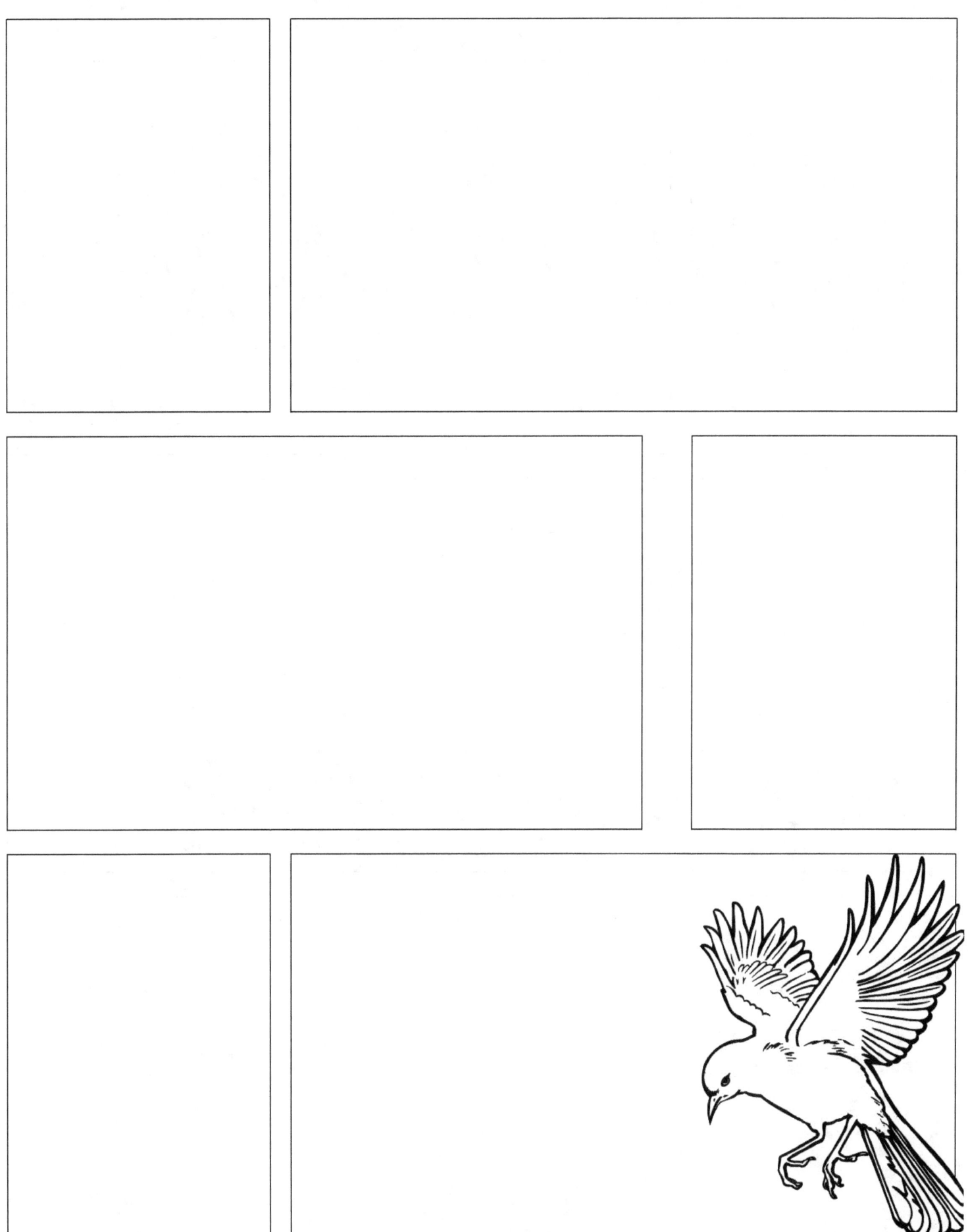

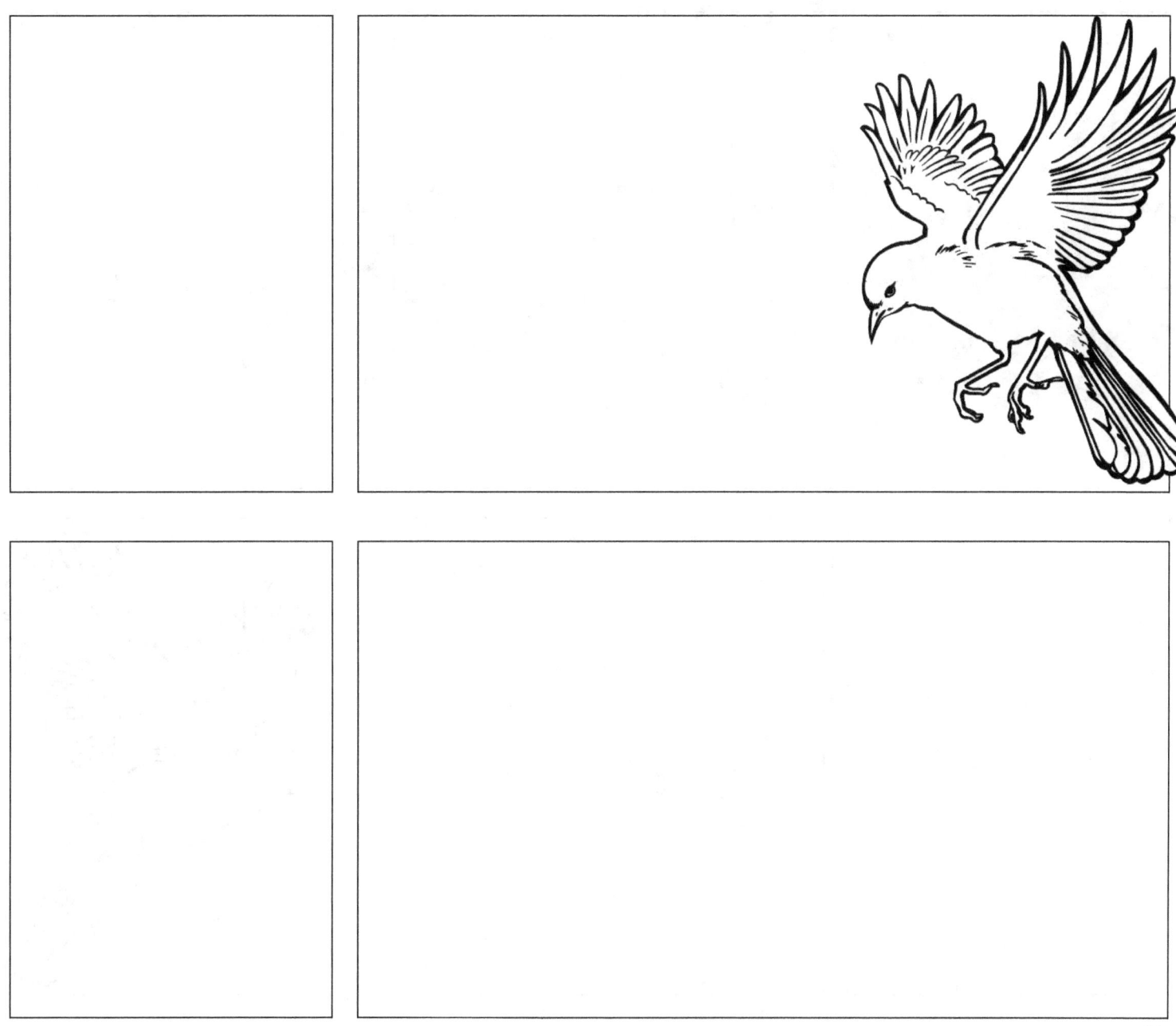

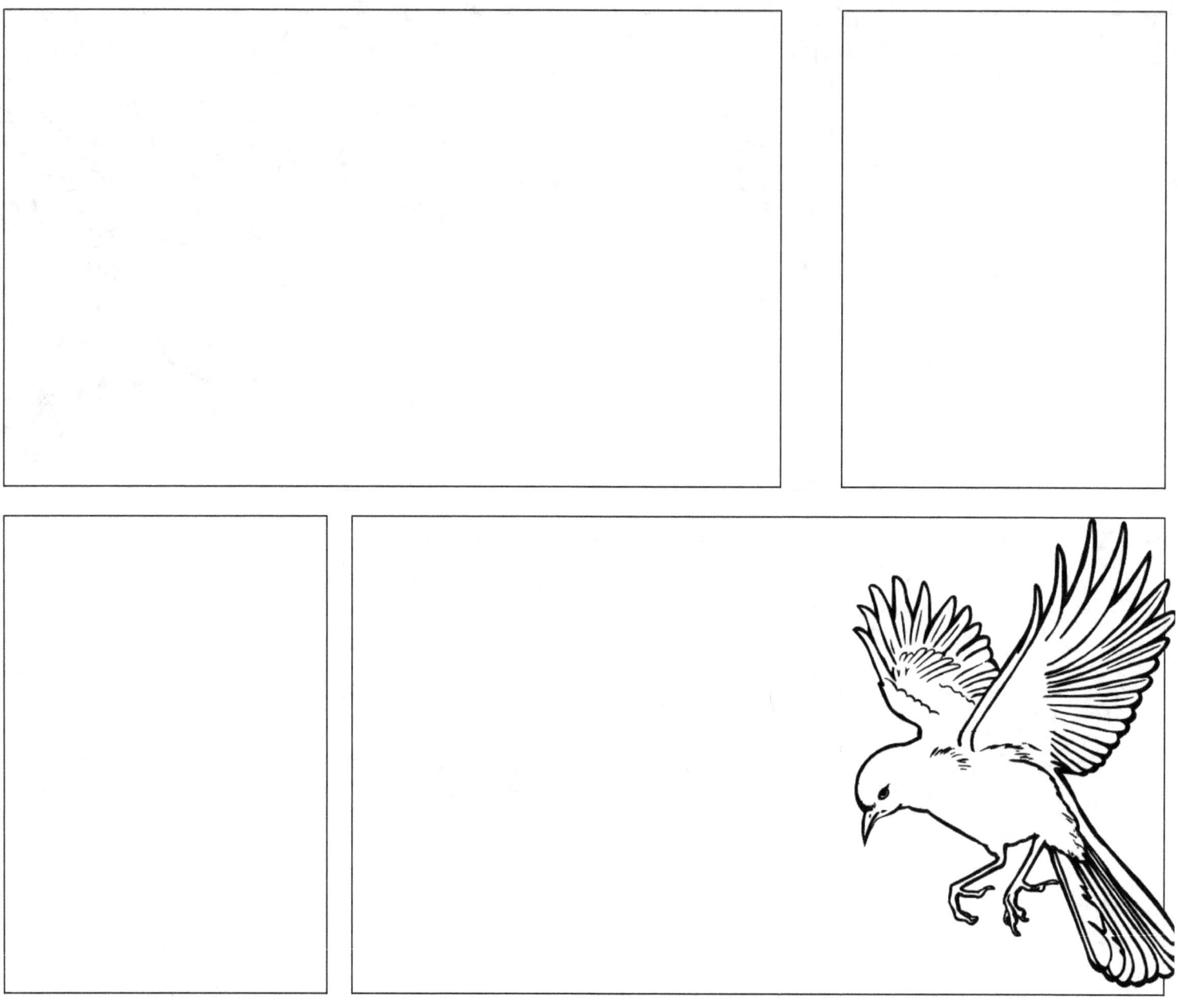

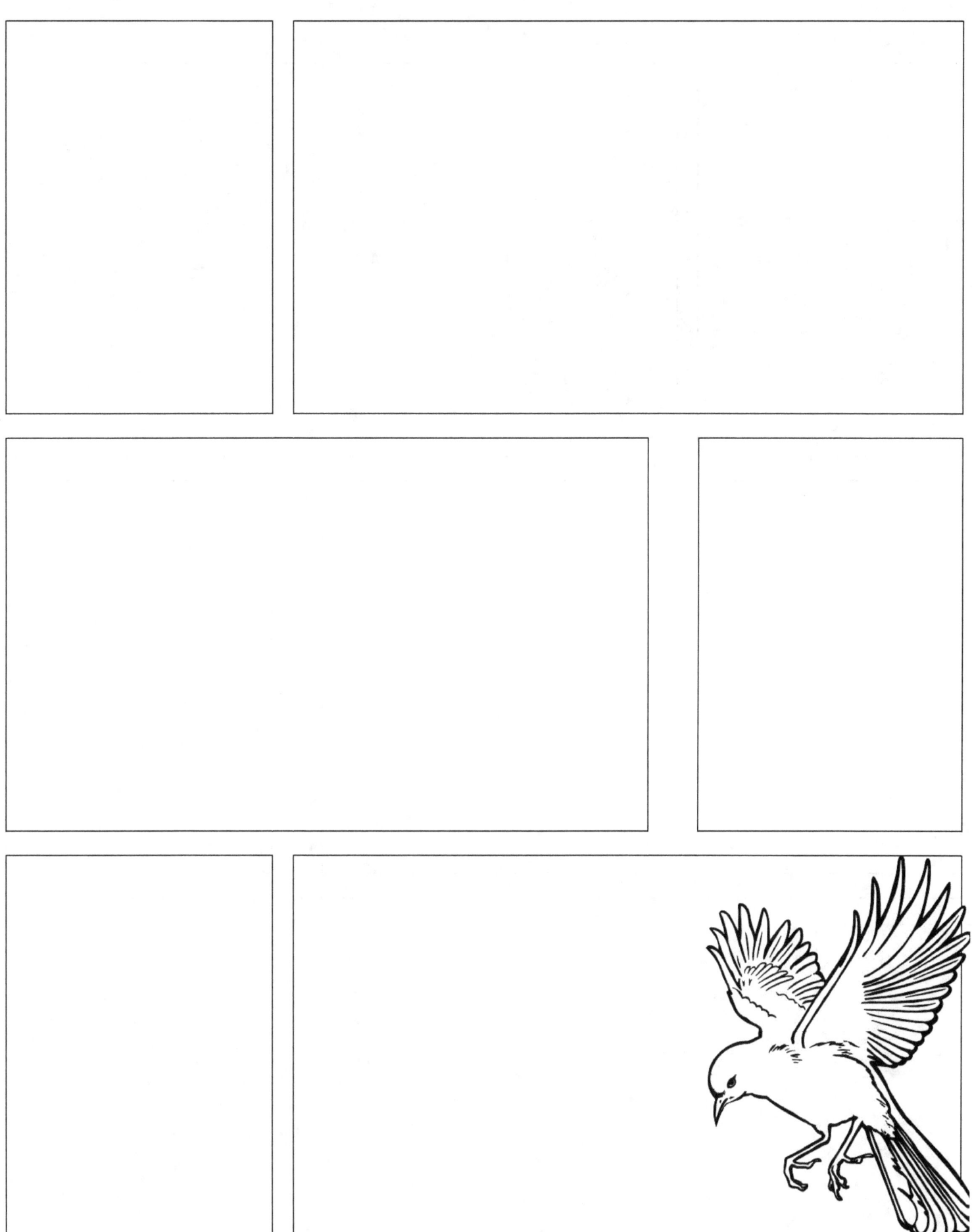

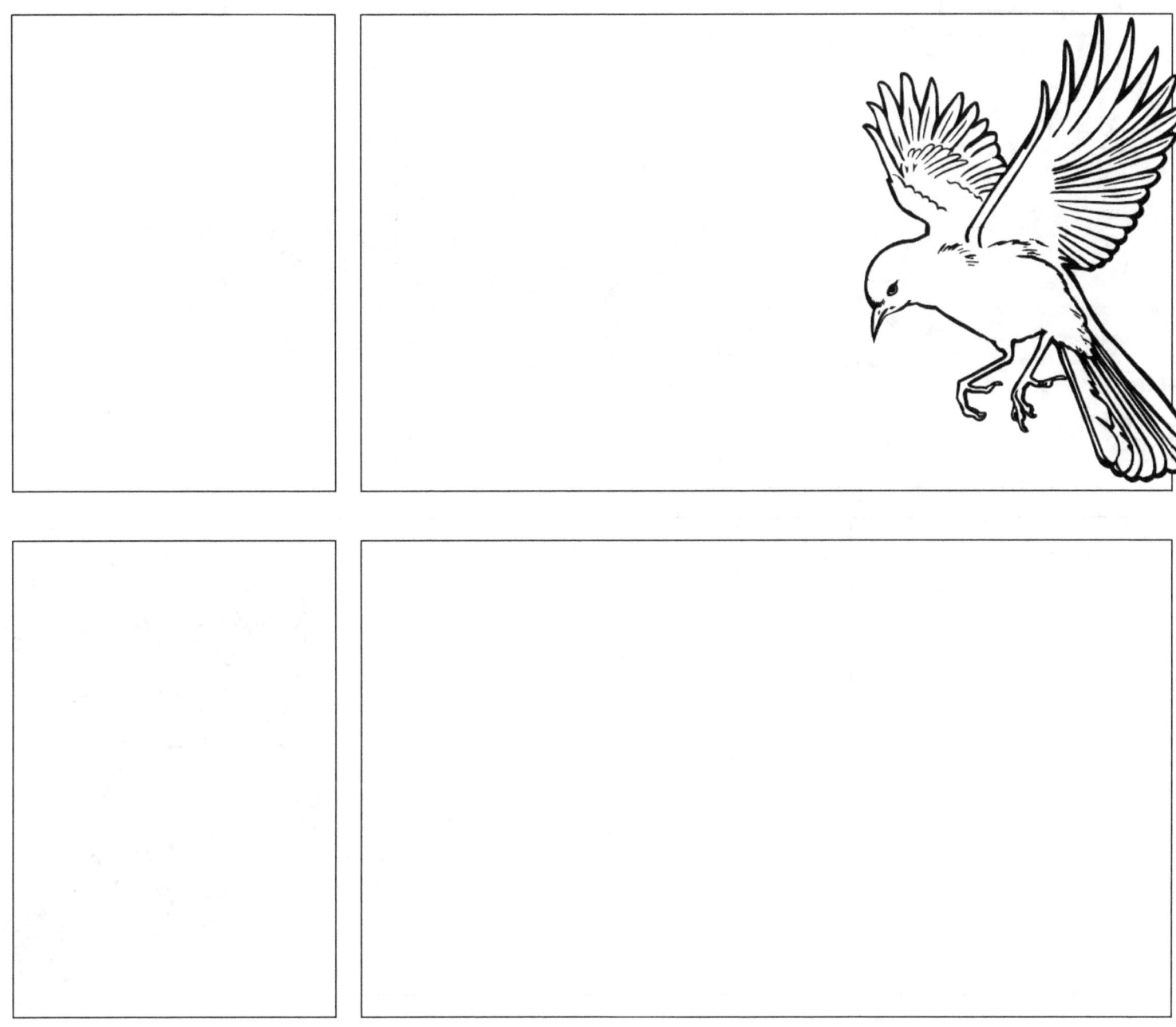

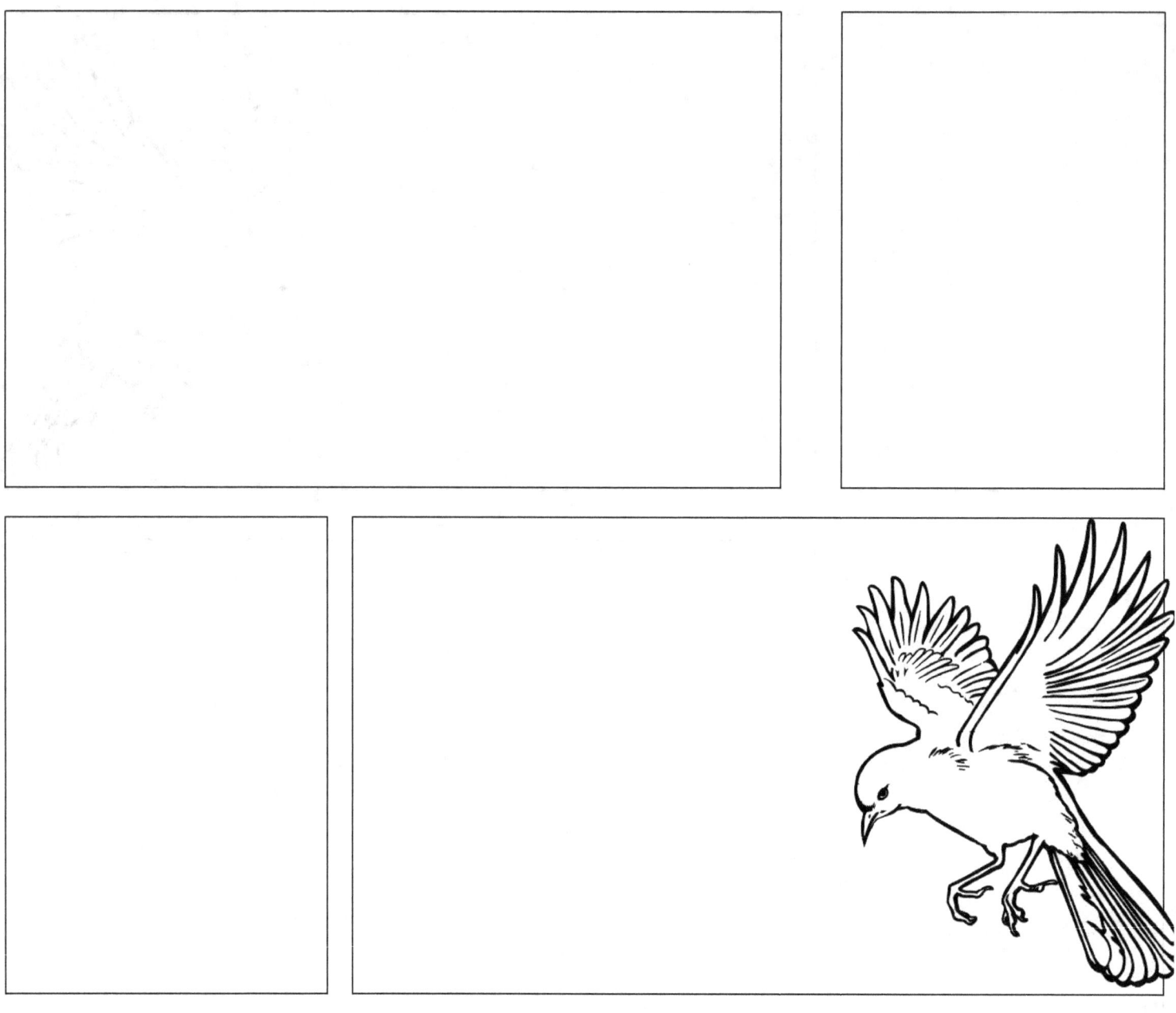

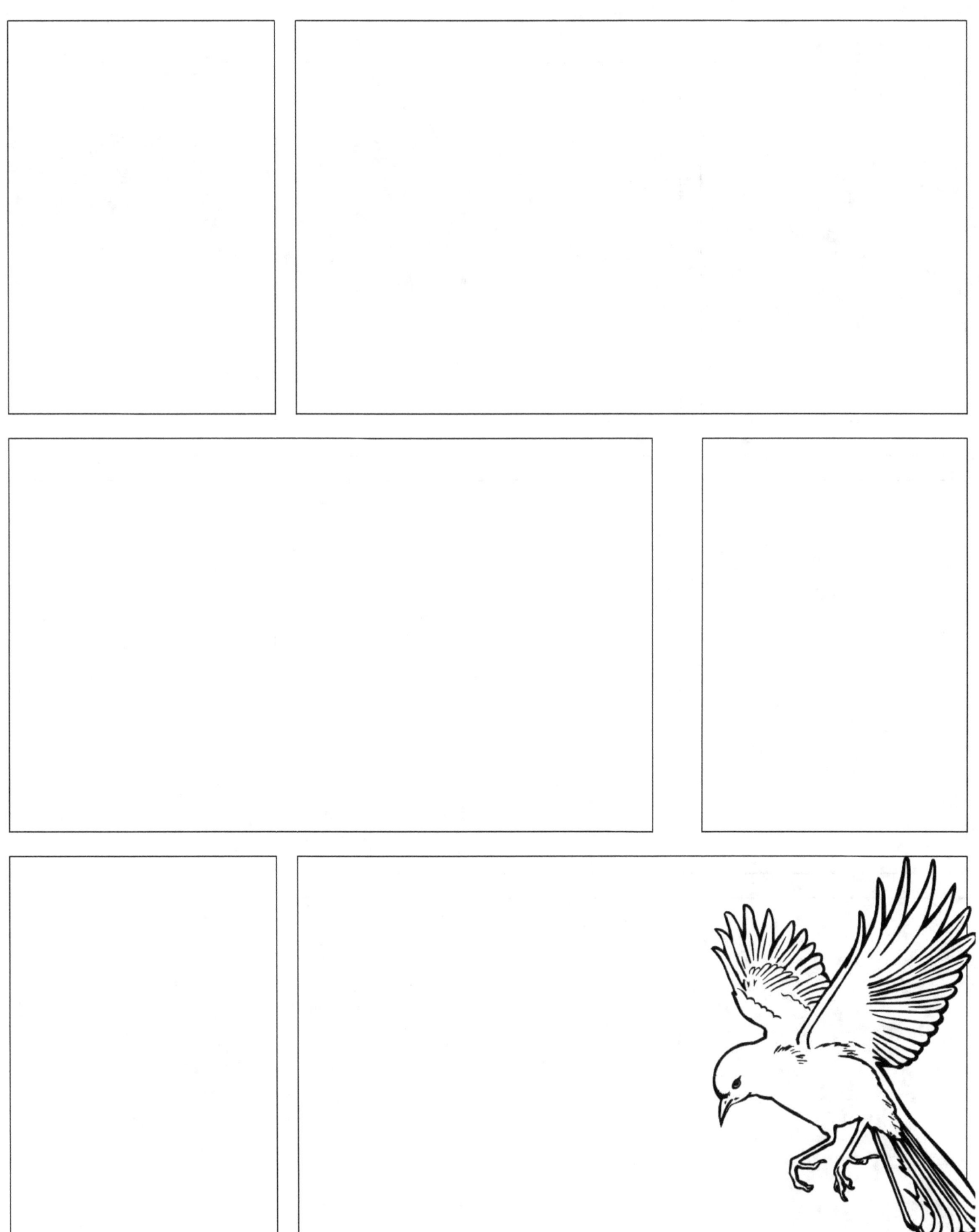

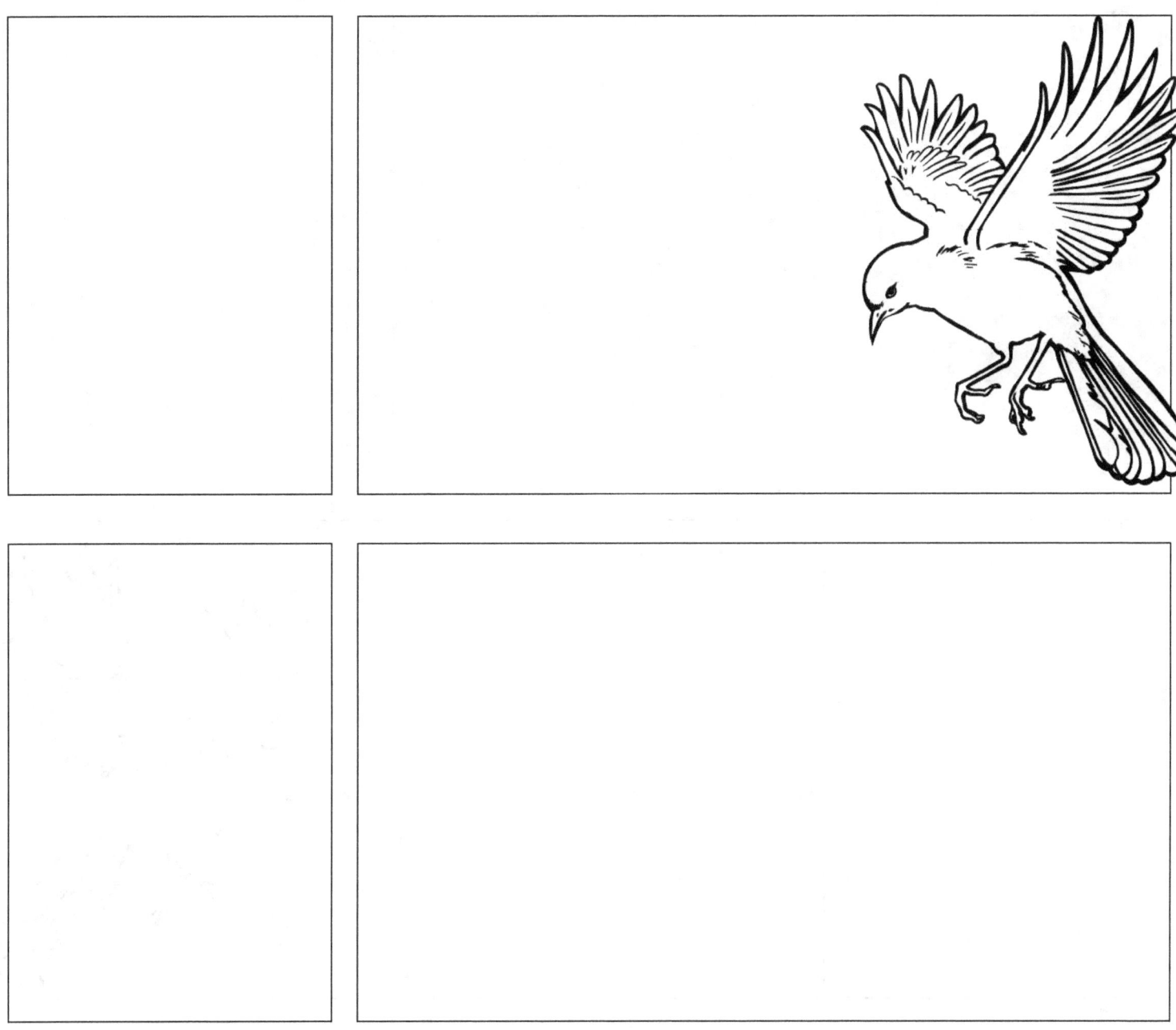

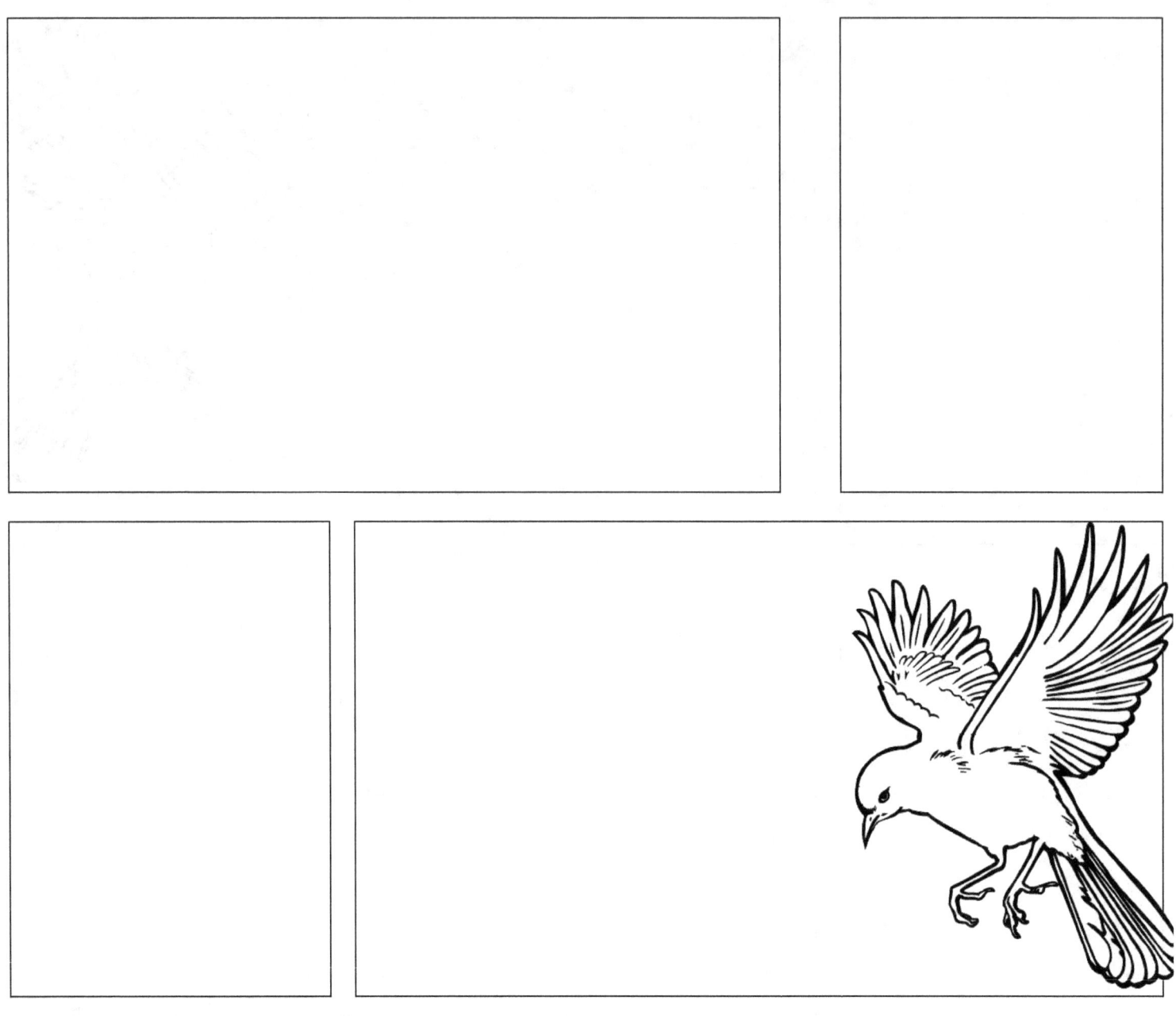

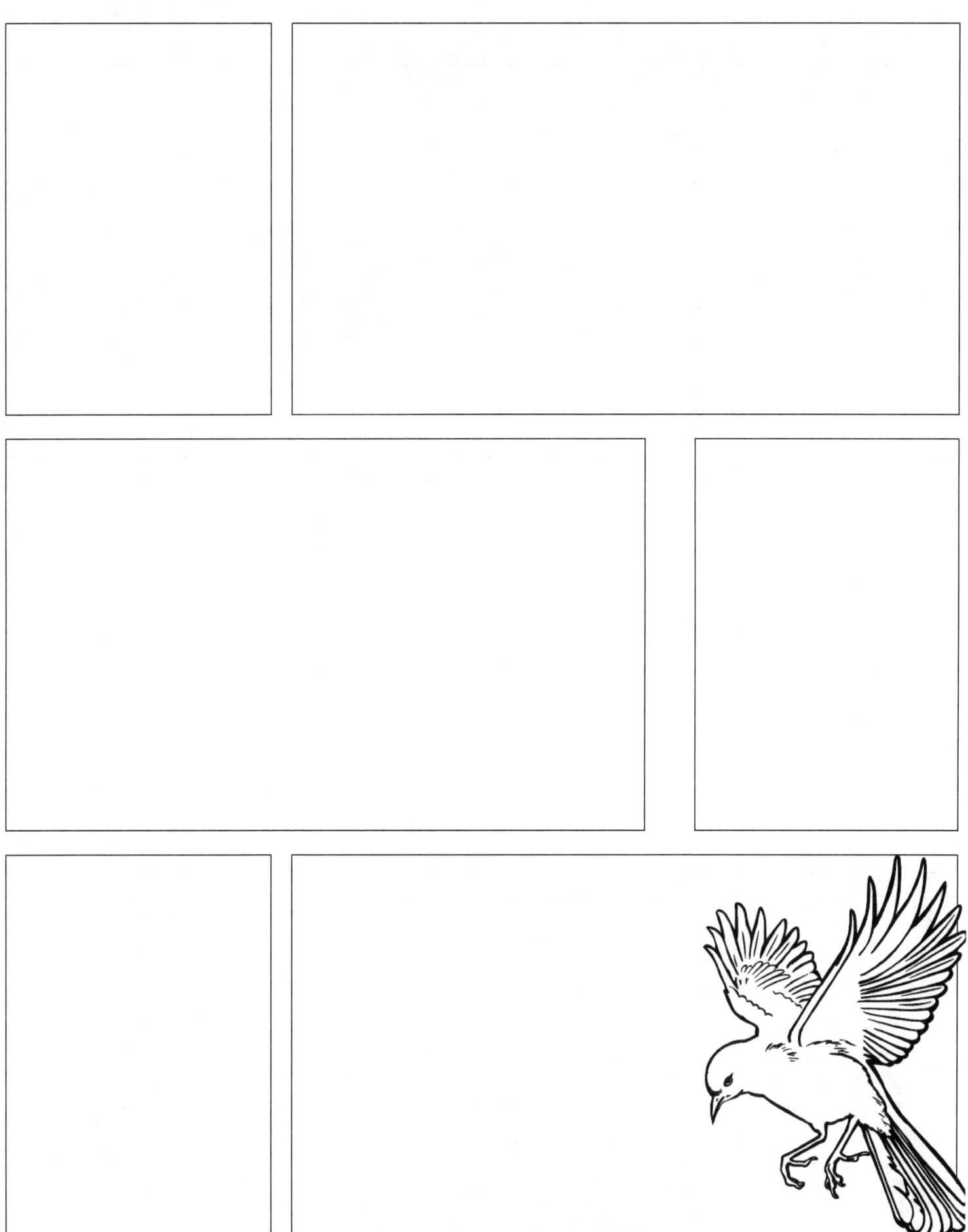

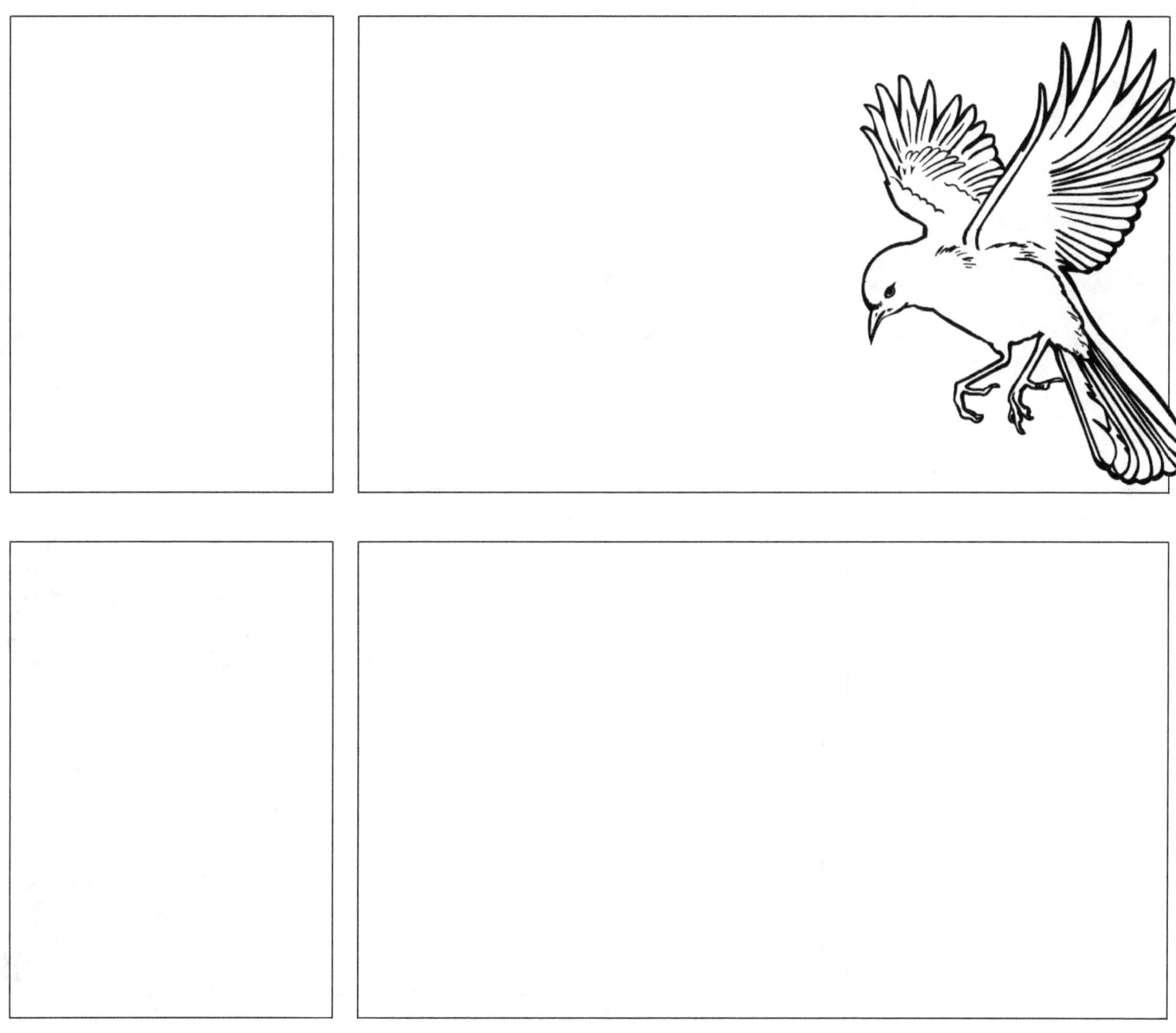

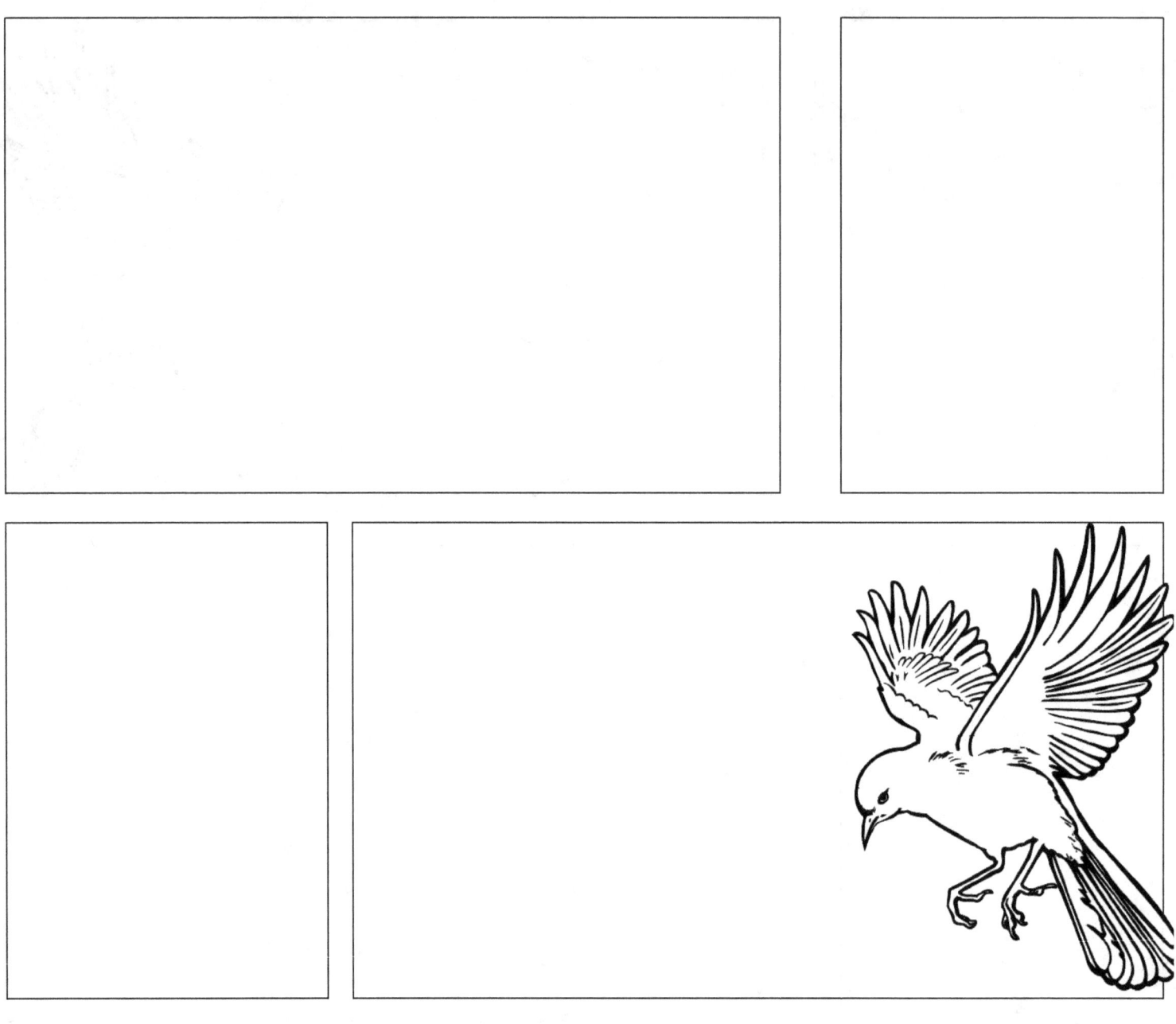

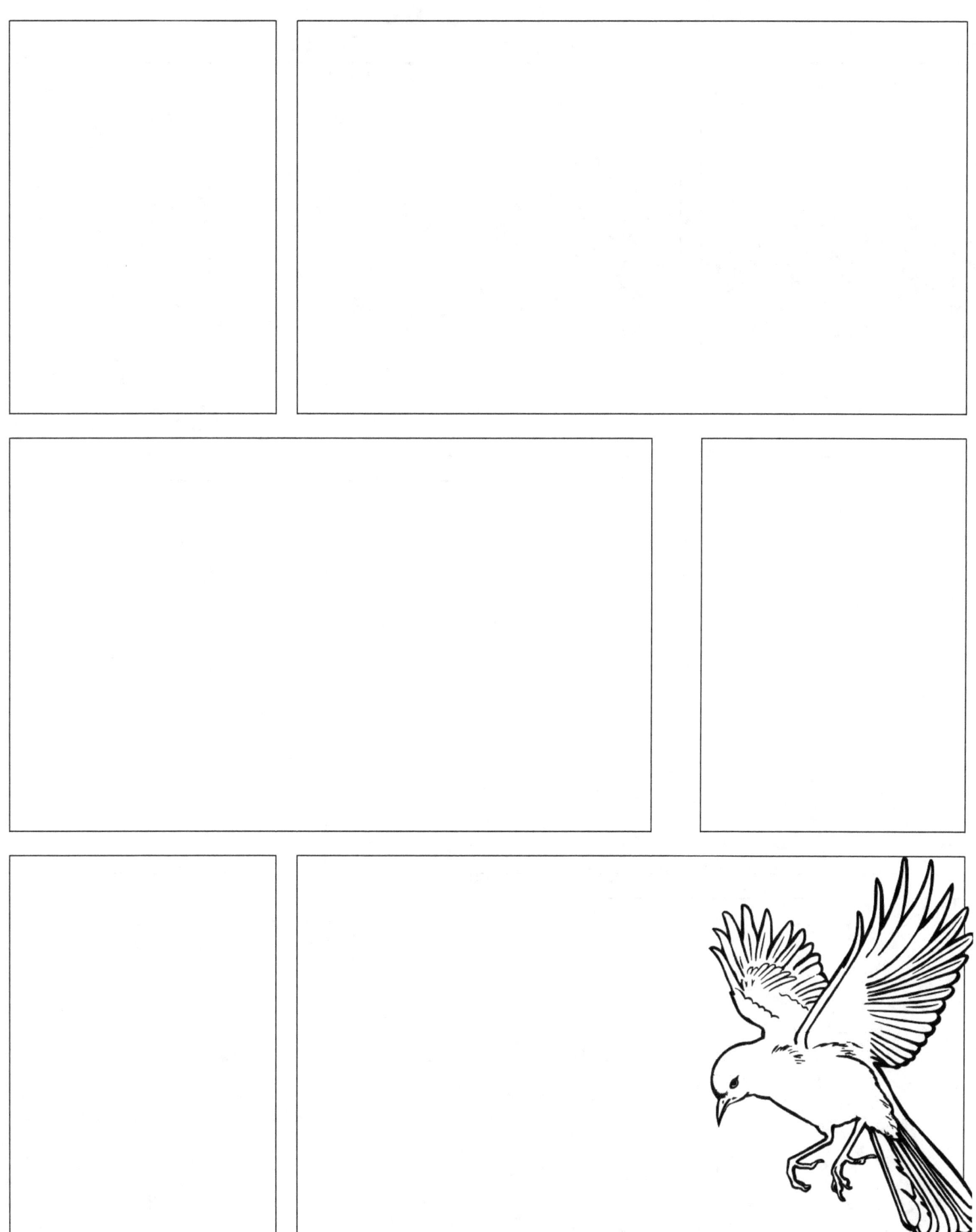

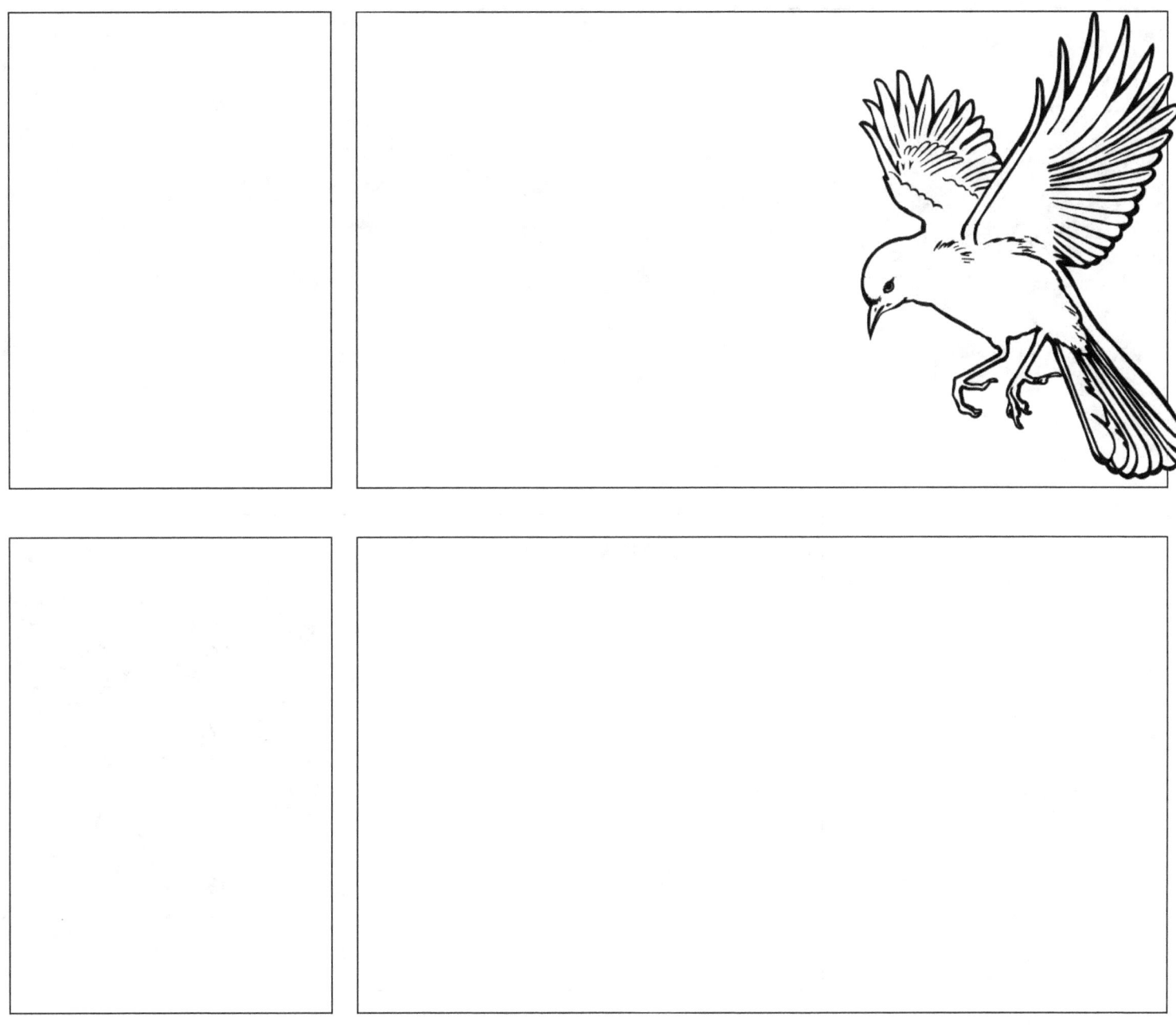

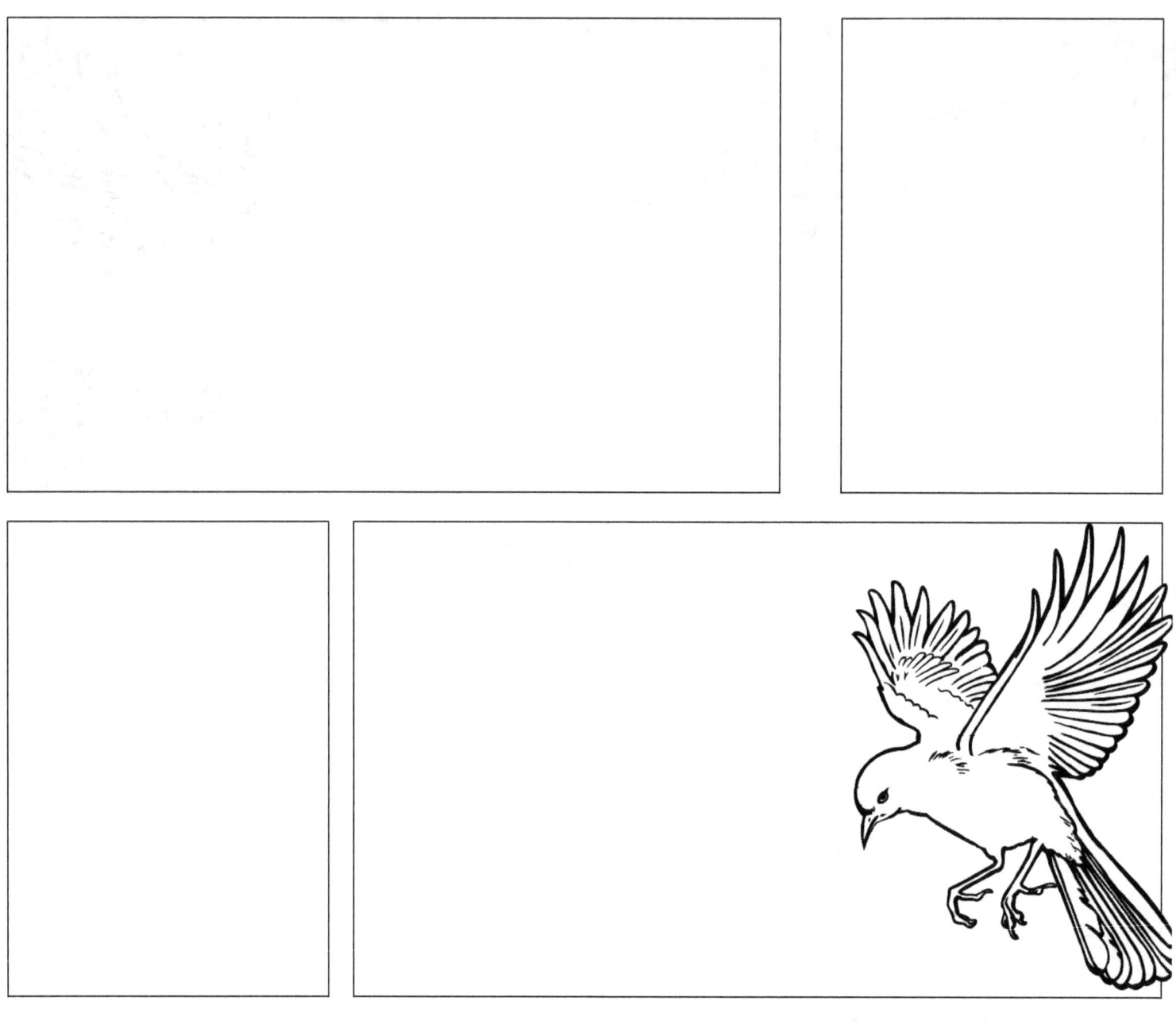

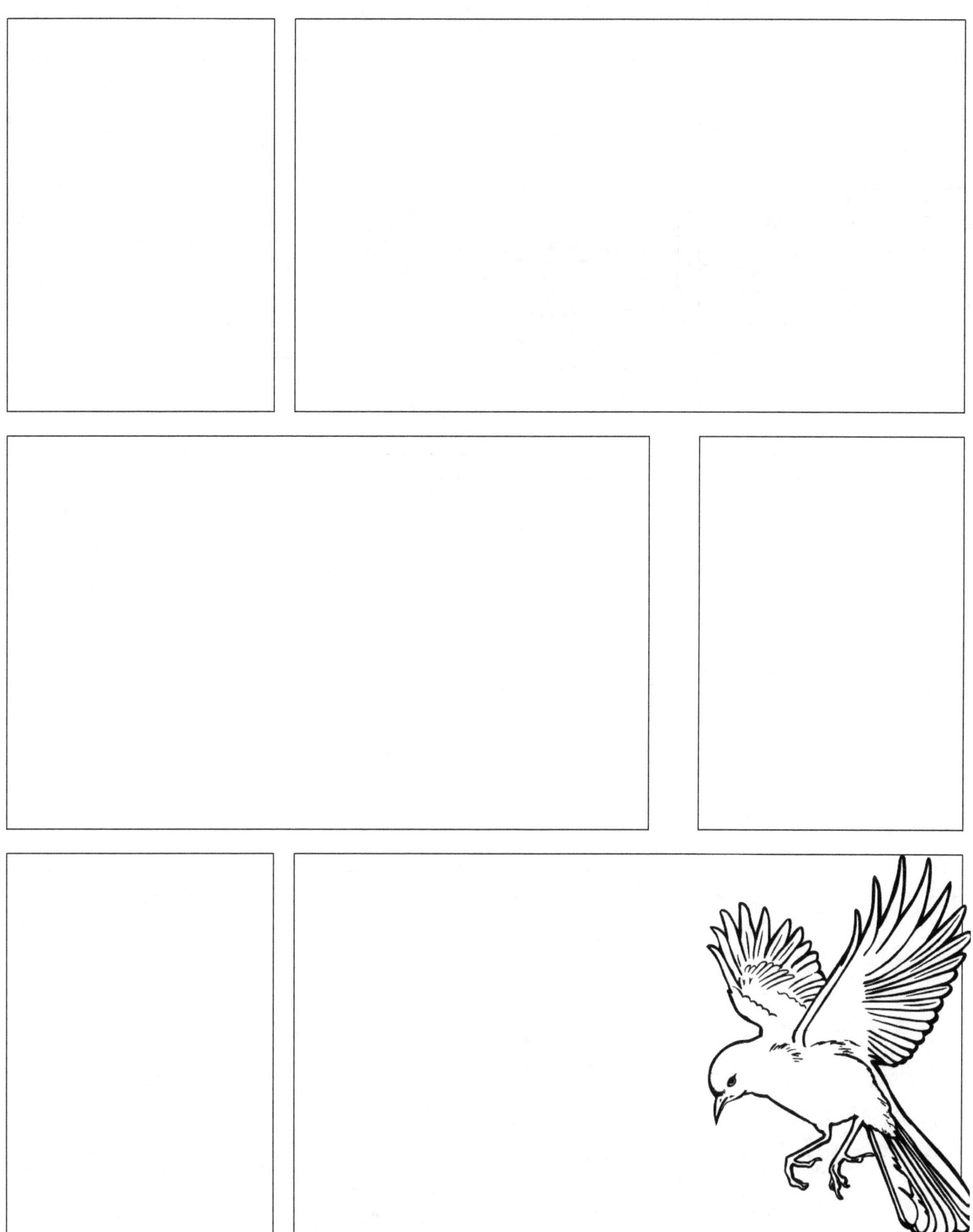

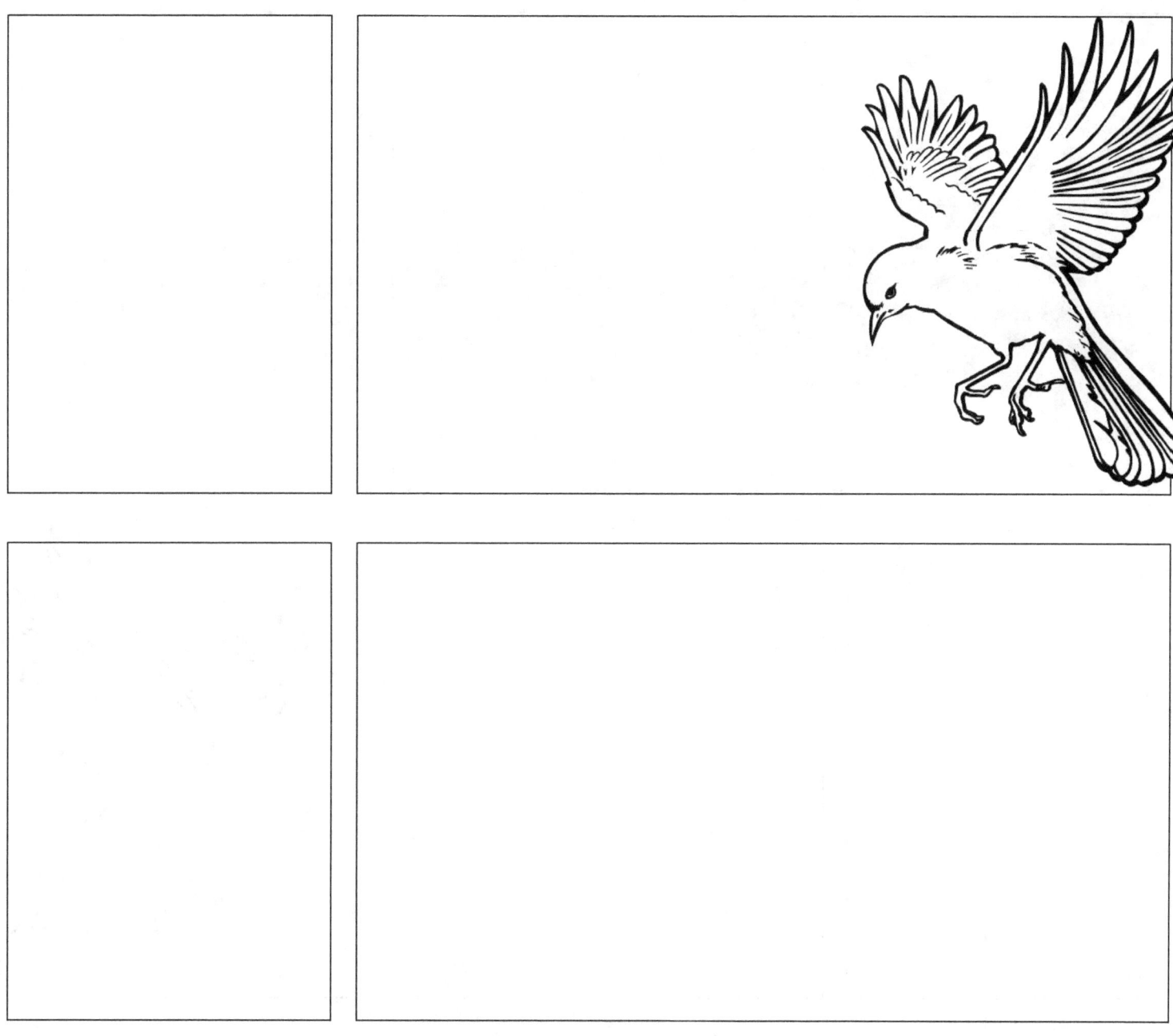

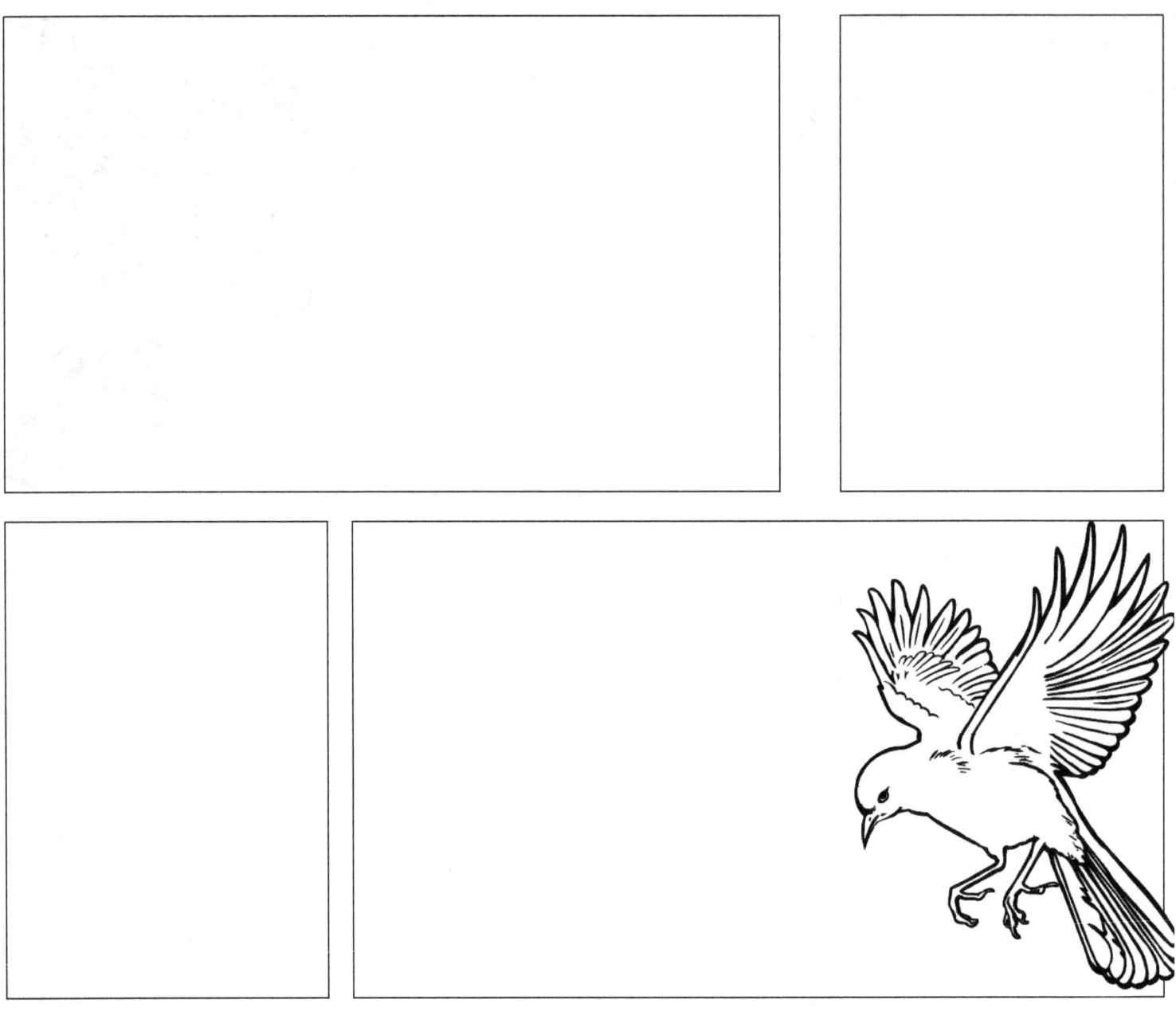

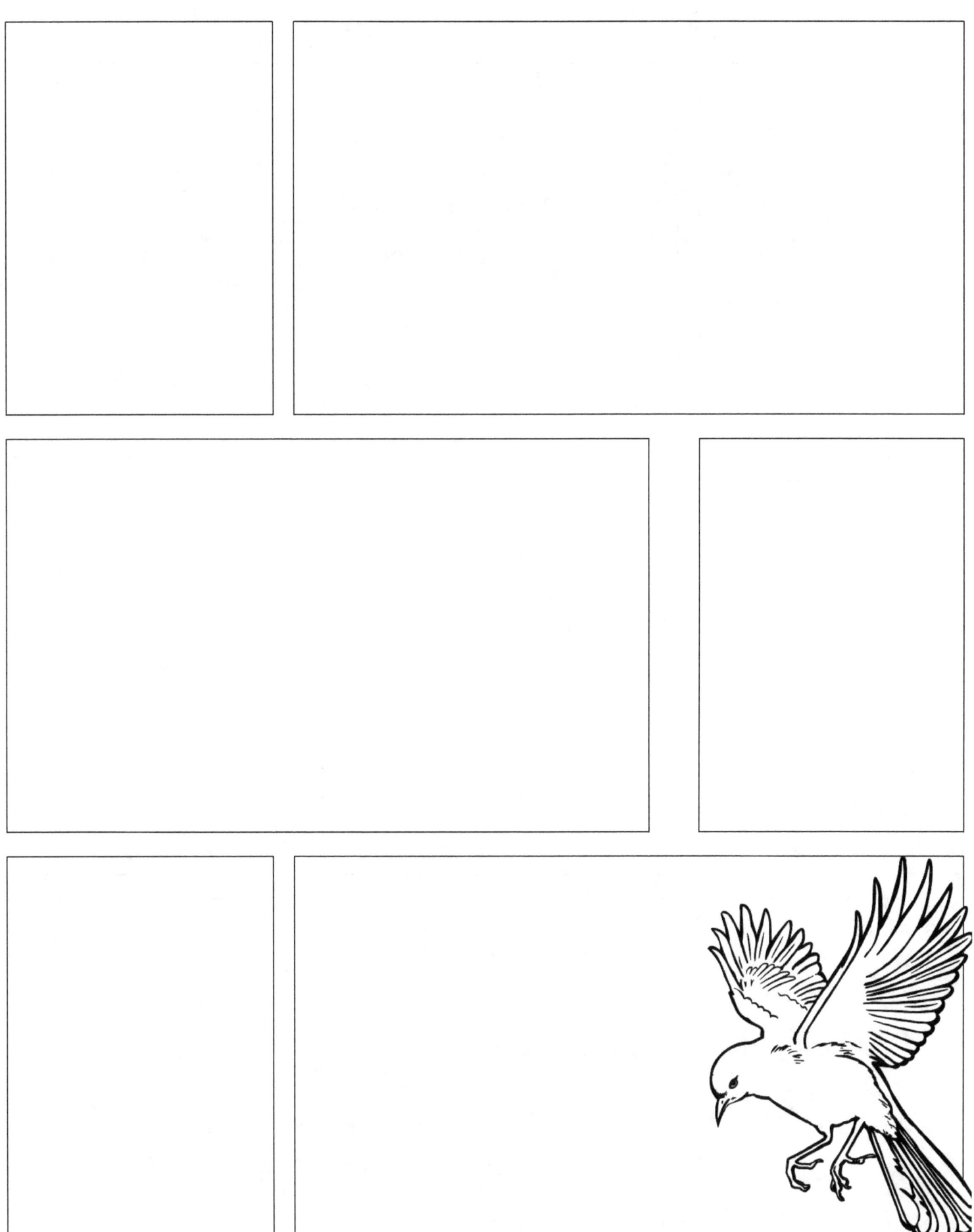

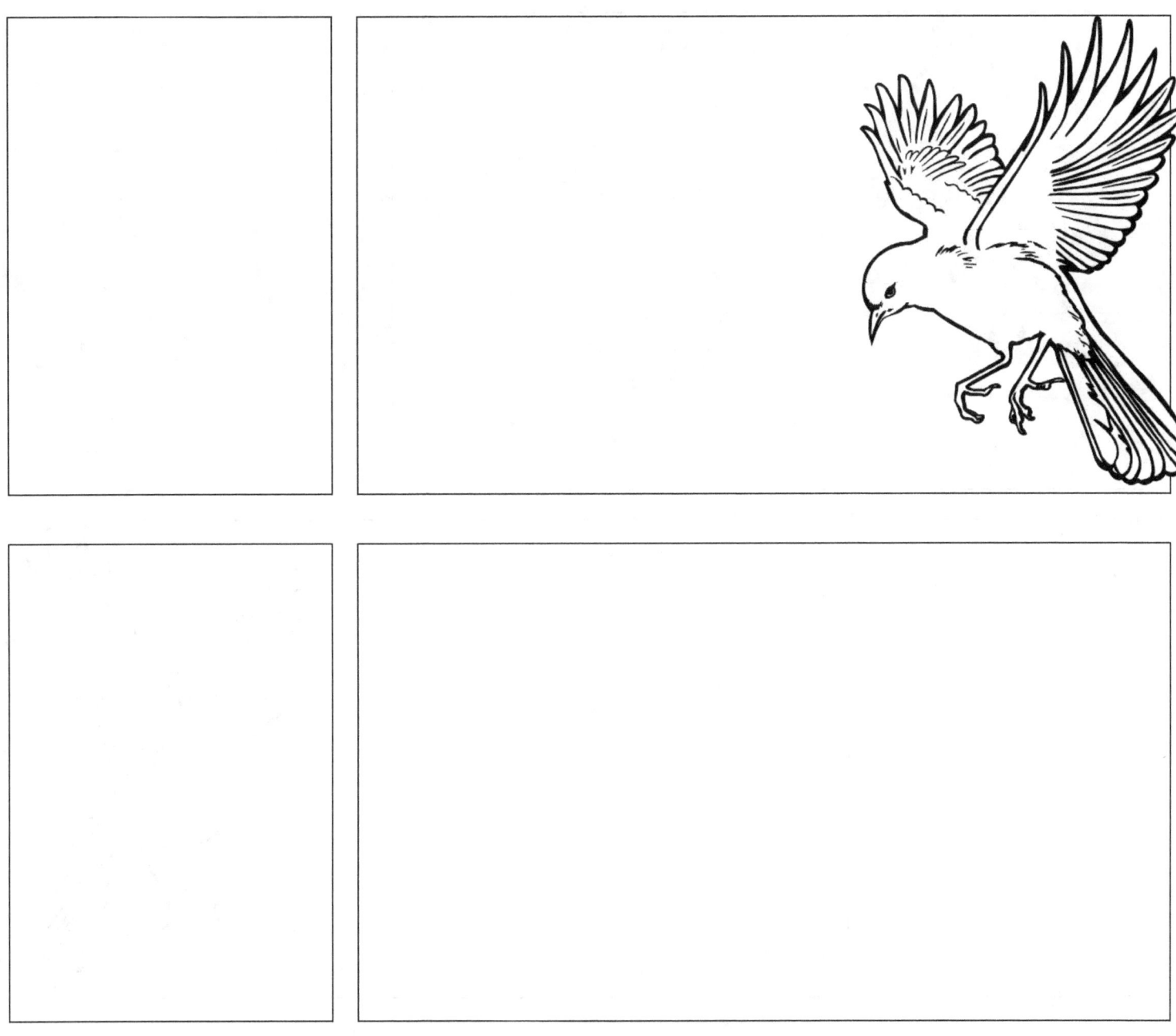

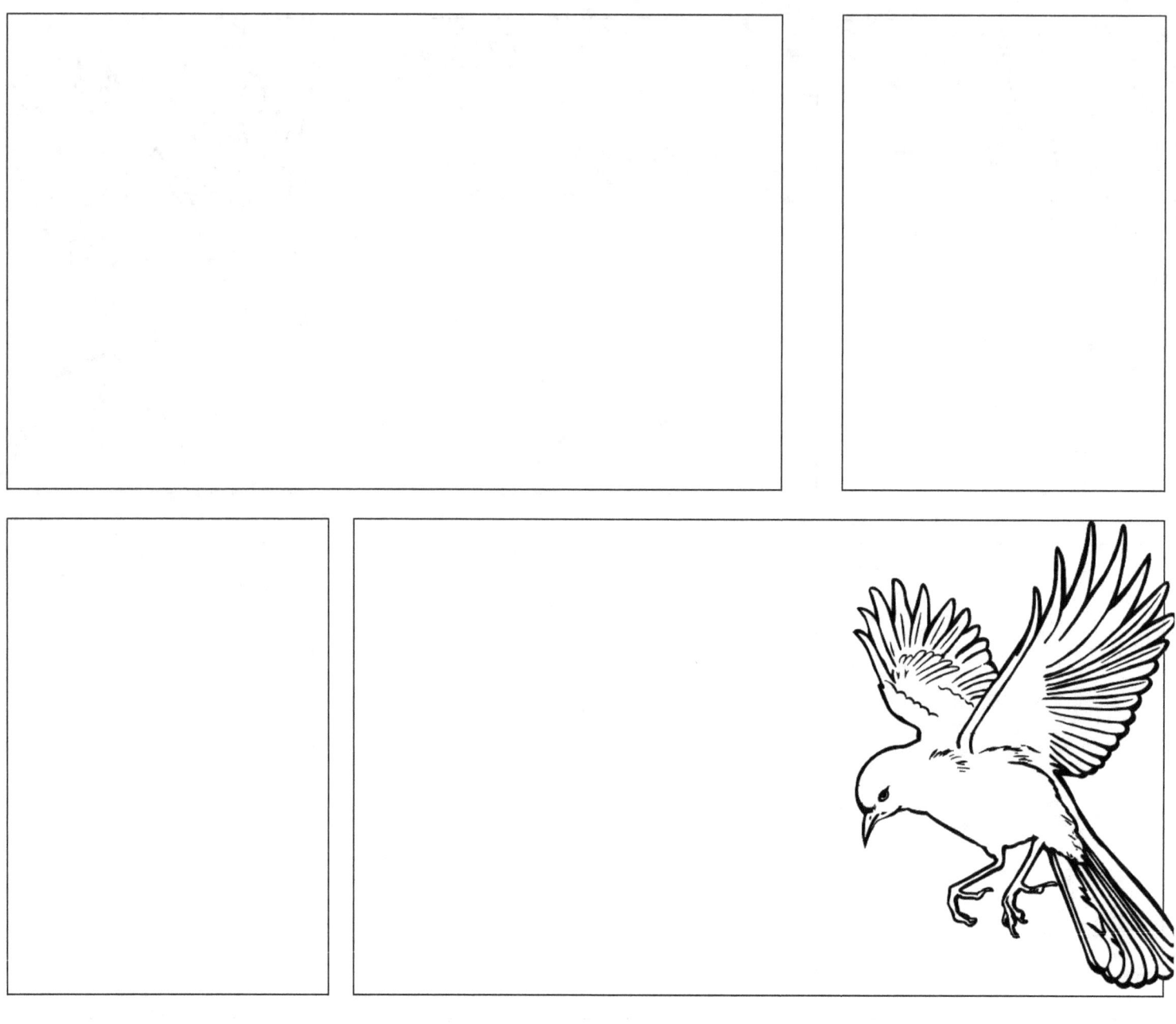

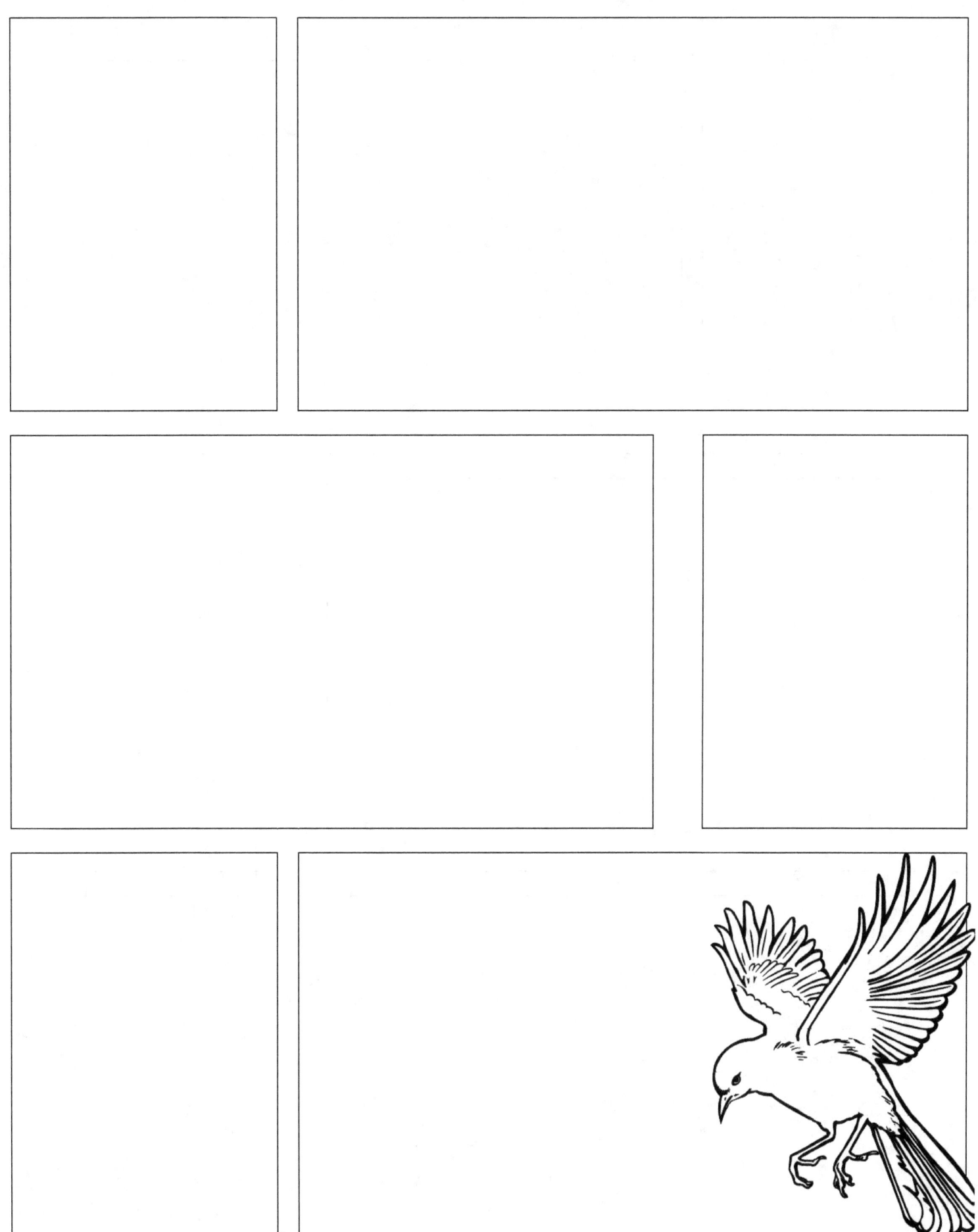

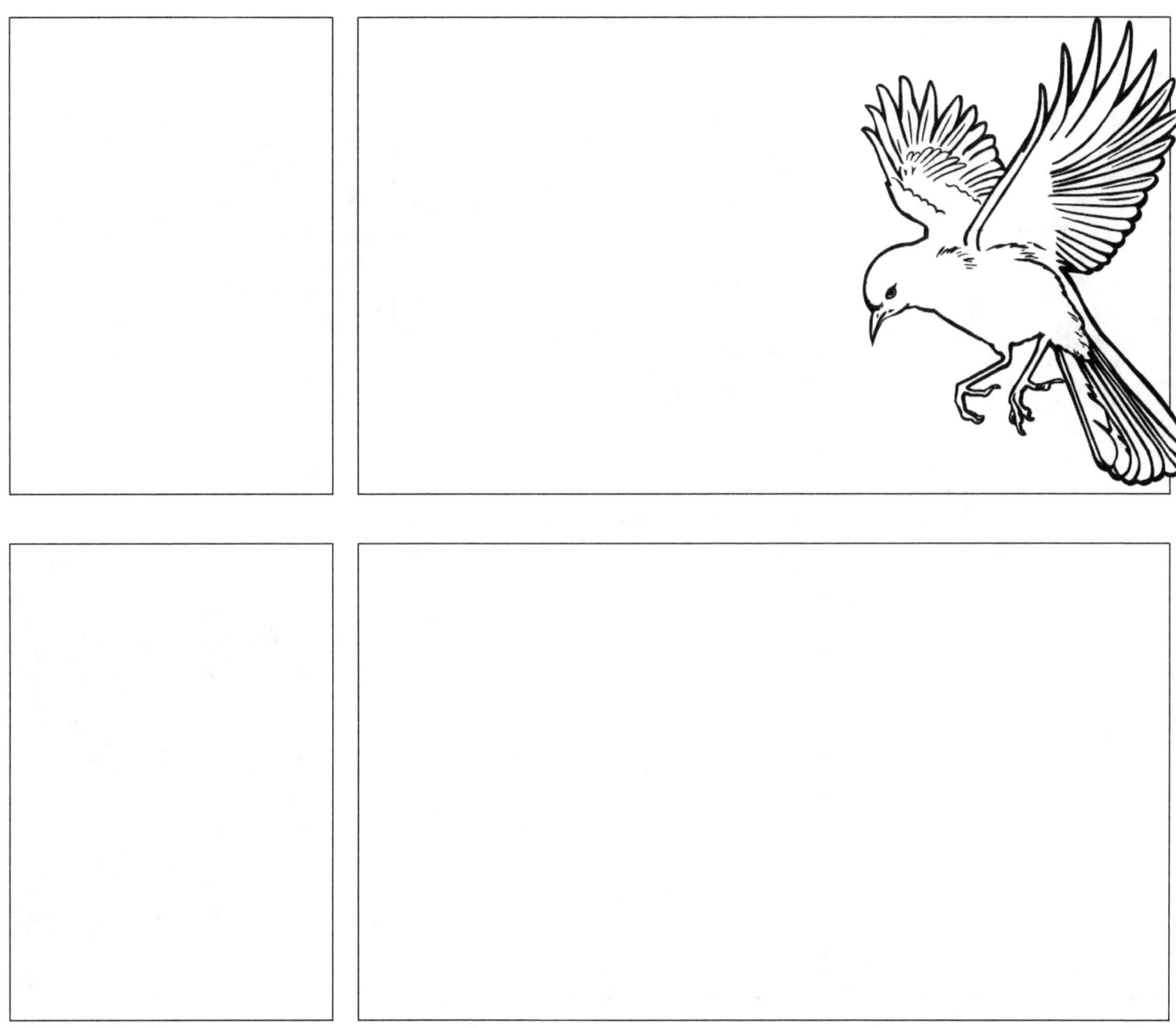

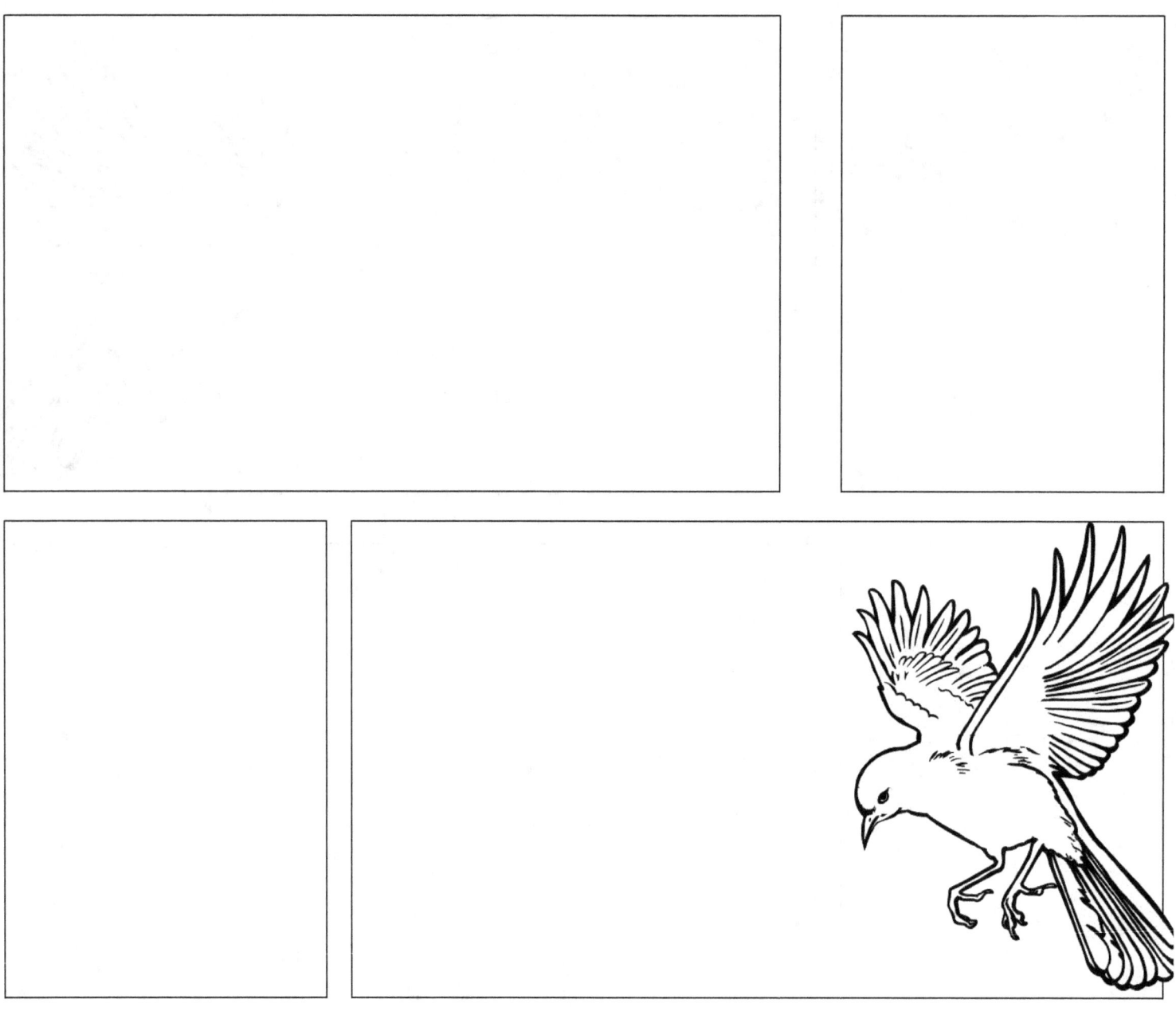

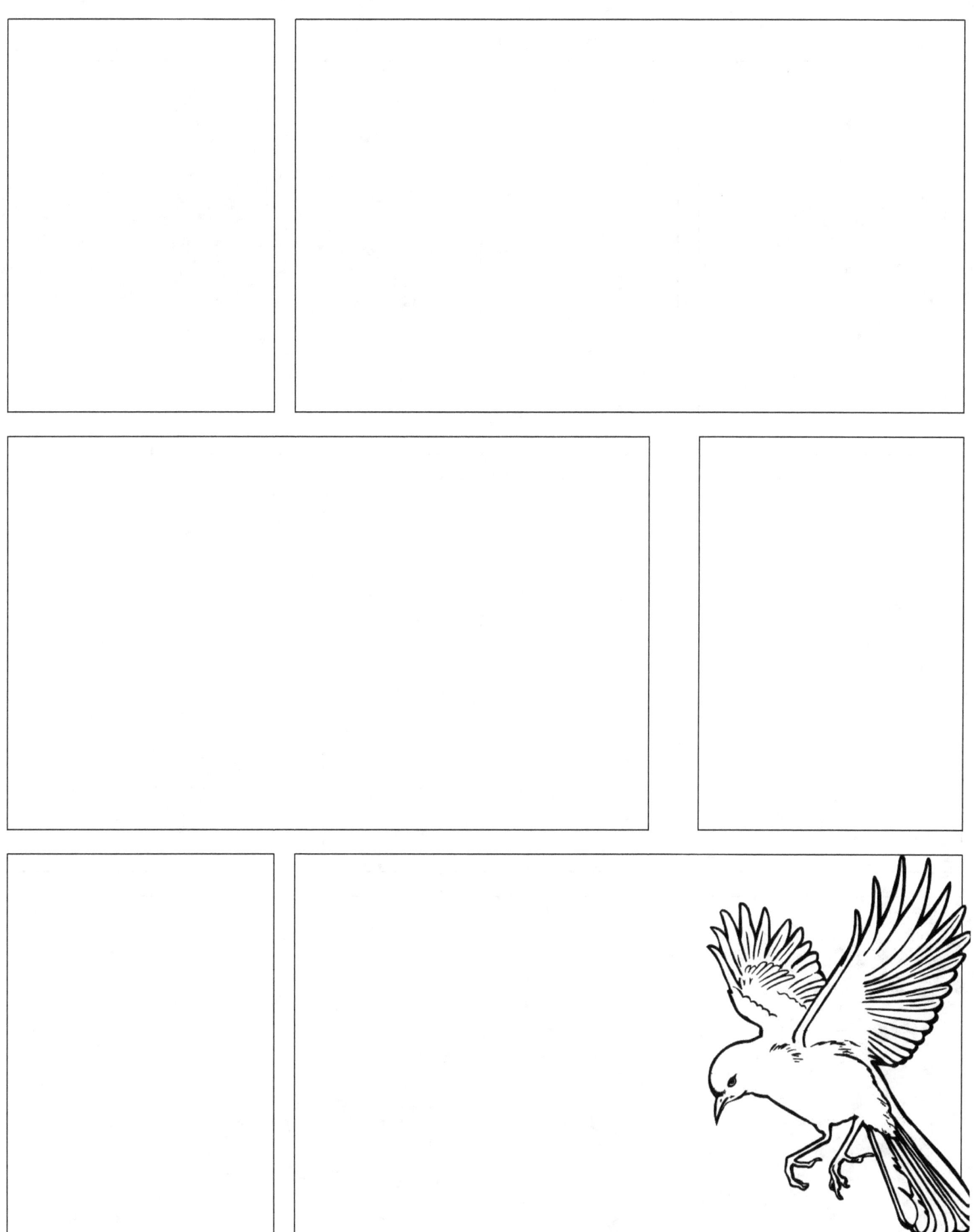

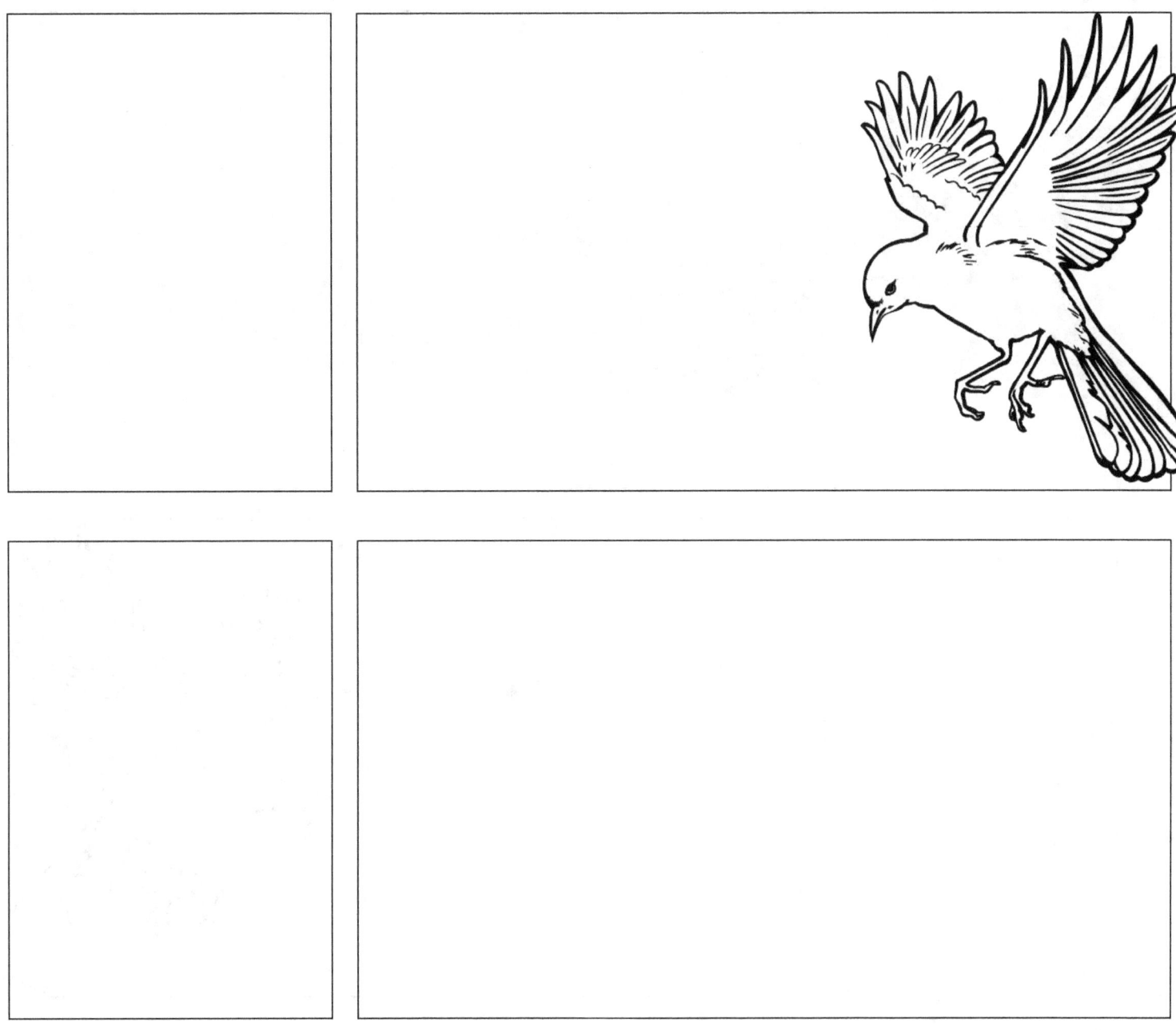

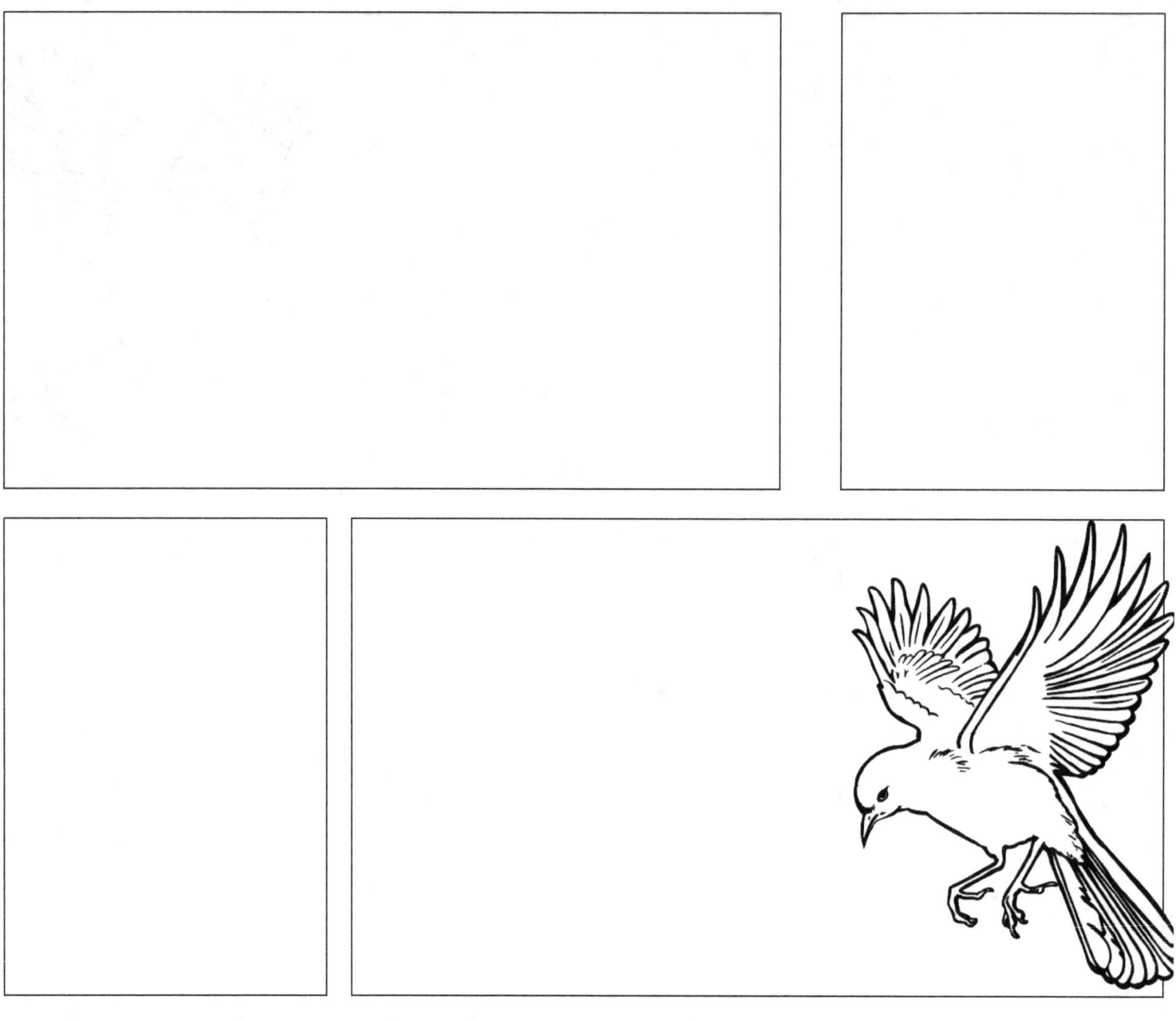

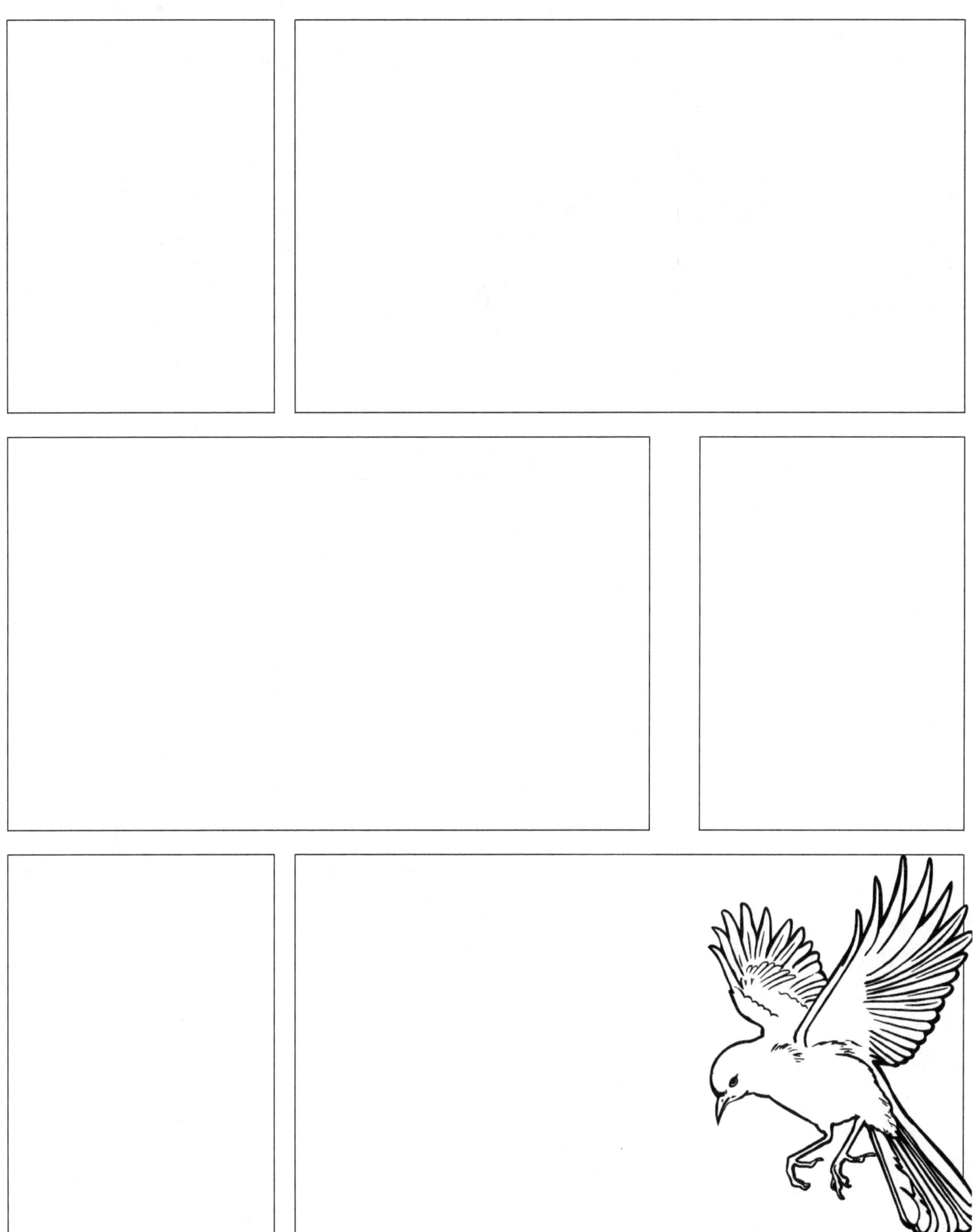

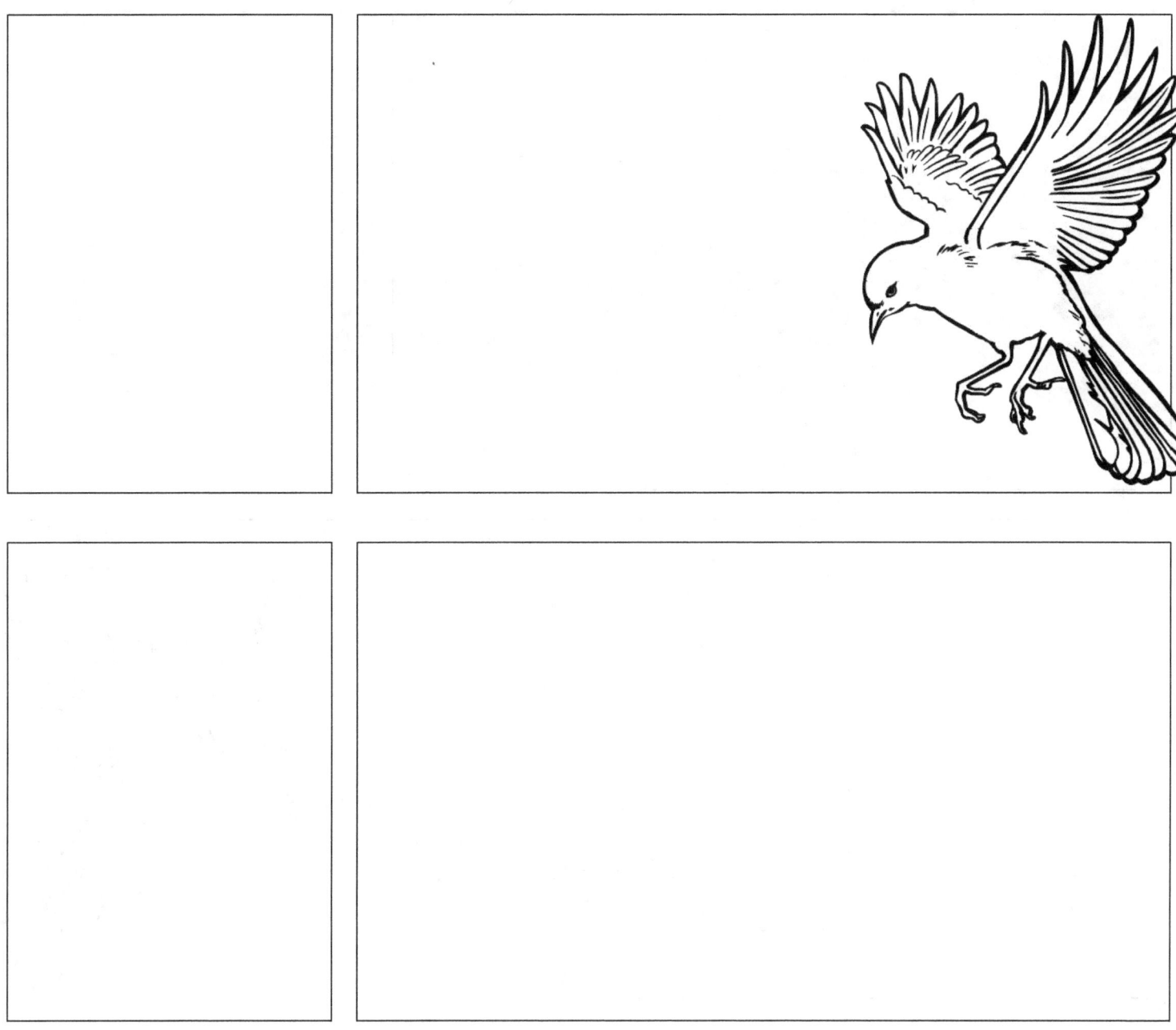

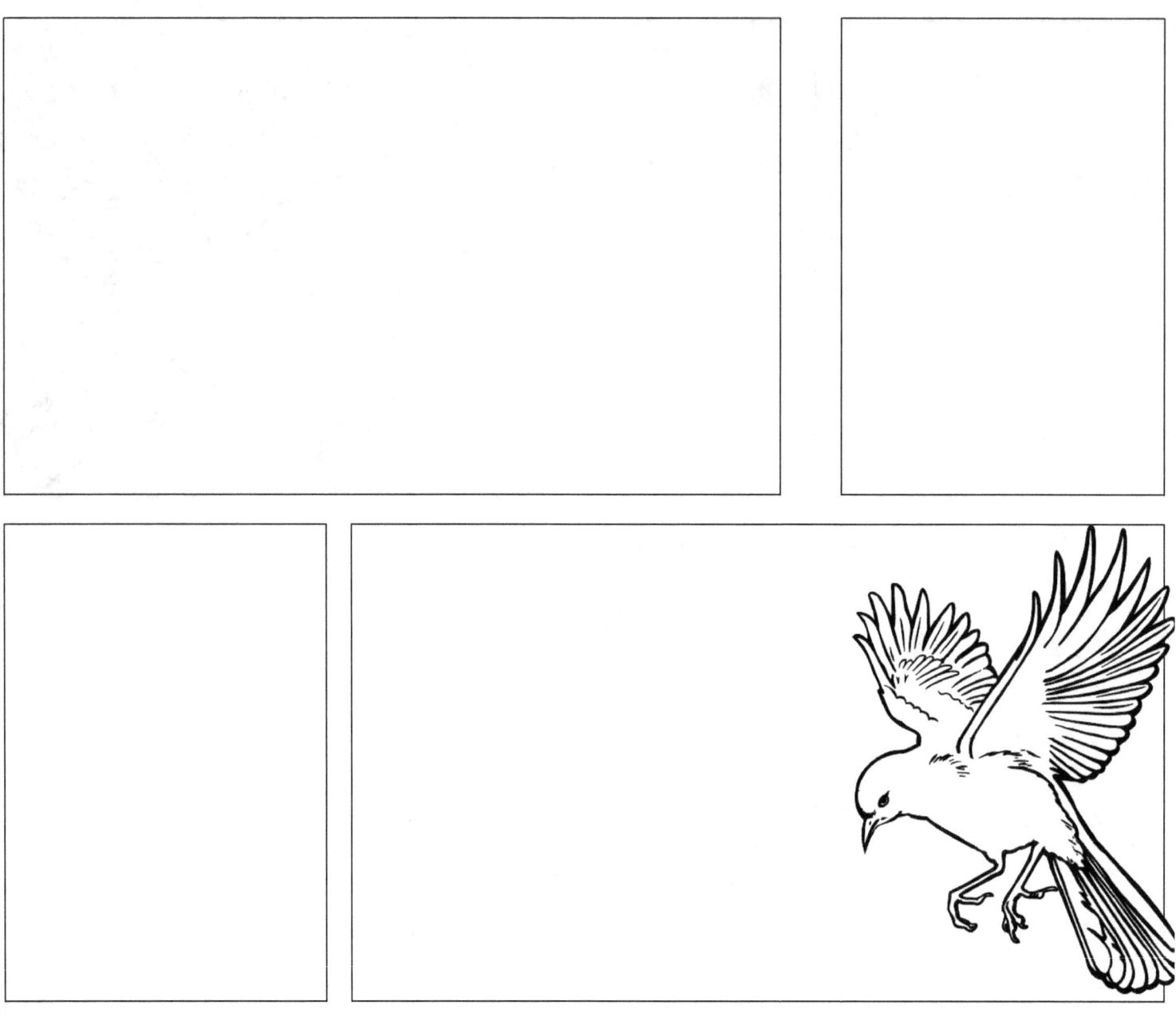

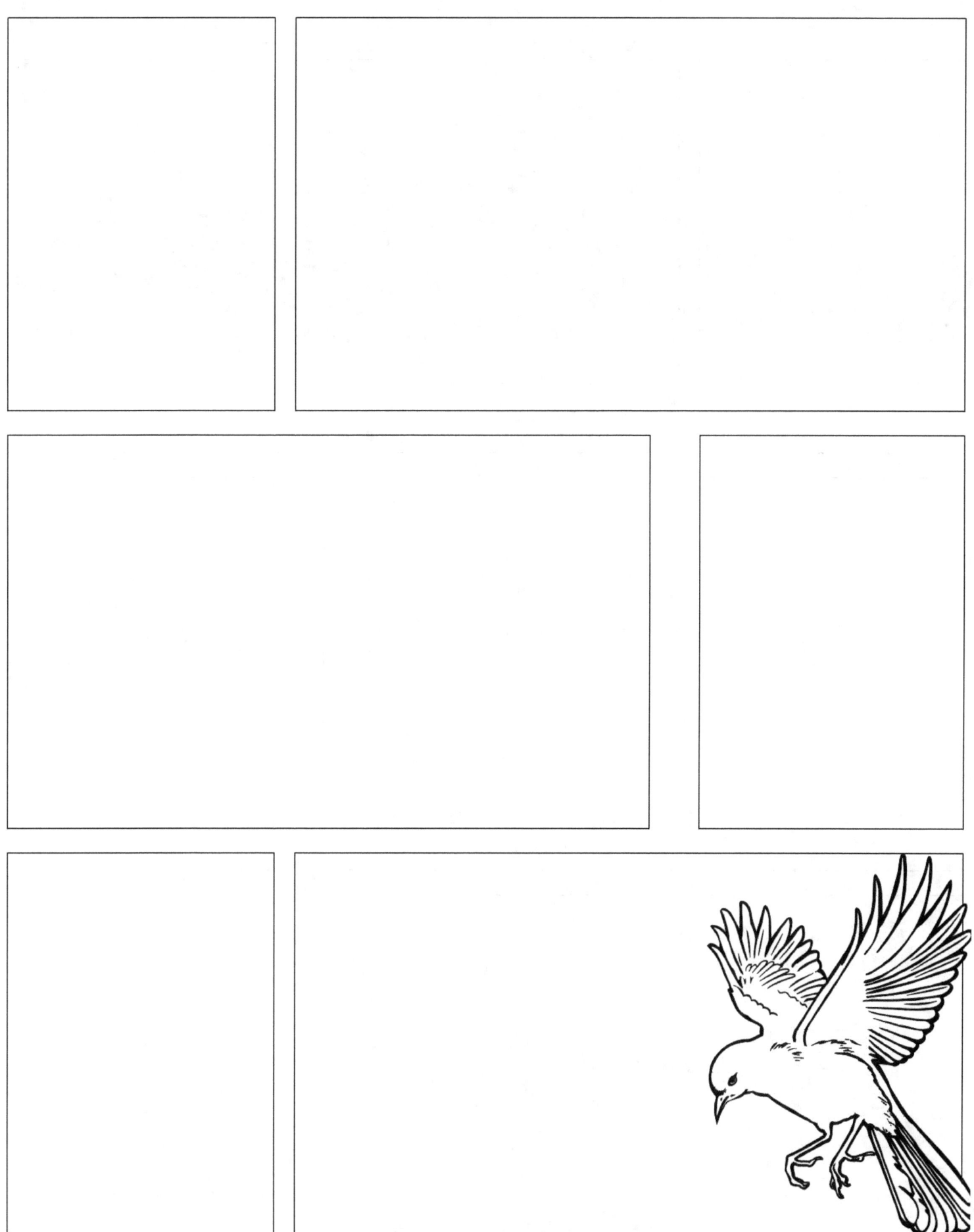

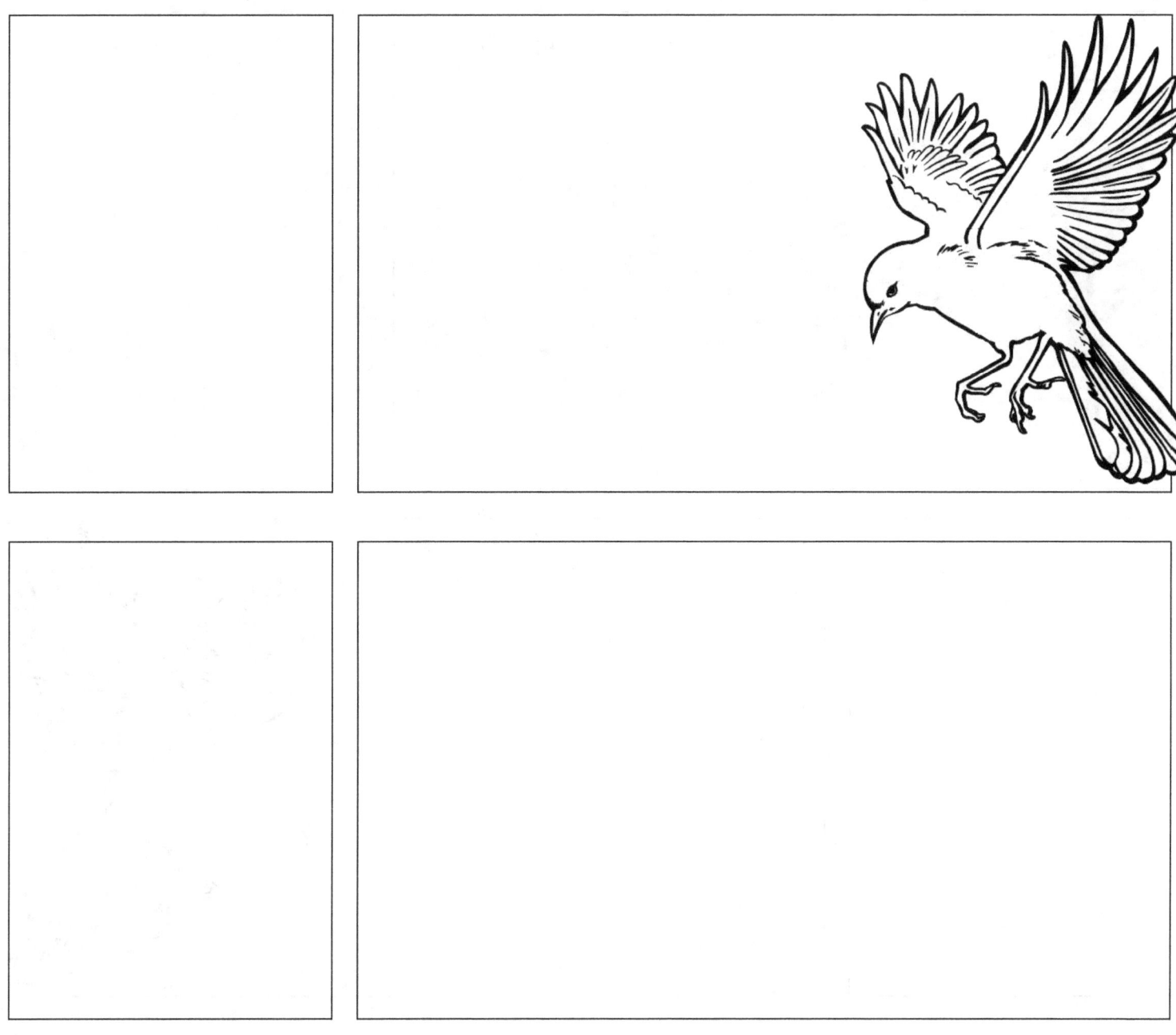

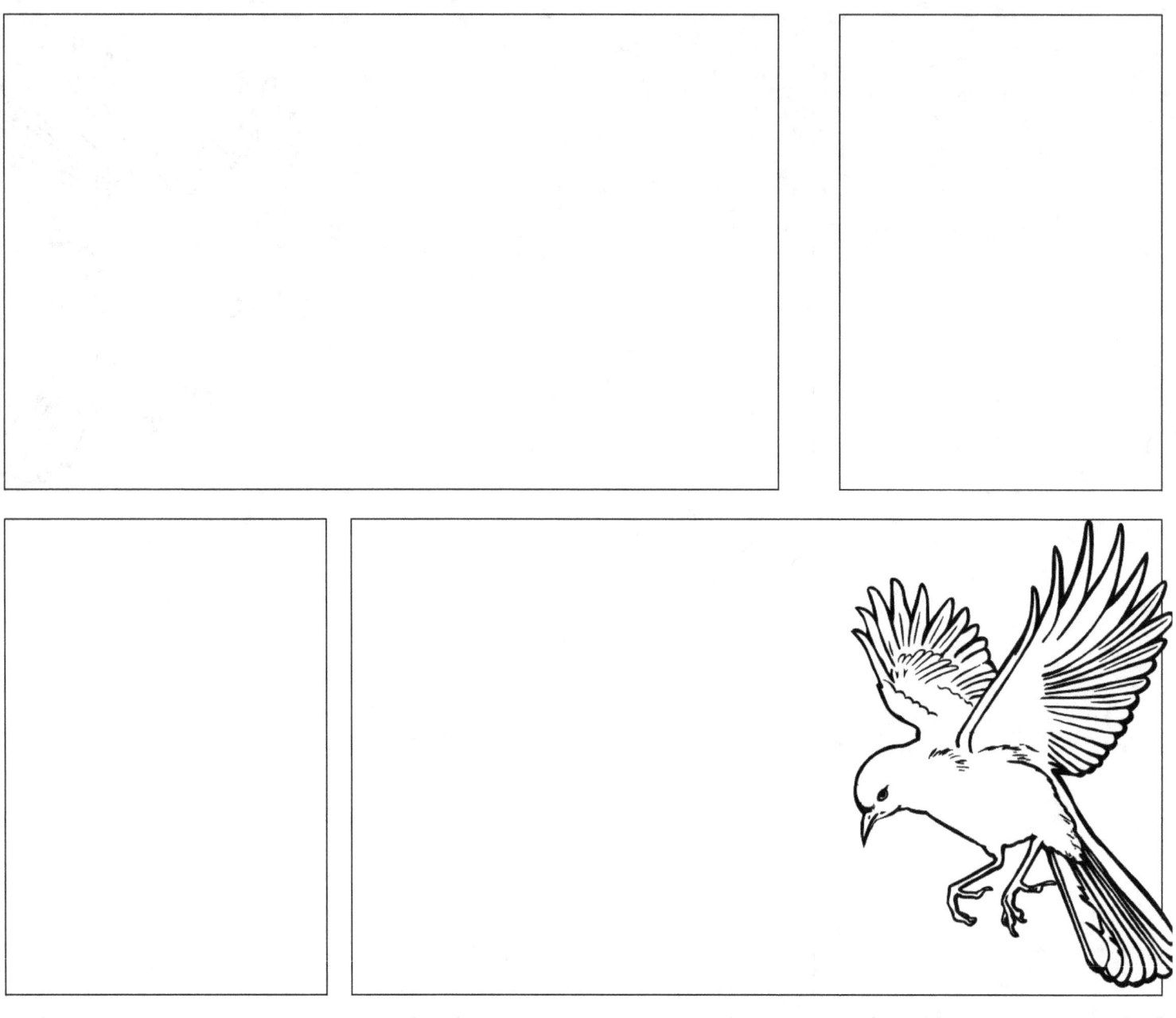

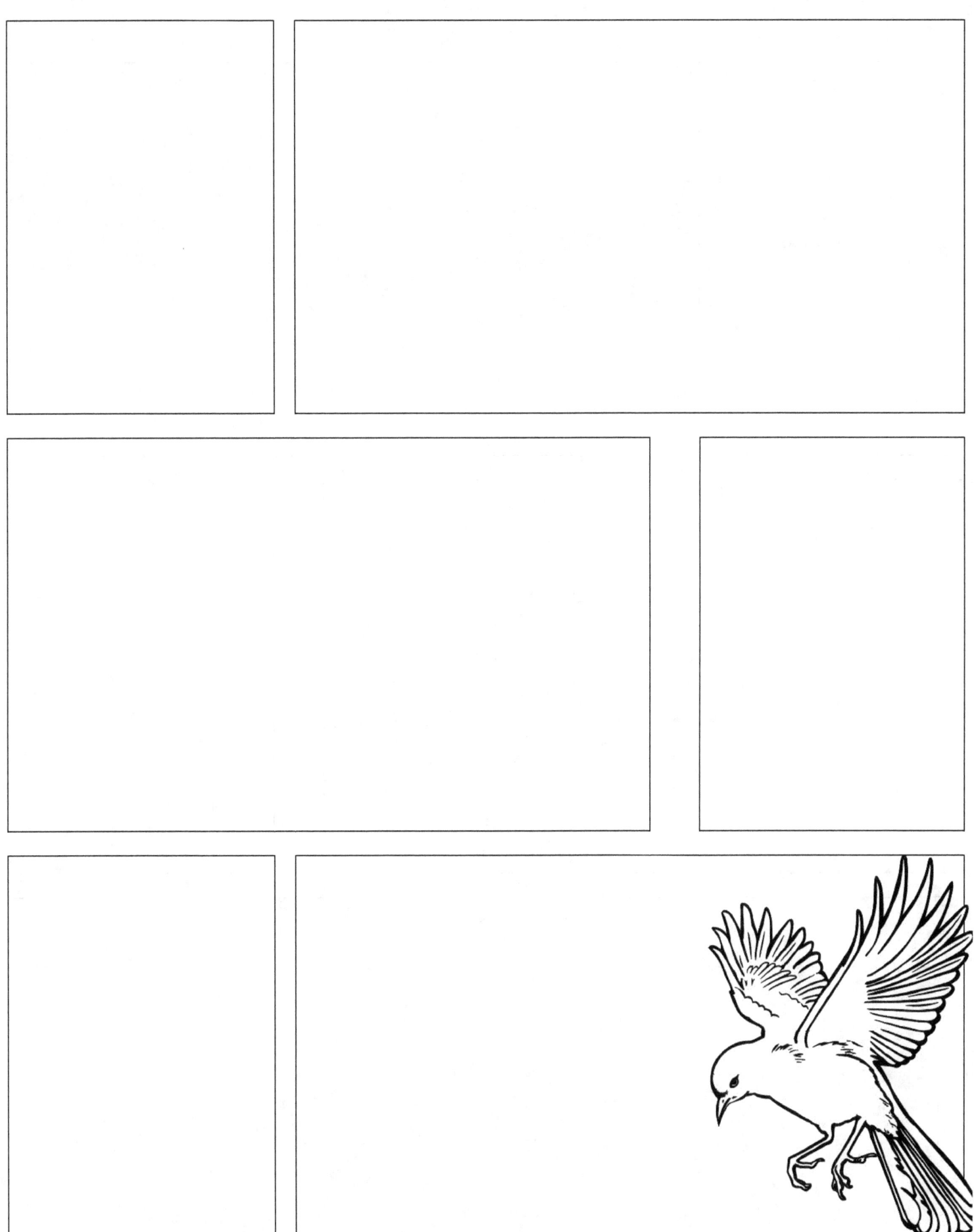

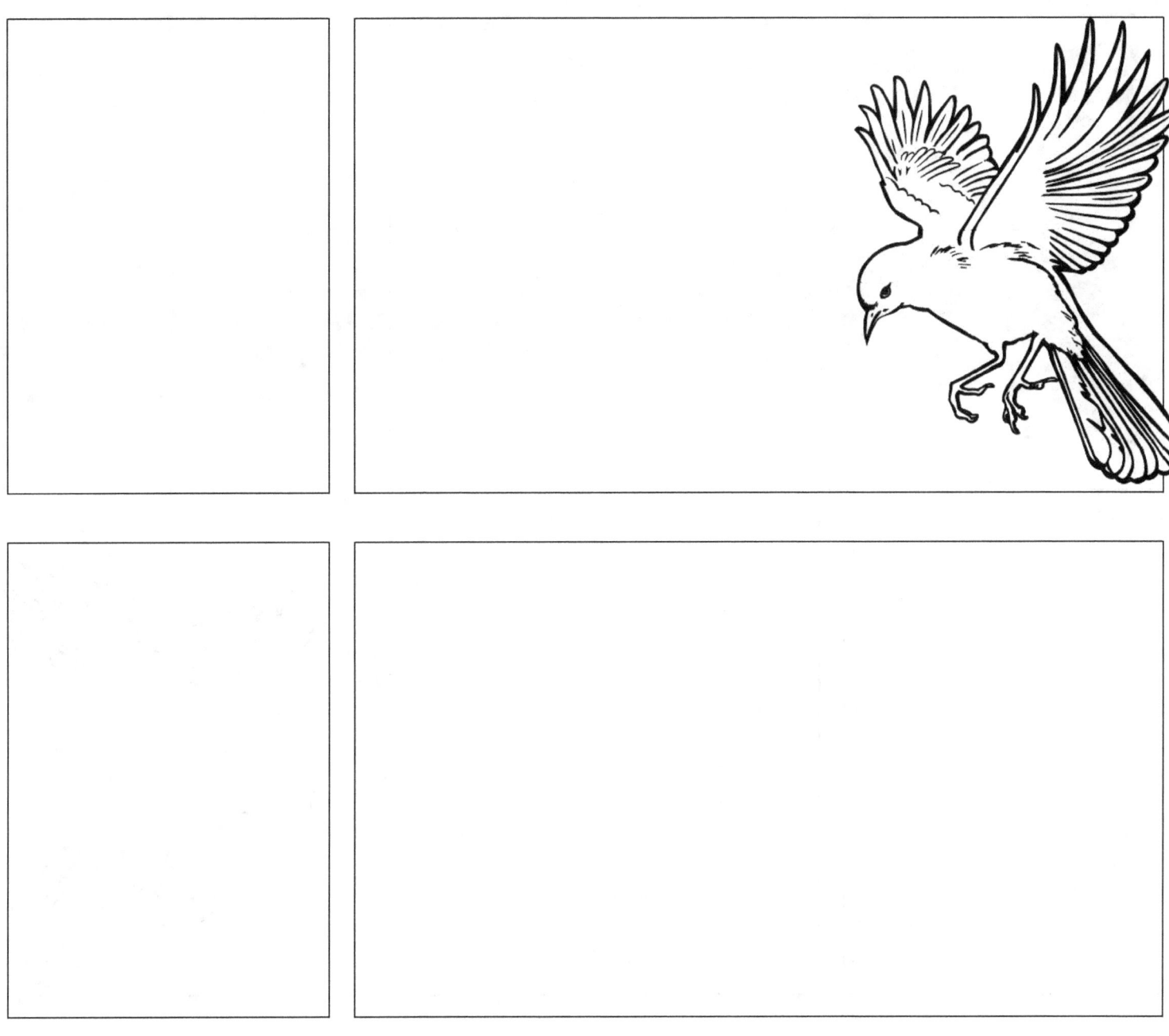

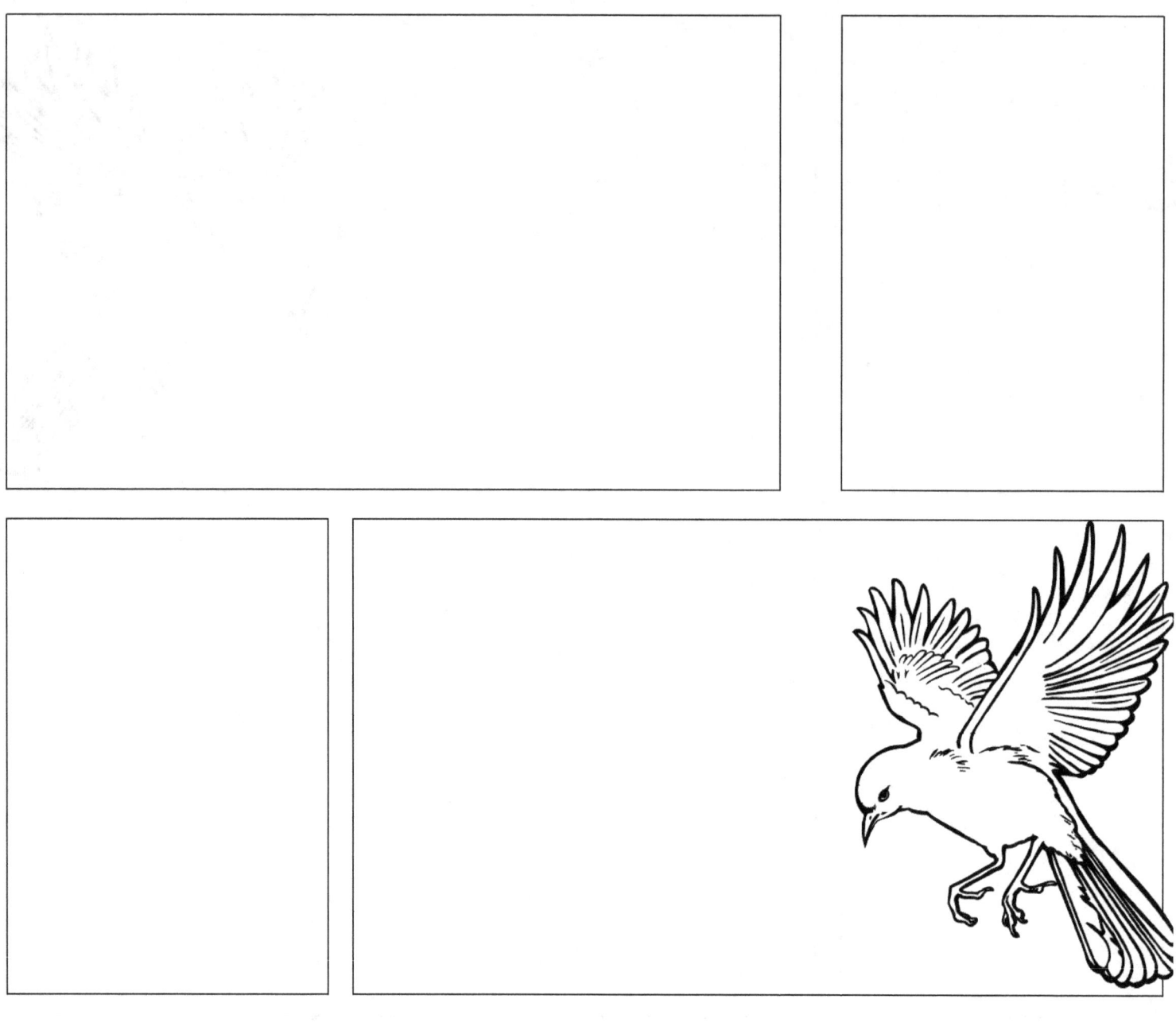

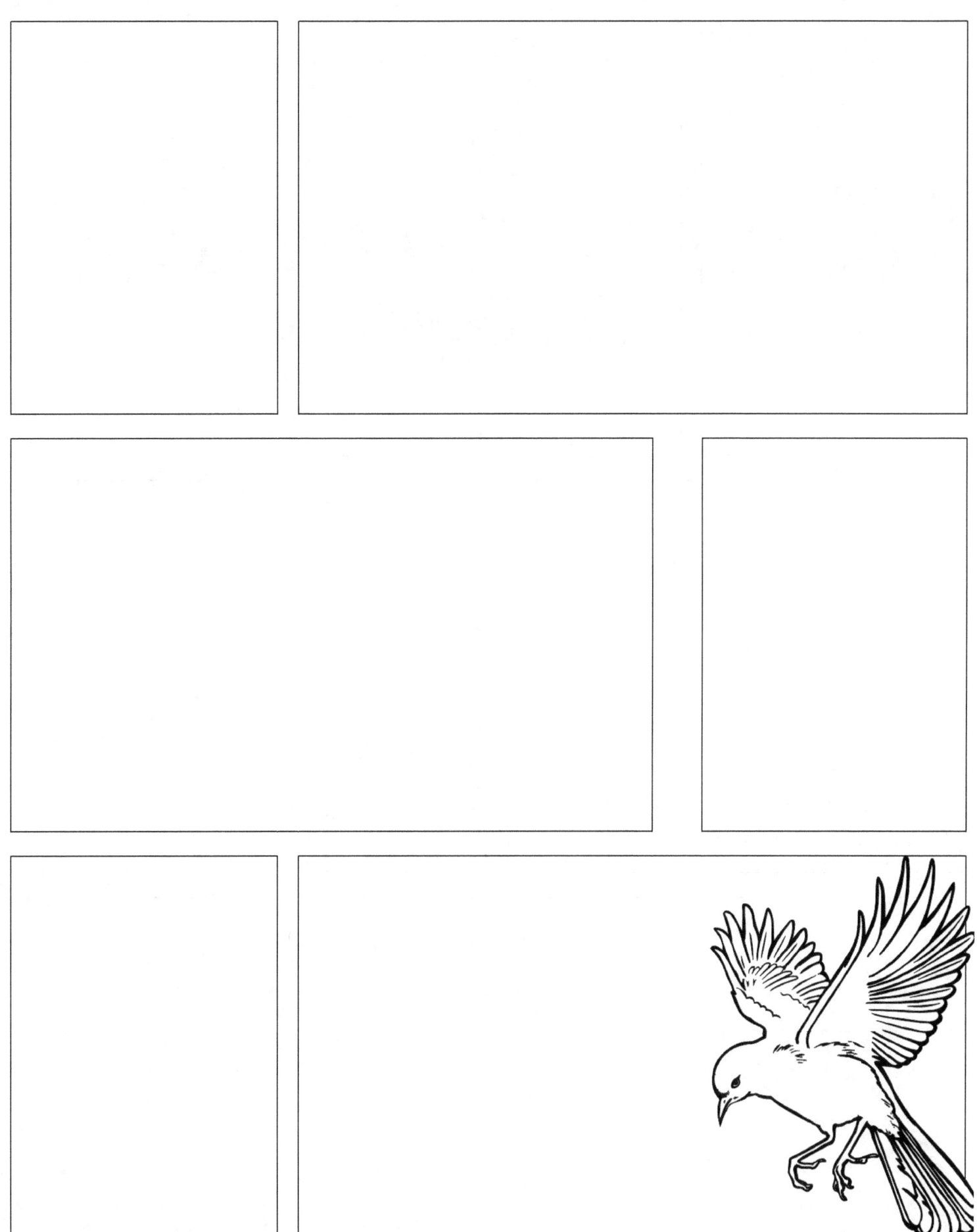

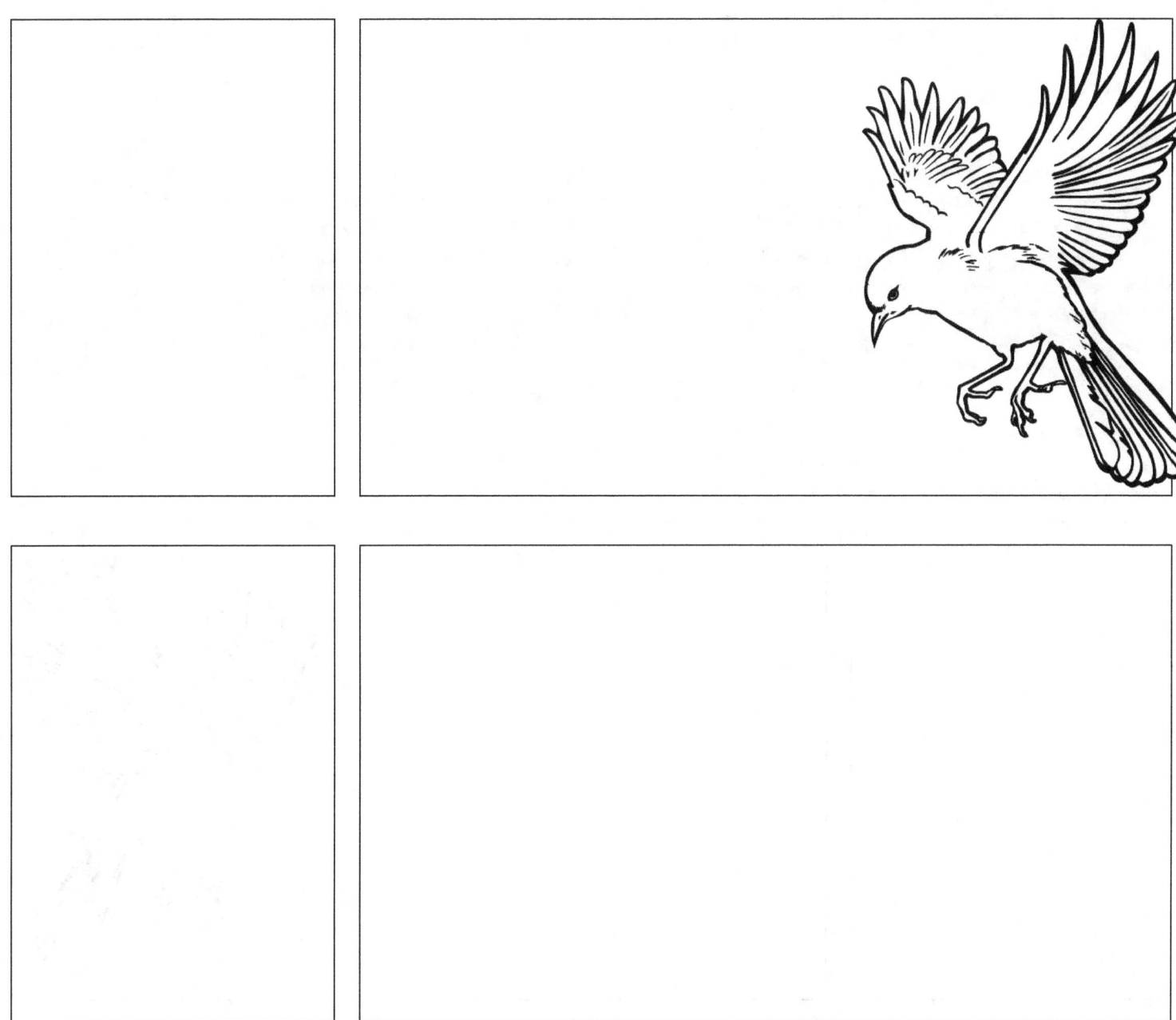

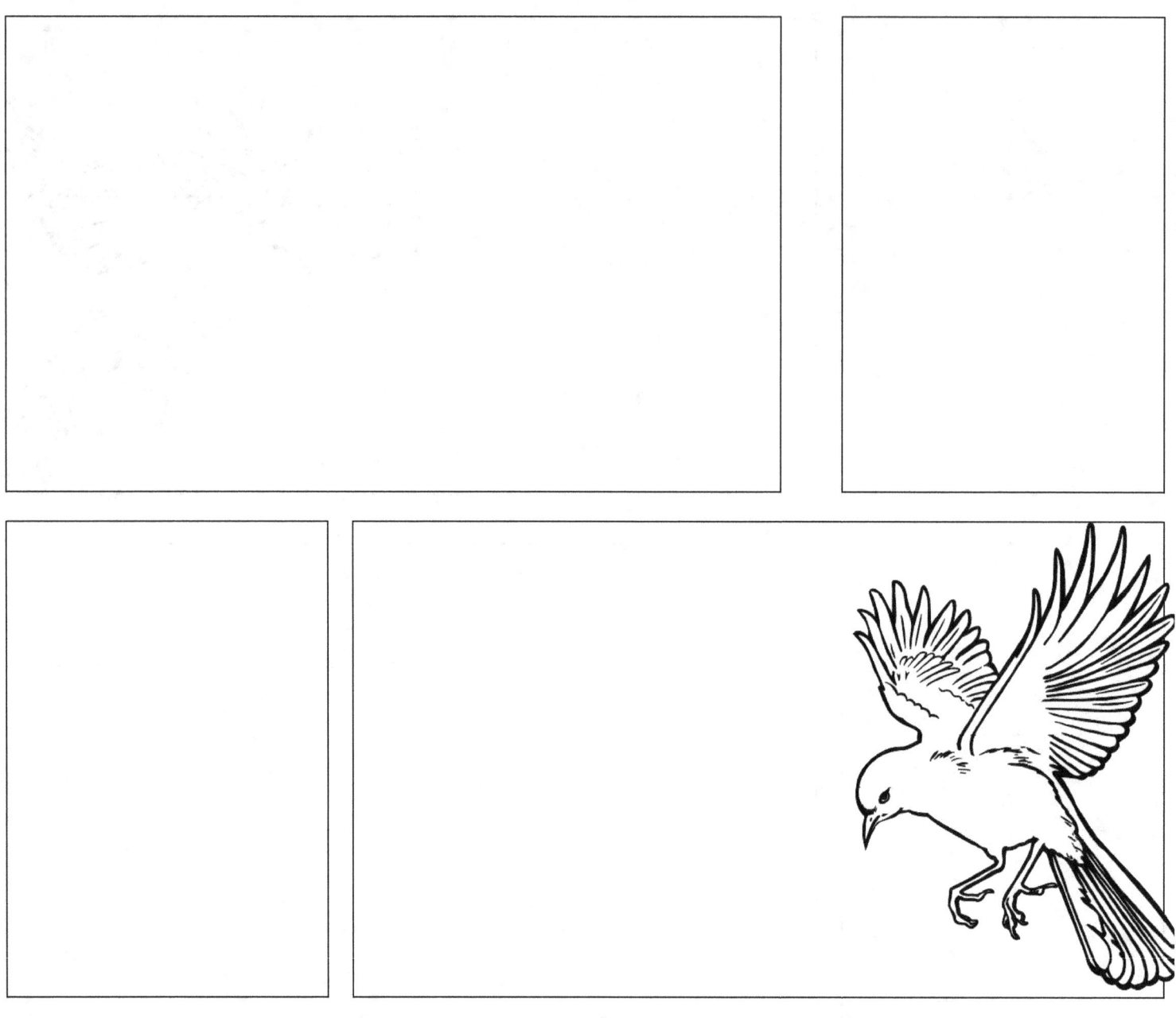

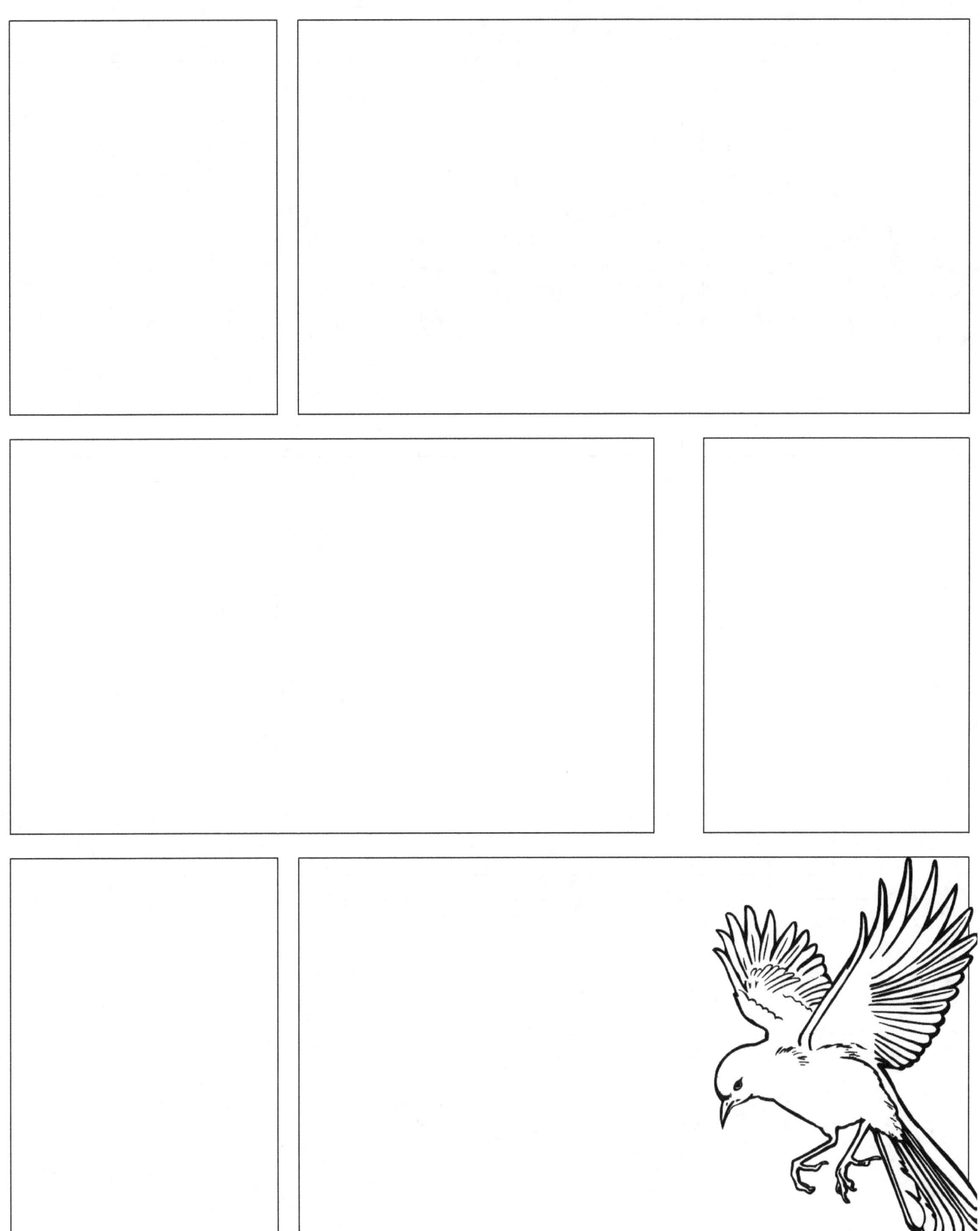

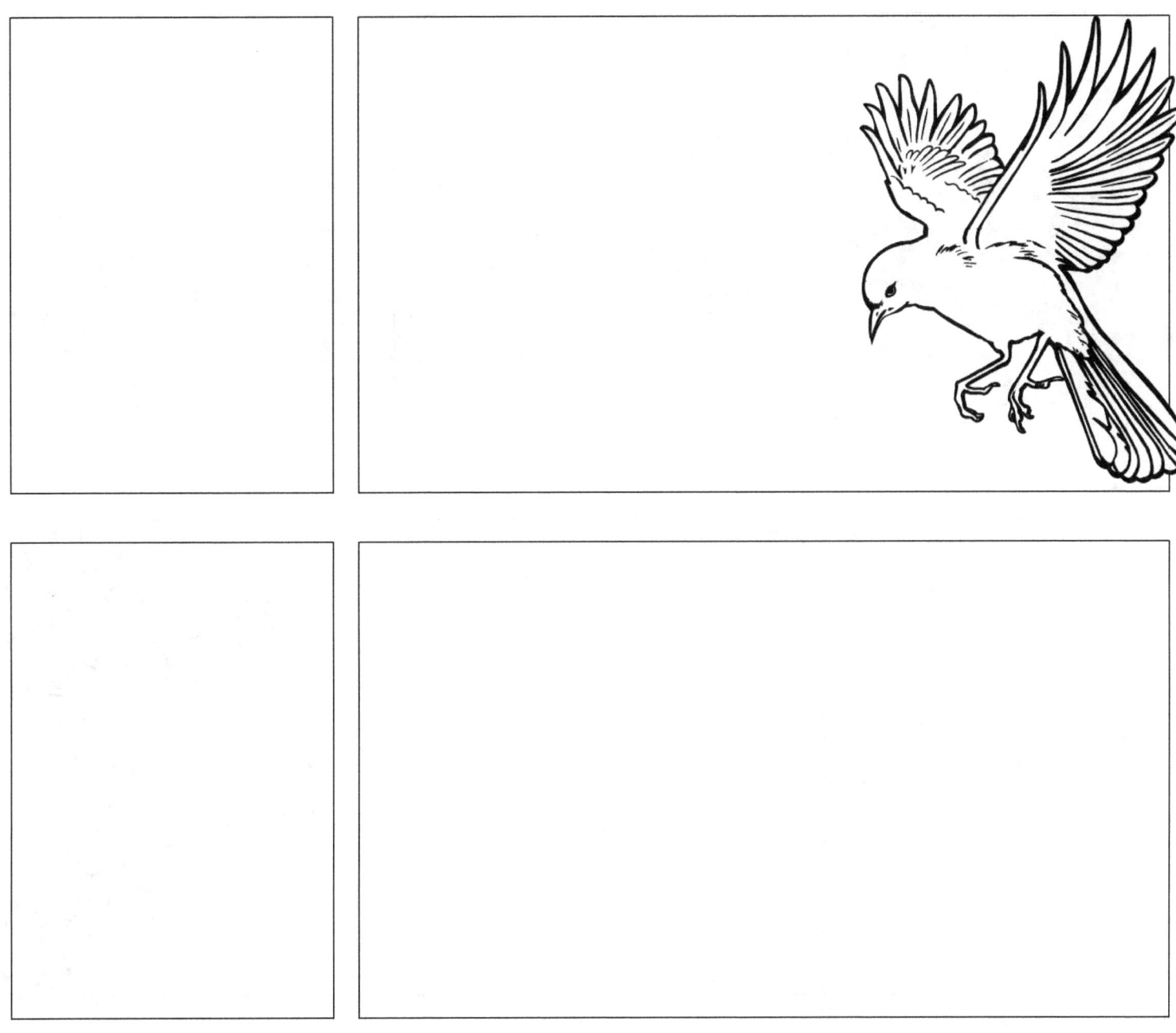

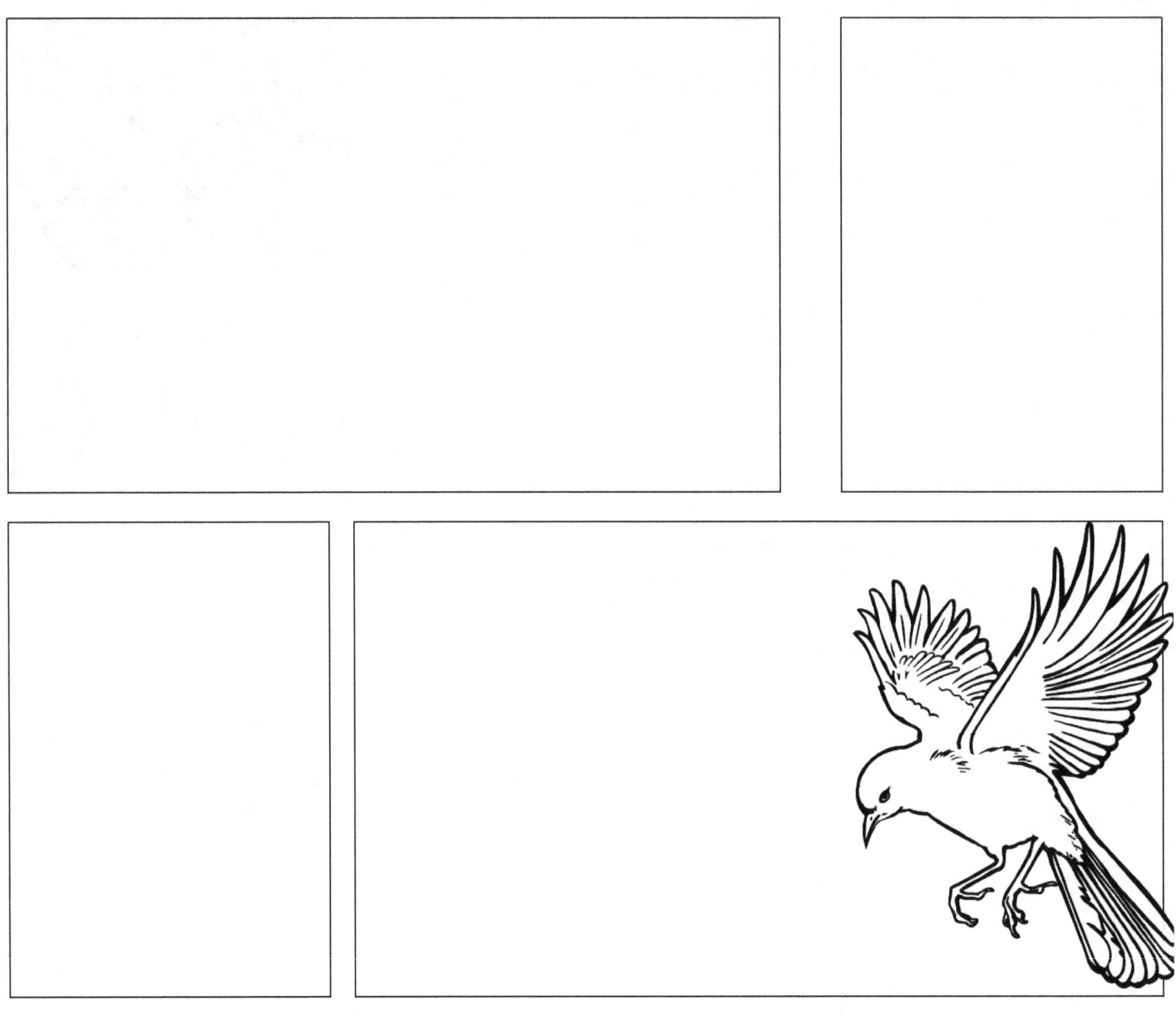

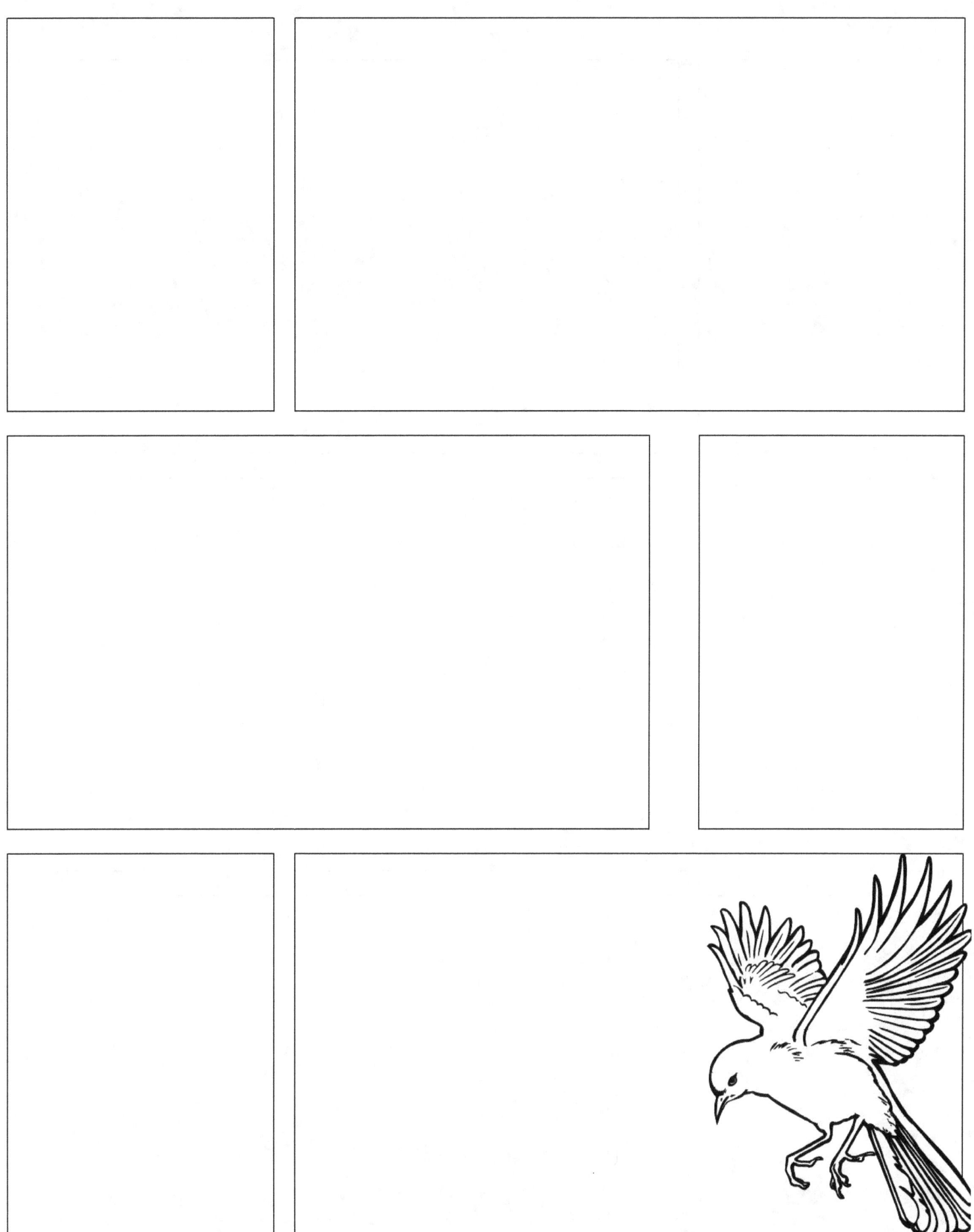

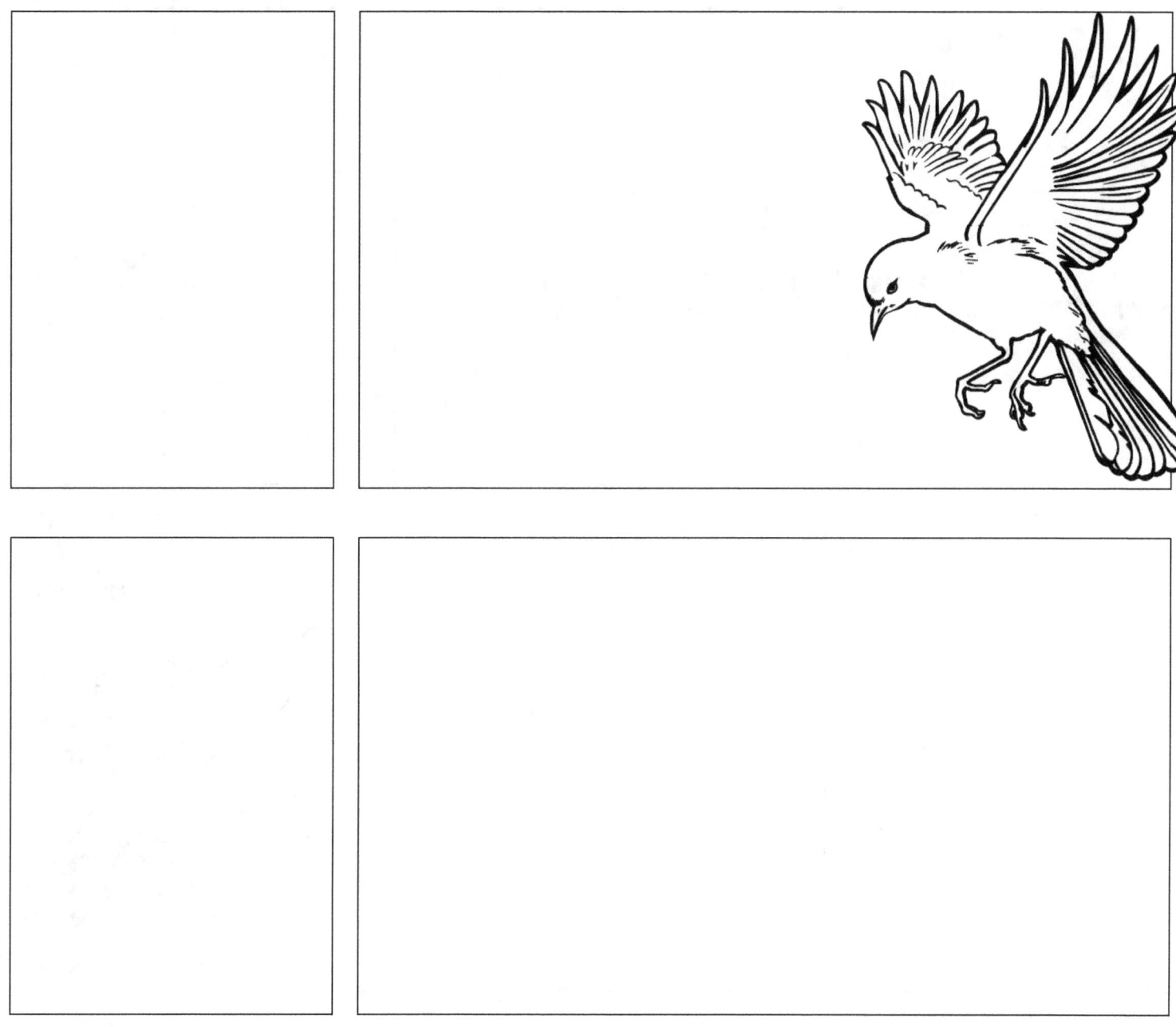

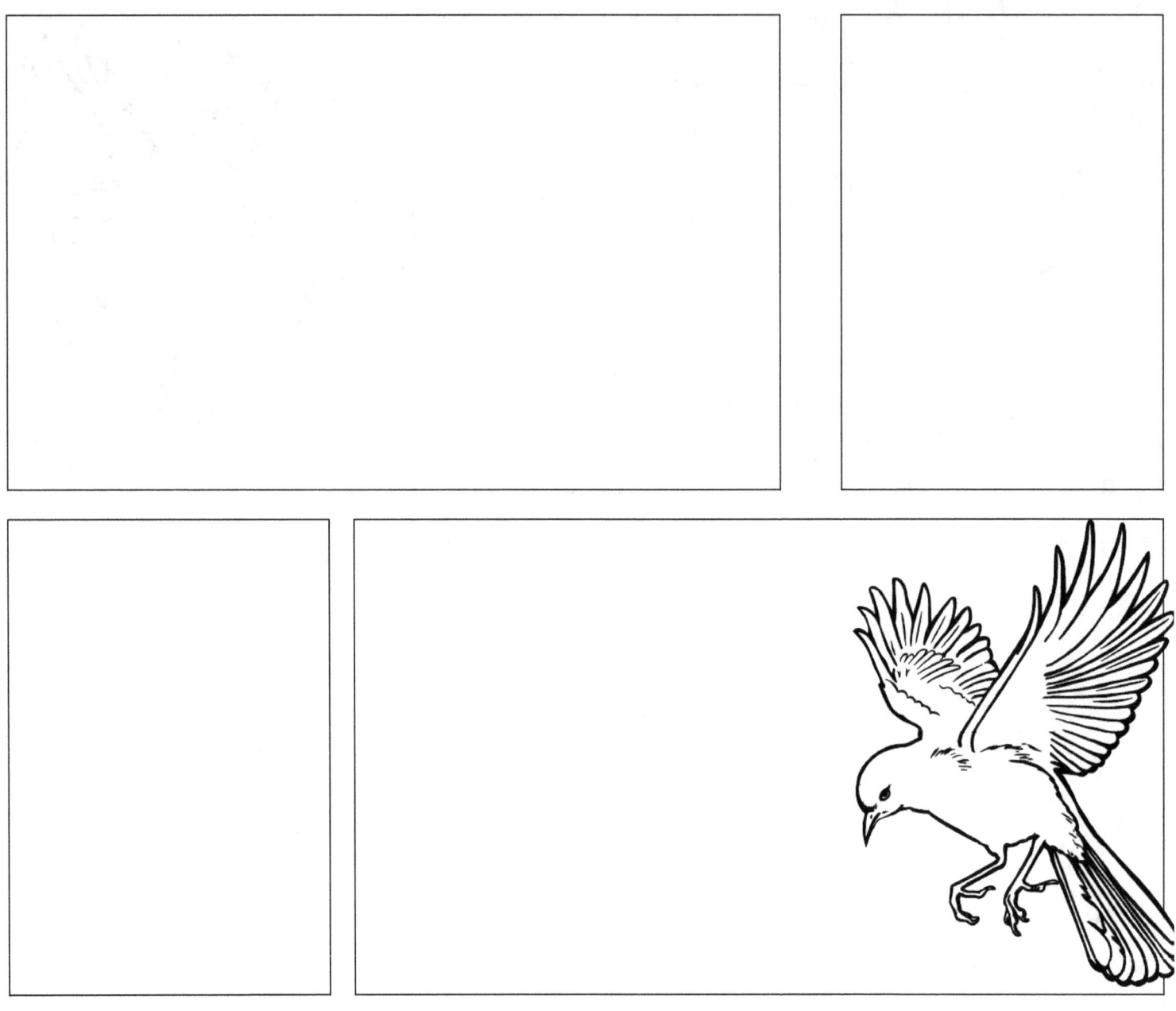

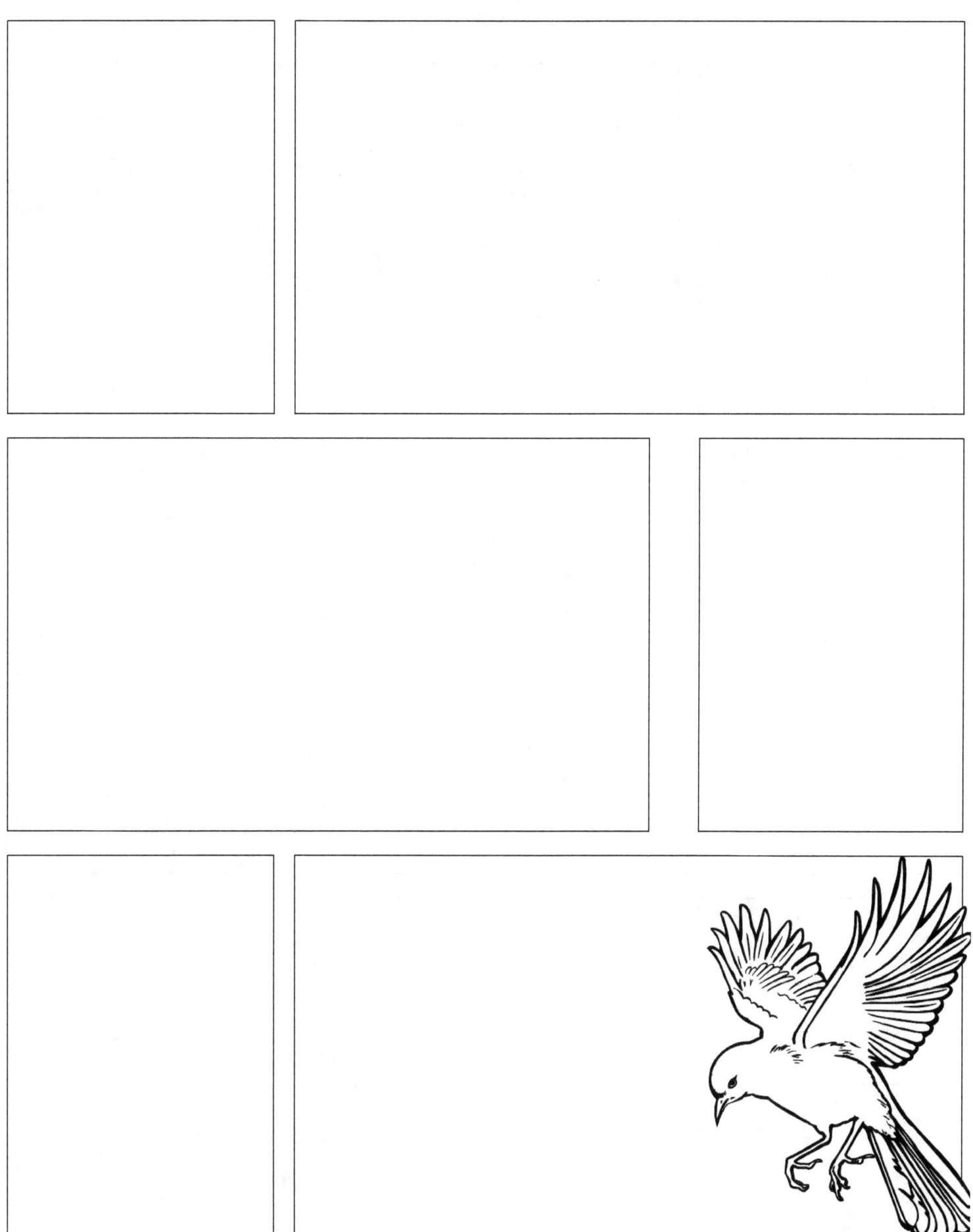

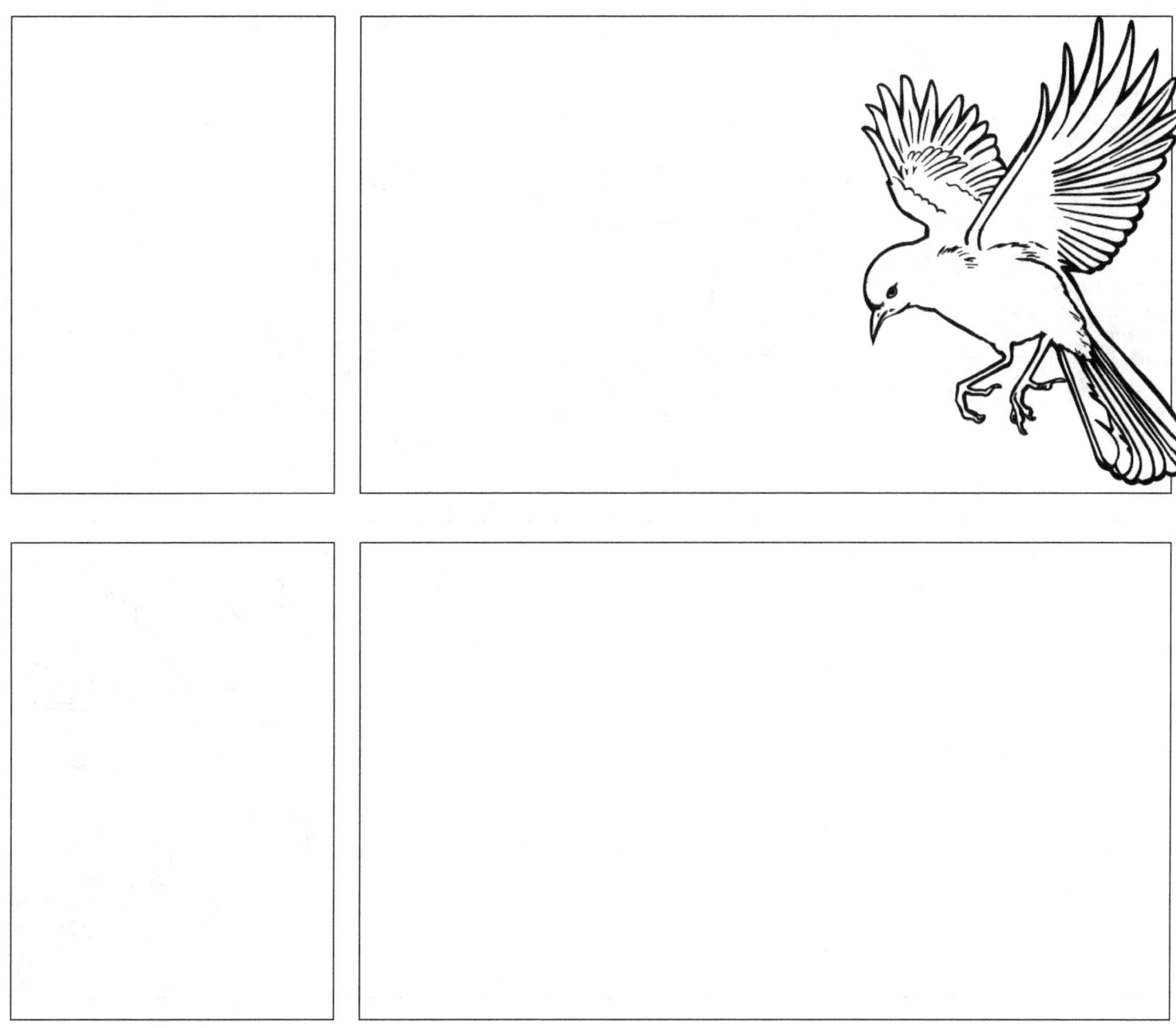

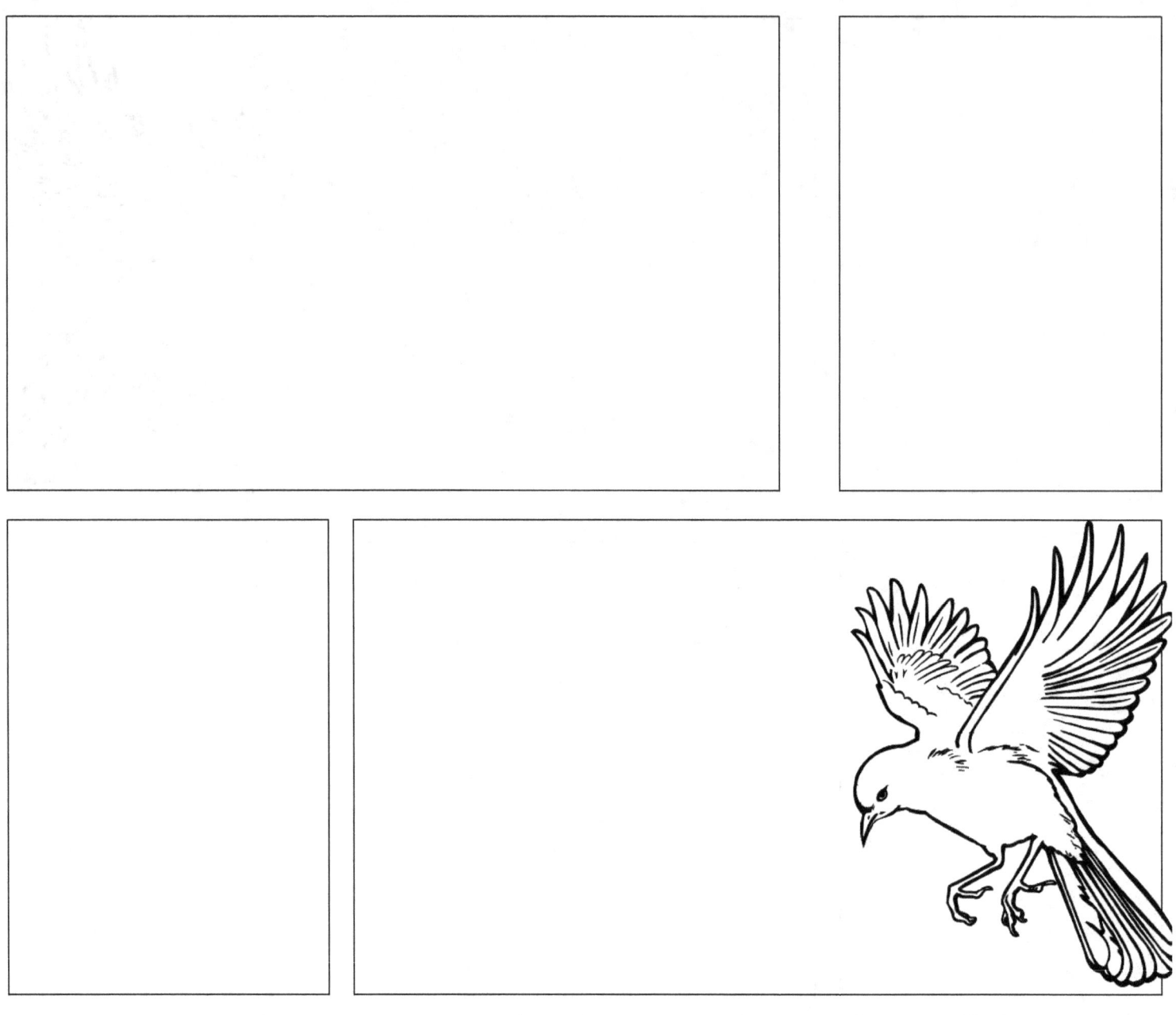

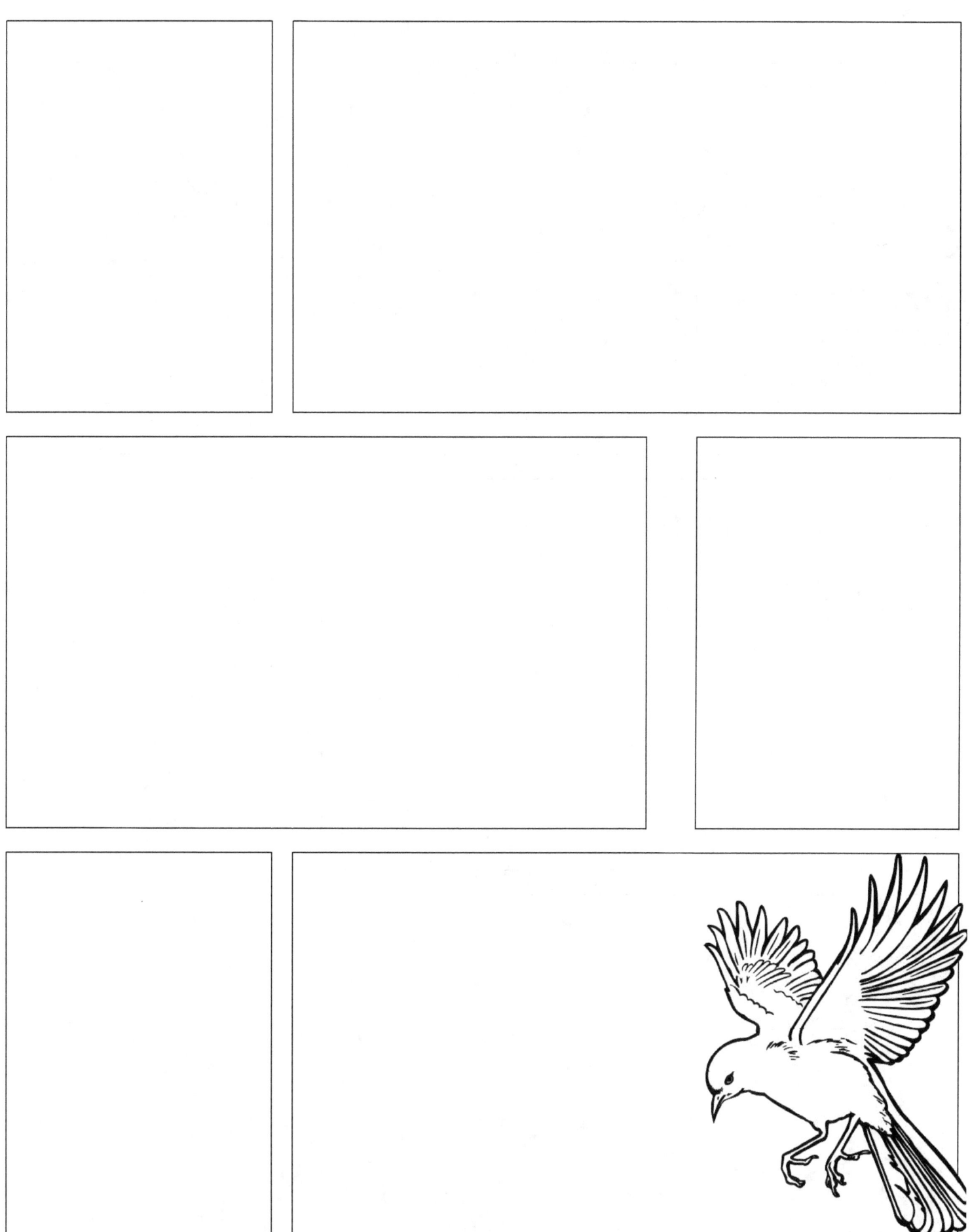

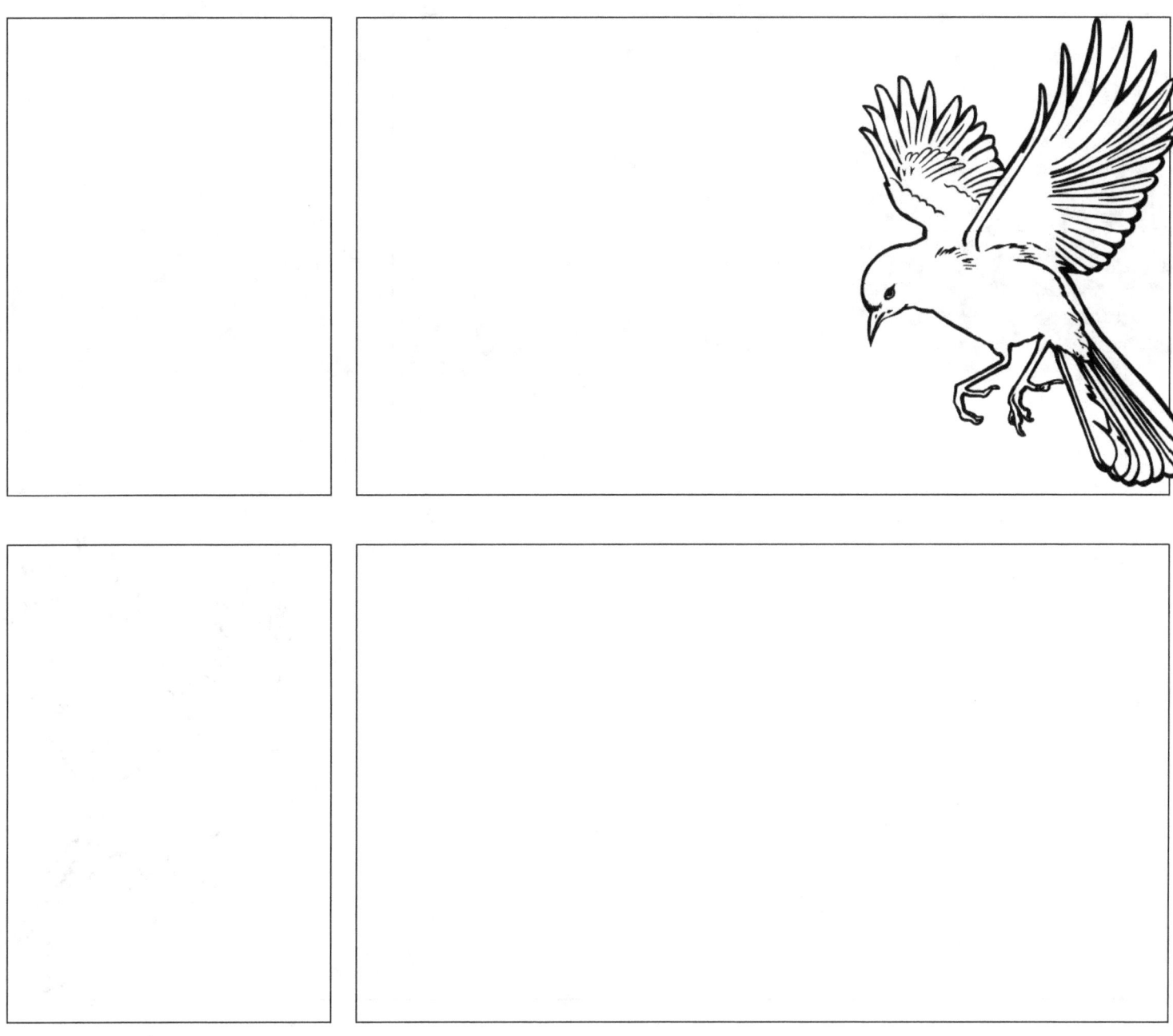

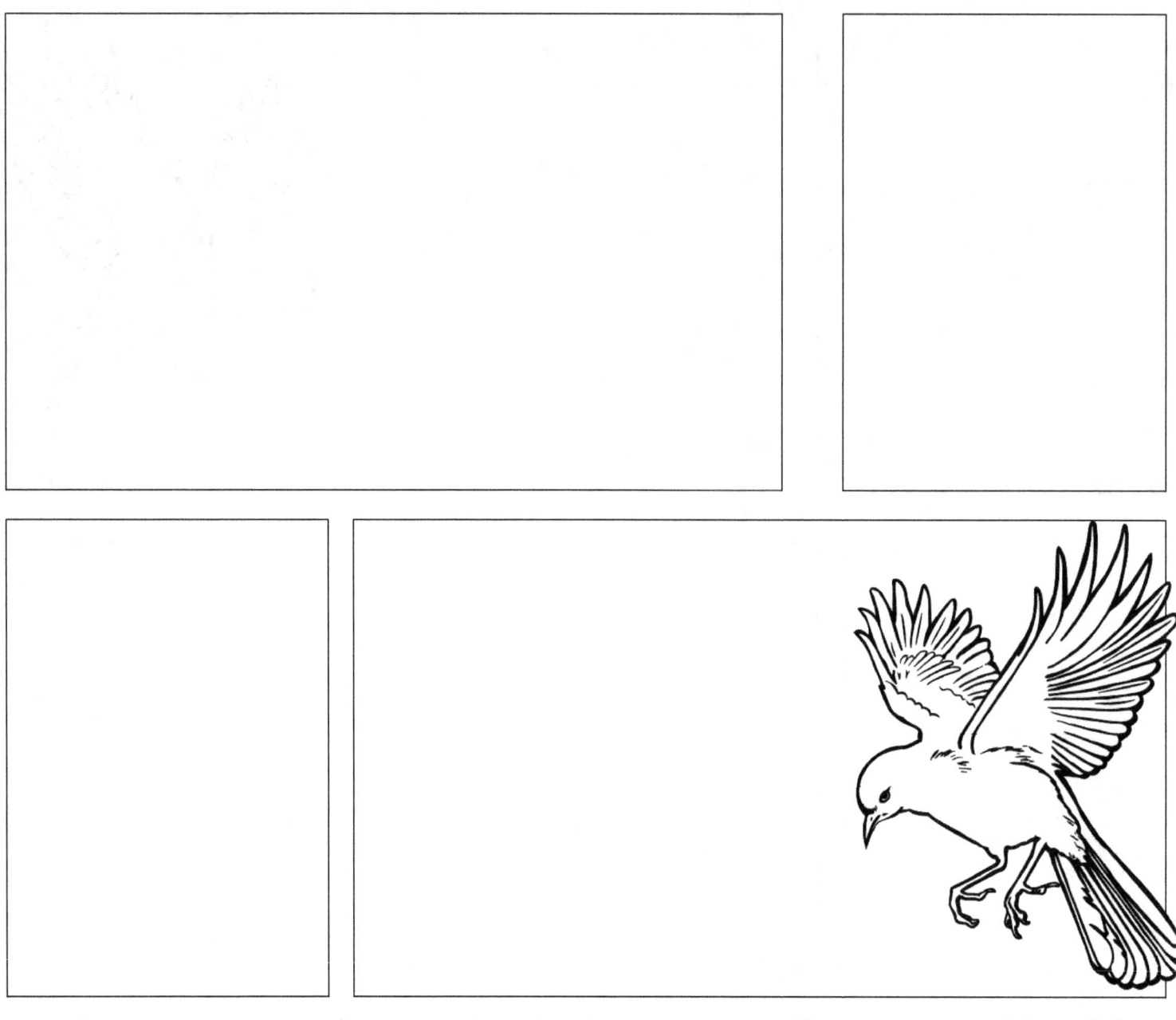

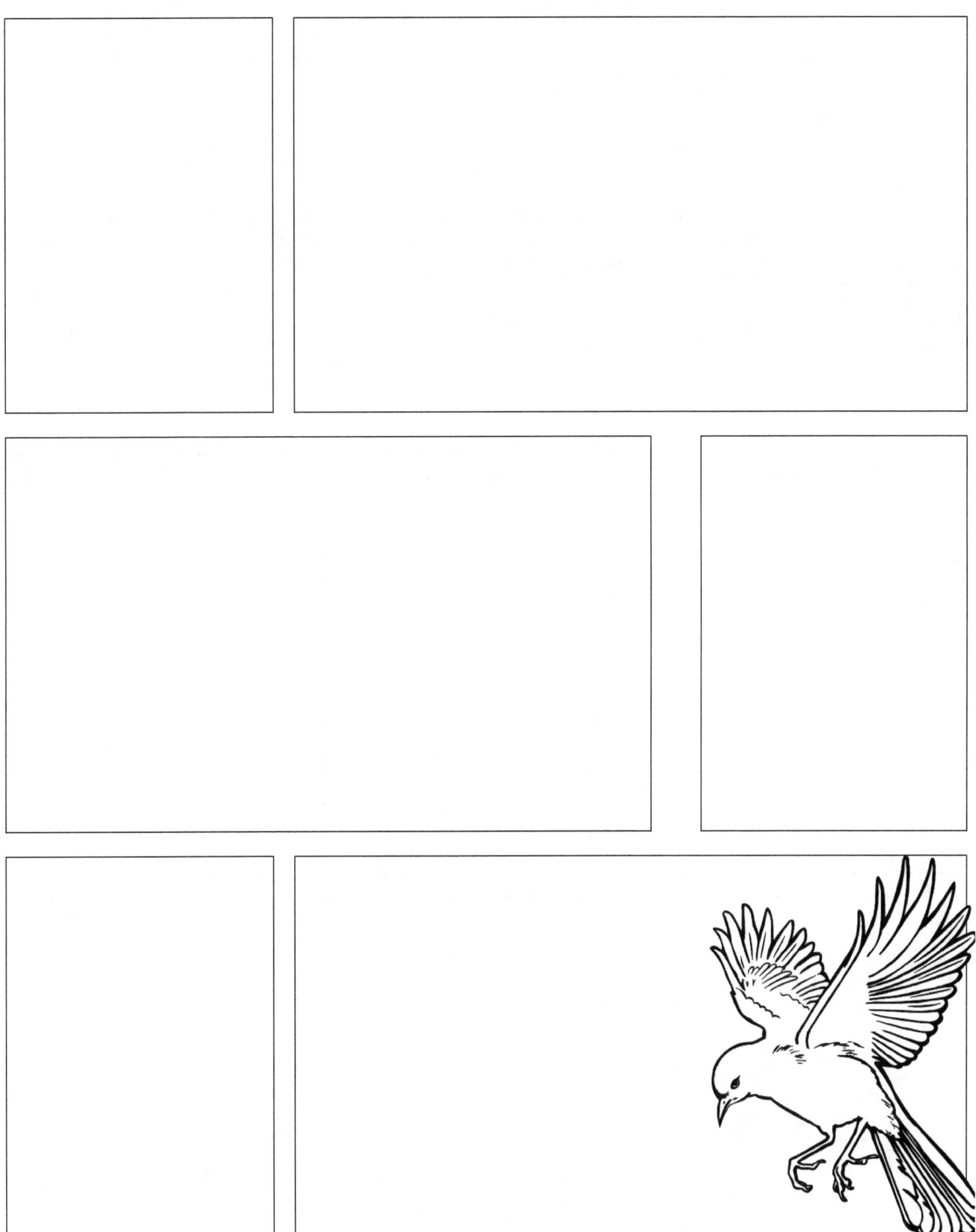

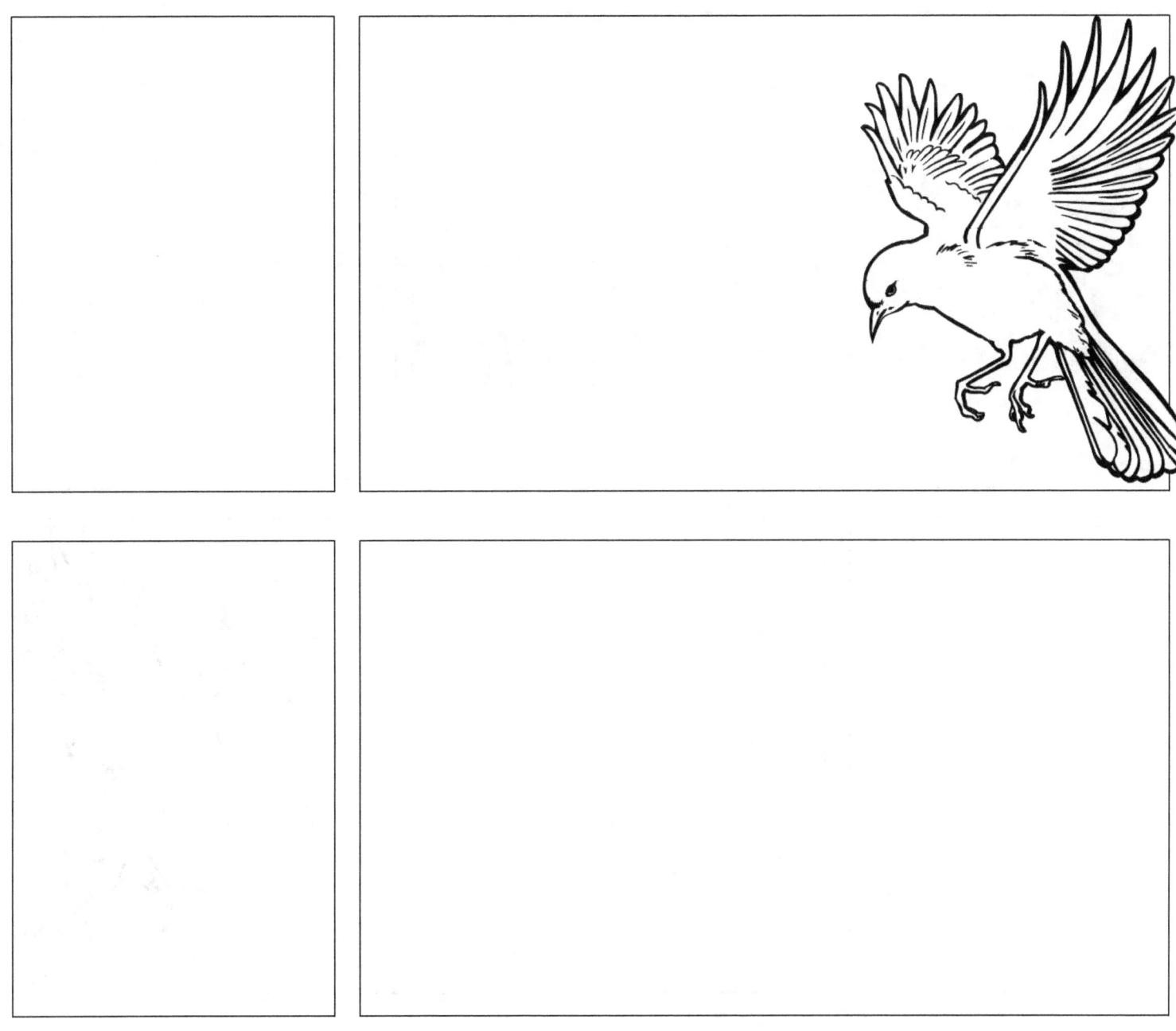

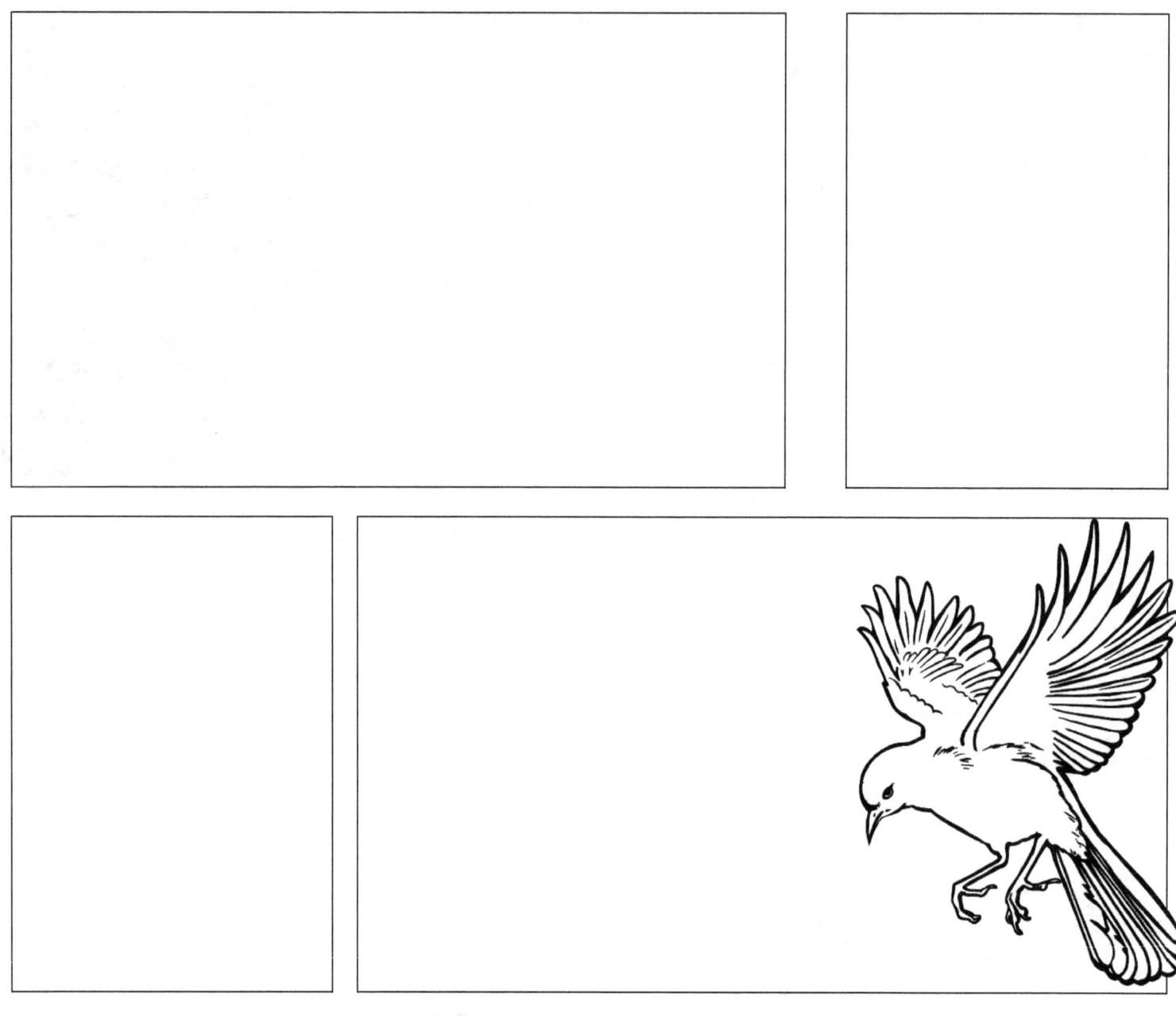

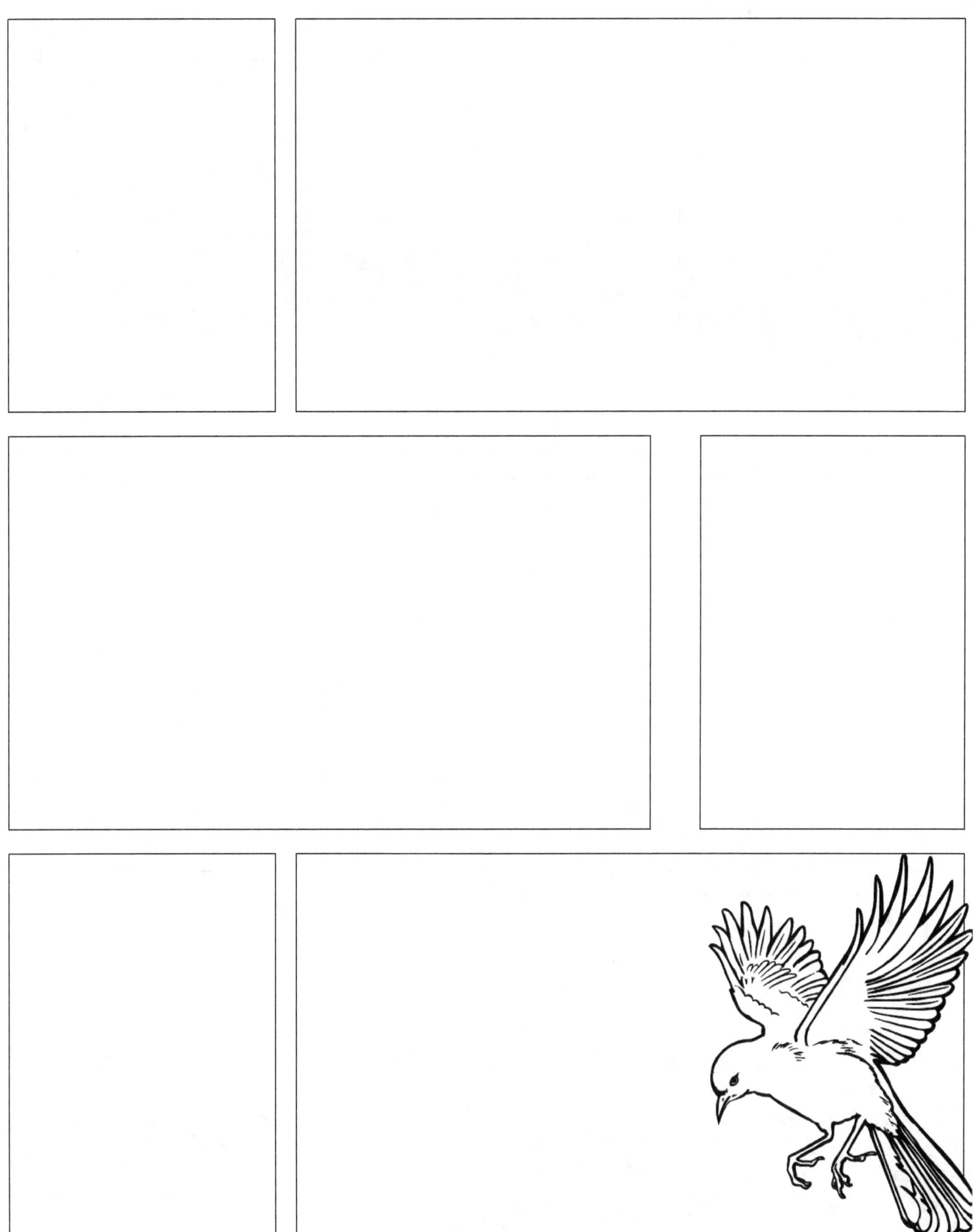

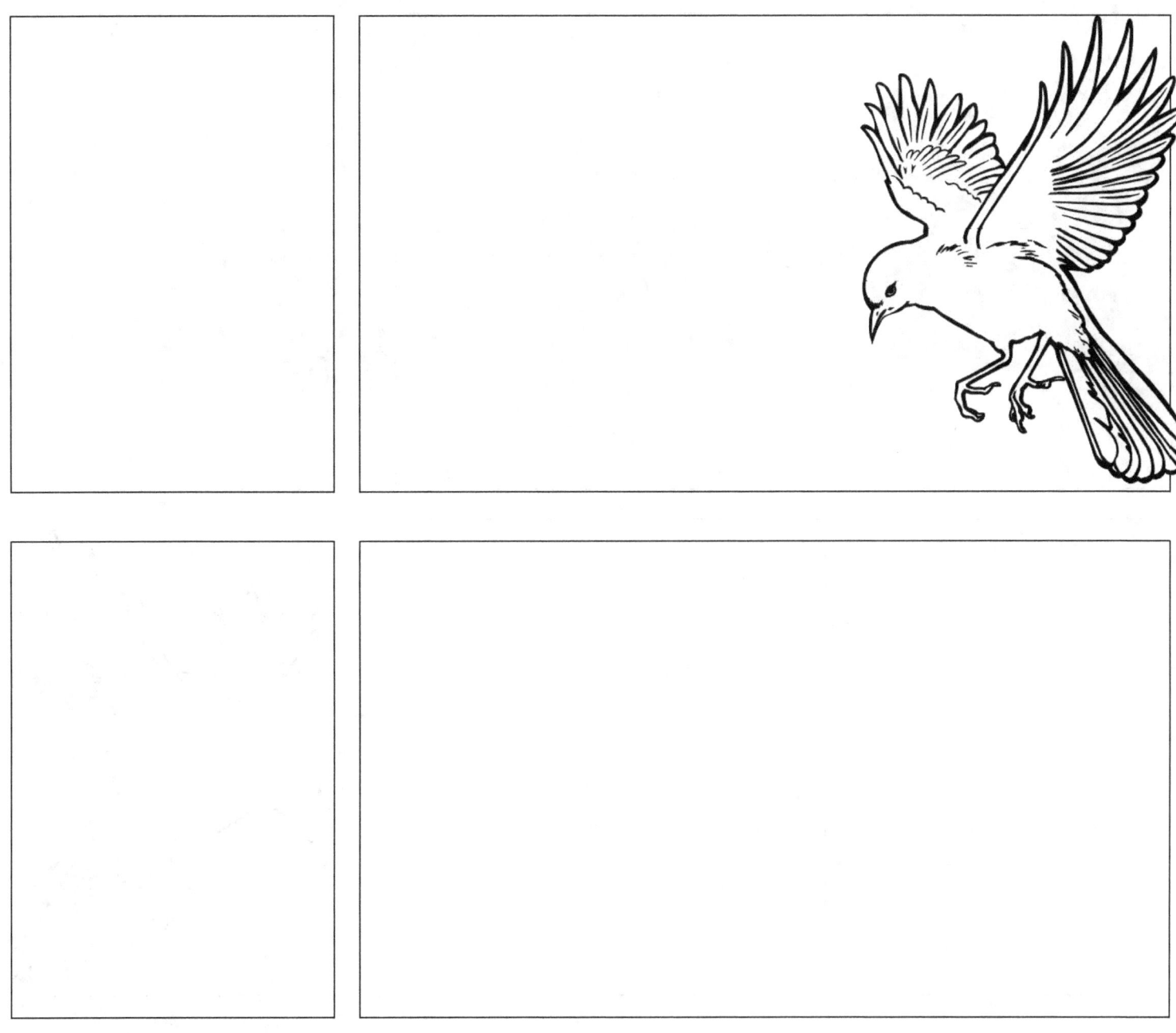

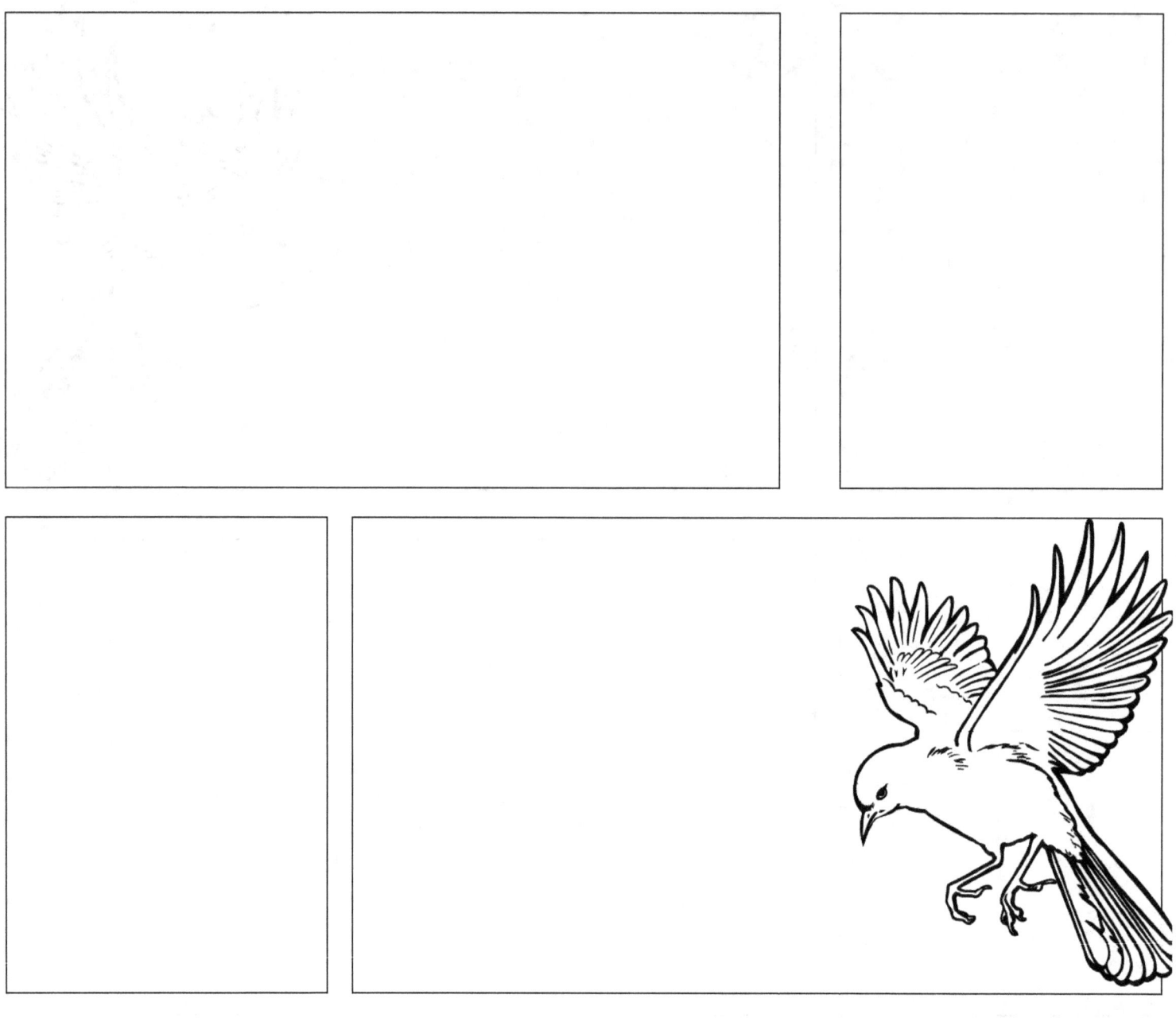

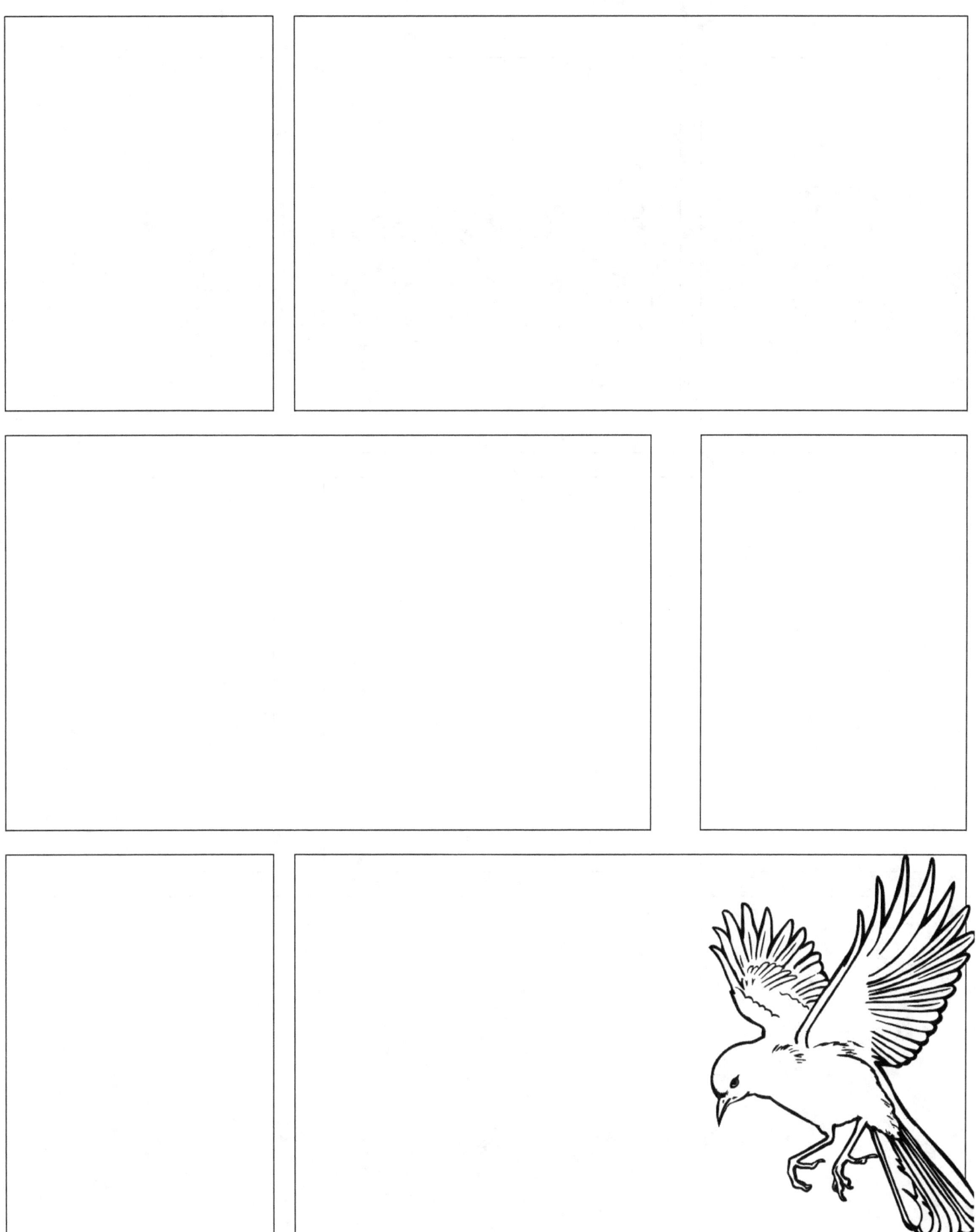

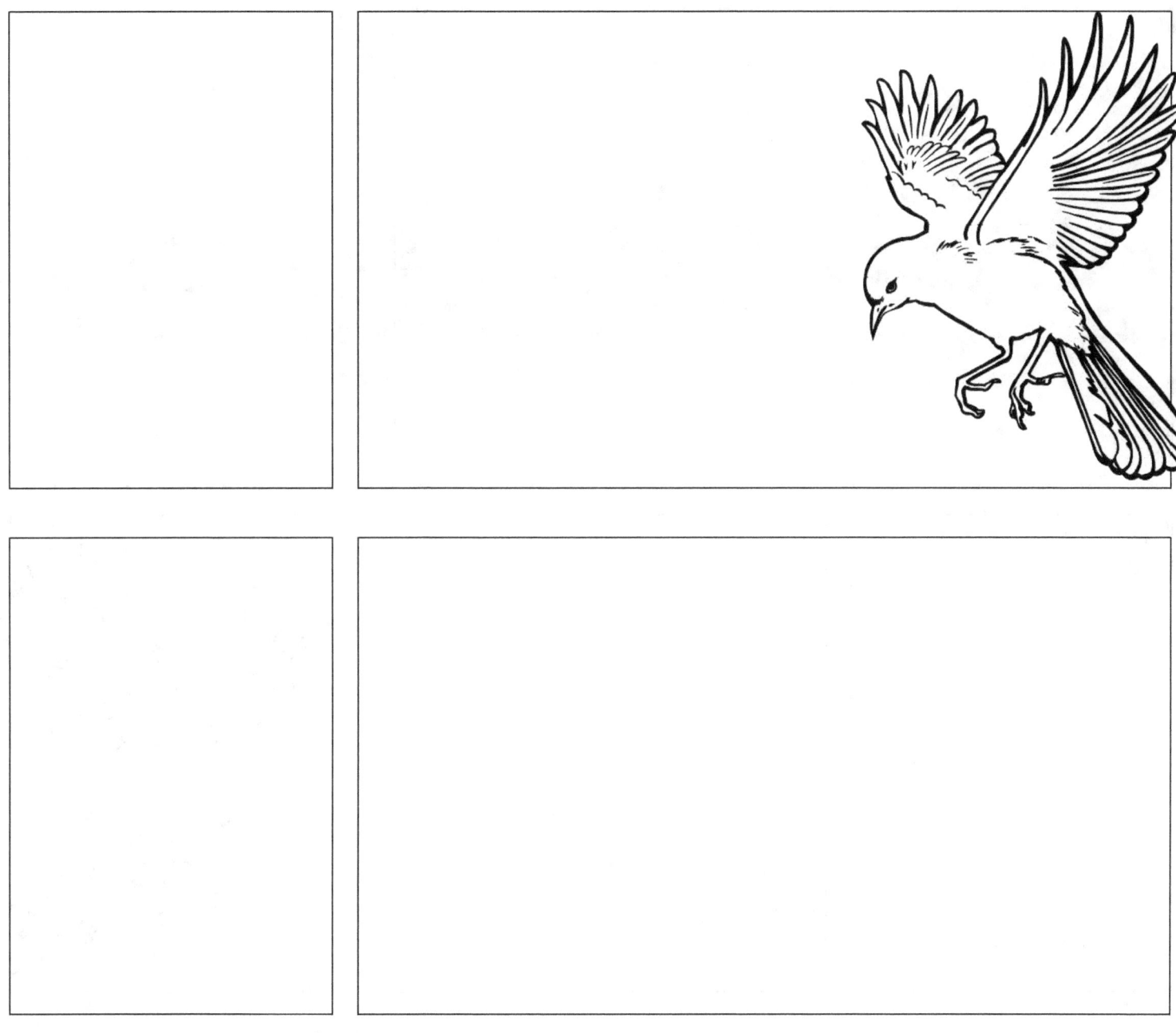

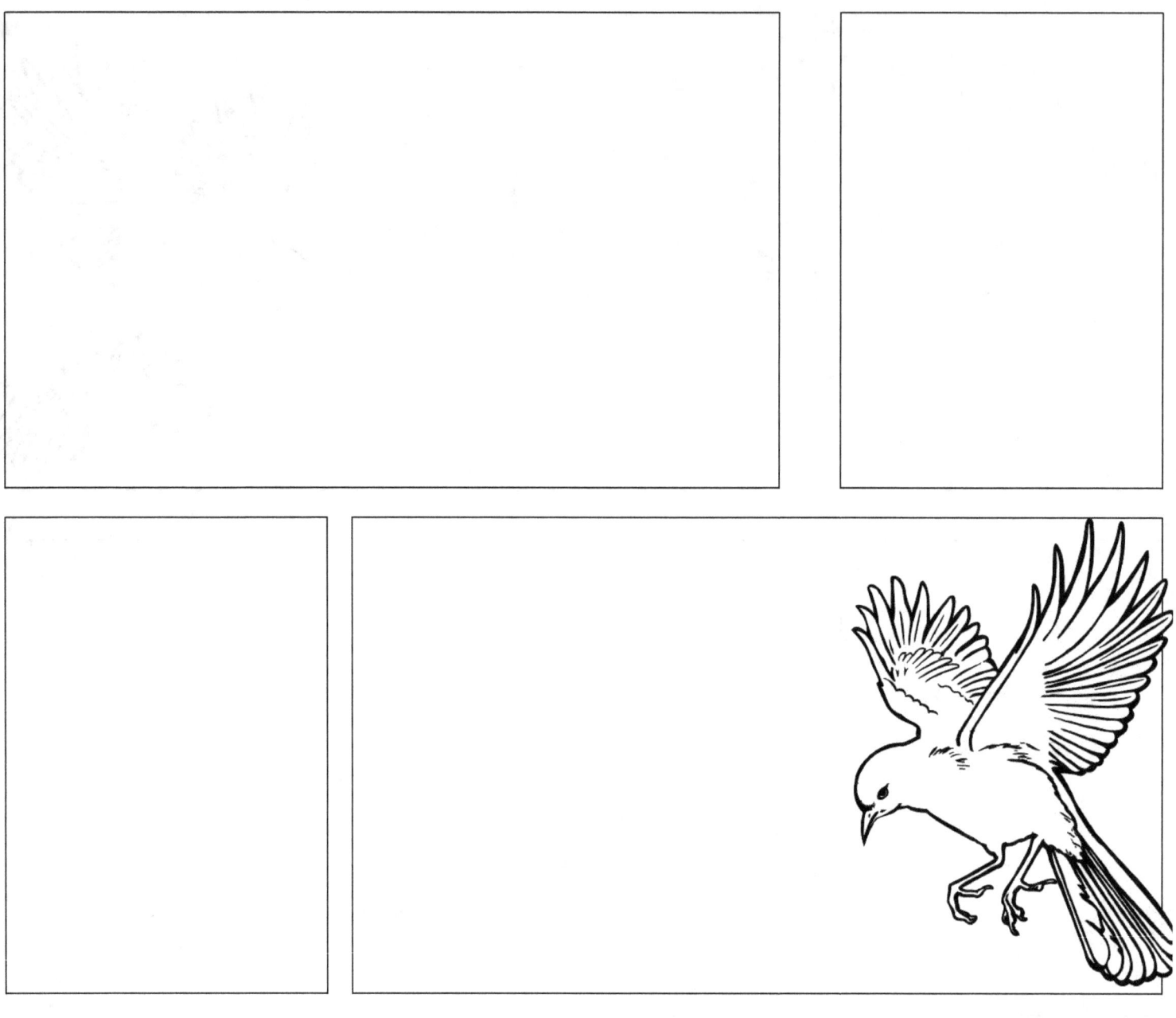

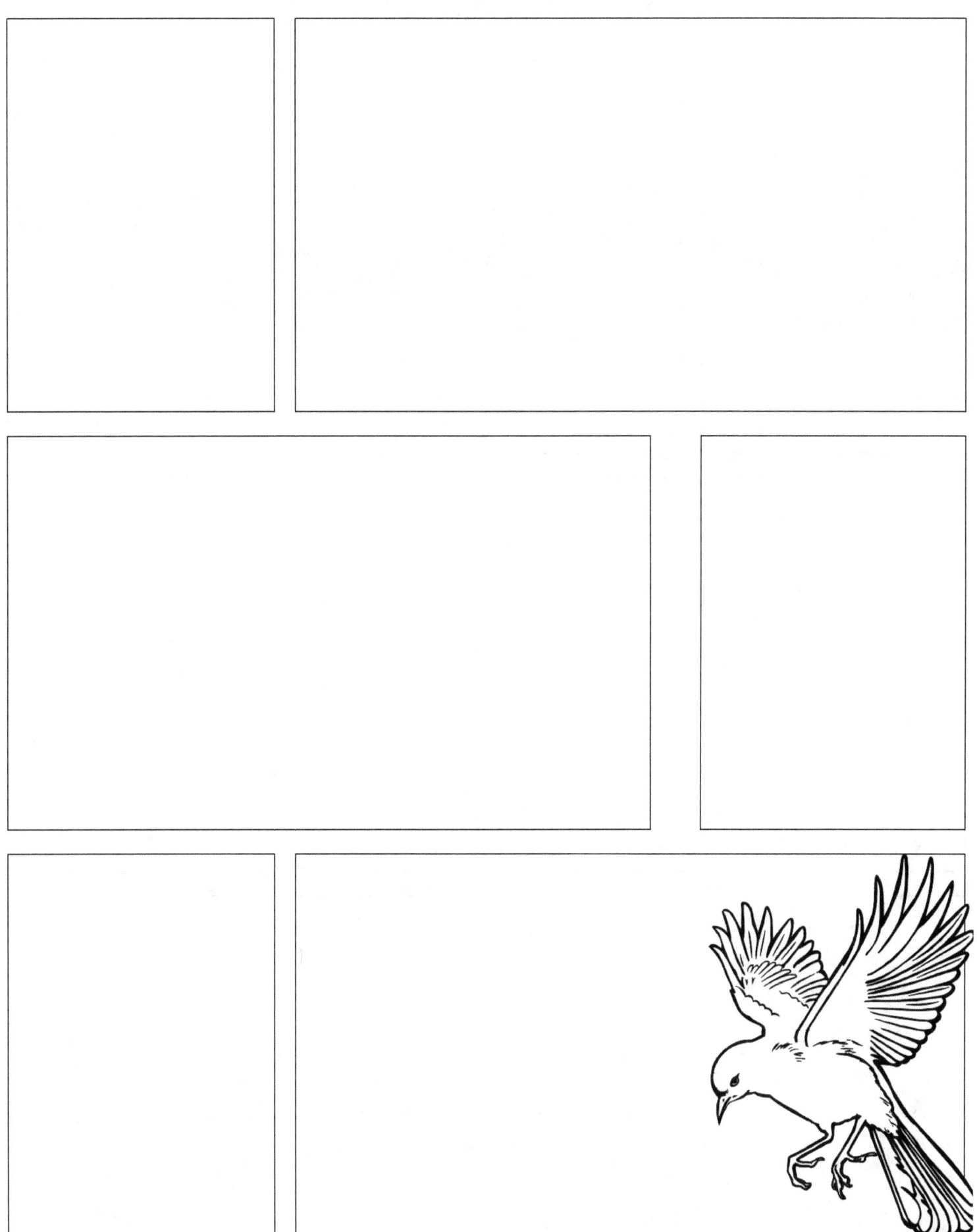

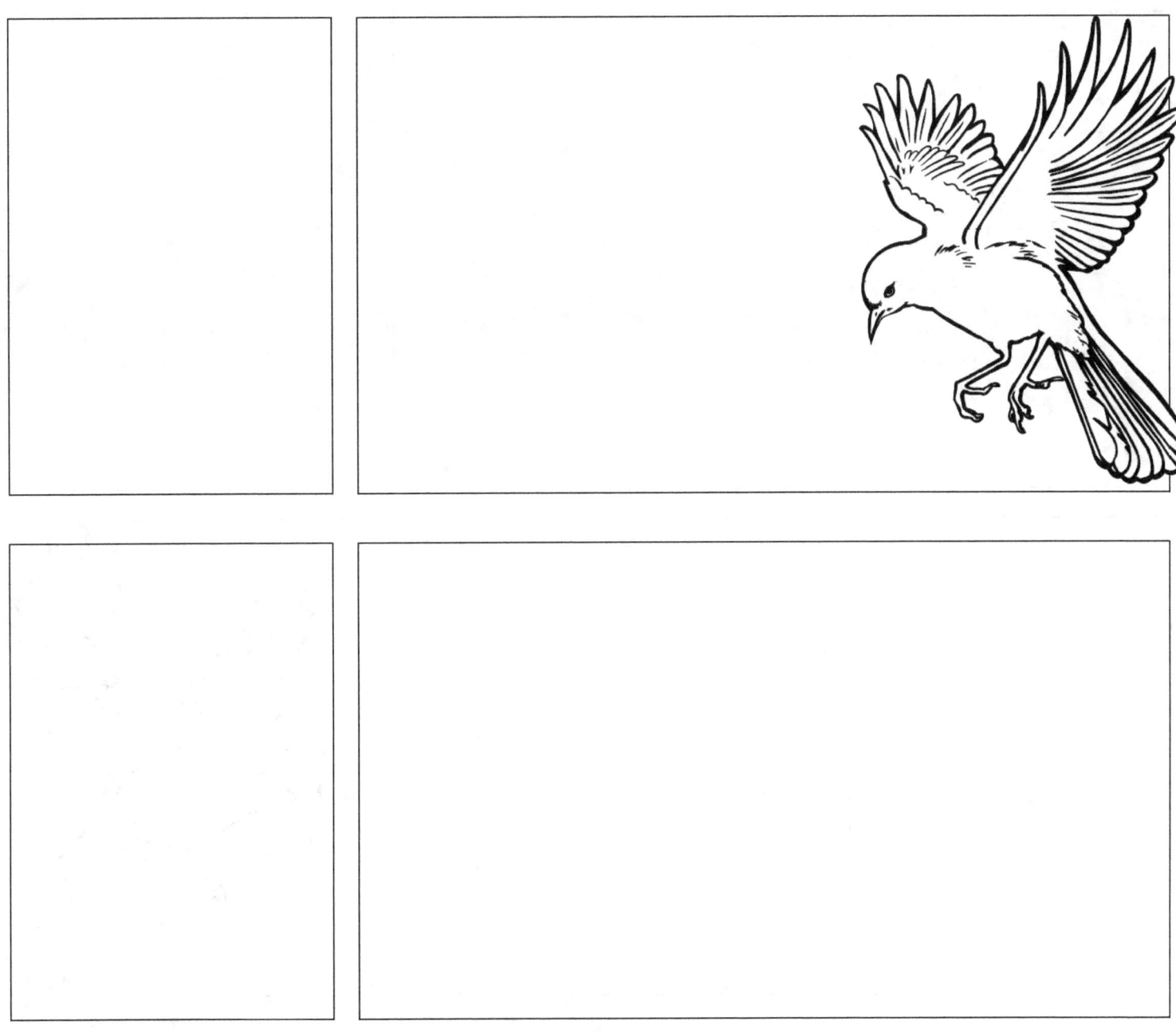

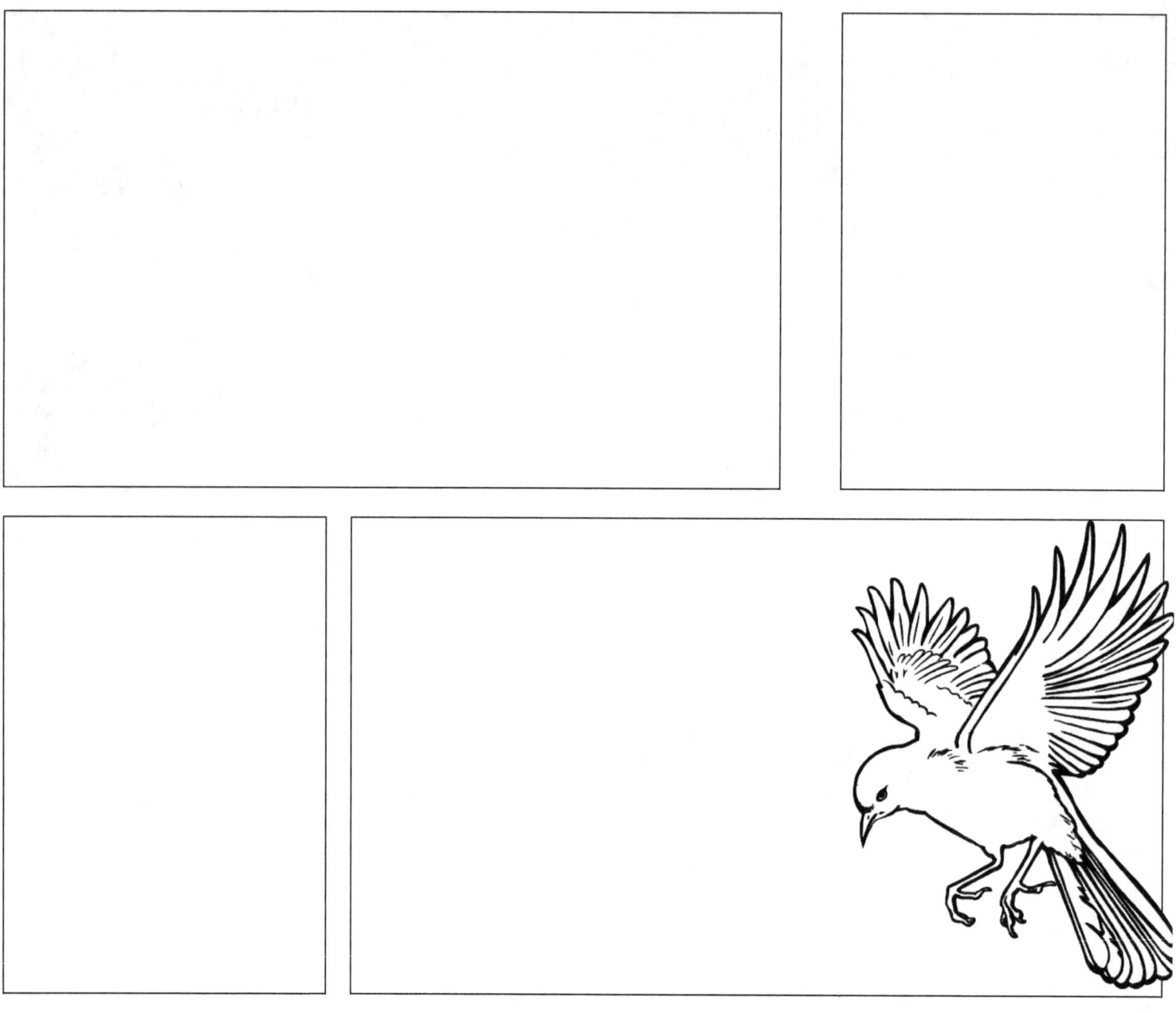

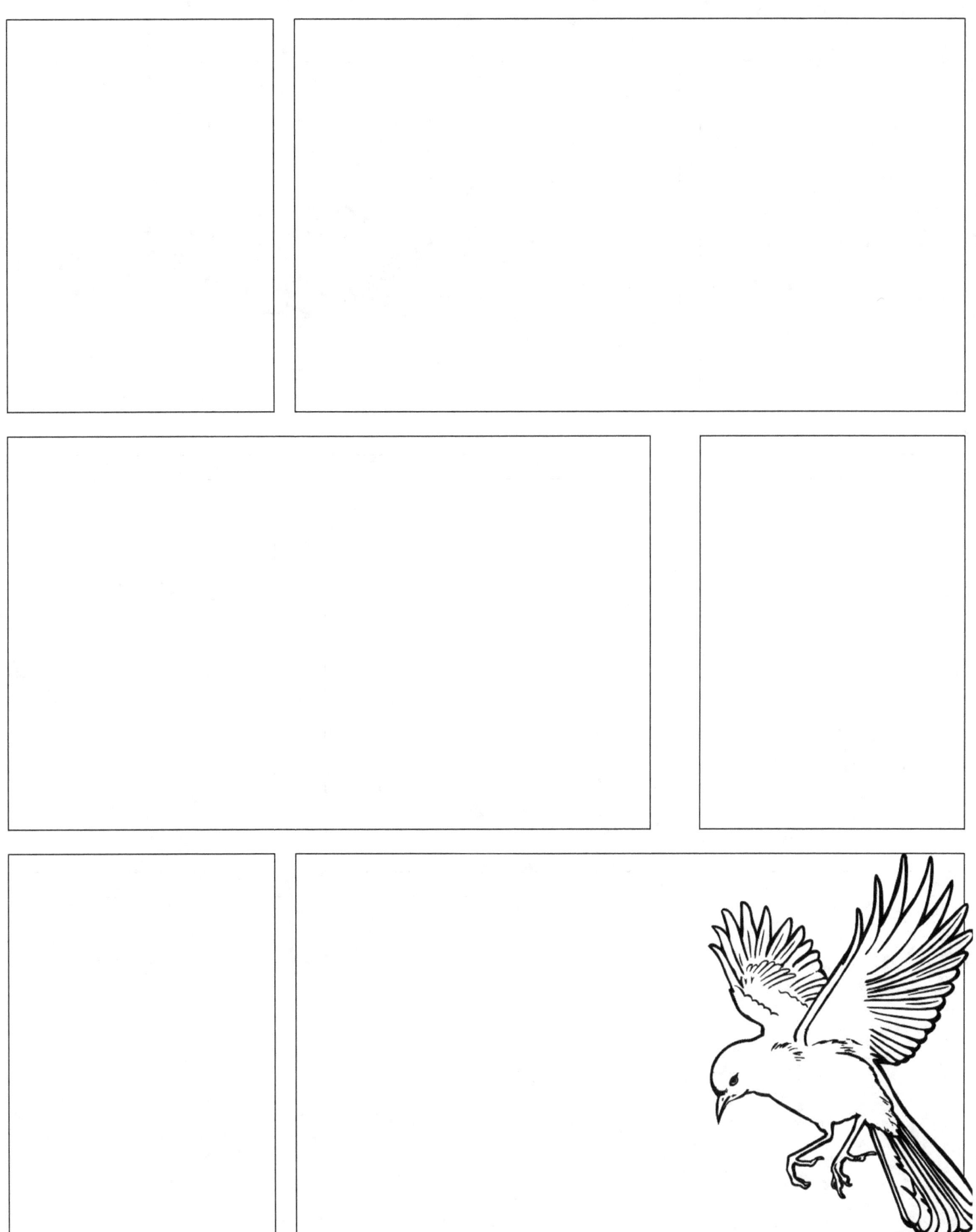

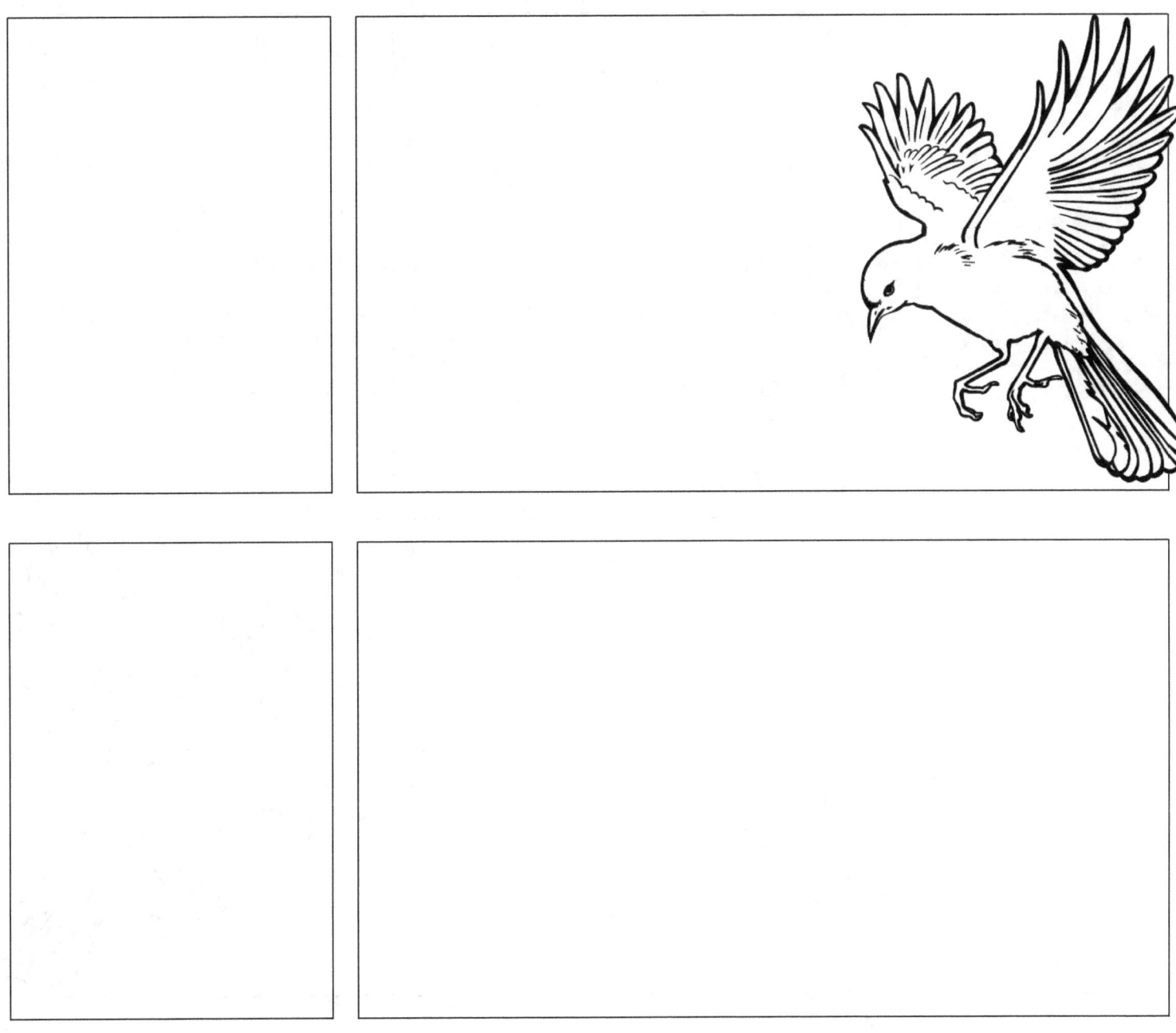

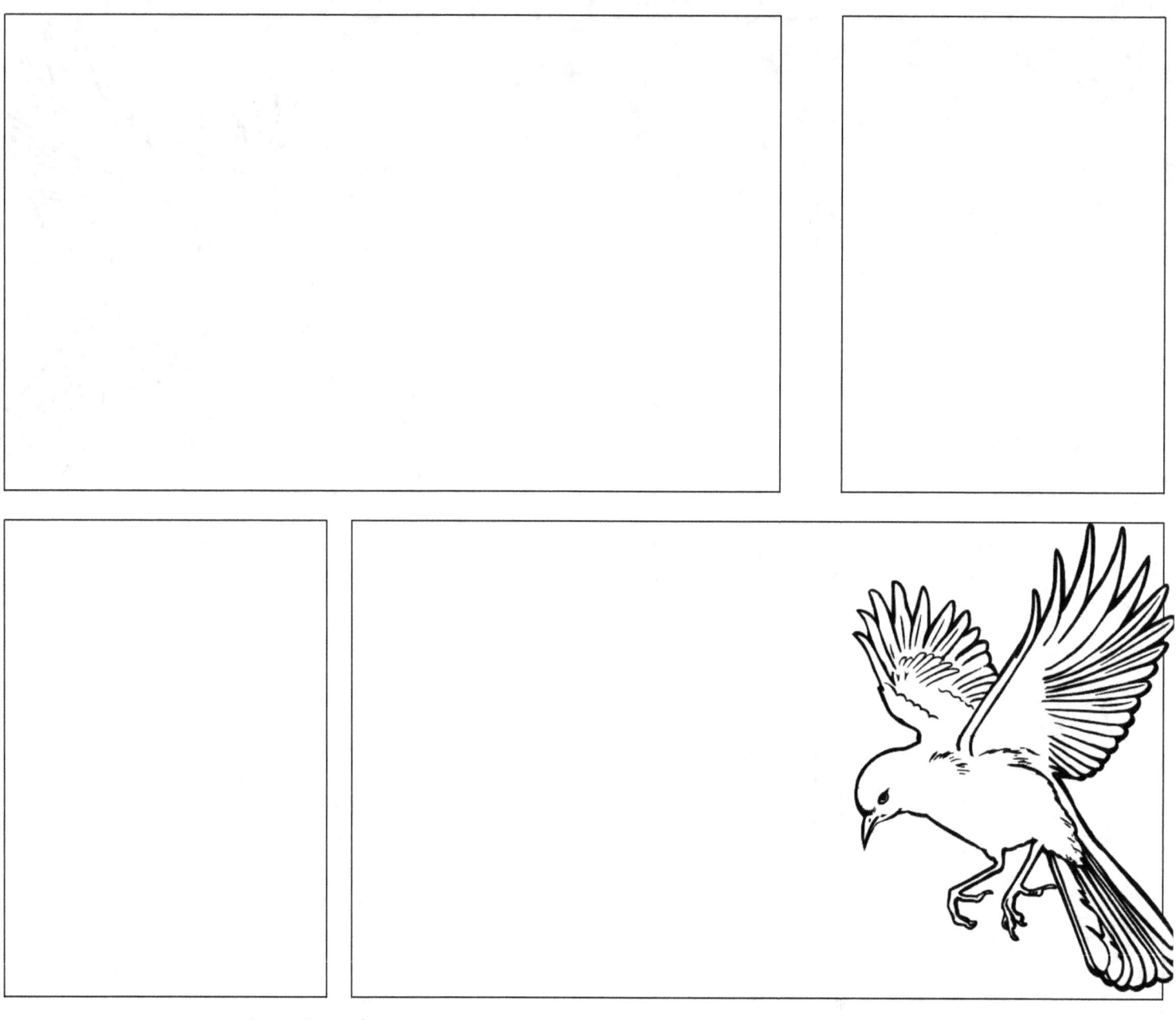

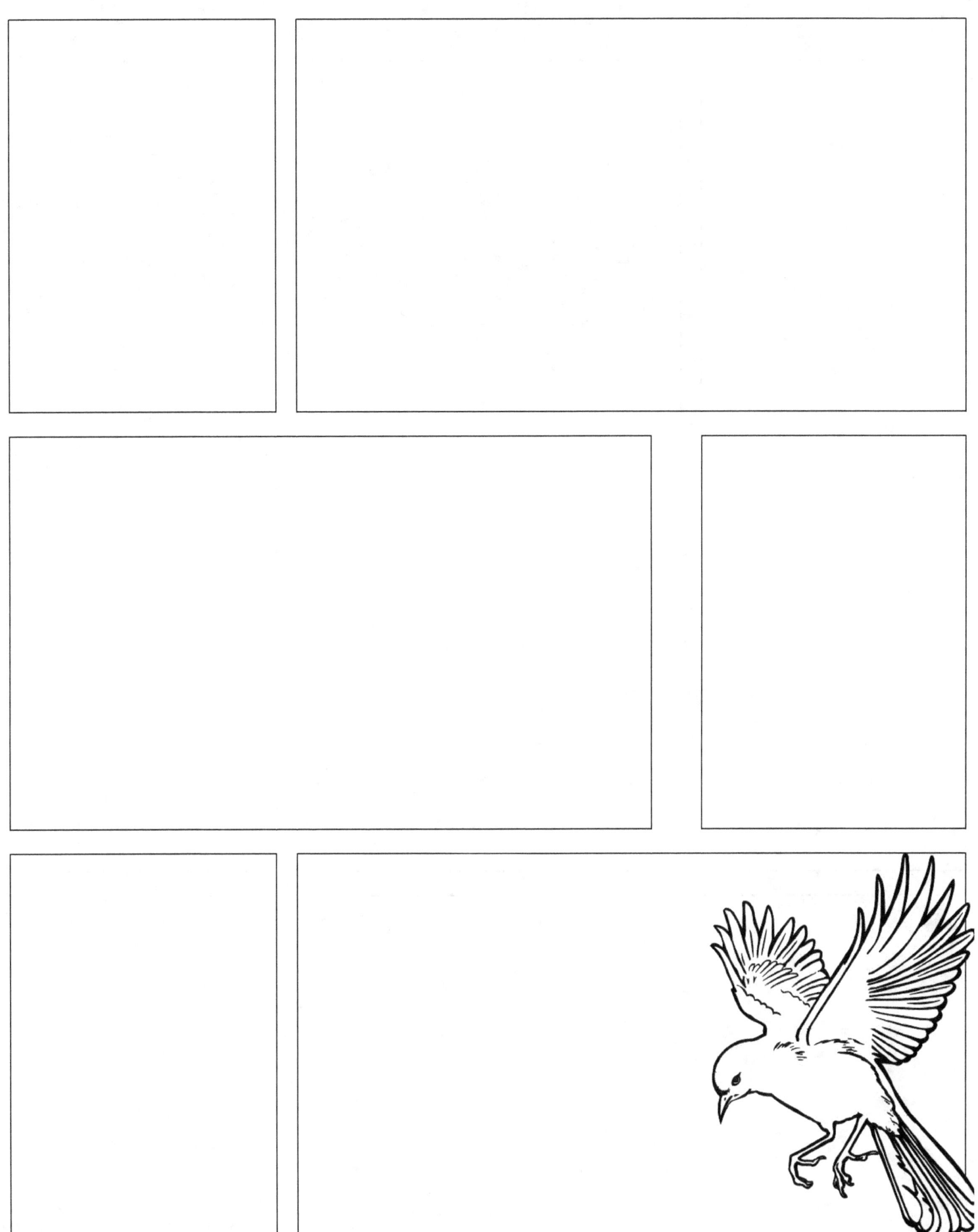

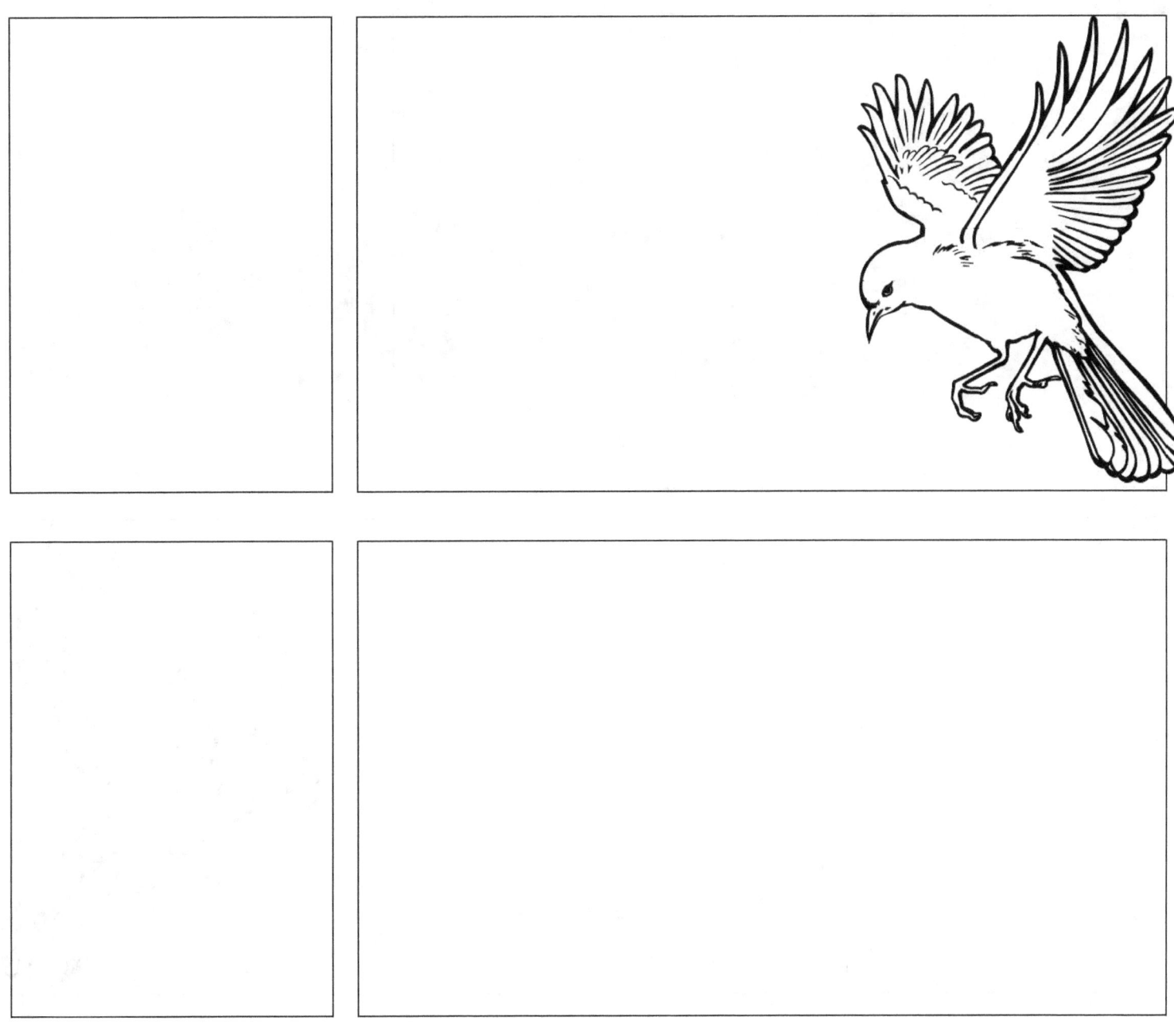

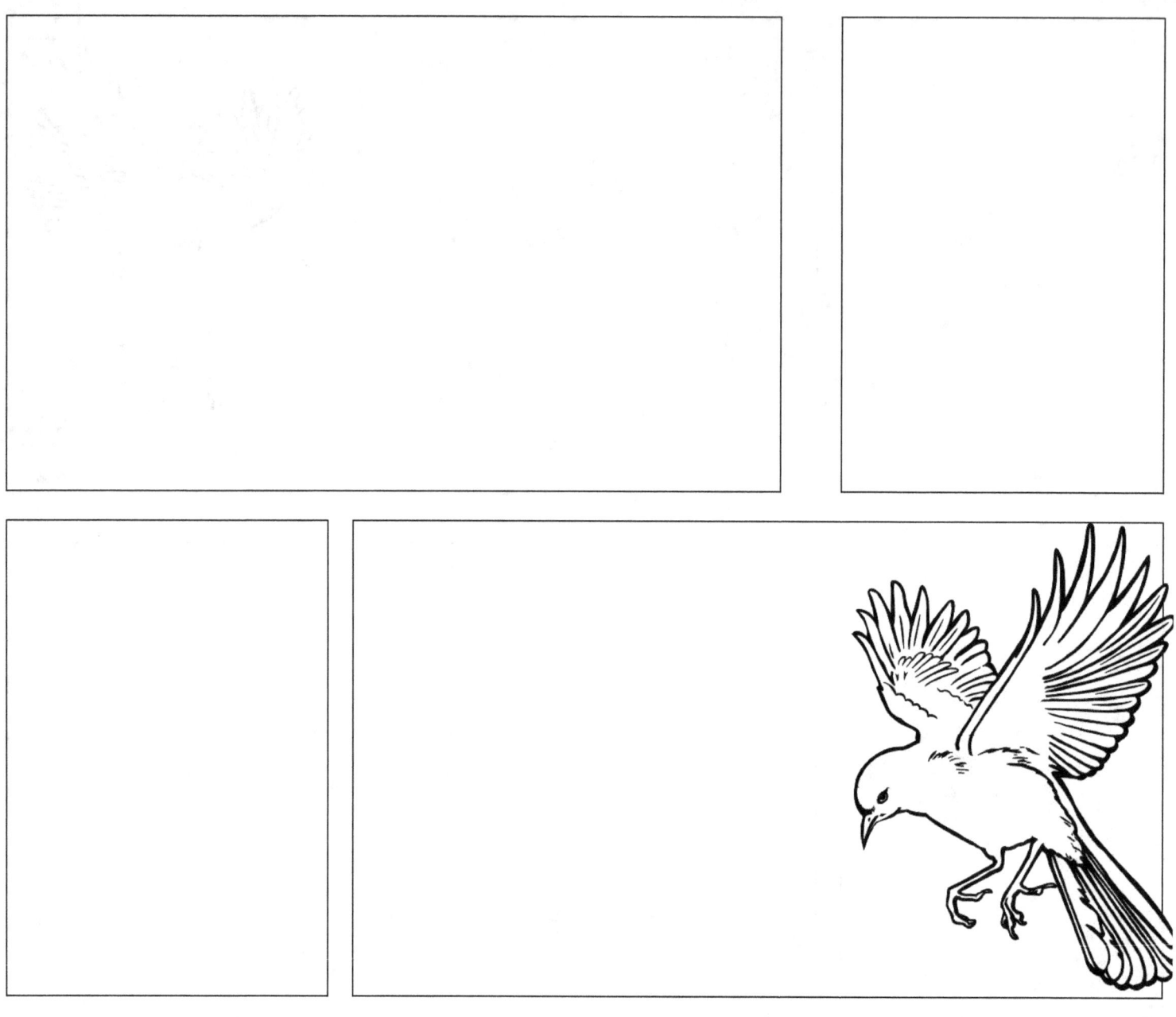

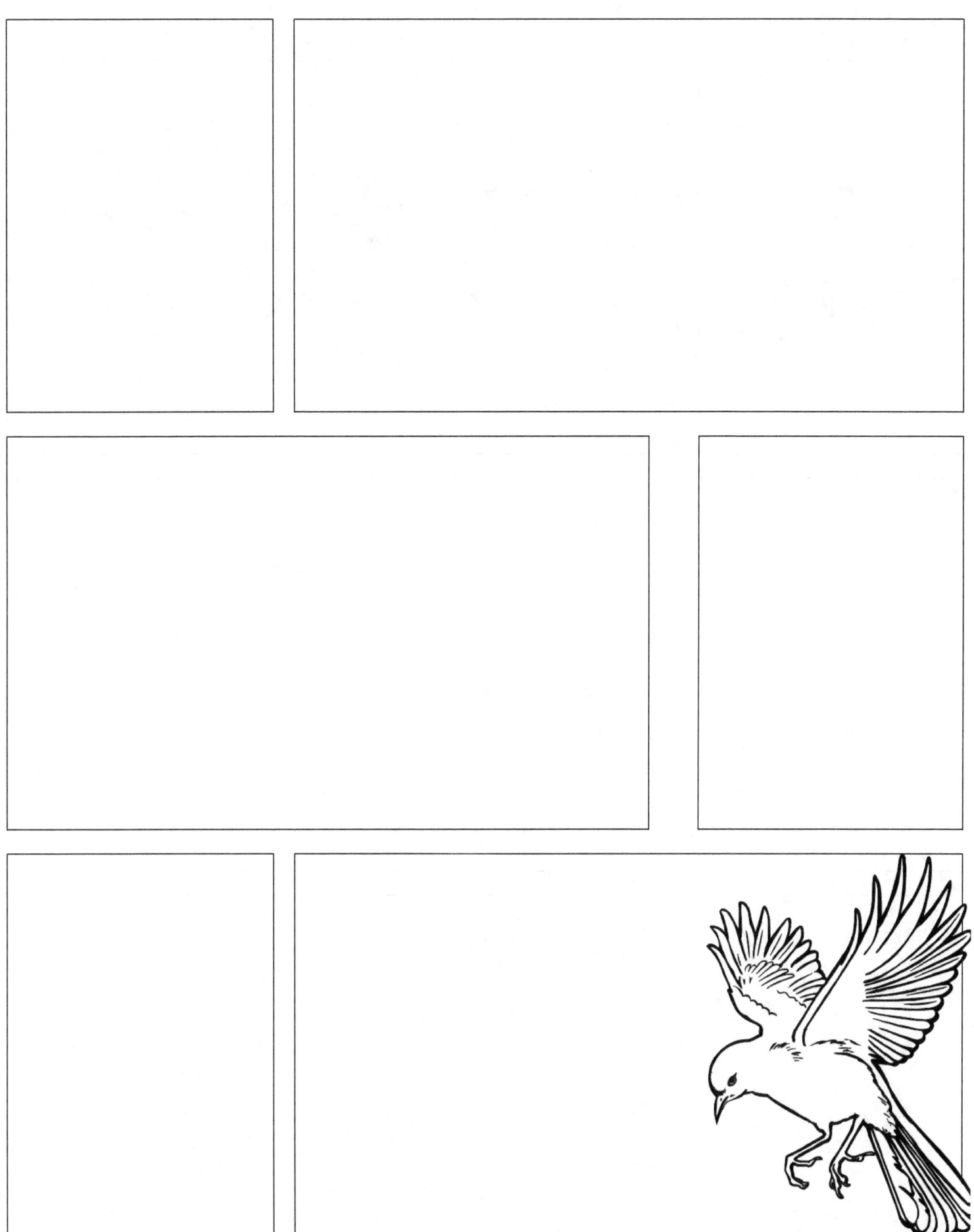

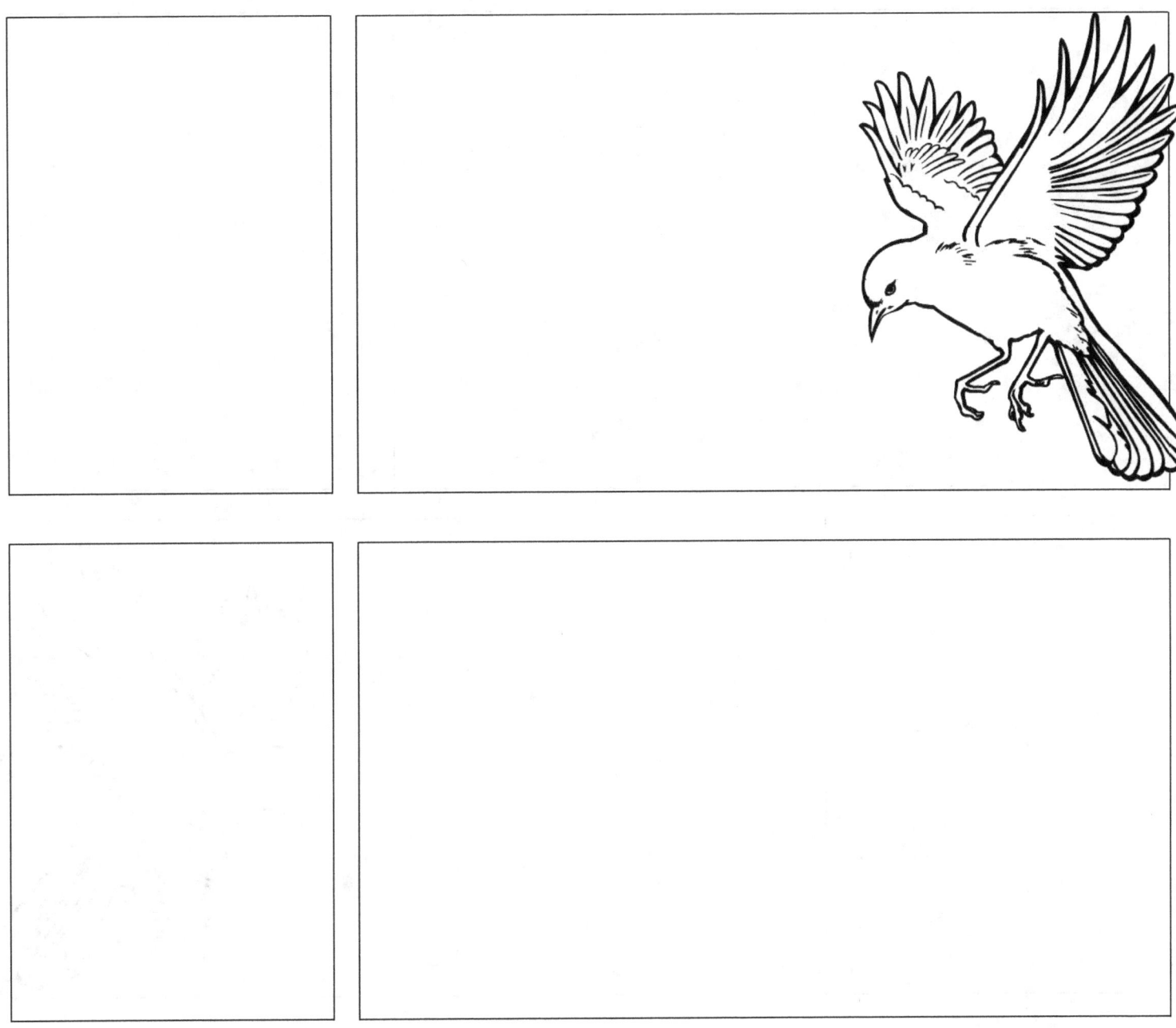

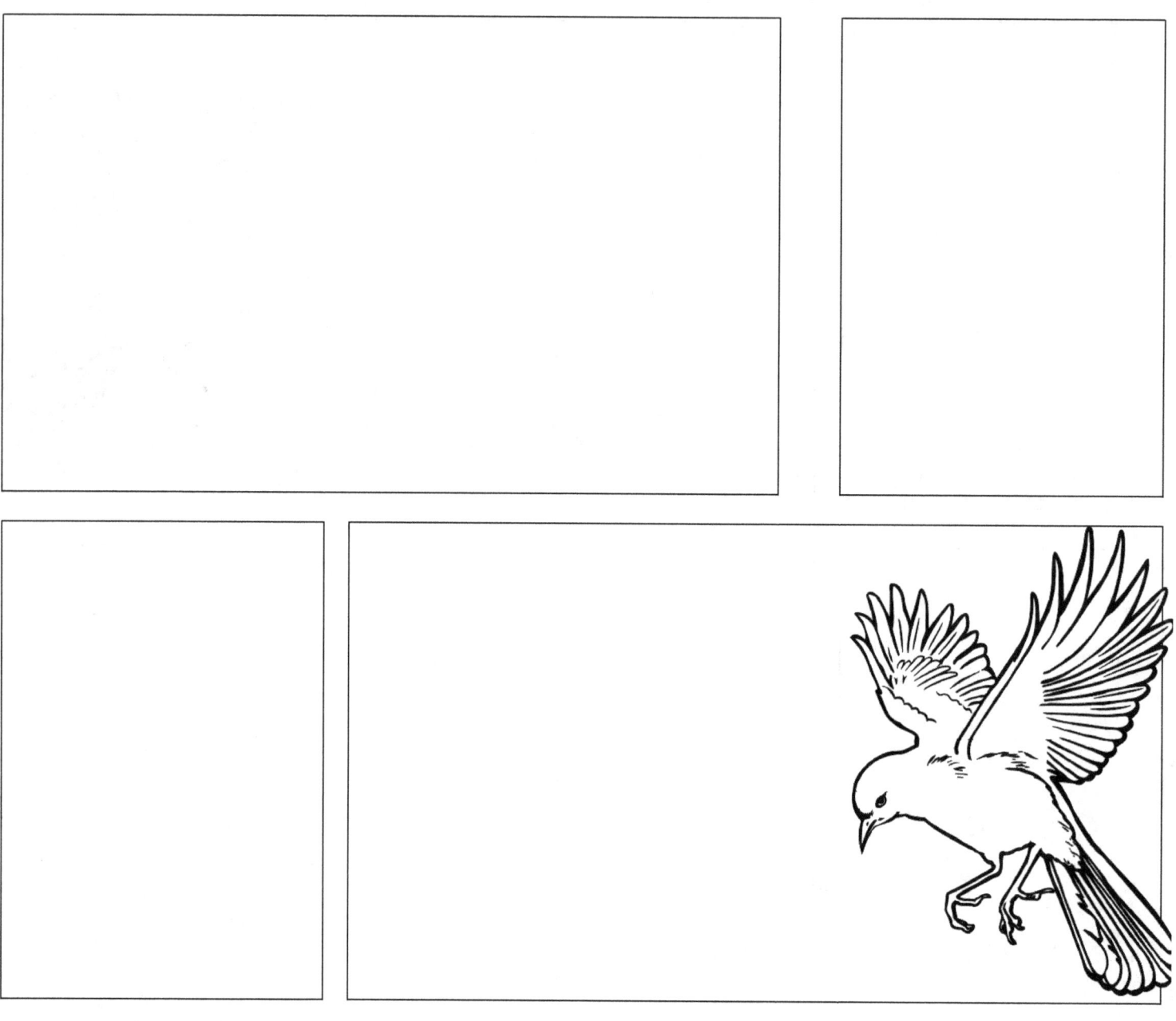

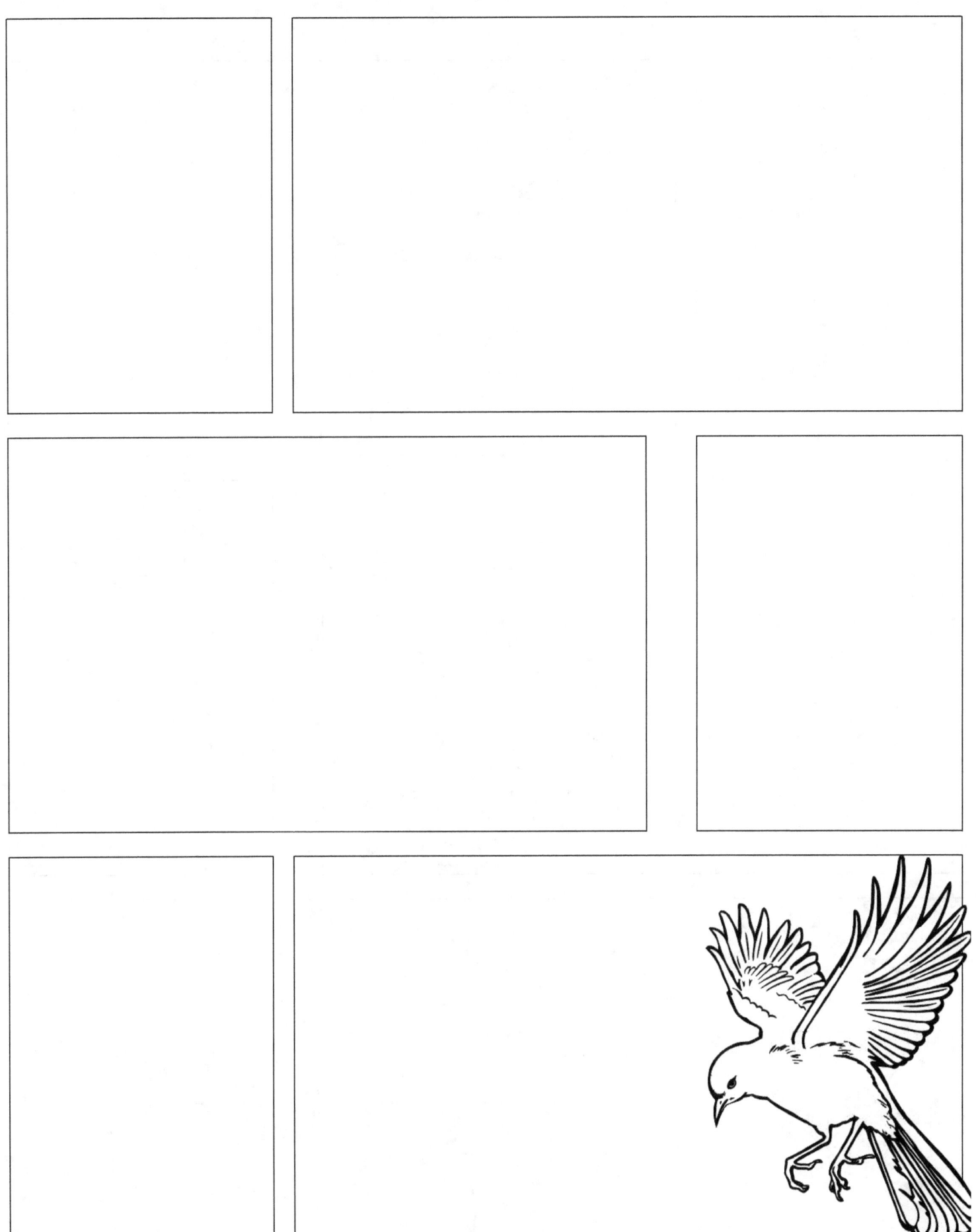

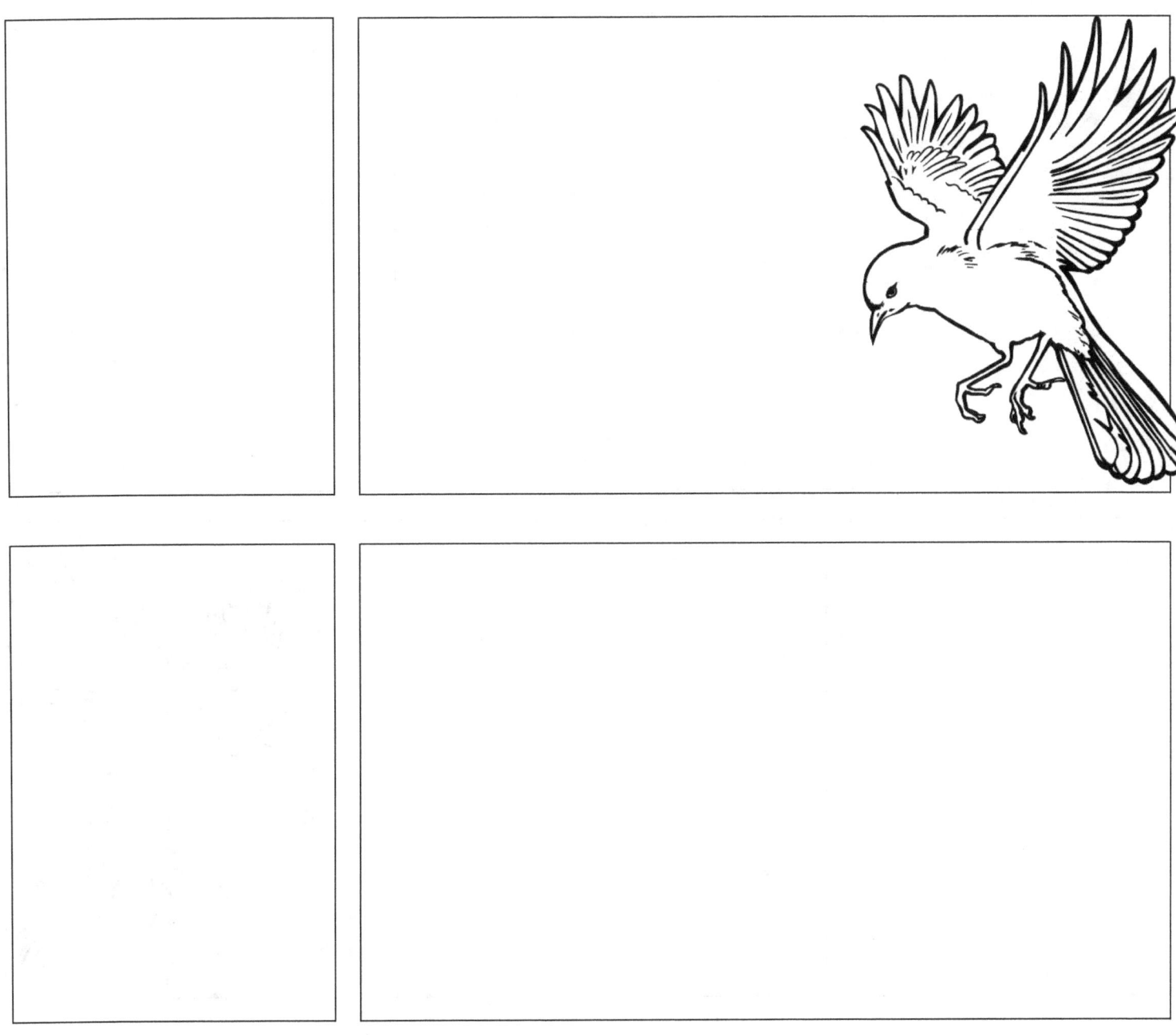

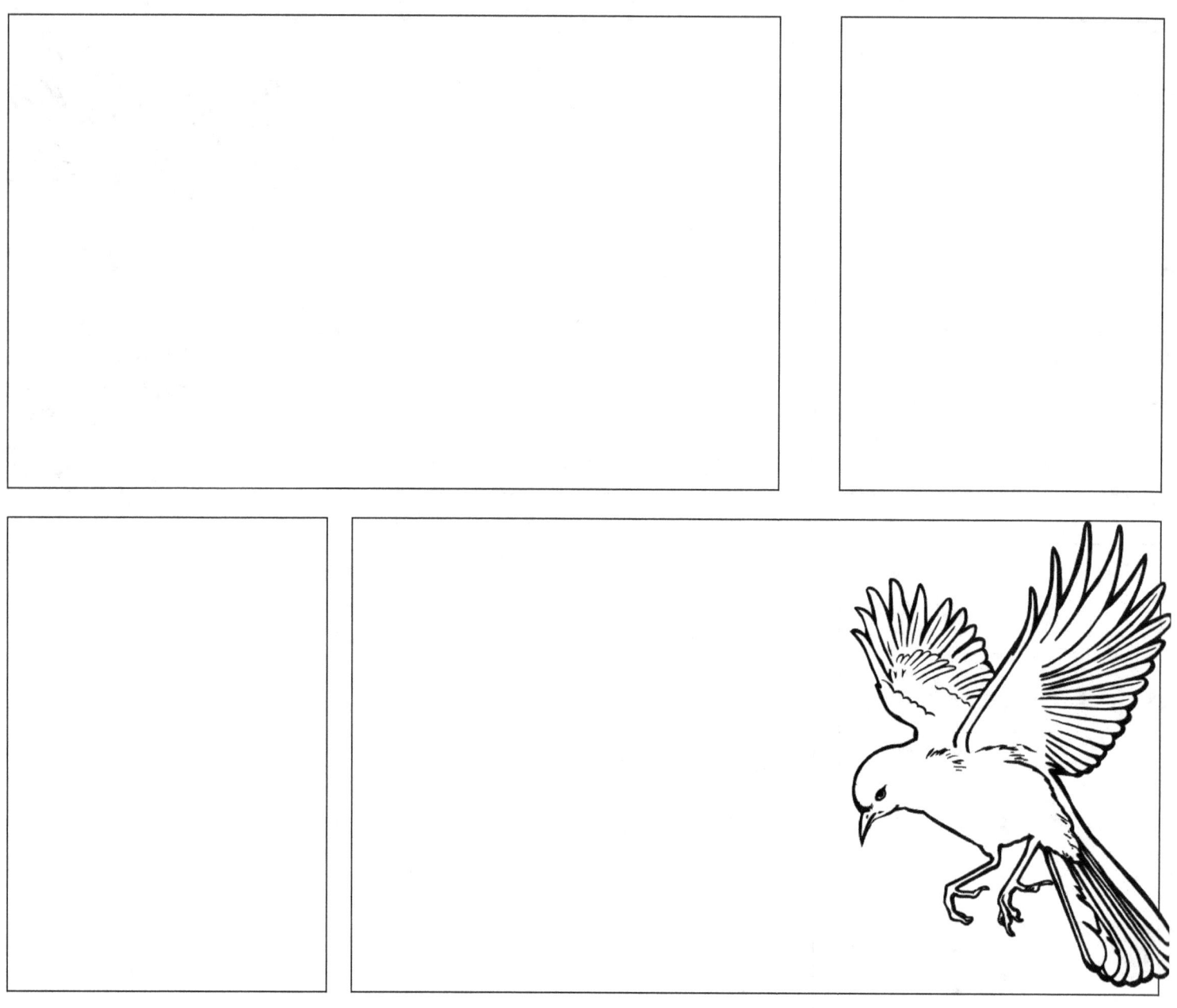

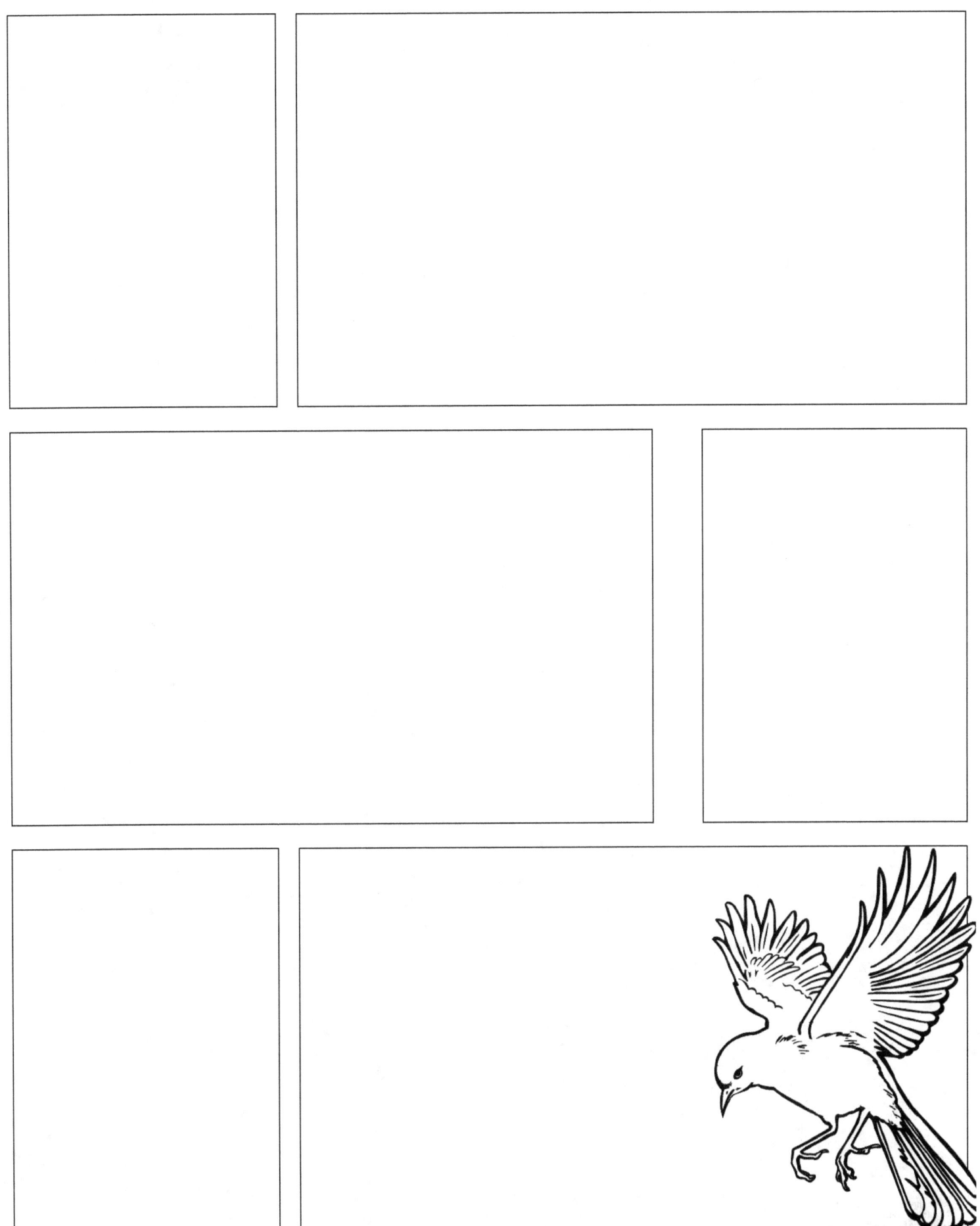

www.ingramcontent.com/pod-product-compliance
Lightning Source LLC
Chambersburg PA
CBHW060410220526
45465CB00008B/2831